RUMBLES OF THUNDER

RUMBLES OF THUNDER

POWER SHIFTS

and the

DANGER OF

SINO-AMERICAN WAR

STEVE CHAN

Columbia University Press
New York

Columbia University Press
Publishers Since 1893
New York   Chichester, West Sussex
cup.columbia.edu
Copyright © 2023 Columbia University Press

Library of Congress Cataloging-in-Publication Data
Names: Chan, Steve, author.
Title: Rumbles of thunder : power shifts and the danger of
Sino-American war / Steve Chan.
Description: New York : Columbia University Press, 2022. | Includes
bibliographical references and index.
Identifiers: LCCN 2022014295 (print) | LCCN 2022014296 (ebook) |
ISBN 9780231208444 (hardback) | ISBN 9780231208451 (trade paperback) |
ISBN 9780231557436 (ebook)
Subjects: LCSH: Balance of power. | War—Causes. | United States—Foreign
relations—China. | China—Foreign relations—United States.
Classification: LCC JZ1313 .C475 2022 (print) | LCC JZ1313 (ebook) |
DDC 327.1/12—dc23/eng/20220701
LC record available at https://lccn.loc.gov/2022014295
LC ebook record available at https://lccn.loc.gov/2022014296

Columbia University Press books are printed on permanent
and durable acid-free paper.

Printed in the United States of America

Cover design: Milenda Nan Ok Lee
Cover image: Decha Anunthanapong/Alamy Stock Photo

CONTENTS

5. TAIWAN AS A POSSIBLE CATALYST FOR SINO-AMERICAN CONFLICT

———

176

CONCLUSION

———

206

RUMBLES OF THUNDER

INTRODUCTION

This book challenges much of the received wisdom about Sino-American relations. It will likely be a source of discomfiture, irritation, and even sharp disagreement for many readers. If it is, it will thus offer an opportunity for a vigorous debate. As a Wall Street pundit supposedly said, "I become worried when everyone gets to one side of the boat." Even smart people can sometimes become victims of what we now know as groupthink.[1] Scholars, no less than people in other professions, can exhibit conformity to conventional thinking and narratives.

We see nowadays elite and public opinion coalescing in both China and the United States about the other country's inherent hostility and bad faith and the need to take a tougher stand against it. This is the stuff that contributes to a conflict spiral, each side developing a mirror image of the other. The silencing of dissident voices, whether by self-censorship or otherwise, abets a sense of self-righteousness, contributing to an escalation of mistrust and tension. Hard-liners in each country become their counterparts' best allies as their reciprocal recrimination feeds on each other.

Readers of this book will find many contrarian views challenging mainstream ideas circulated in popular media and academic discourse. Americans will find contradictions to their self-image of the United States as a benevolent, rule-abiding, and status-quo hegemon. The idea that democratic politics, sometimes reflected in populism, is likely to hamper rather than contribute to easing Sino-American tension is also likely to be controversial, even abhorrent, to many American readers. They will find in the following pages criticisms of their country's crusader impulse to convert the world in its image and their leaders' double standards in constructing narratives about Sino-American relations. Many will also likely object to the claim that the United States has in recent years acted more like a revisionist power than China, and that it has done so more assertively and aggressively than China.

At the same time, Chinese readers will be disappointed to hear that it is still a world dominated by the United States and that it will remain so for some considerable time to come. Moreover, they will be disturbed to hear of a pervasive negative image of China in foreign countries—even though foreigners' trust and confidence in the United States also plummeted during the Donald Trump administration and despite popular skepticism about and even resistance to democratic and capitalist institutions.[2] China's values and identities do not appeal to many people in other countries.[3] Despite the supposed success of its development model, Beijing cannot compete with Washington's soft power.[4] Its actions in Xinjiang and Hong Kong and toward Taiwan lead foreigners to see China in a negative light. A country that mistreats its own citizens cannot reassure foreigners that they will receive better treatment. This observation also applies to the United States given its persistent racial inequities and discrimination that have spurred mass protests such as the Black Lives Matter movement.

What citizens and pundits say about another country often reveals more about themselves than the subject of their commentary. Andrew Bacevich observes that "American statecraft is not, in the first instance, about 'them;' it is about 'us.'"[5] Hubris, prejudice, excessive confidence, overweening ambition, and scapegoating and stereotyping are on display on both sides of the Pacific. These human tendencies are in the final analysis the ingredients that can precipitate a dangerous confrontation. After all, people rather than structural conditions make decisions. The pertinent structural conditions include not just what is happening at the interstate level of analysis, such as the shifting power balance between two countries. The domestic alignments of political power and interests are also pertinent. They can alter the nature of political discourse by empowering hard-liners whose rhetoric gives further fuel to popular grievances and self-righteousness.[6]

Talk of an ongoing power transition between China and the United States and the danger of war stemming from this process has been very much in vogue in scholarly, official, and even public discourses. Graham Allison popularized the aphorism Thucydides' Trap,[7] referring to this ancient Greek historian's remark that the shifting power balance between Athens and Sparta was the root cause of the Peloponnesian War. Other scholars, such as A. F. K. Organski, Organski and Jacek Kugler, and Robert Gilpin, also point to power transition as a basic cause of systemic war.[8] The warning that this process may put China and the United States on a collision has even reached the highest levels of government. For example, Chinese president Xi Jinping was quoted as saying, "we must all strive to avoid falling into Thucydides Trap,"[9] and that this trap can be avoided "as long as we maintain communication and treat each other with sincerity."[10]

Although it argues that tension between Beijing and Washington stems from ongoing changes in these countries' power balance, this book departs from the standard script prevailing in the West that typecasts these countries' respective role in international relations with the United States as the dominant power in the role of defending the system and China as the rising power in the role of a revisionist seeking to overturn it. My argument does not mean that China will refrain from efforts to make the international system more congenial to it—just as the United States has tried to export its values and transform the world in its image. It only asserts that China for now sees its interests as largely served by abiding by the current system's rules and norms that have enabled its rise thus far. Conversely and contrary to the customary depiction, the United States has become increasingly alienated from the system it has fostered since 1945, and has acted in ways suggesting that it wants to revise the rules of the game to arrest and reverse its relative decline.

The standard power-transition interpretation is wrong because China is not overtaking the United States and most past power transitions have been peaceful. At the same time, recent power shifts have inclined Beijing and Washington to adjust their foreign policies, causing a deterioration in their bilateral relations. These arguments are not contradictory. It is states' policies and conduct, and not power transitions, that can cause war. This is an important distinction. Further, although all power transitions entail a power shift, not all power shifts produce a power transition (a power shift refers to any change in the balance of power between two countries, whereas a power transition refers to those occasions when a formerly weaker country overtakes a formerly stronger country).

Commitment problem lies at the heart of Sino-American relations.[11] How can a country be sure that its counterpart will remain committed to the terms of a deal when their power relations change in the future, not just when this counterpart becomes stronger but also when it gets weaker? For example, how can the United States trust that China's leaders will honor their commitment to any deal reached now and not demand revising its terms in the future when their country becomes stronger? Conversely, how can China be reassured that future U.S. leaders would honor the terms of a deal when they become dissatisfied with its results (such as when Trump insisted that the North American Free Trade Agreement be renegotiated with Canada and Mexico to secure more favorable treatment for U.S. producers and exporters)? From Beijing's perspective, Washington's words and deeds have increasingly shown that it is abandoning its commitments announced in the three Sino-American communiques concerning its relations with Taipei.

Trust is a fragile thing. It can be easily undermined. When this happens, it takes considerable work and a long time to restore it.[12] Pessimists such as John Mearsheimer and Sebastian Rosato believe that states' intentions are always subject to change and that they cannot credibly bind themselves to their promises.[13] In Rosato's words, "given the [uncertain] nature of intentions, there is little Washington and Beijing will be able to do or say to persuade the other side that it has or will always have peaceful intentions. In tomorrow's Asia, great-power conflict is destiny."[14]

THE ARGUMENTS

This book is the culmination of my research over the past decade or so, seeking to complete my general explanation of the war phenomenon by introducing missing pieces I have not previously been able to address fully. Although it has a specific focus on the contemporary relations between China and the United States, my analysis draws from the general literature on international relations, thus placing this study in a cross-national and transhistoric context.

My explanation of war occurrence points to a constellation of factors. Thus the outbreak of war cannot be explained by a single variable such as power transition. Power shifts among states are a relevant concern but only one factor in combination with other pertinent, interacting variables, including alliance dynamics, domestic political alignment, the practice of realpolitik statecraft, a history of acrimonious relations, the nature of a state's foreign policy agenda (such as its revisionism), and a fuse that can cause conflict to spread. My prior research has addressed some of these factors, and this book discusses the remaining ones, which have not been taken up adequately before. This project is therefore an effort to complete my overall explanation of why wars happen and, more specifically, how the conditions I identify can contribute to a Sino-American confrontation.

It advances the following arguments, some of which are contrary to the prevailing wisdom:

1. Changes in the power balance between the United States and China hold the key to explaining the recent deterioration in their relations. Other competing explanations, such as those referring to China's record on human rights and its assertive foreign policy, do not fare nearly as well and thus power shift is an important part of why international tensions rise and wars happen, though not in the way usually depicted by power-transition theory.

2. The discipline's common practice of equating a state's possession or production of material resources with its power is seriously mistaken because a state's political capacity to deploy effectively its resources must also be considered. A failure to come to grips with this issue and others means that we do not even have a solid empirical basis to establish that a power shift has occurred and, if so, when and by how much.

3. Concerns over China's catching up to and even overtaking the United States are both greatly exaggerated and premature. (America's structural power will enable its global domination for some considerable time to come.) What is significant is that distorted rhetoric about an impending U.S.-China power transition contributes to misperception and abets a self-fulfilling prophecy of a coming war between them.

4. Domestic political alignment and policies are the primary determinants of a state's foreign policy and its growth trajectory (and thus its international position), meaning that foreign policies are often undertaken

for domestic partisan reasons and national economic growth is often hampered by myopic self-defeating policies. This claim suggests that a country should devote more time and effort to get its own house in order rather than seek to hinder another country's rise.

5. Taiwan is the most likely catalyst for a Sino-American confrontation, and recent trends suggest that leaders in Beijing, Washington, and Taipei are facing a more dangerous situation brought about by their rhetoric and their domestic constraints. The United States and China are separated by considerable physical distance and do not have any direct territorial dispute. For a variety of reasons, however, they are most likely to come to blows over Taiwan.

In the following discussion, I offer the reasons for my claims, my critique of the existing literature, and my overall explanation of the war phenomenon. I then present the puzzles or questions that motivate the various chapters and thus the logic behind the structure of this book.

POWER SHIFT IS ONLY PART OF THE STORY

A rising China in and of itself need not be the only or even the most important reason for increased tension and an elevated danger of conflict. Whether power transition is or is not responsible for these phenomena and, if so, how much and under what circumstances is a matter for empirical investigation. In the one and only instance in modern history (that is, since the Congress of Vienna in 1815) when the leadership baton was passed from one hegemon to another, a rising United States overtook Britain peacefully. Of course, one can argue that these countries shared a cultural affinity, racial identity, liberal institutions, and close economic ties, and that many of these conditions do not exist in Sino-American relations today.[15] Yet Anglo-American relations were acrimonious, even hostile, during much of the nineteenth century, and London and Washington came close to blows on several occasions.[16] The factors often cited to have contributed to the peaceful outcome of this transition are constants (that is, they were present during both tense and cordial times in these countries' relations) and as such cannot explain the evolution of these relations from acrimony to amity. The one indisputable factor that changed during this evolution was of course the balance of power shifting increasingly and eventually decisively in favor of the United States.

The standard explanation for the peaceful Anglo-American transition has a distinct post hoc flavor. A moment's reflection tells us that shared cultural heritage or interlocking economic interests have not stopped Bruderkrieg (German for brother war) in the past, such as when Prussia and Austria fought and civil wars broke out (e.g., in China, Korea, Vietnam and of course, the United States). Countries with intense commercial ties, such as Britain and Germany in 1914, have gone to war. From the perspective of Samuel Huntington's formulation of clashing civilizations,[17] the two world wars were fought among cousins (figuratively and in some cases literally given that Europe's monarchs were closely related by blood). Of course, the obverse also obtains. Many countries that are distant from one another physically, economically, and emotionally have managed to remain on peaceful terms. Some with different political ideologies, cultural traditions, and regime characteristics have gotten along and even cooperated. The Concert of Europe comes to mind as an example of such countries working together to preserve peace and stability.

Emphasizing China's rise as a possible source of international instability overlooks the possibility that a China whose growth has stalled or a China in domestic disarray can also be troublesome. China during the throes of the Cultural Revolution had stood defiantly against the world even though its power then was much weaker than now. A resentful China that feels its aspirations have been thwarted by foreigners or its dignity humiliated by them will be a problem regardless of whether it is getting ahead or falling behind in international competition. As Thomas Christensen puts it, China can "pose problems without catching up."[18]

A singular focus on China and China's conduct is also problematic because, after all, it takes two to tango or tangle. A dominant power in relative decline can initiate a preventive war against a rising but still weaker competitor. Twice in the last century, Germany initiated war, first against Russia and then against the USSR, to eliminate a rising challenger while it still had the upper hand.[19] Both the Soviet Union and the United States considered launching a preventive strike against China's nuclear facilities before it could fully develop its nuclear armament, though obviously both decided in the end not to do so.[20]

The idea that the United States would launch an unprovoked war against China sounds outlandish. However, according to Bob Woodward and Robert Costa,[21] the chairman of U.S. Joint Chiefs of Staff, General Mark Milley, was seriously concerned that Trump might "go rogue" and launch a nuclear war in the final days of his presidency. Milley secretly called his Chinese counterpart, General Li Zuocheng, on October 30, 2020, and again on January 8, 2021, to assuage Chinese concerns that the United States was planning to attack China. He was quoted saying, "General Li, I want to assure you that the American government is stable and everything is going to be OK. We are not going to attack or conduct any kinetic operations against you. . . . General Li, you and I have known each other now for five years. If we're going to attack, I'm going to call you ahead of time. It's not going to be a surprise."[22]

Preventive war[23] is often confused with a preemptive attack,[24] and deliberately so in the case of U.S. invasion of Iraq.[25] The former refers to starting a war to head off a perceived future threat, the latter to undertaking self-defense by administering the first blow to an enemy poised to strike imminently. By definition, a preventive war is a war of choice. The logic for preventive war was given explicitly by President George W. Bush in justifying his decision to invade Iraq ostensibly to deny Saddam Hussein any possibility of acquiring weapons of mass destruction.[26] The public rationale given by the Bush administration for this war—that Iraq had or was about to have weapons of mass destruction and that it had connections with al-Qaeda—turned out to be false. Chinese leaders are certainly aware that the ongoing shifts in the power balance between Beijing and Washington are acutely dangerous for China: they have intensified enough to cause alarm in Washington but are not strong enough to deter its preventive motivation.

Although an important factor, changing power balance does not preordain a peaceful or violent outcome. Just as sometimes power transitions have coincided with the outbreak of war, on many occasions it has not. In recent decades, Japan has overtaken Britain, France, Germany, and Russia economically, and China has also surpassed Japan and those European countries just mentioned without war occurring between them. A moment's reflection tells us that whether the overtaking country or the country being overtaken has a democratic or authoritarian form of government, or whether it is ostensibly a status-quo or revisionist state, appears to not have mattered for the peaceful outcome of these recent episodes of power transition. For instance, in some cases the overtaking country happens to be a putative democratic and status-quo country (e.g., Japan) and the one being overtaken happens to be a putative authoritarian and revisionist country (e.g., Russia). In other cases, the overtaking country happens to be a putative authoritarian and revisionist country (e.g., China), and the one being overtaken happens to be a putative democratic and status quo country (e.g., Japan). As Charles Kupchan remarks, "foreign policy behavior—in particular, the practice of strategic restraint—is a more important variable than regime type per se in isolating the causes for peace."[27] Whereas the structural conditions of the international system are difficult for a state to influence, leaders of a country are more in control of their foreign policy and thus more in a position to influence the prospects of war and peace by practicing strategic restraint.

The other side of the coin is equally important. War can happen in the absence of a power transition, such as when the United States and China fought in Korea. Similarly, when it attacked Pearl Harbor, Japan was hardly in the process of overtaking the United States. In numerous cases, powerful established states have waged war against small or declining states. Recent wars started by the United States against Afghanistan and Iraq are just two examples of history's many lopsided conflicts, including those fought for colonial and imperial conquests against the people of the Global South.

Moreover, contrary to power-transition theory, rising and ruling powers have more often picked on lesser powers and former great powers that have suffered serious decline rather than taking on each other in a direct confrontation.[28] As a former great power that had declined seriously, China was victimized by various established and rising powers (Britain, France, Russia, Japan, and the United States) during its century of national humiliation. The Ottoman Empire, Austria-Hungary, and Spain also come to mind as examples of former great powers that suffered a sharp decline and were picked on by other countries during that decline. Although rising and established states in the select group of great powers have obviously clashed militarily in the past, they have much to lose and comparatively little to gain when they get into a fight against each other. The characterization of transitional warfare breaking out between an incumbent hegemon and a rising upstart is not strongly supported by the historical record.

As Michael Swaine and Ashley Tellis observe,

> the fact remains that direct attacks on a hegemon by rising challengers are rare and infrequent in modern times. The best examples of such a war . . . remains the French attack on the Dutch United Provinces under Louis XIV. Most systemic wars in fact occur because (a) some rising states attack other rising states to consolidate their power but nonetheless manage to precipitate systemic war because the existing hegemon enters the fray on behalf of the weaker side to preempt a future challenge that may be mounted by the stronger rising power (the Italian wars); or, (b) some rising states attack key allies of the existing hegemon or important neutrals in a search for regional gains, which nonetheless precipitates systemic war because the existing hegemon enters the fray on behalf of the ally or the neutral to prevent a shift in the future balance of power (the Spanish wars, the Napoleonic wars, and the First and Second World Wars).[29]

A power transition between two great powers is not a necessary or sufficient condition for war between them. Indeed, just because a war has occurred in the context of an ongoing power transition does not vindicate power-transition theory. This theory's claim needs to be verified and the causal links between changes in the international environment and the decision processes of leaders will have to be specified and confirmed. As we all know, the co-occurrence of A and B does not mean that A causes B or vice versa. The co-occurrence can be fortuitous.

Power-transition theory's original formulation claims that it pertains only to wars fought at the very pinnacle of the international hierarchy—specifically, the struggle between the two most powerful countries in the world for global dominance and control of the international order.[30] In practice, however, this theory has been applied to the study of conflicts among regional powers[31] as well as wars fought by countries not at the top of interstate power hierarchy. Thus, for example, Organski and Kugler include the Franco-Prussian War and the Russo-Japanese War in their analysis,[32] even though these conflicts were not about which of these belligerents should dominate the world or control the international order. Power-transition theory could only depict the two world wars as a German challenge to British supremacy by excluding the United States from its analysis because by the time of these conflicts the United States had already overtaken Britain and Germany never came close to matching U.S. power. "In fact, no rising challenger has thus far succeeded in supplanting any prevailing hegemony by war."[33]

Although power transition may abet war, war can also produce power transition.[34] A reciprocal causal relationship between these two variables is possible. Wars that ended with Germany's and Italy's unifications surely contributed to these countries' rising international position, as did the resolutions of the American, Russian, and Chinese civil wars. World War II also reshuffled the ranks of great powers, demoting some while further securing or strengthening the dominance of others (the United States and the Soviet Union). These observations lead to another important question. The domestic conditions of Portugal, the Netherlands, and Britain—leading global powers in earlier eras—were conducive to successful international competition, and their external expansion in turn greatly enhanced their international power and stature. I return to this point later when discussing the importance of distinguishing domestic from foreign sources of interstate power shifts.

WARS STEM FROM MULTIPLE CAUSES

The many paths that can lead to war are not mutually exclusive.[35] Monocausal explanations of complex social or political phenomena are suspect because usually many factors contribute to their occurrence. As Robert Jervis notes, "Only rarely does a single factor determine the way politics will work out." Similarly, John Gaddis calls attention to how "the convergence or interaction of complementary processes [and] . . . the potential fratricide of contradictory ones" can influence social and political processes.[36]

Shifting power balance becomes dangerous when it is added to other combustible ingredients, producing a dangerous brew. Contentious border disputes, enduring rivalries, recurrent militarized disputes, ongoing armament races, and the bipolarization of competing alliances contribute to a heightened sense of animosity, anxiety, and uncertainty accompanying rapid changes in power balance.[37] Moreover, these power shifts are not just bilateral. A country's gaining or losing ground in the inter-state distribution of power has multilateral, often unexpected, ramifications for the rest of the great-power club.[38] Robert Jervis urges analysts to study the interaction effects among variables and consider their feedback on subsequent events that lead to nonlinear dynamics, such as when the combination of conflict-inducing factors has a multiplier rather than just an additive effect on escalating tension.[39]

Historical grievances and unresolved disputes, when combined with geographic proximity, provide additional reasons that the danger of war increases. Significantly, this perspective argues that "war and violence occur because of *grievances* and not just power."[40] The steps-to-war model explains the process of conflict escalation.[41] These steps include the practice of various forms of power politics. such as provocative military displays, intense arms races, and crisis brinksmanship. They also involve the larger "patron" states being "trapped" or "dragged into war" due to their alliance commitments in a process described as "chain ganging."[42]

Concerns about losing allies played a prominent role in the lead-up to various wars. The Spartans were goaded by their ally Corinth to confront Athens. They were fearful that their alliance would collapse if they had failed to act.[43] Similarly, before World War I, France sought desperately to bind Russia to itself in its effort to contain the perceived threat from Germany, and Germany wrote its infamous blank check to Austria-Hungary in fear of losing its main ally. Whether or not we call them entanglement, these alliance dynamics played a significant role in these conflagrations.

Victor Cha argues that the hub-and-spokes design of U.S. alliances in East Asia has been constructed in part by Washington to maximize its smaller allies' dependency on it and at the same time to minimize the danger that these allies may involve it involuntarily in a war they instigate.[44] As I discuss later, Taiwan would be the most obvious catalyst for a direct confrontation between China and the United States. David Welch describes the dynamics of alliance politics as "pull factors" and domestic politics as "push factors" that in combination with leaders' misjudgments led to the catastrophic Peloponnesian conflict in ancient Greece.[45]

Even though perceptions of changing power balance play an important role in influencing states' actions and policies, it is these actions and policies, not power shifts per se, that endanger peace. "[Their] use of power politics practices (alliance making, crisis initiation, and military build-ups) increases the probability of war."[46] Moreover, states are unlikely to get into a fight for reasons that power-transition theory typically suggests, namely, over which one of them should dominate the world or decide the nature of international order. John Vasquez suggests instead that "any war between the United States and China or the EU-China is not going to come about in order to settle who is the global leader, but will come about through some local territorial war in which one or both sides are brought in."[47]

Hyper nationalism and historical grievances promoted by political entrepreneurs in domestic discourse can add fuel to an already danger-ous mixture of international competition and mutual recrimination.[48] Coalitional politics joining militarists, nationalists, and industrialists also feed this dynamic, such as Germany's naval buildup before 1914.[49] These elements contribute to a tinderbox that can be set off by any spark, such as the assassination of Archduke Ferdinand in Sarajevo. Still, even though these conditions can incline leaders to become more bellicose, the choice for war or peace is theirs to make.

This view in turn suggests that we should not privilege the role of power shifts to the exclusion of other conditions that can elevate the danger of a violent showdown. It also suggests that we should consider other condi-tions that could help reduce tension and mitigate the destabilizing effects ensuing from power shifts. Significantly, changing power balances among countries are largely due to their different rates of economic growth.[50] A country's growth prospects are largely determined by its domestic condi-tions and policies. Foreigners have relatively little influence in affecting its growth trajectory. Officials should focus more on those factors that are within their control to lower the risk of war.

Systemic wars do not happen out of the blue. Typically, a long history leads up to the animosities characterizing the pertinent states' relations. These animosities tend to flare up frequently and their recurrence increases the danger that on one such occasion the outcome will be war. By way of analogy, if a motorist habitually exceeds the speed limit on a winding road during a rainy night, the chances of an eventual traffic mishap are con-siderable. This analogy reminds us that it is usually a combination of dan-gerous factors that contributes to war outbreak. Further, it usually takes a catalyst to trigger a conflagration. For example, if the fictitious motorist has also consumed a few alcoholic beverages, the resulting impairment can be the immediate, proximate cause of a traffic accident. We should therefore look for the most likely trigger to set off a chain reaction that ends in war.

Systemic war stems from a constellation of conditions and practices, including policies to engage in arms race, alliance competition, and provocative military displays. These policies invite reciprocation from other states and interact to produce a multiplicative effect that endangers peace far more than, say, the risk posed by power shift alone (which, as noted, has often happened without triggering war). This acknowledgment suggests that our attention should be directed to policies and conduct more within officials' direct control, such as to avoid armament competition, military provocations, bolstering foreign clients, and rhetorical exaggeration that exacerbate a tense situation. Strategic restraint is more within their reach than the processes of power shifts that, as already mentioned, tend to reflect the uneven rates of economic growth due largely to the domestic conditions and policies of different countries.

This discussion also argues that a country is in a better position to control its future growth than to affect another's. To the extent that power shift is a source of international instability and officials' concern for their country's international standing, it is more pertinent to ask what one can do to promote one's own growth rather than to contain another's. This question obviously pertains to leaders' choice of their domestic policies.

POLICY CHOICES IN THE FACE OF POWER SHIFTS

Studies on power shifts stress this variable to be the decisive factor in determining the danger of war. They do not usually give enough attention to what prudent and feasible policies should be undertaken to reduce this danger. Indeed, as structural theories—structural in the sense that macro conditions at the interstate or systemic level of analysis are preferred over factors pertaining to officials' policy choices to explain an outbreak of war—they imply severe limits on how much human intervention can alter the course of history. After all, the thrust of these presentations is that leaders will be trapped by the same circumstances and will repeat the same mistakes time and again. Their reasoning minimizes the role of human agency. It warns, for example, that contemporary China is a replica of Imperial Germany and will follow its predecessor's footsteps.[51] This type of reasoning by analogy, including references to the Peloponnesian War of ancient Greece as a parallel to contemporary Sino-American relations, essentially overlooks people's capacity to learn from history. It conveys a view of two states locked in dyadic competition, one akin to Lewis Richardson's well-known model of armament and counter-armament pointing to what can happen if leaders do not pause to think before they act.[52]

Some international relations analysts even write as if countries are hardwired to seek power and expand. In their view, it is in the genes of all officials to seek aggrandizement and pursue hegemony. The premise of power-transition theory is that powerful states will always find themselves competing for global control. Mearsheimer expects China to follow the U.S. example, such as declaring its own version of the Monroe Doctrine to evict U.S. influence from East Asia and to establish an exclusive sphere of influence for itself there.[53] He and others expect, and indeed advocate, the United States to join China's neighbors to resist this attempt. Their view suggests that leaders are somehow compelled by their circumstances to act in certain ways, in this case, to expand until stopped by countervailing power. It therefore does not give much consideration to policy choices available to leaders. Instead, it expects them to be trapped again and again by their circumstances, thus to repeat the tragedies of bloodshed despite history's warnings (as suggested by the titles of Mearsheimer's and Allison's books).

In a critical response to Mearsheimer and Allison, Jonathan Kirshner remarks that the true tragedy of great power is that "hegemons are too arrogant to make concessions when they should, and too frightened to make them when they must."[54] It is not too little security, but instead too much, that gives hegemons the luxury to pursue aggrandizement abroad out of vainglory, such as Athens' Sicilian expedition that ended in disaster. Kirshner counsels that even great powers need to recognize other countries' power and the limits of their own power and to avoid costly self-defeating blunders such as Vietnam and Iraq.

It is odd that despite offensive realism's emphasis on all states' ostensible impulse to increase their power, it treats the United States as an exception to this generalization and sees it as a defender of the status quo after it had secured its own regional hegemony in the Western Hemisphere.[55] Somehow, the United States is exempted from the impulse to seek more power, a motivation that is attributed to all other countries, even though it is in the best position to do so simply because it has been the strongest country in the world and other countries are less able to restrain or stop it. In a similar vein, power-transition theorists dichotomize all states as ostensibly committed to the status quo or, alternatively, as seeking to overturn it. They see some states, the established ones, as being satisfied with what they already have and will not seek or demand more. They do not bother to ask how these established states came to possess what they have. The status quo in their analyses can refer to either the existing interstate distribution of power or the nature of international order. In either case, their view suggests a bias favoring the maintenance of the existing interstate power distribution and the existing international order, even though both are in fact always being contested and in the process of evolving. Established states, even a unipolar power such as the United States, do not cease trying to improve their capabilities or to alter the rules of international order more to their liking.[56]

Offensive realism avers that global hegemony is impossible to attain and by implication, does not see the United States as the global hegemon today. It also does not explore why Washington would want to resist a possible bid by Beijing for regional hegemony in East Asia or be alarmed by Beijing's prospects of succeeding in this gambit given the enormous differences distinguishing the current situation in East Asia from the one prevailing in the Western Hemisphere in the latter half of the nineteenth century. As Kirshner has asked, why would Beijing want to launch a bid for regional hegemony in view of the disastrous experiences of other would-be regional hegemons in the past (Germany, Japan, the Soviet Union)? Moreover, why should one assume that Beijing is incapable of drawing lessons from the one and only instance of a peaceful power transition, namely, those policies and conditions characterizing Anglo-American relations in the second half of the nineteenth century? The U.S. ascent to becoming a preeminent power was greatly assisted by the fact that it did not have to face serious foreign threats to its security not only because of its lucky geographic location but also because it was largely spared the distraction of having to compete for international influence in its home region. This success, it should be evident to Chinese leaders, was also related to Washington's general aversion to foreign ambition beyond the Western Hemisphere during its ascent.[57] There is surely no shortage of analyses by both foreign and Chinese scholars offering advice to Beijing (and Washington) based on ostensible lessons drawn from these histories.[58]

Naturally, Beijing would prefer to be East Asia's hegemon and Washington would prefer otherwise. But what are the benefits and costs for each country to pursue policies to realize these respective objectives rather than feasible alternatives, including letting events take their natural course rather than trying to influence them, especially if even massive efforts are likely to be ineffective in affecting the course of history and can even turn out to be counterproductive?

It takes at least two to make war or peace. The other side of the ledger to the characterization of a rising power as an ambitious upstart is the policy choices made by the ruling power and its allies. Do they choose to accommodate the rising power and if so, what are the reasons for this choice?[59] Similarly, if they choose not to accommodate, what again is their rationale? Although Mearsheimer expects with great confidence that the United States would resist a possible Chinese bid for regional hegemony in East Asia,[60] this is not a historical inevitability, as the U.S. experience itself demonstrates. Britain and France were initially too absorbed in their rivalry to check the U.S. ascendance, and subsequently London decided to appease the United States to better confront Germany, a threat nearer to home.[61] This last remark does not deny huge differences between the world prevailing then and the one today. The larger point, however, is that accommodation is at least theoretically an option, and whether to adopt it is a policy choice even though its negotiation can be quite challenging. As T. V. Paul writes, "The process of accommodation in international relations is exceptionally complicated, as it involves status adjustment, the sharing of leadership roles through the accordance of institutional membership and privileges, and acceptance of spheres of influence: something established powers rarely offer to newcomers."[62]

This discussion argues that leaders of China and the United States remain coauthors of their destiny. They are not condemned to repeat the historical tragedy that has visited some countries caught previously in the dynamics of power transition. For the United States, the question is whether it can or wants to stop China's rise and if so, at what price. Washington has professed publicly that its engagement policy was intended to alter China's political system and convert its people's values and identities. This was such a tall order that it was almost certain to fail. The goal of introducing regime change and installing a liberal democracy on alien soil seems quite elusive even in Washington's experiences in the Middle East concerning countries far smaller and weaker than China.[63] Surely, few Americans would agree with the proposition that a foreign power can unilaterally and decisively transform their political and economic institutions or alter their values and identities. One could only assume that the rhetoric for promoting changes inside China to convert it into a liberal democracy is more intended for domestic political consumption than entertained as a serious foreign policy goal.

Rather than trying to change China's internal characteristics, a more pertinent question is whether the United States can live with a China aspiring to a similar position in its home region as the United States itself has occupied in the Western Hemisphere. Of course, it will make an enormous difference whether Beijing uses military means to pursue this goal or gains (or regains) this position as a result of peaceful evolution. By regaining, I refer to China's return to regional preeminence based primarily on its legitimacy and authority as in East Asia's traditional Sinocentric order before this country's "century of humiliations" at the hands of Western and Japanese imperialists.[64]

The last remark in turn raises another question. Can China be stopped from establishing a dominant position in East Asia regardless of Washington's wishes? By the late 1800s, London had evidently decided that the U.S. rise to regional hegemony was unstoppable,[65] and that in the expectation of having to face threats from other quarters to the British Empire it would be wiser to befriend the emergent behemoth than to alienate it. Britain's choice effectively recruited a powerful ally to help it prevail in the subsequent Great War even though it was the weaker party in a contest against Imperial Germany. Britain practiced smart or selective appeasement. In contrast, by taking on all perceived threats to their authority in the hope of establishing a reputation for resolve to deter future challengers, the Spanish Hapsburgs dissipated their energy and weakened their power by fighting on multiple fronts.[66] Donald Trump's America First policies alienated traditional U.S. allies and, in the Joe Biden administration's view, unwisely failed to mobilize the collective strength of the Western camp to confront China.[67]

London's policies reflected the prevailing multipolar international system at that time, whereby a declining hegemon could appease one rising power (or several) in order to more effectively focus its attention and resources on the threat from another rising power. In addition to accommodating the United States, London conciliated with France and Russia, and it even reached out to Japan to form an alliance in the Asia Pacific.[68] In contrast to before World War I, the United States enjoys a unipolar status today even though China has in recent decades managed to improve its relative position. Moreover, Washington can count on many powerful allies, a tremendous asset to add to its already preponderant power and one that Beijing cannot hope to match in the foreseeable future. These differences incline the United States to not accommodate a rising China. Factors suggested for the peaceful Anglo-American transition, such as cultural affinity and racial identity, would imply the same conclusion.

Traditional scholarship on balance of power has much to say about states' incentives to prevent any of them from gaining too much power and especially a unipolar status that carries an overwhelming advantage over the rest of the world. This scholarship, however, is relatively silent on what can explain the U.S. rise to this status and, moreover, how other countries should manage the situation after Washington has already secured its unipolar status. These remarks point naturally to an important difference between what the literature has to say about how the rest of the world should behave (or can be expected to behave) toward a rising power before it attains unipolar status versus how it should behave after the international system is already unipolar.[69] Moreover, the terminology and category of rising powers in the existing literature curiously omits a dominant power that is becoming even more so, to the point of standing head and shoulders above others. Consequently, the rising power label is applied selectively to a country, such as China, which has managed to close the gap separating it from the United States somewhat, but significantly was not applied to the United States after the breakup of the Soviet Union when its power became even more preponderant. This tendency is another example of U.S. exceptionalism in the literature. The United States is exempt from generalizations about rising powers, such as when they are suspected of entertaining a revisionist motivation.

FOCUSING ON POLICY RATHER THAN POWER

That the United States is likely to remain the world's only superpower for some time to come[70] does not mean that its current advantages will endure indefinitely. The unipolar status it has enjoyed since the USSR's dissolution is unprecedented in modern history. What the future holds will depend most particularly on Chinese and American growth trajectories in the coming decades. These countries' relative economic performance will largely reflect their respective domestic conditions and policies. Foreign policy officials and scholars of international relations have a professional bias that focuses on the influence of a country's external environment on its domestic performance. We know, however, that even a devastating defeat in foreign war would have only a transient effect on a country's growth, which typically rebounds to its prewar trajectory in about two decades, as the postwar experiences of the defeated Axis powers make clear.[71]

Allison,[72] like power-transition theorists,[73] argues that when a rising power catches up to a ruling power, the danger of a war between them is elevated. Why, then, was Sparta alarmed by Athens' rise in the tale of Thucydides' Trap? Was this Spartan reaction to Athens' rising power or to its policy of imperial expansion that had led to its increased power?[74] Athanassios Platias and Vasilis Trigkas remark that "it was not *solely the increase* of the Athenian power but the *character of Athenian power* that exacerbated Spartan fear,"[75] specifically, its aggrandizement and efforts to undermine Sparta's alliance. Thucydides attributed no moral superiority to Athens, a supposed democracy by the standards of its time, that had established a "tyrannical empire." In Pericles' words, "Nor can [the Athenians] now give [the empire] over for already [their] government is in the nature of a tyranny, which is both unjust for you to take up and unsafe to lay down."[76]

James Lee argues similarly that Sparta was objecting more to Athens' imperial expansion than being fearful per se of its growing strength.[77] Indeed, the Corinthians in their effort to lobby Sparta to fight Athens had complained that the Spartans were too lethargic and oblivious to rather than alarmed by the challenge from Athens. Athens had expanded its empire, forcing other Greek polities to pay tributes to it and to contribute to its war chest. Lee therefore questions whether Thucydides would have agreed with Thucydides' Trap as formulated by Allison.

In invoking Thucydides' Trap, it is important to consider the extent to which China's rise has been based on its domestic growth as opposed to its imperial expansion. It is relevant to ask whether this country's rise is related to its recruiting formal and informal allies, building overseas military bases, launching military attacks on other countries, and supporting and promoting its multinational corporations across the globe. Or does this profile perhaps better fit the United States? China has but one formal ally (North Korea) and one overseas base (in Djibouti). The United States operates 766 military bases and installations (as of 2006) in seventy-seven foreign countries.[78] China's incidence and magnitude of involvement in foreign wars, military interventions, and militarized interstate disputes have been much lower than those of the United States during China's recent decades of rise or, for that matter, than when the United States was itself a rising power during the late nineteenth century. Although China's rise has benefited greatly from its participation in the global political economy, few would disagree with Michael Swaine and Ashley Tellis that the main reason for its rise is its domestic economic transformation.[79]

THE PRIMACY OF DOMESTIC POLITICS AND POLICY

Current discourse on power shifts in international relations tends to give short shrift to a country's domestic conditions and policies as the principal source for such changes. It often takes the observed power shifts as a given without asking what have caused them. As Robert Gilpin first argued some time ago,[80] differential rates of economic growth are what produce power shifts among countries. The fundamental factors responsible for interstate power shifts are located within countries. Moreover, how well a country performs relative to its peers depends on not only its relative endowment in material resources, but also what it does with these resources.

Commenting on the poor U.S. management of the COVID-19 pandemic, Francis Fukuyama points to three decisive factors: leadership, social trust, and policy capacity.[81] Home to just over 4 percent of the global population, the United States accounted for about 20 percent of the total infections worldwide and about 15 percent of the fatalities as of January 13, 2022.[82] Countries with a smaller resource base than the United States have often done better in containing this virus. Similarly, and more pertinent to the question of economic growth, East Asia's developmental states (e.g., Singapore, Taiwan, South Korea) have outperformed economically their counterparts elsewhere in the world with more natural resources and larger domestic markets (e.g., Brazil, India, Russia) because of their social capital and policy capacity.[83]

In discussing the extent and speed of interstate power shifts, the existing literature tends to emphasize aggregate measures of tangible assets, such as the size of a country's gross domestic product, its export volume, and its stockpile of weapons. These measures of physical bulk tend to exaggerate China's power. Indeed, one well-known indicator of national strength (the Composite Index of National Capability) showed that shortly before its collapse the Soviet Union had overtaken the United States. These indicators, relying on data such as the size of a country's population, military personnel, energy consumption, and steel production, are simply inadequate, indeed misleading, in informing us about relative national power in the era of globalization with extensive cross-border investment and production.[84] They also overlook the importance of a country's ability to pioneer leading industries and develop cutting-edge technologies,[85] the key determinants of its economic vitality. I return to this topic in chapter 2 and argue that we cannot rely confidently on current indicators to tell us whether and, if so, when a power transition has happened.[86] In other words, our analyses of power shifts and transitions rest on questionable evidence.

Parenthetically, that aggregate measures of bulk can be misleading is underscored by the fact that in the 1830s and perhaps even later, China still had the world's largest economy—just when it was entering its century of national humiliation. China, of course, has long had the world's largest population and one of its largest territories. After all, Britain and other leading global powers preceding it (Portugal and the Netherlands) did not have the largest army, population, or home territory. In fact, they were dwarfed by rivals such as Spain, France, and Russia, which were much bigger in physical size. The strength of leading global powers had typically stemmed from their entrepreneurship, competitive institutions, innovative capacity, and naval prowess.

The dominant current treatment of interstate power shifts does not give enough attention to intangible assets, referring to a government's effectiveness in extracting, mobilizing, and deploying the available resources,[87] as well as to a people's dedication to its collective purpose and its willingness to endure joint privation. Outcomes of war often reflect these intangible aspects of policy capacity.[88] Thus, even though Israel has a smaller territory and population than its Arab adversaries, it has prevailed in many of their armed contests. Also, despite eventually losing its war against the United States, Japan's performance in World War II exceeded what one would have expected from its comparatively small resource base because it was more effective in extracting and mobilizing these resources from its society. Larger and more affluent countries sometimes underperform relative to their counterparts with a smaller resource base because of their more limited policy capacity.

Although cultural stereotyping has fallen to ill repute, national ethos is still relevant. It is hard to imagine that people in Singapore, Taiwan, Korea, or Japan protesting their government's mandate to wear face masks during a pandemic on the grounds that it violates their personal freedom. It is also difficult to imagine national cases comparable to surveys showing that a large proportion of Republicans (49 percent) in the United States would refuse to be vaccinated against COVID-19 apparently largely on the basis of their distrust of government authority.[89] Michele Gelfand and her colleagues present an interesting study showing the association between a culture's "looseness" or "tightness" on the one hand, and its management of the pandemic on the other. Differences in cultural norms evolve to reflect evolutionary advantage in addressing collective threats.[90]

Interstate power shifts reflect not just another country's performance but also one's own performance. Relative to influencing another country's performance, it is more within the power of leaders to influence their own country's performance, not that this is easy to do. The USSR's self-defeating policies had more to do with its demise than U.S. efforts to undermine it did. In competing against China, American leaders face entrenched partisanship, electoral cycles geared to appealing to the medium voter, and a political system designed to favor veto groups and blocking coalitions that hamper long-term commitment and planning. A country's extent of usable power is often limited by its self-imposed impairments or domestic dysfunctions such as that reflected by the collapse of bipartisan consensus in support of Washington's traditional liberal internationalism,[91] hampering (for example) its announced intention to "pivot to Asia."[92] Charles Kupchan and Peter Trubowitz remind Americans that an effective internationalist foreign policy requires a strong domestic foundation based on elite consensus and popular support.[93]

A recent poll conducted by the Public Religion Research Institute shows the extent of political division, disaffection, mistrust, and misinformation affecting U.S. politics. Ariel Edwards-Levy reports that 56 percent of Republicans believed that the 2020 presidential election was rigged and stolen from Donald Trump, and that 23 percent of them held conspiratorial beliefs propagated by the QAnon movement.[94] Those with conspiratorial beliefs tended to mostly or completely agree with the following statements: "the government, media, and financial worlds in the United States are controlled by a group of Satan-worshipping pedophiles who run a global child sex trafficking operation," "there is a storm coming soon that will sweep away the elites in power and restore the rightful leaders," and "because things have gotten so far off track, true American patriots may have to resort to violence in order to save our country." Fourteen percent of the U.S. public professed that they mostly or completely agree with these propositions. Roughly the same percentage said that they will never accept Biden as president, including 29 percent of those who identified themselves as Republicans or leaning Republican.[95] The same survey reports that 32 percent of Americans believed that Biden's victory in the 2020 election was due to voter fraud; 73 percent of Republicans believed it.

Self-inflicted injuries due to incoherent and counterproductive policies can be more damaging than adversaries' policies.[96] I have mentioned Thucydides' maxim that the rise of Athens and Sparta's consequent fear was the root cause of the Peloponnesian War. However, Pericles' warning to his fellow Athenians as told by Thucydides may be even more apposite. Pericles cautioned his compatriots "not to extend your empire at the same time as you are fighting the war and not to add self-imposed dangers, for I am more afraid of our own mistakes than the strategy of our opponents."[97] Considering the disastrous economic, social, and political consequences of the Great Leap Forward campaign and the Cultural Revolution, China inflicted far more harm on itself than the United States could have done. For both China and the United States, the greatest threat to their economic performance and international standing come from their domestic sources.[98]

POLITICAL INCENTIVES AND CONSTRAINED CHOICES

Structural forces can push and shove, but people still make decisions (even though not necessarily under circumstances of their choosing). These decisions tend to reflect leaders' domestic incentives rather than their countries' foreign circumstances. As the venerable U.S. congressman Tip O'Neill once observed, "all politics is local." Trumpism remains even after Trump has left office. Nearly 47 percent of Americans voted for Trump in the 2020 election. Future U.S. leaders will have to face this political reality, which is likely to reduce their policy space with respect to how to deal with Beijing. Any overture by Biden to China is likely to encounter opposition from Republicans and be used by them as a political weapon to accuse him of being soft on Beijing and engaging in appeasement policy.[99] Thus far, the China policies of the Trump and Biden administrations show more continuity than difference.

Even though they can rarely agree on other issues, Republicans and Democrats have convergent views on what U.S. policies toward China should be. Liberals are outraged by China's abuses of human rights, its authoritarian government, and its alleged predatory trade practices that threaten American jobs and wages. Conservatives are hostile to its communist ideology and concerned about the danger that China's rise poses to U.S. primacy. Thus Beijing finds itself in the crosshairs of U.S. politics. Trump obviously thought getting tough on China was a winning campaign strategy. He derisively called COVID-19 "Kung Flu" and used the metaphor of rape to describe how China's commercial policies have hurt American workers. The prospect of conciliating with China obviously faces a strong headwind if China-bashing is perceived to be politically rewarding. This phenomenon in turn implies that Washington is likely to insist on concessions from Beijing before undertaking any moves to bring about a rapprochement. But if, as suggested in chapter 1, the basic reason for the deterioration in Sino-American relations can be traced to the shifting power balance between the two countries, it is not clear what kind of concessions from Beijing would satisfy Washington.

On the other side of the Pacific, Chinese leaders also face the political reality of strong nationalist sentiments. Mass media in China have increasingly taken on a strident, confrontational tone, in part echoing popular views and in part abetting these views. They also often feature sensational and misleading news. A dangerous brew is developing, reflecting overconfidence in China's growing strength and anger at U.S. moves perceived to be deliberately blocking its legitimate aspirations and manifesting patently double standards of judgment. Kupchan and Trubowitz have counseled American leaders to dial back their rhetoric and adopt a more pragmatic approach in dealing with China.[100] Chinese leaders should also follow this advice in managing their country's relations with the United States.

Ironically, as China's political system has become more open to public input and as Chinese leaders become more sensitive to this input, they no longer enjoy the discretionary power commanded by their charismatic predecessors such as Mao Tse-tung and Deng Xiaoping. Although China is not a democracy, the democratization process empowers masses whose views tend to be more nationalist and confrontational than the elite's. Domestic netizens often criticize the Chinese government for being too soft in dealing with the United States and Taiwan. Americans who want to see a more democratic China need to be cognizant that countries undergoing the democratization process can be more prone to getting into foreign conflict.[101]

As Allison points out, Americans should be careful about wishing the Chinese to be "more like us" given that a democratic United States undertook numerous military interventions and wars abroad when it was a new and rising power on the international scene.[102] Mearsheimer quotes Henry Cabot Lodge saying that during the years of its ascendance, the United States had compiled "a record of conquest, colonization, and territorial expansion unequaled by any people in the nineteenth century."[103] Germany's territorial conquests looked puny by comparison. Americans also have often been seized by a crusading spirit and missionary zeal to convert the rest of the world in their image—even though polls show that

Americans generally have a low opinion of their politicians and are increasingly skeptical of their political institutions. This impulse to spread liberal values has ironically inclined the United States often to engage in illiberal practices.[104] China has thus far not sought to propagate its values and export its system of government.

In the language of two well-known political theories, Chinese leaders' policy "win set" has shrunk,[105] and the "selectorate" that they need to answer to has grown.[106] *Win set* refers to the range of foreign deals politically acceptable and feasible given a leader's domestic environment; *selectorate* refers to the size of the leader's political constituency and the minimum number of supporters required for the leader to retain power. Ceteris paribus, leaders who are accountable to a larger number of constituents and who need to form a larger winning coalition from a more diverse constituency to keep power face greater political constraints and a smaller win set. Thus ongoing developments tend to make it more challenging for any Chinese leader, including Xi Jinping, to gain domestic acceptance or ratification that is necessary for any deal with U.S. leaders, who are also increasingly facing similar political predicaments at home.

Naturally, no deal is possible unless the two sides' win sets overlap. Significantly, politically strong and secure leaders have a larger win set—that is, they have greater discretion to compromise with foreigners to reach an agreement because they are less constrained by the need to seek domestic approval for this deal. Leaders in both Beijing and Washington appear to have become more hemmed in by their respective domestic political environment. Former U.S. secretary of agriculture John Dunlop was quoted saying, "bilateral negotiations usually require three agreements—one across the table and one on each side of the table."[107] Thus the stars must be aligned domestically in each country for them to achieve an international deal. The windows for reaching a compromise must be simultaneously open in both countries.[108]

Domestic politics is important in shaping officials' menu of feasible policies and their political motivation in selecting from this menu. Domestic environment serves as a transmission mechanism that converts developments in the external environment, such as interstate power shifts, into meaningful political stimuli for leaders to respond to. Their response may very well be a decision not to respond with alarm when overtaken by another country, such as when China overtook Japan and Japan overtook Russia. Their response may also be to undertake a policy of rapprochement and reconciliation. Just as domestic politics may cause a tendency to inflate foreign threats and vilify foreign adversaries, they can work in reverse, such as in transforming former enemies into friends. Kupchan shows that domestic processes were important in the evolution of Anglo-American relations from adversarial to amicable.[109] Political entrepreneurs played a leading role in framing events for domestic audiences. Their narratives influence public perceptions and sentiments, which can in turn affect the menu of feasible policies available to leaders and their proclivity to select from this menu.

As noted, domestic politics are an important and integral part of the policy environment in which leaders must operate. Officials do not suddenly forget about domestic politics when they make foreign policy. In other words, they do not stop being political animals when formulating foreign policy and overlook these policies' domestic ramifications. They do not artificially compartmentalize domestic and foreign considerations.

BRINGING DECISION-MAKING BACK IN

Contemporary commentators routinely cite Thucydides and, as already mentioned, even name the danger of a collision between a rising state and a ruling state after him.[110] Most, however, fail to connect power shifts at the interstate level of analysis to decision-making at the individual or group level. They therefore fail to provide a causal link connecting power shifts between countries to their leaders' policy choices.[111] Yet how changes at the interstate level are constructed narratively matters for how individual Americans react to them, such as their level of trust in China and their preference for a tougher stance against it. Moreover, people's instincts and disposition, such as the strength of their nationalism and inclination to avoid uncertainty, mediate the influence of media narratives.[112] Thus the effects of power shifts depend on how the issues are framed and how individuals react to these frames.

Why should power shifts raise the danger of war? Writing some 2,500 years ago, Thucydides pointed to the fear aroused by Athens' rise in

Sparta as the leading cause of the Peloponnesian War. Although often invoked by U.S. officials, scholars, and even popular pundits, the invocation does not usually address directly Thucydides' claim. Thus these commentators do not say whether they agree that an established power's fear of a rising power is the reason for their conflict. They do not seem even to be aware of the implied irony in suggesting this parallel between relations among ancient Greek polities and contemporary Sino-American relations.

Those people who invoke Thucydides do not ask whether the established power's fear (or anxiety or sense of insecurity) is warranted or misplaced. The burden for instigating conflict is usually placed on the rising power without much analysis or discussion. Commentators and analysts also do not ask how well this analogy from the ancient past fits the contemporary world.[113] For example, does today's United States, the established power, suggest a suitable replica for ancient Sparta, an agrarian society and political oligarchy featuring a powerful infantry and one that lived in constant fear of rebellion by its slaves? Does today's China, the rising power, provide a reasonably similar profile to ancient Athens, a democracy by the standards of its day and a commercial polity whose wealth and power derived from its naval prowess? The differences between ancient Greece and today's world are important.[114] When used inappropriately, historical analogies can obscure and mislead rather than illuminate.[115] The routine and facile invocation of Thucydides' Trap often betrays a superficial understanding, suggesting a "confirmation bias" and "selective presentism."[116] For example, its proponents do not ask whether intervening events, such as the advent of nuclear weapons and modern democracy, and today's heightened nationalism make analogies from the distant past inappropriate.

Paul MacDonald and Joseph Parent argue that "given the relatively gradual rate of U.S. decline relative to China, the incentives for either side to run risks by courting conflict are minimal."[117] Also offering a relatively sanguine view, Ja Ian Chong and Todd Hall remark that "much less hangs in the balance for either [China or the United States]" today than did in the Anglo-German rivalry before World War I.[118] In a similar vein, warning against facile historical analogies, Etel Solingen points out that China's economy today is far more internationalized than Imperial Germany, and its commercial partners are similarly more internationally oriented than Imperial Germany's strategic ally Austria-Hungary and its opponents Serbia and Russia.[119] Thus she concludes that "arguing that China in 2014 is Germany in 1914 is neither precise nor constructive."[120] In this and other instances, historical analogies can seriously mislead when applied to the contemporary world. As already mentioned, in warning about Thucydides' Trap, analysts often overlook that Athens was a maritime and commercial power with an outward orientation. It was also a democracy in the context of ancient Greece. In contrast, Sparta had an oligarchy and agrarian economy whose power stemmed from its infantry. It was also highly militarist but had an inward outlook. Do these characteristics correspond respectively to contemporary China and the United States, and can we afford to disregard obvious discrepancies in drawing parallels between ancient Greece and today's world?[121]

Many scholars attribute their contemporary understanding to Thucydides and invoke his name to give their own analysis an aura of authority and timelessness. "We tend to read IR [international relations] concepts back into classical texts and periods not because they are brilliantly trans-historical, but because presenting them as such is a legitimation strategy for our presentist arguments."[122] Although contemporary references to Thucydides typically characterize him as a realist and the idea of Thucydides' Trap suggests that this ancient historian saw the interstate distribution of power as the primary determinant of war occurrence, even a casual reading of *The History of the Peloponnesian War* suggests that Thucydides attached great importance to the influence of national character, individual personalities, and human emotions.[123] Thucydides was not a structuralist who privileged the role of interstate power balance in his explanation of war as his much-quoted maxim implies. His nuanced account highlights the greater importance of human agency, teaching "us that even though internal passions and external forces may exert much force, humans are in control of themselves and morally aware; they can only blame themselves for their failures."[124]

In addition to fear, Thucydides' masterful account gives us reason to believe that other human emotions such as greed, honor, arrogance, prejudice, and hubris had also played a role in motivating the ruinous conflagration that befell the ancient Greek world.[125] These human frailties as well as the pursuit of glory or personal or national self-esteem rather than power shifts have historically been the more common and direct causes of war.[126] Further, various cognitive and affective biases can distort people's judgments and elevate the danger of war.[127]

One source of distortion stems from the so-called endowment effect, which inclines people to value more highly what they already have than that not yet in their possession (such as the sale price of the house they own versus the asking price of the house they want). Another is the anchor effect, suggesting that people who have suffered a recent setback do not update their situation as quickly and as sufficiently as their counterparts who have made a gain. Still another tendency is loss aversion, which inclines people to run greater risks to avoid or reverse a loss than they are willing to accept in pursuing a prospective gain. These propositions from prospect theory have received abundant support from experimental research.[128] The theory's insights have also been applied to the study of foreign policy.[129] Experimental research supports the view that individuals tend to prefer hostile policies against others when they suffer a loss in power relative to when they experience a gain in power.[130]

Yet despite its evident relevance to theories about interstate power shifts, prospect theory has not been given enough attention in studies of this phenomenon, perhaps because its propositions go against the ingrained belief that wars are instigated by cocky upstarts—that is, by rising powers that challenge dominant ones. Susan Shirk, a political scientist and former deputy assistant secretary of state in Bill Clinton's administration, avers that "History teaches us that rising powers are likely to provoke war."[131] This generalization, however, typically exempts the United States when it was a rising power. Contrary to prevailing U.S. narratives, prospect theory suggests that a dominant but declining power is more risk acceptant and thus more inclined to take rash actions than a rising power is. Moreover, failures to adapt to a new political reality brought about by changing power balance can stem from tardy and inadequate adjustment by a declining hegemon to trim its international role and downsize its sense of entitlement. Conversely, prospect theory would lead us to hypothesize that a rising state is more inclined to adopt conservative policies to preserve the gains it has already made rather than undertaking risky policies that may jeopardize these gains.

One can also come at the question of why power shifts should engender war from a rationalist perspective. If the current trend is making a rising power stronger, why should it not let this trend be its friend, letting the ongoing process to further extend its ascendance? Why would it want to precipitate a premature confrontation with the established power that is still stronger, a conflict that will likely end in its defeat? Thus it would be odd for German leaders to start a war against Britain if they had expected to displace the latter in short order as the world's dominant power. Why should they not wait if by doing so they could gain mastery of the world, or at least that of Europe, peacefully? Something must be missing in the standard narrative provided by power-transition theory to explain Germany's actual conduct.

Similarly, if Chinese leaders can be confident that their country would eventually overtake the United States, they would want to bide their time and avoid a premature confrontation. They should realize that the most dangerous time for their country is when it can be perceived by the United States to present a rising threat but when it is not yet strong enough to deter the United States and, if deterrence fails, to fight it successfully. China is currently facing this most acute window of vulnerability, when it is improving its international position enough to cause concern and even alarm in Washington but when it is still considerably weaker than the United States.

This observation in turn raises the question why Chinese leaders would or should want to irritate, even provoke, the United States. Plenty of discussion has been held in China in recent years about whether it should jettison Deng Xiaoping's famous advice for its leaders to adopt a low profile and bide their time, replacing his motto with a more assertive foreign policy. One possible interpretation of this switch in Beijing's general policy orientation is that its leaders believe that China has already gained enough strength to stand up against the United States. If so, they are in my view making a serious mistake of underestimating U.S. strength and in danger of falling victim to overconfidence, arrogance, and hubris. Another possible interpretation of putative Chinese assertiveness, such as in referring to Beijing's conduct in its sovereignty disputes in the South China Sea and East China Sea, is that this behavior is often a reaction to its counterparts' actions.[132] Still another interpretation is that alleged Chinese assertiveness reflects mainly Western political construction because Beijing's conduct has not actually changed in any significant way even though its power has increased.[133] Alistair Johnston, for example, criticizes prevailing Western discourse on a more assertive China for selecting on the dependent variable, poor specification of causal arguments, and overlooking Beijing's prior behavior. Western media and blogsphere are responsible for creating an echo chamber, amplifying popular memes, and creating a "discursive tidal wave" that promotes a simplistic and distorted view of reality. Here we see an example of political entrepreneurs at work and their influence in framing and propagating popular narratives.[134]

Prospect theory argues that people's decision processes often contradict the rationalist premise typically attributed to them. It shows that people do not follow cost-benefit calculations as rational decision-making suggests. The rationalist logic would incline us to expect Beijing to refrain from demanding full and immediate adjustment of its status to reflect its newly gained capabilities. It would prefer a more gradual adjustment for fear of alarming other countries, especially the ruling hegemon. It would accept an incremental process to raise its international profile and stature because it expects further improvements in its capabilities in the future. But when Beijing becomes more insistent in being compensated immediately and fully for a prestigious status or material allocation that is commensurate with its capabilities, this change in its demand would imply a belief that its growth trajectory is poised to stall or even decline so that it is no longer sensible for it to bank on further gains in the future and thus to defer gratification of its current or recent attainments.[135] This reasoning suggests that a China whose continued ascent is in jeopardy could be more troublesome than a growing China—a proposition that presents another contrarian view to the conventional wisdom.

This conventional wisdom, reflecting power-transition theory, claims that a rising power has a revisionist motivation to challenge the existing international order because this order is rigged to favor the dominant power and its associates. With its rise, the newcomer will have more capability to challenge the existing order and hence poses a danger to international peace and stability. This logic, however, overlooks the fact that a rising newcomer now acquires a larger a stake in the existing order that has permitted and even facilitated its rise and it therefore has less incentive to overturn it. Conversely, a dominant power in decline now has more incentive to change the rules of the game to reverse its setback and it still commands the greatest capability to promote this change. It is not clear why a dominant power in decline should be forever committed to the existing international order, one that is no longer working to its advantage.

A rationalist perspective raises the question of why Chinese and U.S. leaders would want to fight when they should know all too well that fighting can be costly. Leaders of belligerent countries have in the past run the nontrivial risk of losing not only their country's territory or sovereignty, but also their personal power and even lives. As James Fearon explains,[136] war is inefficient because both prospective belligerents would be better off if they could settle their differences without going to war. That they still sometimes go to war can only mean that bargaining has failed, that is, they have been unable to come to an agreement about who is entitled to what. War then becomes a way for each side to demonstrate on the battlefield its (relative) power and to substantiate its demand for entitlement. In Mark Twain's words, what makes a horse race is a difference of opinion.

This discussion suggests that the leaders of at least one belligerent state must believe that their country's power entitles it to greater tangible and intangible compensation (e.g., land, prestige) than it is currently receiving. Put differently, the rationalist perspective argues that if a country's relative power accords with its relative share of benefits received from the international system, it could not credibly threaten to go to war because fighting will not improve its share of benefits. Thus, as Robert Powell indicates,[137] when the international distribution of power corresponds with the international distribution of benefits, the danger of war is the smallest—regardless of whether the balance of power is shifting in favor of one country or another. Returning to Vasquez's remark, it is a sense of grievance, or a feeling of relative deprivation that one has been undercompensated or underrecognized in light of one's actual accomplishments, that motivates war.[138]

This view implicates the rising power as the aggrieved party, one that is motivated to revise and challenge the existing order. At the same time, the leaders of the established state must also believe that their country is entitled to at least the same compensation (whether tangible material or intangible considerations such as influence, deference, respect, or status), if not more, to dispose it to accept a fight. Significantly, if the established power is experiencing a relative decline, this perspective points to the possibility that its refusal to trim its international role or to downsize its sense of entitlement can also be a source of conflict.

Thus, again, it takes two to make war. One side insists on having its place in the sun. The other refuses to accommodate. Interwar Japan, for example, belatedly learned that the door to becoming a member of the select club of great powers was shut to it. The perspective just presented accords with the views of earlier theorists on power transition,[139] who acknowledged forthrightly that the rules of international order are rigged to favor established countries to the detriment of latecomers. Recent commentators and analysts, however, have often taken the position that these rules and the international order embodying them are somehow a settled matter, neutral in their effect on distributing international benefits, and even sacrosanct, when in fact they are always in flux and subject to constant negotiation and renegotiation.[140] This position suggests a status-quo bias.

BEIJING'S AND WASHINGTON'S CHOICES

Naturally, both the United States and China would like to be a dominant power, globally or regionally, to further ensure their safety and enhance their influence. However, the pertinent question is not whether being a global or regional hegemon would make a country safer or more influential. Instead, it is for the United States to determine whether efforts to maintain this hegemony could in the end make it less safe and influential and for China, whether bidding for it would also make it less safe and influential.[141]

If the United States has already established an unassailable regional hegemony in the Western Hemisphere, to what extent can a China dominant in East Asia compromise U.S. security and survival? (Mearsheimer's offensive realism avers that it is impossible for any country, presumably including China, to achieve global hegemony.) Would Washington's insistence on maintaining its global preponderance engender imperial overstretch and result in weakening rather than strengthening its long-term international position and influence?[142] Swaine and Tellis warn that "a U.S. victory would be truly fleeting if, in the process of successfully combating . . . [Chinese] assertiveness, it enervated itself to the point where another rising power assumes global leadership simply because the victorious but now exhausted hegemon has no further capacity to resist."[143] Recent debate among U.S. scholars shows divided opinion on whether the United States should "come home" or not.[144] Should Washington trim its international commitments and reset its policy agenda to give more priority to domestic issues or should it continue its active international role and maintain forward deployment of its military assets abroad?

For Beijing, how large would be the increment of additional safety it would acquire by becoming East Asia's regional hegemon relative to its current situation? Further, what is the probability that it will be successful in establishing this regional hegemony given the devastating consequences that Germany, Japan, and the Soviet Union experienced in undertaking similar quests in the past? It seems that this prospect is not very bright. As Kirshner remarks,[145] four (twice by Germany in the two world wars) of five such bids in the past have ended in failure. Only the United States had succeeded, and only under rather unique historical circumstances.[146] The odds of success are thus only one in five based on this historical record (even when we exclude failed bids to dominate Europe by Napoleon's France and the Spanish Hapsburgs).

Any rational leader in Beijing should be able conclude that China is already largely safe from any threat of foreign invasion or occupation. Its basic security and survival are not in any doubt. If history provides any lesson, however, the odds are stacked against it in a bid to gain regional hegemony using military force. Such a gambit would most likely be counterproductive in causing a countervailing coalition to form against China, diminishing rather than enhancing its security and influence, even threatening the survival of the Communist Party if not the country, should there be a war pitting China against a much more powerful opposition. Of course, the difference in how Beijing seeks to establish its regional influence, whether by military conquest or economic interdependence, is tremendous. The latter approach is far less likely, from Beijing's perspective, to provoke an adverse reaction and has until now already expanded Beijing's regional influence significantly.

Thus the facile assumption that, solely because of the ongoing power shift between them, the United States and China are on a collision course needs to be subjected to critical scrutiny. This remark does not of course suggest that leaders are immune from stupidity or to deny that they can repeat their predecessors' mistakes. Arguments pointing to Thucydides' Trap or power transitions inducing war are intended to suggest that officials can be overwhelmed by the circumstances they find themselves in. Hubris, ambition, overconfidence, arrogance, greed, fear, ignorance, and even a sense of honor can cause them to misjudge and stumble into war. This remark in turn brings us back to the argument that changing interstate balance of power does not in itself precipitate war. People's decisions do.

Leaders are forward looking. They try to anticipate the future and make plans accordingly. China in early 2021 overtook the United States as the leading destination for foreign direct investment. It is the largest trading state in the world and the leading commercial partner for many countries. Its economy is expected to surpass that of the United States in the next decade. These developments suggest that, according to the rationalist logic, China's leaders should and would be leery of upsetting the international order that has enabled its rise thus far. China's increasing weight on the world stage also means that it will be difficult for Washington to bypass Beijing in any collective effort to manage global problems such as climate change and contagious disease.

Being forward looking does not mean that leaders will forget the past. Path dependency reminds us that actions taken today can limit options available tomorrow and it is sometimes difficult to reverse the ill effects of past actions. Although a debate on who started it can always be had, it is relatively clear that the recent impetus for deglobalization in the form of reversing liberal policies on trade and immigration has come primarily from the West. Similarly, the initiative to economically decouple from China has come from Washington. The effects of these developments and the harm done by the Trump administration in turning the United States away from multilateralism and in confronting China on a variety of issues will be felt for some time to come. As I discuss in chapter 4, these U.S. policies have political ramifications in redistributing the interests and influence of various Chinese stakeholders, and they are likely to enhance the domestic position of those with a more inward-looking and nationalist policy orientation at the expense of others with a more internationalist outlook.

Timing is obviously important. As already mentioned, Germany started a preventive war against Russia in 1914 and again against the Soviet

Union in 1941.[147] In Stephen Van Evera's view, "the First World War was in part a 'preventive' war, launched by the Central powers in the belief that they were saving themselves from a worse fate in later years."[148] German Chancellor Bethmann Hollweg reflected this view in 1918 when he acknowledged that "Yes, my God, in a certain sense it was a preventive war." He had explained Germany's decision to bring on a confrontation in 1914 when "war is still possible without defeat, but not in two years!"[149] "Our military men." he added, "were fully convinced that now [July 1914] they could *still* come out of a war victorious; but in a few years, i.e., 1916, after the completion of the Russian railroads, [this] would no longer be so."[150] Helmuth von Moltke, chief of the German General Staff, was reported by Foreign Secretary Gottlieb von Jagow in May 1914 to be worried that "In two to three years Russia would have finished arming. Our enemies' military power would then be so great that he did not know how he [Moltke] could deal with it. Now we were still more or less still of match for it. In his view there was no alternative but to fight a preventive war so as to beat the enemy while we could still emerge fairly well from the struggle. The Chief of Staff therefore put it to me that our policy should be geared to bringing about an early war."[151]

Adolf Hitler expressed similar views before World War II, warning that "favorable circumstances will no longer prevail in two or three years' time," and that Germany would face "certain annihilation sooner or later" if it did not launch a preventive war at a moment most propitious to it.[152]

I do not mean to suggest that the United States is considering a preventive war against China. Still, given these two countries' relative growth rates, when would it be too late for Washington to confront Beijing? It is still possible now to block China's further ascent, but this effort may be too late in ten or fifteen years. By then, the costs to the United States would be higher and the probability of success lower. As British prime minister Robert Salisbury commented ruefully on his country's lost chance to check America's rise, "It is very sad, but I am afraid America is bound to forge ahead and nothing can restore the equality between us. If we had interfered in the Confederate Wars [on behalf on the South] it was then possible for us to reduce the power of the United States to manageable proportions. But two such chances are not given to a nation in the course of its career."[153]

Nevertheless, it is worth asking whether America's rise was stoppable even had Britain tried. Surely, the United States was able to rise faster because it did not have to face the distraction of coping with foreign challenges and hinderances. As Yongping Feng points out,[154] "it is difficult to imagine that . . . the United States would have managed its ascendance so smoothly" had Britain decided to block its rise. But even had it done so, it could have only delayed, not prevented the ultimate outcome. This policy, however, would likely have made the United States its implacable enemy. The history of these countries' relations and the outcomes of the two world wars would then have likely turned out quite differently.

Some readers may object to introducing preventive war in this context, arguing that democracies do not wage preventive wars.[155] They may point to moral or ethical reasons that would inhibit democracies from engaging in this practice because it contradicts their values and identities. They may also suggest that democratic institutions and the citizens of democracies would not support starting a war to head off a potential, and therefore uncertain, threat in the future. However, as mentioned, the United States did consider attacking China's Lop Nor nuclear facilities when China was still at the early stage of developing its nuclear arsenal.[156] It also considered using nuclear weapons against China during the 1958 Taiwan Strait crisis.[157] An analysis of Israel's decision processes leading up to its 1956 Sinai campaign and its 1981 airstrike against Iraq's Osirak nuclear reactor, the Bush administration's decision processes culminating in the U.S. war against Iraq in 1991 and again in 2003, and the Clinton administration's planning for an airstrike against North Korea in 1994 suggests that the preventive motivation was present in all these cases. Moreover, democratic institutions such as the legislature and media did not stand in the way of these decision processes, and public opinion in fact supported preventive war.[158] The Clinton administration did not go through with its plan to attack North Korea, but this decision was based on a cost-benefit analysis, not moral or ethical reasons.

THE BOOK'S PLAN

The preceding discussion provides my overall explanation of the war phenomenon. It reports the conclusions of some of my earlier research. The rest of this book addresses other building blocks of my explanation, ones I have not until now had an opportunity to fully develop. It takes up the following puzzles or questions.

In chapter 1, I ask why relations between the United States and China have deteriorated so seriously, even though China's society and economy have become more open, its diplomacy has become more engaged with multilateral missions and international institutions, and its foreign policy rhetoric and conduct have become less bellicose than they were in the Maoist years (and indeed relative to the United States in terms of the frequency and scale of resort to armed force abroad)? After considering alternative explanations, I conclude that the shifting power balance between the two countries offers the most persuasive answer.

Given this conclusion, it is important and necessary to address what power is and how to measure it. Chapter 2 argues that our current conceptualization and measurement of power shifts are woefully inadequate. Standard indicators of relative national power cannot answer puzzles such as why have weaker and smaller countries often performed better than their stronger and larger counterparts on the battlefield (e.g., Vietnam, Afghanistan), in their respective economic growth (e.g., Singapore, Korea), and in managing their public health, such as in coping with the COVID-19 pandemic. I argue that these phenomena are due to the differences in the relevant actors' political capacity to effectively mobilize and deploy their material resources. This crucial factor, political capacity, has not been given enough attention in the literature.

The issues discussed in chapter 2 pertain to the power relationship between two countries. They seek to compare, for example, the United States with China in specific encounters or issue areas. More pertinent to the discourse on global domination and challenges to this domination is a state's overall strength derived from its positions in and connections to international military, financial, and information networks. These positions and connections refer to a country's structural power, which is the focus of chapter 3. Relative to the dyadic power relationship between two countries in specific contexts, structural power is far more pervasive and relevant to the exercise and maintenance of global hegemony. Chapter 3 explains why the often-heard lament of a U.S. decline is overblown, and why the U.S. advantage in structural power will persist for some time to come. Thus it questions whether a power transition between the United States and China is in fact under way, even while acknowledging that China has narrowed the gap separating it from the United States.

Chapter 4 follows the adage from former House Speaker Tip O'Neill that "all politics is local." It explains why developments inside both China and the United States have constrained their leaders' policy space (that is, their political wriggle room to reach a compromise with their counterpart). Popular mood and political partisanship have instead made scapegoating foreigners and rhetorical exaggeration more prevalent. The hard-liners in both countries have become their counterparts' best allies in creating both an echo chamber of reciprocal recriminations and mirror images of hostility. In short, domestic political dynamics are increasing the danger of foreign conflict. The same domestic dynamics shape a country's economic policies and conditions. They can produce political gridlock and even self-defeating policies that hamper long-term economic growth, which is the key determinant of a country's relative position in the international hierarchy. Thus a country's foreign policies and its international relations have their roots in its domestic politics. This proposition explains why sometimes politicians pursue policies that are manifestly detrimental to their country's international position but that tend to make them more popular among domestic constituents. Significantly, public opinion in the United States and China has turned quite sharply antagonistic against the other, and politicians on both sides are far more likely to reflect and even abet this popular mood than going against it. The important takeaway from this chapter is that power shifts in themselves have an indeterminate effect on interstate relations. Political entrepreneurs in domestic competition seek to frame these developments to advance their partisan cause, so that some of such developments are seen as inconsequential and even positively and others are interpreted as serious threats to national security.

Chapter 5 asks the question of why Taiwan? Why is Taiwan again becoming a flashpoint even though Washington conceded some time ago, albeit ambiguously, that this island is part of China. Why, despite Taiwan's relatively low importance in affecting the international balance of power, are influential voices in Washington now demanding that the United States intervene militarily if China mounts an assault against Taiwan (even when memories of the Afghan debacle are still fresh)? Why, on the other hand, cannot Beijing just "let it go"? In this chapter, I explain how domestic politics and public opinion in China, the United States, and Taiwan are making a compromise more difficult to reach even as recent military developments may incline Beijing to resort to arms. The discussion in this chapter shines a light on how domestic politics motivates and interacts with foreign policy. It also highlights how a local and bilateral dispute may become the fuse igniting a wider conflict.

Finally, in the conclusion, I summarize this book's main arguments and review the policy challenges that both Beijing and Washington face.

1

POWER SHIFT EXPLAINS BETTER WORSENING SINO-AMERICAN RELATIONS

Recent discourse in China and the United States leaves little doubt that the elites and publics of both countries have increasingly come to view each other as competitors, even adversaries, in technological, economic, and security matters. Although the Joe Biden administration is widely perceived as favoring a less confrontational approach than its predecessor, few signs in its early days suggest that tension in Sino-American relations will quickly abate.[1] The meeting held in March 2021 in Alaska between top Chinese and American foreign policy officials suggests that neither side is eager to reach an agreement to dial back bilateral tension. At least publicly, these officials appeared intent on broadcasting to their respective domestic audiences that they would stand their ground. As one source remarks, "Washington has been talking tough, expecting 'extreme competition' between it and Beijing in the coming years."[2]

This source quotes President Biden saying in a speech given at the State Department that the United States would "confront China's economic abuses; counter its aggressive, coercive action; push back on China's attack on human rights, intellectual property, and global governance." In response, China's top diplomat Yang Jiechi, director of the Office of Central Commission for Foreign Affairs, told Secretary of State Antony Blinken that the United States should "rectify its mistakes made over a period of time and work with China to uphold the spirit of no conflict, no confrontation, mutual respect and win-win cooperation, focus on cooperation and manage differences," and stressed that "the two sides should respect each other's core interests and choices of political system and development path, and manage their domestic affairs well." Yang Jie-chi pointedly noted that "it is not for the U.S. alone to evaluate its democracy,"[3] suggesting that even many Americans have questioned the state of democracy in the United States. When celebrating the one-hundredth anniversary of the founding of the Chinese Communist Party, Xi Jing-ping, China's president, said pointedly that "China welcomes helpful suggestions, but won't accept sanctimonious preaching."[4]

These exchanges reflect significant discord and rising antipathy relative to these countries' relations as recently as a decade ago, and offer a sharp contrast to the days when they were practically allies during the Nixon, Ford, and Carter administrations in their joint effort to oppose the Soviet Union. Those who are old enough may still remember Americans' love affair with China's pandas during those heady days. What happened?

HAS ENGAGING CHINA BEEN A FAILURE?

One often hears that U.S. policy to "engage" China was a mistake based on illusions of reforming China and that it has not worked.[5] This conclusion has led to a new consensus that the United States should now adopt a tougher policy toward a more assertive or aggressive China. This discourse, however, fundamentally mischaracterizes U.S. policy toward China since the 1970s. This policy has always been a mixture of engaging Beijing while balancing and containing its influence.[6] For instance, President Bill Clinton summoned two U.S. carrier groups to the Taiwan Strait in 1996; during Clinton's administration, the United States had also bombed China's embassy in Belgrade in 1999 (Washington explained that it was an accident, but most Chinese do not believe this explanation); and a U.S. electronic surveillance plane EP-3 and a Chinese fighter jet collided off China's Hainan Island in 2001 during the George W. Bush administration. More recently, Washington opposed Beijing's hosting of the 2008 Summer Olympic Games and lobbied other countries (mostly unsuccessfully) not to join the Asian Infrastructure Investment Bank initiated by China in 2016. The reorientation of U.S. military posture, commonly described as its "pivot to Asia," had already started in 2004 rather than later in 2011, as usually thought.[7]

To attribute China's recent assertiveness or aggressiveness to the failure of U.S. engagement policy and to use this claim to justify more balancing and containment is therefore disingenuous. China's assertive or aggressive behavior could also be blamed on the limits of a policy of balancing and containment, and even argued to be a reaction to U.S. efforts to balance and contain it. Moreover, it is a matter for debate whether China's behavior has in fact become more assertive or aggressive in recent years (relative to its conduct, say, during the Maoist years). Naturally, one does not hear the reverse of the common narrative in the United States, suggesting that China's policy of rapprochement and engagement with the United States has failed because it has not made the United States less assertive or aggressive, given Washington's promotion of various color revolutions and military interventions abroad since the Cold War's end, and its policy toward Taiwan.

In promoting democracy abroad, Washington has been highly selective, as shown in its discrepant treatment of popular movements in Ukraine and Armenia; the main reason distinguishing its policies toward these countries appears to be whether their government has an anti-Russian orientation. Arman Grigoryan concludes that "contrary to the popular narrative, the West has supported democracy only when that support has been reinforced by material interests, and rarely, if ever, when it has posed a threat to such interests."[8] One does not need to be a foreign policy expert to recall that Washington was not greatly upset when military forces overthrew elected governments in South Korea and Egypt and, indeed, was itself complicit in the violent overthrow of such governments headed by Iran's Mohammad Mossadegh and Chile's Salvador Allende.

It is not always clear what advocates of a "firmer" or "tougher" U.S. policy toward China have expected a policy of engaging China to accomplish. If they had expected to transform China into a full-fledged liberal democracy like the United States, and to convert the Chinese people's values and identities in close alignment with those of Americans, the expectation has indeed not been met. But that is such a tall order that one would not expect anyone to have realistically entertained. Moreover, as Graham

Allison remarks,[9] Americans would not presumably want China to imitate Washington's policies when the United States was a rising power, such as declaring the Monroe Doctrine to exclude European influence from the Western Hemisphere and to undertake frequent armed interventions in neighboring countries. He notes that during the late 1800s and early 1900s, "The US [had] declared war on Spain, expelling it from the Western Hemisphere and acquiring Puerto Rico, Guam, and the Philippines; threatened Germany and Britain with war unless they agreed to settle disputes on American terms; supported an insurrection in Colombia to create a new country, Panama, in order to build a canal; and declared itself the policeman of the Western Hemisphere, asserting the right to intervene whenever and wherever it judged necessary—a right it exercised nine times in the seven years of TR's [Theodore Roosevelt's] presidency alone."[10] Allison thus warns Americans to be more careful in wishing the Chinese to be "more like us."[11] If Xi Jinping were to act like Theodore Roosevelt, he would be pursuing much more aggressive policies to expand China's influence in its home region.

If Washington's policy of engaging China was intended to have more modest goals than a thorough transformation of China's political system and society, one cannot as easily argue that this approach has been a failure. China's society and economy have surely become more open since the 1970s. Its political system has also become less authoritarian. It has reformed its economy to emphasize private enterprises and to open it to foreign companies' operations. It is now deeply embedded in the global economy, with foreign trade taking up a larger percentage of its gross domestic product than in the United States and foreign investment accounting for a higher portion of its economy than in Japan. If human rights encompass security from hunger, diseases, illiteracy, and poverty, China presents arguably the most successful story in history to have lifted the greatest number of people in the least amount time from these deprivations.[12] Beijing's foreign policy has also seen a sea change since the days of its revolutionary stance promoting the violent overthrow of foreign bourgeois governments, rejecting agreements to limit nuclear armament, and opposing various international organizations including the United Nations. If the intent of U.S. policies toward China is to promote Beijing's integration in the global economy and to encourage its involvement in multilateral diplomacy, then these policies have in fact been a "fantastic success."[13]

I now review various popular but specious explanations of why Sino-American relations have worsened. They are grouped into two broad categories, China's internal and external conditions or policies.

CHINA'S INTERNAL POLICIES

NATURE OF CHINA'S AND TAIWAN'S POLITICAL SYSTEM

None of the preceding remarks suggests that Beijing's policies and practices are beyond reproach. It is not a liberal democracy like the United States. This said, it is also difficult to deny progress since Richard Nixon visited Beijing in 1972 or since Jimmy Carter announced formal diplomatic relations with it in 1978. As Michael Swaine and Ashley Tellis,[14] who can hardly be considered apologists for Beijing, remark, "Although China is by no means democratic today [2000], there is little doubt that a slow process of democratization has been under way since 1978. The sphere of personal freedoms has increased; the capricious exercise of state power has been reduced, especially as far as threats to the lives of Chinese citizens are concerned; and the development of institutions pertaining to the rule of law, the respect for property, the adjudication of disputes, and the exercise of power is gradually under way."

Referring to the VDem dataset on political liberalization, Alastair Johnston paints a mixed picture for changes in China's domestic political situation.[15] On the one hand, this dataset's index of "liberal democracy" shows no change since Mao Tse-tung's death. Its index of "freedom of expression" shows a dip from when Jiang Zemin and Hu Jintao were in power and remains comparable to the days when Deng Xiaoping was the paramount leader. On the other hand, the index on "equality before law and individual liberty" shows a slight improvement from the Deng era to the current period under Xi Jinping. The overall picture suggests that despite no change in Chinese people's political rights, some gains in their personal liberty are evident. This assessment is also supported by the

Freedom House's annual reports discussed later. Like Swaine and Tellis, Johnston concludes that with major exceptions, such as the government's treatment of religious freedom, "Chinese society is more pluralistic than any time since the 1950s."[16]

Arguably, even after Beijing's military crackdown against protesters at Tiananmen Square in 1989 (which was motivated by the fear that the fate of communist regimes in Eastern and Central Europe might befall China),[17] the United States got along with China better than today. Although the administration of George H. Bush imposed sanctions on Beijing, it worked to contain a serious deterioration in bilateral relations and to restore these relations in relatively short order. In contrast, Sino-American relations have been in a steady decline in recent years, and there is, at least of now, little indication that the Biden administration is interested in returning to the state of these relations before the Donald Trump and even Barack Obama administrations.[18] A policy of pivoting or rebalancing to Asia, clearly with China as its target, was initiated before the Obama years,[19] whereas the intensification of trade and technological tension occurred during Trump's tenure. In its early days, the Biden administration showed an interest in invigorating the Quad (as the Quadrilateral Security Dialogue with Australia, India, and Japan is known), with China clearly as its intended target. Biden held a virtual (electronic) meeting with the leaders of the other three countries in March 2021, pledging commitment to a "free, open, secure" Indo-Pacific.[20] In contrast to the phenomenon shortly after the end of the Cold War that suggested a breakdown of traditional coalitions, the Quad points to a reversal of this trend and portends a more polarized pattern of alignments given that China and Russia have also been moving closer together.

The general transformation of China's political economy suggests that this country has moved increasingly away from both the model of a command economy and its history of political repression and authoritarianism as highlighted by the Cultural Revolution and the Tiananmen Square crackdown. In the years immediately after China and the United States established formal diplomatic relations, these countries were practically speaking allies in their joint opposition to the USSR. In recent years, however, their relations have become more contentious, even hostile. Elementary logic suggests that Beijing's professed communist ideology, its one-party rule, and its repression of human rights cannot be the only reasons, or even the main ones, for worsening Sino-American relations. Washington, after all, did not let these concerns stand in the way of rapprochement and even cooperation in the 1970s and 1980s, when Beijing's practices were more egregious and its record more objectionable. Its official ideology and one-party rule have not changed and as constant factors, they cannot explain changes in U.S. attitudes and policies about China.

Many of the reasons Washington gives for criticizing and opposing Beijing today are simply not believable. Consider U.S. policy toward Taiwan, which provides an example contradicting Washington's public rationale. U.S. support for the island was strongest when it was ruled by Chiang Kai-shek's authoritarian regime under martial law and when it was dominated by a single party (the Kuomintang). As the Kuomintang's iron grip slowly relaxed, Washington's support for Taiwan waned and on January 1, 1979 it switched diplomatic recognition to Beijing and started to withdraw U.S. military installations from the island. The trendlines belie the rhetoric that one hears today that the United States must support Taiwan because it is a democracy. It appears instead that the nature of Taiwan's political system does not matter very much to Washington. Indeed, in the years immediately after Beijing and Washington established formal diplomatic relations, the United States aligned more closely with China—just when Taiwan was becoming more democratic.

In 1977, before the U.S. diplomatic recognition of China and de-recognition of Taiwan, Freedom House gave political rights and civil liberties in China each a score of 6 (on a scale of 1 to 7, 7 being the worst) and Taiwan a score of 5 for its people's political rights and 4+ for its civil liberties.[21] Since then, China's scores have remained relatively stable (it was rated 7 for its citizens' political rights in many subsequent years, the score for its people's civil liberties remaining at 6), whereas Taiwan's ratings improved to outstanding levels (1s) for both its people's political rights and civil liberties in 2016. Indeed, in Freedom House's recent ratings, Taiwan's scores were better than those for the United States. For example, in its new rating system Freedom House gave Taiwan 38 (out of 40) on its people's political rights and 56 (out of 60) on its people's civil liberties in 2021, relative to -2 and 11 for China and 32 and 51 for the United States.[22] This discussion's larger point is that domestic authoritarianism clearly cannot explain the differences in Washington's policies toward Beijing and Taipei and in the evolution of these policies over time.

Washington's Taiwan policy is derivative of its China policy. Taiwan is important to the United States because it is important to China, providing Washington an important leverage to influence Beijing—or a thorn to irritate Beijing. Those who argue that Taiwan's political system and its people's right to self-determination are intrinsically important to Washington need only recall what happened to South Vietnam after many years of U.S. assurance that it would not abandon Saigon. The Trump administration was clearly anxious to withdraw U.S. troops from northern Syria and Afghanistan. It extracted U.S. troops from northern Syria in October 2019, abandoning the Kurdish forces there allied with the United States, and—over the objections of its ally, the Afghan government—made a hasty deal with the Taliban to pull out all U.S. troops from Afghanistan by May 1, 2021.[23] Overruling the Pentagon's objection, Biden subsequently changed the date of U.S. troop withdrawal to September 11, 2021. The Kabul government quickly collapsed after the United States pulled out its forces in August. The Taliban took over in eleven days. Many argue that the rapid disintegration of the Afghan government can in part be attributed to the perception that Washington had abandoned it. Future U.S. policies toward Iraq will offer additional evidence on the strength and reliability of Washington's commitment to this ally. After the U.S. debacle in Afghanistan, Taipei publicized that Washington had reassured it that its situation is different from Kabul's and that the United States remains committed to its defense.

RIGHT OF SELF-DETERMINATION

Washington's rhetoric concerning a people's right to self-determination also sounds hollow in view of its ambivalence and even opposition to the demands of Palestinians, Kurds, Biafrans, and Bangladeshis. This is also true of its condemnation of Crimea's secession from Ukraine after a plebiscite held by Crimea's residents to approve a union with Russia. Joining other Western countries, the United States condemned Russia's annexation. It insisted that Ukraine's entire population should have a say in the matter and that Crimea's secession should follow Ukraine's constitutional procedures—ironically echoing Beijing's objections to Taiwan's independence. More recently, Washington condemned Moscow's recognition of the independence of Donestk and Luhansk, two oblasts seeking secession from Ukraine, as a violation of international law. The parallel is obvious, Beijing seeing Taiwan as a breakaway province. The overwhelming majority of the international community, including the United States itself, recognize Beijing as the legitimate government of China, with only fourteen tiny states maintaining diplomatic relations with Taipei. Official Washington routinely expresses its concerns about the rights of Tibetans and Uighurs in Xinjiang, but not often about the people living in Kashmir under Indian rule or Palestinians living in territories occupied by Israel.

Nor, if one is to recall history, did Abraham Lincoln tolerate the Confederacy's attempt to secede from the Union. As Barry Buzan and Michael Cox remark, "Parallels could in fact be drawn between the ruthless military anti-secessionism and rejection of self-determination that underpinned the US civil war, and China's similar current attitudes towards Tibet, Taiwan, and Xinjiang. Abraham Lincoln and the Chinese Communist Party would perhaps have understood each other quite well on this question. The United States has been more fortunate in that its unity question was largely laid to rest after the Civil War, and did not much affect its peaceful rise. For China, the unity question is still not fully resolved, especially over Tibet and Taiwan. It plays significantly into China's international image, and therefore into its wider foreign policy and IR [international relations]."[24]

The United States was fortunate that although Britain considered intervening on the Confederacy's side, it eventually decided not to involve itself in the U.S. civil war and therefore "lost" its last chance to divide the United States and prevent it from becoming the behemoth that it eventually became. As noted in the introduction, British prime minister Robert Salisbury lamented this lost opportunity. In contrast, China's unfinished civil war can be largely traced to President Harry Truman's decision to order the Seventh Fleet to intervene in the Taiwan Strait shortly after the outbreak of the Korean War, thereby preventing a communist assault on the Kuomintang's last bastion and saving it from the dustbin of history. Throughout the Chinese civil war, the United States had backed the Kuomintang and provided it with large amounts of aid. When seeking to understand the current state of Sino-American and Russo-American relations, one should not overlook the legacies of Western (including U.S.) intervention in their respective civil wars.

Washington did not object to those secessionist movements that tore apart former Yugoslavia, even resorting to bombing Serbia in Kosovo's campaign for independence. Moreover, as mentioned, it promoted and supported Panama's break from Colombia. The entire legal justification for U.S. military intervention in the Korean and Vietnam wars was based on the claim that these conflicts were not civil wars but instead instances of international aggression that started when one side (namely, the communist north in both cases) crossed an international border to invade the other, and that this behavior was therefore tantamount to international aggression.

Finally, invoking Washington's support for the right of Taiwan's people to determine their own future is misleading and even disingenuous because it has been the U.S. policy to prevent not only China from taking over the island militarily—but also Taiwan from declaring formal independence.[25] This policy has been specifically designed to discourage Taipei from carrying out the majority preference of its people favoring secession, a provocation that would incline Beijing to respond by resorting to force. Indeed, Washington did not try to hide its displeasure with other milder forms of provocation by Chen Shui-bian (Taiwan's former president representing the Democratic Progressive Party) in pursuit of his pro-independence agenda and openly favored Kuomintang's candidate Ma Ying-jeou in his successful bid to become Taiwan's subsequent president in 2008.

VIOLATIONS OF HUMAN RIGHTS

In narratives on worsening relations between China and the United States, one also often hears criticisms of China's record on human rights, including its mistreatment of the Uighurs and its suppression of Hong Kong's demonstrators. Critics of China, however, tend to overlook the plight of Palestinians and America's own racial and ethnic minorities. They do not often mention the internment of Americans of Japanese descent during World War II, the deportation of about a million people of Mexican descent (including many who were U.S. citizens) during the 1930s, and the forcible removal of Native Americans from their ancestral lands to be relocated to "reservations" (such as that remembered by the Cherokee people as the Trail of Tears). The enslavement of African Americans and government-mandated discrimination against them and people of Asian descent (such as the Chinese-Exclusion Act that banned Chinese immigrants from the United States) are legacies whose effects continue to be felt today (as demonstrated by the Black Lives Matter movement and Stop Asian Hate protests). It was also not so long ago that schools in Australia, Canada, and the United States subjected children of indigenous peoples to abuses and forced assimilation. None of these remarks should be construed to condone China's mistreatment of its citizens but should remind Westerners to remember their own history of exploitation and discrimination and refrain from what Xi Jinping has described as "sanctimonious preaching."

Ironically, the United States once labeled the East Turkestan Islamic Movement a terrorist group and only removed this designation in November 2020. This is a separatist group seeking Xinjiang's independence from China and was designated by the United Nations as a terrorist group in 2002 for its alleged associations with al-Qaeda and the Taliban.[26] Beijing has used this group's activities, some of which were violent, as a justification for its crackdown in Xinjiang. Several Uighurs who fled China to live in Afghanistan were seized by the United States and incarcerated as enemy combatants at Guantanamo without any legal proceedings.[27] They have since been released and resettled outside China. Their saga suggests that Washington's concern for the Uighurs' plight likely reflects its deteriorating relations with Beijing rather than a genuine interest in protecting the Uighurs' human rights.

U.S. secretary of state Antony Blinken stated publicly that he stood by his predecessor Mike Pompeo's condemnation of Beijing's commission of "genocide" in Xinjiang and its confinement of Uighurs in "concentration camps."[28] The deployment of these words contradicts conventional usage.[29] From Beijing's perspective, it is also inflammatory. This rhetorical escalation also contrasts with U.S. officials' behavior of deliberately shunning the use of the "g-word" when Hutus were massacring Tutsis out of a concern that this word would increase pressure on the Clinton administration to intervene in Rwanda.[30] Although many other countries have been critical of China's policies in Xinjiang, they have been reluctant to describe them as genocidal.

How would the United States describe its facility at Guantanamo Bay, Cuba, where suspected supporters of al-Qaeda and ISIS (the Islamic State of Iraq and Syria) have been subjected to torture such as water-boarding and detained indefinitely without having any charge brought against them? Congress has refused to relocate them to the United States, where they would be protected by the constitutional requirement of legal due process. Beijing also sees hypocrisy when leading Americans condemn Trump supporters who stormed the Capitol as insurrectionists or seditionists but laud rioters demanding Hong Kong's independence as pro-democracy demonstrators and overlook their occupation and vandalization of Hong Kong's Legislative Council. The National Republican Committee censured two of its House members (Liz Cheney and Adam Kinzinger) for joining the Democrats' investigation of the January 6 riot, claiming that they were participating in "persecution of ordinary citizens engaged in legitimate political discourse."[31]

There have in fact been fewer casualties and arrests during recent protests in Hong Kong than during many similar mass demonstrations occurring at about the same time in Bolivia, Chile, Colombia, Ecuador, France (Gilets Jaunes), Iran, Iraq, Lebanon, and the United States (Black Lives Matter), in some cases significantly fewer. Other and older examples include when British soldiers shot and killed thirteen Catholic civil-rights protesters in Northern Ireland (remembered as Bloody Sunday) on January 30, 1972. In contrast, no one died from police action in the recent Hong Kong protests. Western media and official statements reacted very differently to these episodes.

The people of Hong Kong of course had no political say about their government when it was a British colony, and police suppression of pro-Beijing demonstrators in the summer of 1967 was much more brutal and violent and resulted in many more casualties. What was remarkable about Hong Kong's recent protest movement is that Beijing did not order its soldiers garrisoned there to suppress the demonstrators (or call on its troops stationed in areas adjacent to Hong Kong), as some pundits expected in a possible repetition of the Tiananmen Square crackdown. In this case, what did not happen is as important as what did happen. In juxtaposition, Trump had complained that U.S. governors were not forceful enough in dealing with demonstrators protesting the death of George Floyd. He called on them to "dominate" the protesters and indicated that he was prepared to deploy the U.S. military for domestic law enforcement, even asking whether soldiers could be ordered to shoot protestors.[32]

In these and other episodes—such as the 1980 Gwangju massacre in South Korea when an estimated two thousand people were killed by the pro-U.S. military after overthrowing the previous government, and when hundreds, perhaps even thousands, were killed in the military coup led by Egypt's General Abdel Fattah al-Sisi overthrowing the elected government of Mohamed Morsi supported by the Muslim Brotherhood—Western governments and media did not voice strong concerns about human rights or support for democracy. Until reversed by Biden, Trump had issued an executive order banning people from seven Muslim-majority countries from entering the United States and freezing their application for refugee status. Anti-immigrant sentiments have played a strong part in populist right-wing politics in both Europe and the United States.

Again, this discussion does not condone China's suppression of its citizens' civil liberties. Critics of China argue that human rights are not just an expression of Western values, pointing to the UN Universal Declaration of Human Rights. They are right but they should also go on to acknowledge that this declaration covers not only political rights and civil liberties but also people's economic and social entitlements.[33] Human rights encompass the alleviation of various forms of "structural violence,"[34] including premature and unnecessary deaths caused by malnutrition, lack of access to health care, poor education, criminal violence, income inequality and not least, systemic discrimination. Black, Hispanic and Native Americans are far more likely to suffer from these conditions, and have shorter life expectancy, higher infant mortality, and greater propensity to die from diseases such as COVID-19. In recent years, China has experienced widening disparities between the haves and have nots, but it has also lifted hundreds of millions from abject poverty and illiteracy. Again, the larger point is that we need to consider China's record in a comparative light, contrasting it with its own past and the performance of other countries while considering the extent, direction, and rate of the pertinent change.

CHINA'S EXTERNAL POLICIES

TERRITORIAL DISPUTES

Some people point to Beijing's "new assertiveness" in its foreign policy, such as in its maritime disputes in the South China Sea and East China Sea, as a reason for reconsidering U.S. policy toward China. Beijing has staked out an ambitious though vague claim, the so-called nine-dash line, that asserts its sovereignty over a large area of the South China Sea. It has never clarified whether its claim pertains only to the land features in this area and the immediate surrounding coastal water, or whether it covers the entire ocean enclosed by the nine-dash line, encompassing all the fisheries and undersea resources within it. Beijing has thus far refrained from applying direct military force to enforce its claim and has relied instead on its coastguard and civilian fishing vessels when confronting the other claimant states. Notwithstanding its ambiguity, the scale and reach of Beijing's sovereignty claim in the South China Sea was not unprecedented: consider that when it was a rising power the United States seized from Mexico territories that make up all or parts of today's Arizona, California, Colorado, Nevada, New Mexico, Utah, and Wyoming, and from Spain Guam, Puerto Rico, and the Philippines.

It is reasonable to argue that Beijing's restraint thus far from resorting to direct, overt, and massive military force reflects its still relatively weak capabilities rather than its unwillingness to use force. This reasoning suggests that when and if Beijing becomes stronger, it will be more disposed to use force. It argues that the jury is therefore still out on Beijing's propensity to use force. Naturally, when a country has used massive, overt, and direct military force to invade or attack another country as the United States did in Afghanistan, Iraq, and especially much smaller countries such as Grenada and Panama that cannot be in any way construed to present a material threat to it, the same logic would lead one to conclude that it must have both the ability and willingness to undertake physical coercion. In these cases, the U.S. resort to coercion is often described as just "muscular" as opposed to international aggression. As with a country's treatment of its racial minorities and political dissidents, its actions toward neighbors that are much smaller and weaker communicate important information to foreign audiences about its trustworthiness.[35]

China has put military installations on those islets in the South China Sea under its control and undertaken land reclamation projects to enlarge these land features. These are the largest military programs and land reclamation projects undertaken by the various claimant states but China was not the first to do so.[36] Washington has objected to China's seizure of the contested islets and its alleged obstruction of freedom of navigation. However, unlike Beijing, which has joined the United Nations Convention for the Law of the Sea (UNCLOS), the United States has declined to do so. Beijing has invoked UNCLOS's special provision to reject the International Arbitration Tribunal's authority to adjudicate a competing claim filed by the Philippines to contest China's sovereignty assertion in the South China Sea. The United States, however, has also rejected the ruling by the International Court of Justice that it had violated international law when it mined Nicaragua's harbors.

Washington and its allies have charged Moscow with war crimes, even genocide, in its invasion of Ukraine, and Western media suggest that Russian leaders should be prosecuted for these crimes. However, in 2020 the Trump administration objected to investigators looking into alleged war crimes committed by Americans in Afghanistan. It imposed sanctions on prosecutors working for the International Criminal Court (ICC), freezing their financial assets and banning their families from entering into the United States[37] It also threatened to sanction anyone who cooperates with ICC investigations looking into allegations of war crimes committed by Americans. In 2021, the Biden administration reversed these policies, but Secretary of State Antony Blinken stated that the United States continues to "strongly disagree" with ICC's investigations in Afghanistan and Palestine and would "vigorously protect current and former United States personnel" from any ICC attempts to exercise jurisdiction over them."[38] Allison has observed that all major powers, not just China, have refused to accept international legal verdicts that contradict their perceived national interest.[39]

Similarly, even though states often proclaim legal principles to condemn others' actions, they disregard these principles when they are inconvenient. For example, freedom of navigation did not prevent Washington from "quarantining" Cuba in 1962, a euphemism used to avoid the legal implications of imposing a naval blockade on another country. Putting the shoe on the other foot, what would its reaction be if Beijing were to impose a naval quarantine on Taiwan? After all, Taiwan occupies a geostrategic position relative to China comparable to Cuba's position for the United States—even setting aside the issue of contested sovereignty.[40]

Trump administration's recognition of Israel's annexation of territories conquered from Arab countries again raises doubts about the extent to which China's conduct in the South China Sea disputes is the real reason for deteriorating relations between Washington and Beijing.

Washington had taken, at least initially, an ambiguous stance on Argentina's military takeover of the Falklands/Malvinas in 1982 although it was quick to condemn Saddam Hussein's invasion of Kuwait and subsequently led an international coalition to forcefully evict Iraqi forces from Kuwait.

Significantly, except possibly for the Diaoyu/Senkaku Islands, China's territorial claims date back at least to 1949. These claims have not increased as China's power has grown.[41] Moreover, China has settled most of its land borders largely based on unequal treaties it was forced to sign in the nineteenth century. Its assertion of sovereignty in the South China Sea predated the establishment of the People's Republic in 1949. The nine-dash line had originated from its predecessor, the Kuomintang government. Beijing's dispute with Tokyo over the islands in the East China Sea is also not a recent phenomenon. It has long preceded China's recent rise, and Taiwan has also advanced the same claim for these islets. When referring to this dispute on his visit to Japan in 1978, Deng Xiaoping stated, "We believe that we should set the issue aside for a while if we cannot reach agreement on it. It is not an urgent issue and can wait for a while. If our generation do not have enough wisdom to resolve this issue, the next generation will have more wisdom, and I am sure that they can find a way acceptable to both sides to settle this issue."[42]

The tacit agreement between the two sides was to maintain the status quo and postpone its resolution to an indefinite future date. Rising tension in recent years can be traced to the decision by Prime Minister Yoshihiko Noda's government to purchase three of the disputed islands from their private owners in 2012. This action was perceived by Beijing to have violated the tacit agreement.

China shares a land border with fourteen sovereign states. In contrast, the United States has only two, Canada and Mexico. This is important because border disputes tend to be the most common reason for militarized crises and interstate wars.[43] It is typical for multivariate analyses studying the causes of militarized disputes and wars to introduce control variables to discern the true effect of a proposed independent variable on the dependent variable. For example, in studies that hypothesize democracies to be more peaceful than autocracies, analysts control for the effects of a country's status as a great power, its economic size or wealth, its physical distance from a counterpart, its trade intensity with this counterpart, this counterpart's regime character, and so on. In the absence of such statistical controls, it would be plain for all to see that democracies such as the United States, Britain, France, India, and Israel are at or near the top of any list counting the frequency of a country's involvement in resort to arms, whether war, militarized dispute, or unconventional use of force (such as drone attacks and even the assassination of foreign officials and nuclear scientists).

My point is that if one introduces the number of contiguous neighbors as a control variable, China does not appear to be more war- or dispute-prone than others, especially relative to the United States. Ceteris paribus, one would expect countries with many contiguous neighbors to have a higher incidence of militarized disputes and wars and, conversely, countries with fewer neighbors to have a lower incidence. The former should have more "opportunity" to become involved in these conflicts. This logic is no different from the expectation that motorists who drive many miles are likely to have more traffic accidents compared to their counterparts with a lower mileage.

Beijing has settled all its land borders save those with India, Nepal, and Bhutan, and these settlements often reflect terms more favorable to China's counterparts.[44] Beijing's policies and conduct in its remaining maritime disputes have not changed significantly from its past stance or practice. China has not become more aggressive in its land or maritime disputes even though it has gained more military and economic power over time.[45] Thus, it is not clear how "new" or "assertive" China's recent behavior has been.[46] What is clear, however, is that in the past forty or so years, China has fought fewer wars and been involved in fewer militarized disputes than the preceding decades (e.g., the Korean War, the Sino-Indian border war in 1962, the Sino-Vietnamese border war in 1979, several episodes of intense bombardment of Matsu and Quemoy in the Taiwan Strait in the 1950s and 1960s), and relative to many other major powers. These include the United States, which has fought more foreign wars and has been involved in more militarized interstate disputes than any country since 1945, and often by a wide margin in not only frequency but also intensity in pairwise comparisons with other major powers. The incidence of Washington's military intervention abroad has risen after the Cold War's end, increasing from forty-six between 1948 and 1991 to 188 between 1992 and 2017.[47]

It helps to see China's conduct in a comparative context, especially juxtaposing it against that of the United States. Appropriate consideration should be given to the incidence as well as scale of these countries' use of force abroad. China's contested sovereignty in the South and East China Seas and its border dispute with India are simply not comparable to the massive and overt use of U.S. armed forces to invade and occupy Afghanistan and Iraq, or to attack Libya, Serbia, and Syria (and smaller countries such as Panama and Grenada). Singapore's former ambassador to the United Nations, Kishore Mahbubani, was quoted saying that even during the relatively peaceful administration of Barack Obama, the United States had dropped twenty-six thousand bombs on seven countries in 2016 alone, whereas China has not fired a shot across its border since 1979 when it fought its last war with Vietnam.[48] Although the incidence of China's resort to overt and large-scale force has decreased over the past four decades, objections to its alleged assertive or aggressive foreign policy have ironically increased. Thus the trendlines in this case again point in a direction opposite to that often given in public accounts in the United States trying to explain the recent deterioration in Sino-American relations.

MASSIVE MILITARY SPENDING

Critics of China have also expressed concern about its efforts to modernize its military, seeing its large and increasing military spending as prima facie evidence of its foreign ambitions. Why would Beijing want to spend so much money on its military unless it harbors aggressive intentions? Donald Rumsfeld, former U.S. secretary of defense, voiced this view when he said in 2005, "Since no nation threatens China, one must wonder: Why this growing [Chinese] investment [in defense]?"[49] Rumsfeld and others do not pose the same question about the United States, which faces a much more benign security environment. It enjoys not only a more favorable geostrategic situation with only two contiguous and much weaker neighbors, but also a large network of allies and a huge advantage in military technology and assets as the world's only superpower.[50]

Despite all this, in 2020 the United States spent more on its military than the next eleven highest countries combined. Its military spending that year was 3.1 times larger than China's, accounting for 3.7 percent of its gross domestic product relative to China's estimated 1.7 percent.[51] At one time shortly after the end of the Cold War, the United States accounted for nearly half of the total amount of global expenditure on military (in 2020, it accounted for 39 percent). Rather than the proverbial 800-pound gorilla in the room, it is the 330,000-pound blue whale in a class by itself. Not only did Washington outspend China militarily by a large margin, most of the other countries with high military spending are its formal or informal allies. In 2020, the top twelve such countries included India, Britain, Saudi Arabia, Germany, France, Japan, South Korea, Italy, and Australia. Other than China, Russia was the only exception to these countries being allied or aligned with the United States. It is difficult to imagine that any U.S. strategic planner would want to change places with their Chinese counterpart. Parenthetically, arms export by the United States has exceeded China's by a huge margin. Moreover, Washington exports more arms to autocracies that violate human rights and those countries torn by civil war.[52]

Why does a country continue its massive military expenditures when its physical survival and security from foreign invasion are no longer in doubt? Defensive realists of course posit that a state spends on the military to protect its survival and security. Described as internal balancing, this practice is sometimes pursued concomitantly with external balancing, referring to a state's policy to join alliances to augment its prospects for survival and security.[53] Offensive realists argue instead that even after ensuring their survival and security, states are motivated to continue their expansion because they are interested in accumulating more power and aspire to become the world's only and undisputed hegemon.[54] Ironically, this characterization fits the United States better than any other country.

Given its level of military spending, it is odd for Washington to complain about Beijing's defense expenditures. It is also strange that many self-professed realists who advocate a get-tough policy on China see a greater balance of power between China and the United States to be a source of threat to international peace and instability. Realists of different stripes have traditionally argued that a balance of power (or an equal distribution of power) facilitates international stability. Some even argue that it is sometimes necessary to go to war to preserve this balance. According to them, it is natural, expected, and even desirable that states undertake balancing policies. They often, however, exempt the United States from this generalization when it comes to other countries such as China seeking to balance against preponderant U.S. power.[55] They are inclined to see these other countries as revisionists seeking to overturn the status quo, thus posing a threat to international peace and stability. Nowadays many of the same self-professed realists often point to power transition as a threat to international stability and peace—that is, they see China's closing the power gap separating it from the United States as a source of concern and even alarm. They therefore reverse the traditional realist propositions that states ought to and will balance against a stronger counterpart, arguing instead that keeping an imbalance of power in favor of the United States is desirable for peace and stability in the Asia Pacific.

In contrast to some dominant formulations of realism that see all countries as alike (they all operate under the same systemic pressure of anarchy and are thus consumed and motivated by the same preoccupation to ensure survival and security or to expand power for its own sake), those who now argue a greater balance of power (or an ongoing process of shifting power bringing about this greater balance of power) threatens peace and stability suggest that states are after all different in their motivations.[56] Some states are ostensibly status quo powers interested only in keeping what they already have, whereas others are revisionists seeking to expand their influence and overturn the existing international order. Here we see another example of international relations scholarship adjusting to changes in official relations among states, adjusting their explanations and prescriptions from the dominant power's self-centered perspective. As I argue in chapter 3, knowledge is power and, as creators and propagators of knowledge, international relations scholars are inevitably and deeply embedded in the power relations they study. Although they profess an interest in objective analysis, their discourses and practices are not independent of the power politics of international relations. Thus, as Robert Walker observes, "Theories of international relations are more interesting as aspects of contemporary world politics that need to be explained than as explanations of contemporary world politics."[57]

UNFAIR TRADE PRACTICES

One also hears frequent complaints about China violating the rules of fair trade. However, its record on complying with the World Trade Organization's (WTO) rulings has been far better than that of the United States and the European Union, according to Daniel Drezner.[58] He observes that after the financial crisis of 2008–2009, "China, far from acting like a spoiler, acted primarily as a responsible stakeholder to reinforce the pre-existing rules of the global economic game."[59] More complaints have been voiced about the United States resorting to unilateral protectionist measures than about any other country, including China and the European Union. "The United States has made more frequent use of WTO exceptions to protect domestic industries from foreign competition than any other country," and foreign countries "have initiated more complaints at the WTO against the U.S. for violating trade-exception rules than against any other nation or region, including the European Union."[60]

Fareed Zakaria writes in the same vein, referring to "a 2015 report by the financial services giant Credit Suisse [that] provides a useful tally of nontariff barriers against foreign goods put in place by major countries between 1990 and 2013. With a total count of almost 450, the United States is in a league of its own. Next is India, then Russia. China comes in at number five, with one-third as many nontariff barriers imposed as the United States. The picture hasn't changed much in the years since."[61] Among the newly emergent economies of BRICS (Brazil, Russia, India, China, and South Africa), "China is consistently ranked as the most open and competitive economy."[62]

These remarks put Washington's allegations of Chinese trade malpractices in a comparative context and make it less likely that these malpractices are the true reason behind the recent deterioration in bilateral relations because the United States is not immune from the same criticisms. Although the United States accounts for about 13 percent of the total value of the world's imports, it is the target of a disproportionate number of complaints submitted by other countries to the WTO alleging protectionist practices. These complaints account for 42 percent of all those referring to antidumping claims, 34 percent of all those referring to subsidies and countervailing duties, and 44 percent of all those referring to safeguard provisions.[63] When the United States faced challenges from Japan's automobile industry, it resorted to measures such as orderly marketing arrangements and voluntary export restraints to impose limits on imports from that country.

Countries, including the United States, have practiced varying forms of protectionism to nurture their infant industries in the early stages of their economic development. When they reach a more mature stage, they abandon obsolescent industries that have declining comparative advantage while seeking to open foreign markets for their firms that have gained international competitiveness, even dominance. Thus differences in their stages of economic development can explain a considerable part of the nature and degree of state intervention in the marketplace. The more advanced economies' turn to preach free trade has been described as "kicking away the ladder" for those who come after them.[64] Naturally, advanced countries do not cease entirely to protect their politically sensitive sectors like agriculture or to eschew state intervention to assist strategically important sectors.

Kristen Hopewell questions the stark dichotomization between "free market capitalism" and "state capitalism" that one often encounters in prevailing discourse on the differences between the United States and China.[65] She points out that the United States has a long history of state intervention and trade protectionism, and the Trump administration's policies were not a break from the past. Washington is guilty of many of the practices that it accuses Beijing of. Just like China, the United States has sought to open foreign markets while restricting foreign ownership and investment in strategic sectors such as shipping, energy, and communications. It has also undertaken massive state-funded projects to assist research and development in aerospace, informatics, communication technology, biotechnology, and nanotechnology. Federal grants, tax incentives, subsidized loans, and procurement contracts have supported large firms such as Boeing and Tesla. Hopewell reports that U.S. government subsidies have accounted for over 40 percent of the revenue from corn and sugar; 50 percent for cotton, wheat, and barley; 60 percent for rice; and 70 percent for milk.[66] She concludes, "The United States has actively intervened in the markets to protect and promote its economic interests and maintain its primacy, including using state intervention to promote its dominance in cutting-edge industries, and reverting to trade protectionism when facing competitive threats. Furthermore, the American hegemon has used its considerable power in the global trade regime to push for liberalization in its own areas of economic competitiveness while ensuring that international trade rules still allow considerable scope for its own trade protections and interventionist policies."[67]

Similarly, others have remarked that the dichotomization between market economics and mercantilism is facile and that Washington's professed support for open markets is instrumental. "The point is not that there is hypocrisy in the world—that states espouse liberalism while following *la raison d'état*—though that is also true. The point is that economic liberalism, a force that many hype will pacify international politics, may not be the dominant political ideology of the twenty-first century, as it appears on the surface."[68]

China has without question become more deeply embedded in the international political economy in the last four decades. Its economy has become more open such that its "weighted mean applied tariff" has fallen from 30 percent in 1992 to 4 percent in 2017.[69] Such development can be seen to suggest that Washington's policy of engagement has succeeded, whether judged by China's past conduct or current practice. Naturally, China's economic opening has benefited it enormously. Why then would it want to overturn the current economic order? Although a rising China has acquired a greater capability to do so, it should have less incentive to disrupt the international economy now that it has a larger stake, which in turn should incline it to be more interested in maintaining the order it has benefited from. That a state with a large stake in the existing order should be its defender is after all the rationale for suggesting that a ruling state cannot but be a status quo power. The same logic would suggest that a declining state should have a greater incentive to agitate for changing this order to arrest or reverse its decline and that if this state is still a preponderant power, it also still has the greatest capability to effect such change.

PROTECTING TAIWAN'S AUTONOMY

Next is the issue of Taiwan. China's critics point to Beijing's threats to undermine this island's autonomy but overlook the historical fact that the United States had insisted until the 1970s that Taiwan was part of China (albeit China under the rule of its ally, the Kuomintang or Nationalists) and that the government in Taipei represented the mainland as well the island (thus, with Washington's support, the Kuomintang government in

Taipei was accepted as the legitimate representative of China, the whole of China, in the United Nations until 1972) even though it no longer exercised any control over the mainland. Were it not for the intervention of the U.S. Seventh Fleet shortly after the outbreak of the Korean War, the Communists would have successfully invaded this last bastion of the Nationalists under Chiang Kai-shek. Beijing's stance on Taiwan as an inalienable part of China has not altered over the years, which as a constant again cannot explain changes in Sino-American relations over time. The United States has been the revisionist on this question, altering its policy positions on more than one occasion.

In its joint Shanghai communiqué with China in 1972, "The United States acknowledges that all Chinese on either side of the Taiwan Strait maintain there is but one China and that Taiwan is a part of China. The United States Government does not challenge that position. It reaffirms its interest in a peaceful settlement of the Taiwan question by the Chinese themselves."[70] Former U.S. secretary of state Henry Kissinger states bluntly that "[for] us [Americans] to go to war with a recognized country where we have an ambassador over a part of what we would recognize as their country would be preposterous."[71] Although some U.S. politicians invoke Taiwan people's right to self-determination, it is also clear that Washington does not support the island's political independence even if most of its voters decide to pursue it. Washington wants to prevent the likely consequence of such a declaration, a decision by Beijing to resort to force to prevent Taiwan's independence.

Although the United States has pledged to reduce armament sales to Taiwan over time, it announced $5.1 billion in this transaction in 2020 alone.[72] After observing a tacit agreement with Beijing to refrain from having any high-level official contact with Taipei, the Trump administration in its waning days abandoned this practice. In August 2019, U.S. secretary for health and human services Alex Azar visited Taiwan and met with its president, Tsai Ing-wen; U.S. secretary of transportation Rodney Slater had also visited Taiwan in 2000. The Azar visit was followed in November by that of U.S. rear admiral Michael Studeman, a high-level official overseeing intelligence in the Asia Pacific. U.S. ambassador to the United Nations Kelly Craft had planned another visit to Taiwan just days before Biden's inauguration, only to cancel it at the last minute ostensibly due to the imminent change of administration. In the early days of the

Biden administration, Washington deliberately publicized a photo show-ing Taiwan's top envoy to the United States, Hsiao Bi-Khim, meeting in the U.S. State Department with Sung Kim, U.S. acting assistant secretary of state in charge of the Bureau of Asian and Pacific Affairs, on Febru-ary 10, 2021. This event indicated another serious departure from the pre-vious U.S. policy that banned meeting Taiwan's officials in governmental buildings,[73] another provocation in Beijing's eyes. In March 2021, the United States again departed from its long-standing policy since break-ing diplomatic relations with Taiwan in 1979. The U.S. ambassador to Palau, John Hennessey-Niland, accompanied Palau's president on an offi-cial visit to Taipei, becoming the first U.S. ambassador to do so in nearly forty-two years. Finally, on his visit to Taiwan in March 2022, former U.S. secretary of state Mike Pompeo said in a speech that the United States should formally recognize Taiwan as a country.[74] As these incidents make clear, it is not just China that engages in policies or practices seeking to revise the status quo or existing (albeit informal) understandings.

ALLEGATIONS OF FOREIGN INTERFERENCE

Taiwan's status is the most critical issue in Sino-American relations. Bei-jing has all along insisted that this status is an internal Chinese affair and that it objects to any foreign interference. Russia's alleged meddling in the 2016 U.S. presidential election has been a constant feature of U.S. media reports, which have also mentioned possible Chinese and Iranian inter-ference in the 2020 election albeit without any disclosure of relevant infor-mation. To Beijing, these allegations are another case of supreme hypoc-risy, especially given voluminous documentation of U.S. attempts to influence the outcomes of many other countries' elections, starting from at least the Central Intelligence Agency's effort to deny an electoral vic-tory to the Italian Communists in 1948.[75] Washington has also been com-plicit in many covert attempts to overthrow foreign governments, includ-ing some that were democratically elected, such as Iran's Mohammad Mossadegh and Chile's Salvador Allende.

Since establishing formal diplomatic relations with Washington, Bei-jing has professed its support for the Westphalian international order and its core values of state sovereignty and noninterference in other countries' domestic affairs. This change is a U-turn from its revolutionary stance during the Maoist years when Beijing supported armed insurgencies to overthrow pro-Western governments abroad. As Alastair Johnston and Robert Ross suggest, "In contrast to the Maoist era, China propagates no ideology to be spread around through the intervention in the internal affairs of others. Indeed, the predominant ideology that the Chinese leaders promote today is sovereignty and autonomy, and the illegitimacy of intervention in the internal affairs of others."[76] Similarly, Evan Medeiros remarks that "China's international behavior is not ideologically driven, and China is not pursuing a revolutionary foreign policy that seeks to acquire new territory, forge balancing coalitions, or advance alternative models of economic development or global security."[77] Beijing's foreign conduct has been motivated more by economic interest than political ideology.[78] Ironically, it has been the United States, especially since the end of the Cold War, that has pursued a policy of regime change abroad (e.g., Afghanistan, Iran, Iraq, Sudan, Libya, Syria, Venezuela, Grenada, Panama, Nicaragua, Ukraine). In seeking to propagate its values and alter other countries' political and economic systems, the United States is itself a revisionist state.[79] In deploying terms such as *revisionism* and *status quo*, conventional narratives in U.S. academic and official discourse often reverse their customary meaning, so that policies seeking to promote change in the international order are described as defending it, whereas policies espousing support for the traditional Westphalian principles are characterized as attempts to revise it.

CYBER ESPIONAGE AND ELECTRONIC HACKING

The Trump administration blocked Chinese companies such as Huawei from accessing the U.S. market and technology and lobbied other countries to also issue similar bans in their respective plans to install 5G networks. Washington claims that Chinese internet companies can engage in surveillance activities and be required by Beijing to turn over their clients' private information. The irony has not escaped Germany's Economic Minister Peter Altmaier, who notes that it was the United States that had surreptitiously taped Angela Merkel's telephone conversations in 2015 and that "The US also requires its companies to provide certain information needed to fight terrorism."[80]

Edward Snowden, a former subcontractor for the National Security Agency, disclosed that the United States undertook extensive mass surveillance programs with the cooperation of European governments and U.S. telecommunication companies.[81] The U.S. National Security Agency reportedly penetrated the Chinese internet company Huawei with the witting or unwitting support of U.S. telecommunication companies.[82] Public media have also reported a U.S. attempt to plant listening devices on a Boeing aircraft sold for use by China's president,[83] and that it surreptitiously introduced computer programs intended to compromise information systems installed in various Chinese institutions. Widespread reports also circulated on its and Israel's infiltration of the computer virus Stuxnet to undermine Iran's nuclear program. This attempt destroyed about one thousand centrifuges in Iran's possession and caused significant damage to its nuclear program. Alleged Iranian attempts to penetrate U.S. information systems followed this subversion.

The United States has powerful capabilities to wage cyber warfare and has initiated digital offensives against other countries' networks.[84] As Jon Lindsay observes, "the [cyber] threat from China is exaggerated whereas the threat to China is underappreciated;" moreover, "the magnitude of the gap between China and the United States in the balance of cyber power . . . is potentially growing, not shrinking."[85] Washington has implied that espionage to collect data pertinent to "national security" is permissible, but not for the purpose of commercial gain or economic advantage. It is not clear what is the legal basis for this distinction which is blurred in practice. In short, "hacking" is not being undertaken just by the Chinese. Disclosures by Edward Snowden showed extensive electronic surveillance by the U.S. government, pertaining not only to the collection of foreign communications but also telephone calls (domestic and foreign) made by U.S. citizens. Allegations that Beijing has been more egregious in such activities are one sided and again do not explain the recent deterioration in Sino-American relations.

RESPONSIBILITY FOR COVID-19

Former U.S. president Donald Trump and Secretary of State Mike Pompeo both suggested publicly that the COVID-19 virus originated from a Chinese laboratory in Wuhan. In his interview with ABC News on May 3,

2020, Pompeo stated that "enormous evidence" supports his allegation but declined to offer any details. His allegation followed a similar claim by President Trump on April 30 that he had "a high degree of confidence" that the virus had come from a Chinese laboratory.[86] He too refused to provide detail to support his assertion.

These claims contradicted the views of most scientists that the virus was likely to have originated from bats. Dr. Anthony Fauci, a leading U.S. expert of infectious diseases, said, "If you look at the evolution of the virus in bats and what's out there now, [the scientific evidence] is very, very strongly leaning toward this could not have been artificially or deliberately manipulated."[87] The same news source noted that Pompeo's and Trump's statements contradicted their own Office of the Director of National Intelligence, which had announced on April 30, 2020, that the "Intelligence Community also concurs with wide consensus among scientists that the Covid-19 virus was not man-made or genetically modified."

Still, inside the Trump administration "there [was] an appetite to use various tools, including sanctions, canceling US debt obligations and drawing up new trade policies, to make clear to China, and to everyone else, where they [felt] the responsibility lies."[88] This source observes that despite "serious questions about China's transparency, the Trump administration . . . escalated its effort to blame China for the global spread of the virus as criticism of its own handling of the pandemic has increased." Trump in his public remarks called the COVID-19 virus "Kung Flu," abetting racial animosity and even hate crimes against Asian Americans.

China's management of the virus outbreak has encountered serious criticisms abroad. It deliberately understated the severity of the contagion during its early phase and had tried to silence those who had wanted to warn the government and the public about its deadly consequences. Reacting to these criticisms, Beijing launched a public relations campaign. An editorial in the Global Times responded harshly to Pompeo, claiming that he "had stunned the world with groundless accusations."[89] Chinese media figures bristled at Steve Bannon's suggestion that China should be held liable for financial damages caused by the pandemic,[90] and questioned whether Washington would be willing to apply the same logic to itself because the 2008 Great Recession had originated from its financial mismanagement, one that was, however, caused by human error rather than nature.

In his Senate confirmation hearing in January 2021, U.S. secretary of state Antony Blinken stated that China has "misled the world" on COVID-19 although he has subsequently tried to sidestep this issue.[91] Available evidence suggests that Chinese authorities had initially downplayed the severity of this disease. Any additional evidence of their malfeasance still awaits documentation by independent and impartial international experts. In late March 2021, the World Health Organization issued a report stating that the COVID-19 virus most likely originated from bats and was transmitted by an intermediate animal host to human beings. It considered the introduction of this virus through a laboratory incident to be "an extremely unlikely pathway."[92] The United States, along with thirteen other countries, however, criticized this report and demanded a full, transparent investigation. In May 2021, Biden ordered the U.S. intelligence community to investigate the virus' origin and to report back to him in ninety days.[93] This report, though, indicated continued disagreement within the U.S. intelligence community about the origin of the virus.[94]

The charge of misleading the world comes to mind in other contexts, such as when the George W. Bush administration tried to persuade the international community that Saddam Hussein had a program to develop weapons of mass destruction as well as connections with al-Qaeda.[95] These were the public reasons the Bush administration gave to justify the U.S. invasion of Iraq and they turned out to be false. U.S. presidents lied to the world on other occasions, such as when Dwight Eisenhower misrepresented the U-2 spy plane shot down in Soviet airspace in 1960 as a strayed weather research aircraft from the National Aeronautics and Space Administration, when John Kennedy tried to conceal the U.S. role in the Bay of Pigs invasion of Cuba in 1961, when Richard Nixon sought to cover up the White House's role in the Watergate break-in in 1972, when George H. Bush declared "read my lips, no new taxes" in accepting the Republican Party's nomination to be its presidential candidate in 1988, and when Bill Clinton stated in his televised speech in January 1998 that he "did not have sexual relations with that woman, Ms. Lewinsky." Still other instances include Franklin D. Roosevelt's disingenuous allegation of an unprovoked attack on U.S. destroyer USS *Greer* by a German submarine in 1941 in the run-up to the U.S. entry to World War II and Lyndon B. Johnson's claim, to gain congressional passage of the Gulf of Tonkin Resolution to escalate the Vietnam War, that U.S. destroyer USS *Maddox* was attacked by North Vietnamese torpedo boats in 1964.[96] Most recently, Donald Trump claimed that the 2020 election was "stolen" from him. In a meeting with high-level U.S. foreign policy officials in March 2021, China's top diplomat Yang Jiechi strongly rebutted Antony Blinken's statement demanding China adjust its conduct to conform to international rules, arguing that the United States "does not have the qualification to say that it wants to speak to China from a position of strength."[97]

EXTRAJUDICIAL KILLINGS

The United States has not accused China of committing extrajudicial killings, but President Biden has publicly labeled Russian President Vladimir Putin "a killer" for his suspected role in poisoning the opposition leader Alexander Navalny.[98] This charge has led to the Kremlin's decision to recall its ambassador to the United States. Significantly, even after publishing a report indicating that Saudi crown price, Mohammed bin Salman, had given his personal approval to kill *Washington Post* journalist Jamal Khashoggi, Washington did not designate him "a killer." Nor did it issue any criticism of Israel, which was widely suspected in assassinating Iran's nuclear scientists. The United States has itself resorted to drone attacks abroad to kill suspected terrorists, including at least one U.S. citizen (Anwar Nasser al-Awlaki), without due process, and the head of Iran's Revolutionary Guard Qasem Soleimani in January 2020 near the Baghdad International Airport. Such conduct belies professed commitment to international norms.

In sum, most reasons often given by U.S. officials, pundits, and even academics to explain the recent deterioration in Sino-American relations are not credible. In some significant respects, such as refraining from using armed force abroad, joining international institutions and accords, undertaking domestic economic reform, opening itself to the global economy, and improving its people's life conditions, China has moved in a direction that Washington should find congenial. In other respects, such as its territorial contests and suppression of domestic dissent, Beijing's policy stance and conduct either have not changed or have become more moderate since its border war with Vietnam in 1979 and its bloody crackdown of the Tiananmen Square protesters in 1989. David Kang remarks that "the evidence to date reveals that China is increasingly conforming with, and adapting to, international standards and norms, rather than attempting to subvert them."[99] This observation continues to be valid today.

One may still disapprove of Beijing's behavior, but the direction of change in its policies and conduct is noteworthy. It has clearly abandoned its former support for armed insurrections abroad and opposition to international arms agreements and multilateral diplomacy. It has become an active member of many international organizations and is the largest contributor to UN peacekeeping missions among the permanent members of the Security Council, missions that it had denounced and rejected previously. In still other respects, such as cyber espionage, military spending, and the use of force abroad, its recent behavior does not seem more egregious relative to that of the United States and in fact has been much less bellicose, assertive, and unilateral. Chinese parallels to U.S. actions of waging preventive war, promoting regime change abroad, or undertaking unconventional warfare such as drone attacks on suspected terrorists and even assassinating another country's official (Iran's General Soleimani, for example) are lacking. Finally, recent U.S. actions have progressively undermined those long-standing understandings and agreements that have provided a modus vivendi ensuring stability across the Taiwan Strait.

CHANGING U.S. POLICIES AND OUTLOOK

Just as China has changed dramatically in the five decades since Nixon's visit to Beijing, U.S. policies and conduct have also changed in important ways, especially during the Trump administration. Americans' views and attitudes have become more skeptical and even hostile to various tenets constituting the liberal international order. Sometimes described as the Kantian tripod after this philosopher's well-known treatise on "perpetual peace,"[100] this order has been described as a constitutional pact among established, Western countries.[101] It consists of three pillars: republicanism, cosmopolitanism, and pacific union. These features have been translated to mean democracy, economic interdependence, and joint membership in intergovernmental organizations in the contemporary world. Individually and collectively, they have been shown to promote peace among countries sharing these traits.[102]

The liberal international order has recently come under assault. Democracy or at least its liberal institutions have suffered setback in countries such as Hungary, Poland, the Philippines, Turkey, and even the United States. We have also seen a rise in populism in the West against globalization and international institutions, including anti-immigrant and pro-protectionist sentiments. Britain's departure from the European Union, and Trump's abandonment of international accords and multilateral diplomacy (such as the Paris climate agreement and the World Health Organization, decisions Biden subsequently reversed) are part of this phenomenon. So was Trump's avowed policy to economically decouple from China. Pundits have sometimes described these developments as the onset of a deglobalization process. Explanations for this phenomenon are numerous, but what seems reasonably clear is that its impetus has come mainly from the West led by the United States. Ironically, after promoting the liberal international order for many years, globalization has acquired a strongly negative connotation in some Western quarters; meanwhile, in 2017 and again in 2021 Chinese president Xi Jinping pledged that his country would be steadfast in its support for it.[103]

Some people have questioned whether the post-1945 order has been truly liberal, global, or open, and the extent to which its institutions have restrained the United States from exercising its preponderant power when they hamper its pursuit of important material interests.[104] Some have also predicted that the forces undermining this order are more likely to come from domestic than foreign sources. The charge that a rising China threatens this rule-governed order is therefore not fully in accord with these views. In Zakaria's words, "the liberal international order was never as liberal, as international, or as orderly as it is now nostalgically described. . . . A more realistic image is that of a nascent liberal international order, marred from the start by exceptions, discord, and fragility. The United States, for its part, often operated outside the rules of this order, making frequent military interventions with or without UN approval; in the years between 1947 and 1989, when the United States was supposedly building the liberal international order, it attempted regime change around the world 72 times. It reserved the same right in the economic realm, engaging in protectionism even as it railed against more modest measures adopted by other countries."[105] "In short," he concludes, "China has acted in ways that are interventionist, mercantilist, and unilateral—but often far less so than other great powers."[106]

The United States has been disengaging from the liberal international order that it has supported since 1945. The Trump administration clearly had a pronounced tendency to reject multilateralism in favor of unilateralism. The Biden administration has issued executive orders to return the United States to the World Health Organization and the Paris climate accord. It has also reversed the travel ban against Muslim-majority countries, stopped the construction of border walls intended to stop refugees from Mexico and Central America, and signaled its interest to negotiate a new nuclear deal with Iran. However, it has also continued many of its predecessor's policies, prompting some people to question whether it is "normalizing" Trump's America First tendency while giving lip service to multilateralism.[107]

Washington's skepticisms or reservations about committing itself to international agreements and institutions long predated Trump, and substantial evidence shows that even during the Clinton administration its policy preferences had already drifted farther from the tenets of liberal international order as embodied in the Kantian tripod.[108] For instance, in 1999 the U.S. Senate declined to ratify the Comprehensive Nuclear Test Ban despite Clinton's support for this agreement. In 2002, George W. Bush abrogated the Anti-Ballistic Missile Treaty with Russia. Other well-known episodes predated Trump, such as the U.S. rejection of the International Trade Organization, the Kyoto protocol on global warming, the ICC, and UNCLOS. Some, such as the U.S. refusal to join the League of Nations, even predate 1945. In all these cases, Washington had taken an active part in protracted negotiations on crafting these accords but eventually decided not to join them.

The Trump administration's policies are not an aberration from the past when the United States has recoiled from taking on commitments that it routinely urges others to undertake. However, this administration demonstrated a more extreme tendency to reject multilateral diplomacy and international institutions. During his years in the White House,

Trump pulled the United States out of the Iran nuclear deal (the Joint Comprehensive Plan of Action), the Trans-Pacific Partnership, the Intermediate-Range Nuclear Forces Treaty, the Global Compact on Migration, the United Nations Education, Scientific and Cultural Organization (UNESCO), and the UN Human Rights Council. He criticized the North American Free Trade Agreement as the "worst trade deal in history,"[109] and demanded that Canada and Mexico negotiate a new trade treaty with more favorable terms for the United States. The result was the USMCA Agreement (U.S.-Mexico-Canada Agreement) which came into force in July 2020. Trump also withdrew the United States from the Arms Trade Treaty, the Open Skies Treaty, and the World Health Organization as already mentioned. Further, he boycotted the International Labor Organization, threatened to withdraw from the Universal Postal Union, and held up the World Trade Organization by blocking the appointment of judges to its appellate body. Although the United States presses its allies to contribute more to the cost of collective defense, it is itself delinquent in paying its past dues to the United Nations. Washington demands that Beijing comply with a rule-based international order, but recent events raise doubts about the extent to which Washington is itself committed to those international institutions responsible for developing and enforcing these rules. Western scholars and commentators invoke norms and rules routinely in their discourse, assuming that they are inherently good and overlooking the origins and consequences of these norms and rules.[110] Of course, racial discrimination, colonial conquest, and imperial expansion were once accepted and practiced by Westerners as norms and rules governing the European-centered international system.

CONCLUSION

Most, even all, of the episodes or developments mentioned in this chapter are common knowledge among scholars of international relations. I suspect, however, that many of these colleagues would disagree with my interpretations and conclusions, some strongly. I submit that scholars tend to adjust their interpretations and conclusions in accordance with changes in the state of countries' official relations. When Nixon visited

China, most China scholars and analysts of international relations applauded this development even though China had a more authoritarian government and a more closed society and economy at the time. That it is a polity ruled by one political party with a professed communist ideology (albeit with "Chinese characteristics") has not changed. China was also more bellicose in rhetoric and actual conduct, such as supporting violent insurrections abroad and initiating a fight with Vietnam in 1979 to "teach Hanoi a lesson" (with apparent approval and support from Washington). It had also a military altercation with Vietnam in the South China Sea, specifically, Johnson South Reef in the Union Banks region of the Spratly Islands, in March 1988. Beijing's foreign policy has become less bellicose since then. Yet many Sinologists and analysts of international relations have now signed on to the view of a "new, assertive" China and express the belief that a policy of engaging this country has been a failure.

Thus, despite the vaunted idea of scholarly independence and objectivity, researchers' views can change rather quickly and sometimes inconsistently. For instance, although many self-professed realists see balance of power as a path to peace and stability, they are alarmed when China's rise has brought about a more balanced power relationship with the United States, seeing this development as a threat to regional and even global peace and stability. Similarly, whereas some previously argued that all states behave alike under the pressure of an anarchical world, they now emphasize a distinction between so-called status-quo and revisionist states even though these designations contradict customary usage and existing evidence.[111]

Scholarly discourse, no less than pronouncements by government leaders, can reflect a heavy dosage of social and political construction, often repeating or echoing officials' narratives. This discourse's premises and conclusions can be quite fragile and subject to rapid revision to catch up with the changing reality of official relations. The Kaiser's Germany was once held by leading Americans, including the then future president Woodrow Wilson, as a model of constitutional state, a paragon of bureaucratic efficiency, and an example par excellence of the rule of law. As World War I drew closer, both elite and mass opinions in the United States turned negative against Germany with its leaders now being depicted as Teutonic militarists bent on aggression.[112] A similar reversal of image came when the Shah of Iran was ousted and replaced by the rule of theocrats headed by Ayatollah Khomeini. Scholarly and popular depiction in the United States quickly switched from seeing Iran as a friend to as an enemy. Even though the nature of the government in Tehran remained authoritarian, its official relations with the United States had changed. Similarly, wartime image of an aggressive and conniving Japan was quickly replaced after the war with that of a peacetime ally and reliable bulwark against communism.

This chapter's discussion suggests that as China has become more engaged with the world, the United States (especially under Trump) has increasingly withdrawn from it and has abandoned or weakened many of the institutions that it has supported and even fostered since 1945. Moreover, many of the reasons commonly heard in Washington's complaints about and criticisms of Beijing do not represent a new assertiveness on Beijing's part and at least relative to Washington's conduct in waging preventive war and promoting regime change abroad. Relative to the United States, today's China has not been more disposed to use force in international disputes or to reject multilateral institutions or agreements. Roll-call votes in the United Nations, both in the General Assembly and on the Security Council, reveal that the United States—not China—has found itself increasingly out of step with the rest of world.[113] Do these votes not provide the best representation of international community and international order, given Washington's frequent reference to these concepts? In Johnston's words, "China is not challenging the so-called liberal international order as much as many people think . . . at present China's challenge to order is less deep and wide than the current narrative [prevailing in the West] suggests."[114]

Chinese diplomacy has seen a sea change from its erstwhile support for armed revolution and insurgency against incumbent governments; U.S. policies have moved in the opposite direction to promoting color revolution and regime change abroad. Recent statements and conduct by these governments suggest that the United States has become more revisionist, not China. Especially after the Cold War, U.S. policy has been "revisionism in the guise of liberal hegemony," changing mainly from system maintenance to system transformation.[115] The United States especially and the West more generally have been on the offense, seeking to expand to the global scale the so-called liberal international order (one once limited both geographically and ideologically among liked-minded capitalist democracies in the North Atlantic region plus Japan). Ironically, recent popular opposition to this order and pressures to deglobalize have also come primarily from the West.

What can account for these diverging tendencies and more specifically, the deterioration in Sino-American relations, the question asked at the outset of this chapter? The most likely answer is the shifting power balance between the two countries. Other explanations are not nearly as persuasive because they appear to be decisively secondary in their importance. In some cases, they even suggest better Sino-American relations as China's society and economy have become more open and its involvement in foreign armed conflicts has declined in recent decades. Although Beijing and Washington disagree on many issues, they agree that their bilateral relationship has seen a power shift in favor of China even though the United States still holds the upper hand. My argument that this power shift has been the main factor affecting Sino-American relations is neither new nor unusual.

Moreover, compared with other explanations, the erosion of U.S. primacy can explain better changing U.S. policies and attitudes toward international institutions and multilateral diplomacy. Washington's support for them was strongest after World War II when its power was at its peak. This support has since diminished, especially during the Trump administration, which increasingly pursued a policy of unilateral assertiveness. Changing power balance thus is likely the main determinant shaping the evolution of Sino-American relations though it also behooves us to recognize that this development does not in and of itself increase the danger of war. As suggested in the introduction, the effects of other variables also need to be considered. This last caveat is apposite because U.S. power reached another zenith immediately after the Cold War, but this time Washington acted differently; it did not try to forge another consensual constitutional order but decided instead on more muscular policies to impose its vision on the rest of the world based on an agenda of regime change abroad.

Naturally, we should not exaggerate the speed and extent of shifting power balance. In the next two chapters, I discuss in more detail different aspects of national power and some enduring sources of U.S. strength. The view that China is rapidly reaching the point of challenging Washington's global primacy and even poised to overthrow its hegemonic position suggests more hype than reality. Still, the current tension between the two countries reflects U.S. efforts to block this incipient danger to its primacy.

Even though China is making relative gains and rather quickly and significantly in some areas, it will be difficult for Beijing to displace the United States as the world's lone superpower in at least the next few decades. Although China's economy is projected by some to overtake the size of the U.S. economy in about ten to fifteen years, in 2019 its per capita income was still roughly six and half times smaller than the comparable U.S. figure. It would take considerable time for it to reach the U.S. level of affluence.[116] This development is unlikely to come before 2050, if ever. It would be a mistake to confuse the size of an economy with its vitality and its people's wealth. Even as late as the 1830s and possibly even much later, China still had the world's largest economy, just when it was about to enter its "century of national humiliation" at the hands of Western and Japanese imperialists.

The thrust of this chapter is not to condone China's transgressions, or to complain about hypocrisy and double standard in Washington's practices and explanations of why its relations with China have deteriorated. The larger point is that the prevailing discourse obscures our understanding and hinders prudent policy. As Jonathan Kirshner reminds us, classical realists argue against universal moral judgments that can disguise realpolitik reasons and particularistic interests. They advise that we should always acknowledge the reality of power politics, recognizing others' power as well as the limits of our own power.[117] Strident rhetorical assertions may resonate with domestic audiences and even score political points, but they do not necessarily advance the improvement of international relations. Among the reasons suggested for the deterioration in Sino-American relations, the shifting power balance between these two countries is the leading, even if not the only, factor. This deterioration has less to do with China's regime type or even its current foreign policies than the evolving power balance that, in Washington's view, poses a threat to its international dominance. This discussion suggests that even if China were to become more democratic, bilateral tension would remain if the power balance continues to shift. Mearsheimer suggests that the current tension is not about China; any country, regardless of its ideology or regime character, that approaches the level of U.S. power will be a concern for Washington.[118]

Mearsheimer is right in pointing out that after securing regional hegemony in the Western Hemisphere, a constant and consistent tenet of U.S. foreign policy has been to prevent the rise of another regional hegemon elsewhere in the world.[119] Washington has shifted its support between China and Japan, always favoring the weaker side to prevent the other from gaining a decisive upper hand. Like its hegemonic predecessor Britain, whose policy had alternated between support for France and Prussia/Germany, the United States fought two world wars and the Cold War to prevent Germany and the USSR from securing mastery in Europe. We see the same pattern of divide and rule in Washington's policies toward the Middle East, pitting Iraq against Iran previously and Saudi Arabia against Iran currently. It continues to support Pakistan as a counterpoise, albeit a weak one, against India and deploying India as a counterpoise against China.

This line of reasoning implies that it will be difficult to reverse the current deteriorating relationship between China and the United States— unless of course China's economy falters and its growth rate falls so that the United States is confident of keeping and even extending its primacy. Indeed, the problem seems intractable because how can a country's leaders promise not to grow its economy and to increase its national capabilities? This question poses the classic problem of commitment that James Fearon raised quarter century ago.[120] Moreover, to the extent that power transition introduces issues such as national status, prestige, and honor, including the idea of being the undisputed dominant power in the world, it pertains to issues that defy easy solution for another reason Fearon suggested: namely, these desiderata are inherently indivisible and zero-sum and they impinge on a people's self-image and identity.

I hasten to add, however, that officials in both countries can undertake policies that can ease tension or at least stabilize their relations from further deterioration even though their policy discretion may be constrained by domestic politics. As mentioned, both sides can refrain from hardball politics, eschewing conduct in the playbook of realpolitik, such as participating in armament races, competing for allies and clients, engaging in crisis brinksmanship, and taking part in rhetorical escalation and baiting. These practices can further heighten tension and exacerbate animosity. History teaches us that they rather than power transition per se are the proximate causes for a conflict to spiral out of control.

We do not have a crystal ball to see the future clearly. But if the past may offer some clues about future possibilities, we can perhaps learn something from Russia's and the USSR's experience. Mikhail Gorbachev made large and unrequited concessions to the United States and the West. He withdrew the Red Army from Central and Eastern Europe, allowed allied communist regimes to fall without military intervention, accepted Germany's reunification and even its membership in the North Atlantic Treaty Organization (NATO), and started the process that led to the USSR's dissolution. However haltingly and imperfectly, he also initiated the process that ended the one-party rule by communists and subjected Russia's economy to structural reform. Although the specifics can be debated, few people would challenge the proposition that Russia's political and economic system is more open today than during the Soviet days.

As Charles Kupchan observes, "From Moscow's perspective, Russia for successive years made a series of concessions to the West, including accommodating NATO expansion, reacting with restraint to democratic revolutions in its 'near abroad,' and facilitating strategic access for the United States in Central Asia and Afghanistan."[121] These concessions, however, did not have any effect on NATO's and the European Union's eastward expansion, nor did they discourage demands from the United States and its allies for more concessions. They also did not prevent the return of tension. Others have made similar observations, concluding that the United States had taken advantage of the USSR's demise to extend its geographic and ideological reach.[122] Obviously, today's Russia has declined in stature and power. It is a much weaker country than its former incarnation during the Cold War, but this development did not in itself improve its relations with the United States or the West more generally. It has instead increased Russia's sense of grievance. As a declining power, Russia has asserted more aggressively its demands for status recognition than has China, a rising power.[123] Even though the United States is zealous in protecting its regional hegemony in the Western Hemisphere, it refuses to acknowledge that Russia and China are entitled to a sphere of influence in their respective neighborhood.

What would or should Beijing conclude from Russia's experience? Movements toward greater political democratization and economic liberalization would not in themselves ensure better relations with the United States or the West. Unilateral concessions could invite additional demands for more concessions rather than reciprocity. Instead of reassuring the United States and the West, weakness encourages more pressure from them. If Beijing's officials hold these views, they would face a policy bind. Progress on the Kantian tripod of increasing democratization, economic interdependence, and participation in international organizations cannot stop relations with the United States and the West from deteriorating.[124] Paradoxically, improving national power could lead them to undertake more vigorous containment policies whereas weakened national power could incline to them to pursue more coercive policies. Thus, both favorable and unfavorable power shifts from their perspective could have a detrimental effect on their relations with the United States and the West. These views would then lead to the inevitable conclusion that the United States and the West are implacably hostile because, short of capitulation, relatively little can be done to alter their disposition.

Other important implications follow from this discussion. China's progress on liberalization (with important caveats on its halting and limited nature), integrating itself with the global economy, and participating actively in international organizations (and renouncing its previous policies of supporting insurgency movements abroad, rejecting international peacekeeping missions, and opposing international agreements on arms control) has not helped to improve its relations with the United States or the West more generally. This pattern contradicts the liberal perspective on international relations and bolsters the realist argument asserting the primacy of power balance as a determinant of international relations. In the 1970s and 1980s, much talk, even alarm, circulated in the United States about the economic challenge coming from Japan, a fellow democracy and military ally. Regime type and defense partnership did not dispose Washington to treat this perceived challenge with equanimity. Russia's and China's contrasting experiences—relative power loss in recent decades for Moscow and relative power gains for Beijing—suggest also paradoxically that neither national strength nor national weakness can ensure good foreign relations. When a country becomes weaker, this development invites foreign coercion and even predation (recalling China's decrepit Qing dynasty and its century of national humiliation). When it becomes stronger, this development engenders containment and blocking actions by the established powers, especially when the hegemon is concerned about maintaining its preponderance.

2

CONCEPTUAL AND MEASUREMENT PROBLEMS IN STUDYING POWER

Realists of different stripes agree about one thing: the importance of national power as a determinant of a country's foreign policy and, similarly, the importance of the interstate distribution of this power as a determinant of peace and stability.[1] Focusing on the changing power balance between two countries as they do, power-transition theory and Thucydides' Trap also give national power the pride of place in their analyses.[2] But what is national power and how can we measure it? This topic has been the subject of many studies.[3] Although more attention has been paid to a country's soft power since Joseph Nye's influential writing,[4] most analysts continue to treat and measure national power in terms of a state's production or ownership of stocks of tangible resources such as its economic size, energy consumption, export volume, and weapons arsenal. This chapter discusses serious conceptual and measurement issues that continue to beset research on power transition. To the extent that analysts cannot be confident about when and even whether such a process has occurred, it is impossible to go on to the next step of ascertaining whether this process endangers peace. This chapter's discussion obviously also pertains to the changing power balance between the United States and China, and the effectiveness of these countries' efforts to mobilize and deploy those power resources in their possession.

POWER AS RESOURCES

Following Raymond Boudon and Francois Bourricaud,[5] Ashley Tellis points to the common approach of treating power as resources.[6] "Power, in this conception, is dispositional. It refers not to actual performance but merely to the capacities or assets possessed by any given entity, resources that either may enable certain outcomes to be produced by the very fact of their existence or could be utilized subsequently to produce particular outcomes through intentional action."[7]

The resources in question may incline other states to do something, or to refrain from doing something, simply because of their presence. For instance, a state's possession of nuclear weapons may effectively deter another country from attacking it, or its ability to provide foreign aid may incline another state to vote according to its preferences in the United Nations. In these instances, the state in possession of the pertinent resources may be able to obtain favorable outcomes without trying to actually use these resources in any overt attempt to influence another state's behavior. These favorable outcomes reflect a target state's acknowledgment or awareness that its counterpart possessing the pertinent resources has the capacity to act in certain ways and thereby to bring about certain outcomes. Thus power as resources directs our attention to a state's potential capacity to exercise certain options. For example, a state with a large economic and technological base is presumed to have the wherewithal to develop a strong armament program if it chooses to do so. This proposition does not mean that it will. For example, even though Japan certainly has the necessary economic and technological resources to develop nuclear weapons, it has thus far chosen not to do so. Still, ceteris paribus, the more resources in a state's possession, the larger its menu for policy choices.

However, whether the state with the relevant resources will adopt a particular policy choice and whether it can implement this choice effectively are open to question. That it can do so is just an assumption. Thus the connection between a state's having resources and its ability to act on them cannot be taken for granted. This possession may be a necessary condition for an ability to act but it is hardly a sufficient condition.

Most existing analyses of national power, whether qualitative or quantitative, reflect this approach of treating it as a state's possession or production of physical resources. Perhaps the best-known systematic attempt to measure national power over a long stretch of time is the Composite Index of National Capability (CINC) developed by the Correlates of War (COW) Project at the University of Michigan.[8] This measure summarizes a country's total and urban population, its iron or steel production and its energy consumption, and the size of its defense expenditures and military personnel. These variables stress a country's physical size and thus tend to inflate the power of countries such as China, the Soviet Union, and others that have historically featured large populations, smokestack industries, and massive infantries. Some assessments relying on these variables suggest that China had already overtaken the United States by the mid-1990s, or even in the 1980s, a conclusion most people would likely question.

In contrast to physical size, a country's human capital can be more informative about its capacity. Thus a country's per capita income, not its aggregate economic output, is telling. In 2019, the average U.S. income was 6.38 times greater than the average Chinese income in nominal terms and 3.32 times greater if adjusted for purchasing power parity.[9] This means that U.S. workers have a much higher productivity than their Chinese counterparts. A large population can be a liability if the economy is not productive enough to feed it. In a low-productivity economy saddled with a large population, much of what is produced will be consumed, leaving little to be invested—including investment to improve human capital.

Michael Beckley points to the problem of relying on bulk measures to indicate national power, remarking that until the 1890s China still had the world's largest economy and military even though it was clearly a declining power that had been facing catastrophic setbacks in its encounters with Japanese and Western imperialists.[10] He argues that we should abandon gross indicators of power with net indicators that adjust a country's assets against its liabilities. Even though, according to Pew Research Center polls conducted in 2017, "most people in most countries think that China is overtaking the United States as the world's leading power," this view is mistaken because "the hype about China's rise . . . has been based largely on gross indicators that ignore costs. When costs are accounted for, it becomes clear that the United States' economic and military lead over China is much larger than typically assumed—and the trends are mostly in America's favor."[11]

Beckley compares standard measures of national power, namely, CINC and gross domestic product (GDP), with his own suggested alternative measure of GDP multiplied by GDP per capita. His measure takes into consideration not only a country's economic size but also its economic efficiency or productivity. People's views on the distribution of interstate power can be seriously distorted without accounting for productivity. For example, whereas GDP and CINC show that China was much stronger than Japan in 1930, Beckley's alternative measure indicates the reverse.[12] Similarly, although in 1850 Britain's GDP was only half of India's, its GDP per capita was four times higher and this factor made all the difference in Britain's ability to conquer India.[13] He argues correctly that "many of the cases identified as power transitions may not have involved an actual transition in power, and, conversely, many genuine power transitions may not have . . . been identified as such."[14]

Despite its drawbacks, power as resources is attractive to many analysts because it refers to those phenomena that can be more easily quantified and many of the pertinent variables such as demographic, territorial, and economic size are widely available for many countries over a long period. "The view of power as resources is particularly appealing to theorists of international relations who often treat countries as 'bordered power-containers': the country is akin to a receptacle and the resources it possesses are akin to stock, allowing the latter to be measured, quantified, and compared with the holdings possessed by others. Although there may be disputes about which particular resources, such as population, natural wealth, productive capabilities, and military strength, are best suited to describe a country's national power, the utility of having a standardized set of measurable variables allows for cross-country comparisons and the global rank ordering of nations."[15]

International Strategic Analysis (ISA) presents a ranking of the world's top countries based on its consideration of "economic power, demographic power, military power, environmental and resource power, political power, cultural power, and technological power."[16] It is not clear what data are used for each of these power components or the relative weight given to each of them in deriving the composite indicator. This composite indicator gives an ordinal ranking (thus we do not know the distance separating, say, the United States and China). It is also not clear how this ranking has changed over time or is expected to evolve in the future. ISA reports in descending order the following ranking: the United States, China, India, Russia, Japan, France, Britain, Brazil, Germany, Canada, Saudi Arabia, Australia, South Korea, Turkey, Italy, Indonesia, Mexico, Spain, Nigeria, Iran, Pakistan, Israel, Egypt, South Africa, and the United Arab Emirates. It is not clear which power component mentioned is most important in determining a country's rank position. Given all these reasons, such ranking cannot be easily replicated and has only limited use for international relations.

Naturally, which indicator one uses to measure national power can be consequential for an analysis's conclusions. Ned Lebow and Benjamin Valentino use a country's population multiplied by its gross domestic product.[17] This decision led them to conclude that Spain was dominant from 1640 until Russia overtook it in 1795. In their view, the only two other cases of power transition were the United States overtaking Russia in 1895 and China overtaking the United States in the early 1980s.[18] Contrary to power-transition theory, in all three of these cases the process ended peacefully. If one accepts Lebow and Valentino's measurement of national power—and many people may be highly skeptical of its validity—some forty years have passed since China overtook the United States and yet these countries have thus far managed to stay at peace.

Using another measure, such as a country's gross domestic product, an approach A. F. K. Organski and Jacek Kugler favor,[19] the conclusion would be different, namely, that no power transition has involved China overtaking the United States. Moreover, the Anglo-American transition is the only instance in the modern era (since the conclusion of the Napoleonic Wars in 1815) and it was not followed by war, as power-transition theory would have predicted. This discussion refers only to a positional change between the two leading states in the international system, and therefore does not consider any other countries ranking behind them, as power-transition theory stipulates.

Despite any possible correlation between GDP and the COW Project's CINC for all the countries in the world, this aggregate relationship does not mean that these indicators can be used interchangeably for studying the power-transition phenomenon because, as mentioned, this theory is concerned only with the most powerful states in the international hierarchy. Carsten Rauch documents how assessment of the power-transition phenomenon can be seriously affected by the measure used in one's analysis.[20] If GDP is used, the United States overtook Britain in the 1870s; if CINC is used, it did not do so until the 1890s. In either case, the United States had acted as a dissatisfied, or at least expansionist, power even after overtaking Britain. From the 1870s to the 1910s, it sought to exclude European influence from the Western Hemisphere, extended the U.S. frontier westward, waged war against Spain, fought a bloody anti-insurgency campaign to establish a colony in the Philippines, annexed the Hawaiian archipelago, and intervened repeatedly in Central America and the Caribbean (twenty times just in the Caribbean between 1898 and 1932).[21]

Of course, the U.S. GDP has continued to be the world's largest since the 1870s. Germany, the USSR, and China have not come close to matching it, never mind overtaking it. These countries came, at best, to 77 percent, 45 percent, and 80.7 percent, respectively, of U.S. GDP according to the historical data series from the Maddison Project at the University of Groningen.[22] The obvious conclusion is that no transition between the world's two top powers has occurred since the United States overtook Britain in the late nineteenth century. Consequently, power-transition theory cannot explain any systemic war since that time. Moreover, contrary to the theory's prediction, in the only power transition in the modern era, that between the United States and Britain, the outcome was peaceful.

Whether we should use nominal GDP or one adjusted for purchasing power parity (PPP) can also significantly affect conclusions about the power-transition phenomenon. PPP estimates reflect varying assumptions that can produce very different assessments. At least according to one PPP estimate, China's economy had already overtaken that of the United States in 2013.[23] In nominal terms, however, China had not even reached parity (defined as 80 percent) as late as 2005. That year, China's nominal GDP was estimated to be at 61, 60, and 59 percent of the U.S. GDP by the International Monetary Fund, the United Nations, and the World Bank respectively—in contrast to the much higher figure (80.7 percent) of the Maddison Project for the same year.[24] Thus estimates for GDP figures can diverge widely.

These GDP figures can also differ significantly from CINC. The CINC measure reports that the USSR was the world's most powerful country from 1977 to 1988, and that China took its place in 1996.[25] According to CINC, only three power transitions have occurred since the 1890s, and all of them have had a peaceful outcome. Naturally, most people may have serious doubts about the validity of CINC's assessment of the last two putative power transitions, especially because the Soviet Union collapsed shortly after it was declared the world's most powerful country.

A significant and still unresolved issue in this discussion pertains to whether power transition refers to positional changes between the world's most powerful countries (such as when a country that was ranked second in its power becomes the first), to the absolute distance separating these countries' power, or to one country's proportionate power in relationship to the other. Organski and Kugler originally stipulated that Country B has reached parity with Country A when it has 80 percent of the latter's power.[26] Many power-transition analysts, however, have not followed this definition. Moreover, the exchange between Joshua Shifrinson and Beckley has raised the important question of whether the absolute difference between two countries' power or the ratio characterizing their respective power should be of greater theoretical and empirical relevance.[27]

The approach treating power as resources and its analysis based on the view of countries as "bordered power-containers" face four serious problems. First, in this age of globalization characterized by deep and wide cross-border production chains and investment links, it is no longer sensible to treat countries as self-contained entities. For instance, multinational corporations now operate across the globe even though they are still usually headquartered in any of a few large, developed countries. The physical location where a product is made or assembled is less important as an indicator of national strength than the national identity of the transnational corporations that own and control the most valuable parts of the production process such as a product's branding, design, and marketing.[28] For instance, assembling the iPod accounts for only about 1 percent of its value.[29]

Second, although many of the variables used in the power as resources approach were relevant and helpful indicators of national capabilities during an earlier era, their usefulness for understanding contemporary international relations is questionable. Indeed, a reliance of these indicators can obscure and mislead rather than illuminate the relative power standings of countries in today's world. For instance, production of iron and steel, consumption of fossil fuels such as coal and oil, and the maintenance of a large infantry are outdated indicators and tend to show a country's backwardness rather than its strength. We also know that when a country reaches an advanced stage of economic development, birth rates tend to fall and life expectancy rises. Although it seems reasonable to argue that a country must have a minimum population to be considered a great power, size becomes less important after a certain threshold. As already mentioned, leading global powers in the past, such as Britain, the Netherlands, and Portugal, had much smaller populations than their rivals.

Third, the more important determinants of national power pertain to a country's ability to pioneer new industries at the frontiers of technology. Traditional indicators of national power, emphasizing quantity rather than quality, cannot effectively capture this capacity to make qualitative leaps based on scientific or technological breakthroughs. Britain's leadership in the world was due to its ability to undertake these inventions and innovations, such as in the textile industry and railway construction, that first launched its industrial revolution and subsequently sustained its economic and technological advantages.[30] Advances in nanotechnology, artificial intelligence, genetic engineering, big-data computation, electric vehicle, and communications technology have been mentioned as critical areas for contributing to a country's ability to spur economic growth and maintain its technological edge in today's international competition. Naturally, it takes human capital to make scientific and technological advances. Rather than obsessing over outdated measures, it would be wiser to ask whether China is catching up to the United States in scientific discovery and technological innovation.[31]

Finally, international relations are rarely dyadic, pitting one country against another. Whether voting in the United Nations, undertaking economic sanctions, or winning wars, putting together a winning coalition is critical. Britain led Germany in 1914 in having a more powerful navy and a higher average income. In other respects, Germany held the upper hand. London was able to prevail in the ensuing war because it was part of a more powerful international coalition. Similarly, the Axis powers lost World War II because their alliance was much weaker than the opposition (to compound this weakness, Germany and Japan fought their separate wars without effective coordination). "Struggles for hegemony are rarely dyadic encounters between two powers . . . the strongest surviving state in the winning coalition usually turns out to be the new hegemon after a systemic war."[32] Put starkly, alliances win wars. The obvious implication is that whereas today's China can hardly count on the assistance of any ally in a possible confrontation with the United States, the reverse is not true. Washington has many powerful allies and a vast network of financial ties and military bases that further extend its own already formidable, preponderant power. Few doubt which side Australia, Britain, and Canada would stand on should there be a Sino-American showdown. It is far more difficult to identify China's prospective allies.

POWER AS ABILITY

Possessing resources does not necessarily mean that an actor can put them to useful purposes. These resources must be mobilized and converted in ways that this actor can deploy them effectively to achieve its objectives. Organski and Kugler refer to this as a state's policy capacity.[33] They show that countries with a larger population, territory, and even economy can lose contests to others with fewer resources but are better at exploiting what they have.

Other than the obvious example of Israel's prevailing over its larger Arab neighbors in repeated military encounters, the difficulties the United States encountered in Afghanistan, Iraq, and Vietnam point to this phenomenon, which of course also includes considerations of other more intangible aspects of power such as morale, leadership, strategy, and a people's dedication to its cause and willingness to endure privations. Both Jacek Kugler and Marina Arbetman and Kugler and William Domke use the respective belligerents' effectiveness in extracting resources and exerting themselves to explain the outcomes of different combat theaters during the two world wars and other conflicts such as the Russo-Japanese War and the contest between North and South Vietnam.[34] Their results again show that actual performance on the battlefield depends on the effective mobilization of available resources rather than the mere possession of them.

To give another example that possession of resources is not necessarily tantamount to an ability to reach a higher level of performance or to attain a more satisfactory outcome, oil revenues and exports of other minerals have not always translated into human development given a producing country's limited institutional capacity to mobilize its population and to use its wealth wisely or effectively.[35]

History shows many instances whereby a country with more resources decides not to fully use the resources at its disposal or fails to use them effectively. Consequently, the largest or militarily strongest countries do not always prevail in contests against counterparts with more meager resources.[36] This phenomenon suggests that different kinds of resources generally construed to constitute national power are not likely to be fungible. For instance, a larger economy does not necessarily imply a stronger military that can enable a country to win wars, although a high level of economic development (suggesting a qualitative edge in a country's ability to "produce, maintain, and coordinate complex military systems") does contribute to greater military effectiveness.[37] Naturally, whether to apply all the means available to a country to prevail in a military contest is a matter of policy decision reflecting its leaders' political, economic, and normative considerations. That the United States did not prevail in Korea, Vietnam, and Afghanistan indicates its unwillingness to resort to the full range of its military capabilities rather than its lack of them.

This reasoning calls attention to a conception of power as ability. Originally presented by Boudon and Bourricaud, this refers to "the ability to use . . . resources, which in turn implies, among other things, a plan of use and [the necessity of] minimal information about the conditions and consequences of this use."[38] Tellis goes on to explain that "This notion of power as ability is a valuable complement to the conceptualization of power as resources because it emphasizes intentionality and the active dimension of the actual-potential dichotomy that inheres in any notion of power centered on brute capabilities. This approach, by focusing on the idea of the power 'to do' something, as opposed to the notion of power emanating from a stock of resources, opens the door to thinking about power as strategy in which the processes, relationships, and situations that shape purposeful action all play an important role."[39]

Thus, the possession of (tangible) resources does not tell us the entire story. These resources need to be "activated," which in turn requires an actor to have the requisite policy capacity, as Organski and Kugler argue.[40] The application of available resources also implies intentionality, as Tellis indicates, and, more specifically, a deliberate plan on how the resources in question are to be deployed to pursue defined objectives. Moreover, power as ability depends on a state's relationship with its society because the government needs to mobilize the requisite resources from its society. As Kugler and Domke remark, "power in the global system requires a combination of political capacity and resources."[41] One leading indicator of this capacity pertains to a state's ability to collect revenues, which is exemplified by its tax system.

The idea of political or policy capacity has been further elaborated to include not just a state's ability to extract resources from society but also its ability to reach its citizens. Scholars have applied these twin concepts of states' relative extractive capacity and their relative political reach to study a variety of phenomena pertaining to cross-national policy performance, such as states' relative success in managing inflation, encouraging investment, and promoting economic development.[42] These studies and others, however, do not address how a state's extraction and reach have affected past or can affect possible future power transitions. In their original analysis, Organski and Kugler do not factor in policy capacity in their assessment of whether and when a power transition was occurring.[43] They decided not to consider it on the grounds that their theory pertains to only the leading developed countries, which in their view should have similar levels of policy capacity.

As a general proposition, developed countries have greater political or policy capacity than developing countries. Paradoxically, this observation also implies that the former countries cannot dramatically alter their revenue flows because they have already reached or approached the upper limit of this extraction, principally by taxation on personal and corporate income. In contrast, because they start from a low level of extraction, developing countries have more room to improve their performance. Significantly, although states' extractive capacity tends to vary with their development level (higher for developed countries, and lower for developing countries), this variable is independent of regime types. There is no a priori reason to expect democratic governments to have a greater extractive capacity than authoritarian governments, or vice versa. Both authoritarian Russia and democratic France failed to extract resources effectively during World War I. Meanwhile, in World War II, authoritarian Japan turned out to be the most effective among the belligerent states to mobilize its resources, though not enough to compensate for its much smaller resource base.[44]

"Relative political reach measures the degree to which [a] population accepts the presence of government in their lives."[45] This view suggests that social capital and trust are an important determinant of a government's ability to reach society,[46] including its efforts to promote vaccination against infectious diseases. The size of the informal or underground economy, the rate of labor participation, and the level of enrollment in secondary schools can all serve as proxy measures of a state's capacity to reach society. The number of Americans rejecting government mandate to wear face masks or be vaccinated in a pandemic is another example. All else aside, authoritarian governments with a mass party are more able to mobilize its people if for nothing else but the likely resistance from a democracy's civil society to such mobilization attempts except in national emergencies such as war. It is useful to draw from the literature on developmental states with its insight that both a state's embeddedness in society and its autonomy from society are important.[47] A state's embeddedness in society discourages it from becoming predatory and its autonomy prevents it from being captured by special interests seeking rent.

Political or policy capacity has a third dimension beyond extraction and reach that refer to the input side of those resources to be made available to a state. This third additional consideration concerns what the state does with these resources, the output side. Thus the allocation of resources by the state is also germane if for nothing else than that the available resources can be spent on wasteful projects or siphoned off by graft and corruption.[48] Mark Abdollahian and his colleagues show that Pakistan allocates and uses its resources poorly, in the manner just described, whereas South Korea demonstrates both high political reach and effective allocation.[49]

In developed democracies, political cross-pressure on the state to implement or dismantle different programs is inevitable, including programs to return money to citizens in the form of lower taxes or tax rebates. The struggle for different kinds of public spending is also constant, including the trade-offs between guns and butter. Naturally, such pressure and struggle also exist in authoritarian systems, except that their "selectorate" has a smaller number of pivotal interest groups. At least in theory, authoritarian leaders should have more discretion to reallocate their available resources, whereas democratic leaders are more likely to be constrained by various veto groups from undertaking sharp departures from existing patterns of spending. Indeed, in the United States, many of these expenditures have already been committed to various entitlement programs. "While wealthier societies are more stable and more consistent, they do not necessarily extract, reach, and allocate resources more efficiently than their authoritarian counterparts."[50] Of course, poorer countries tend to score low on all three dimensions of power as ability: extraction, reach, and allocation.

What are the implications of this discussion for the United States and China? As noted, political or policy capacity is independent of regime types and has little to do with "good" or "bad" qualities associated with a government such as democracy, individual freedom, free speech, and personal affluence. As a cross-national generalization, this proposition is likely to be true. In comparing the United States with China, however, these countries' political institutions can provide some additional information on their respective capacities.

Given the nature of a democracy, in which officials face voters in regularly scheduled elections, popular resistance to taxation and the citizens' concurrent demand for more social services put U.S. politicians in a perpetual bind. They have thus far tried to finesse this challenge by resorting to borrowing, raising national debt to about 136 percent of the aggregate economy as of mid-2020 and before the massive $1.9 trillion COVID-relief legislation introduced by the Biden administration and passed by Congress.[51] The pressure to win elections constrains politicians from extracting more resources from society and to reallocate the resources made available to it. As already mentioned, much of the federal government's spending has been committed to entitlement programs. As a democracy with a large selectorate that includes many veto groups, elected officials' freedom to shift resources to alternative purposes is also limited. Of course, crafting a consensus about national priorities becomes difficult in an environment of intense partisanship. Finally, in terms of its ability to reach society, the federal structure hampers Washington's ability and authority to implement national policies such as during the COVID-19 pandemic. Decisions such as to mandate wearing face masks, to distribute vaccines, and to order lockdown are in the hands of fifty governors.

U.S. government institutions enhance the power of minorities to block policies. The electoral college, for example, favors the more rural, conservative states and those that are less populous and diverse. It gives them an oversized influence in presidential elections. If these elections were to be decided by popular vote, the Democratic Party's candidate would be the favorite to win most contests. In the 2020 presidential election, Donald Trump carried most of the country's counties covering a vast amount of its territory but only 29 percent of its economy.[52] In contrast, Biden won far fewer counties but more people. These more urban, diverse, and liberal centers of population contributed to 71 percent of the U.S. economy. The same discrepancies or distortions characterize representation in Congress. With a population of nearly forty million, California has the same number of senators as Wyoming, which has a population of less than six hundred thousand. The rules of the Senate again give the minority party significant power to block objectionable legislation, requiring a supermajority for passage because it takes sixty votes to stop a filibuster. Gerrymandering and the winner-take-all election system tend to also magnify the power of a political minority at the local or state level. With an average of 45 percent support from the electorate, the Republican Party often commands a majority in state legislatures, sometimes taking over as many as 65 percent of legislative seats. Thus, U.S. political institutions explain the phenomenon that legislation, such as on abortion rights and the regulation of firearms, can be stalled despite the wishes of most Americans.

In contrast, with its more centralized government and a single ruling party, the Chinese state is not nearly as constrained. Its top-down political system is better positioned to mobilize and penetrate society. This greater capacity, however, does not imply smarter or more effective allocation of the available resources. The authoritarian nature of the government and weaker institutional checks on arbitrary power give leaders greater policy discretion to make allocation decisions. These traits also mean that the Chinese system does not have strong guardrails to prevent or reverse bad policies. The policy mistakes made during the Great Leap Forward campaign and the Cultural Revolution demonstrate the devastating consequences that can ensue given the nature of China's political institutions. As mentioned earlier, such self-inflicted harm does far more than any damage that foreigners can impose. At least in theory, longevity in office can promote long-range planning and policy continuity that otherwise could be disrupted by alternation of politicians with different political agendas and outlooks.

The general conclusion to be drawn from this discussion is that a state's political or policy capacity matters for its economic and military performance and for its relative position in the international system. Although they are not intended as definitive forecasts, the alternative scenarios sketched by Kugler and his colleagues are still instructive for heuristic reasons.[53] They project that China's economy would overtake the United States around 2035 if it were to maintain high extractive and reach capacity. If this base scenario is altered to reflect low U.S. capacity, it would occur sooner, around 2025. Finally, in a scenario featuring low capacity for both countries or one in which United States maintains high capacity and China shows low capacity, this overtaking would not occur until 2050 at the earliest—if then. Although we may quibble with the specific measures and algorithms used to make these projections, the major point is again that each country controls its own destiny. Its growth prospects are determined primarily by its domestic conditions and policies. Naturally, because international competition refers to countries' relative performance, their position in the world is determined by not only their performance but also that of their counterparts.

POWER AS OUTCOME

The third and final dimension of power refers to power as outcome. As Tellis frames it, "[This] third notion discussed by Boudon and Bourricaud centers on 'the strategic character of power,' namely that 'ultimately it is exercised not only against the inertia of things, but against the resistance of opposing wills.' This conception of power, which focuses fundamentally on the consequences of a given action, comports with the common human intuition of what it means to be powerful: getting one's way. In its strongest form, this understanding of power incorporates the simple question of whether an agent is able to influence the targeted entity to act in a desired way, even if that entails undermining the target's own interests—an idea that was later encapsulated in Robert Dahl's now classic definition of power as the ability of A to get B to do something B would otherwise not do."[54]

In a similar vein, other scholars have discussed power as control over outcomes or events.[55] This view takes the further step of asking whether a state is likely to prevail over another state with a different interest and disposed to oppose its preferences. The key aspect of this conception of power refers to the interactions between two parties. As Tellis explains, this view reflects Dahl's well-known definition of influence as A's ability to get B to act in a way contrary to B's initial intention.[56] Significantly, in this third conception, power is treated as an inherently relational idea. It is not something that exists in abstraction but is instead grounded in specific relations and contexts. Power becomes a useful concept in international relations when it is considered in the context of one state seeking to impose its will on another. The extent to which it can get its way reflects its relative power over the target state. This outcome in turn depends on B's sensitivity and vulnerability to A. Sensitivity "involves how quickly do changes in one country bring costly changes in another, and how great are the costly effects?" whereas "vulnerability can be defined as an actor's liability to suffer costs imposed by external events even after policies have been altered."[57]

For example, the Chinese telecom company Huawei has been subjected to a U.S. ban to access its market and technology. Huawei's reliance on the United States for its continued growth therefore indicates its sensitivity to Washington's actions. Naturally, Beijing would take countermeasures to mitigate the effects of this ban, such as by seeking markets and suppliers elsewhere and developing its own indigenous capabilities. Such adjustments, however, usually take a long time to implement and bear fruit. The effects of the ban even after Beijing's mitigation efforts point to China's vulnerability, which "can be measured only by the costliness of making effective adjustments to a changed environment over a period of time."[58] Note that the adjustments undertaken by Beijing in response to U.S. actions can themselves be costly in addition, of course, to the costs imposed by the initial actions.

A recent project addresses some of the concerns just raised even though it does not indicate B's costs of adjustment or A's actual success in seeking influence.[59] Nor does it investigate whether B in fact has interests that are opposed to A's or for that matter, whether A has in fact sought to influence B. What it does do is to indicate the opportunity for A to influence B and B's potential costs for resisting A's influence attempt, both of which depend on the extent of their interactions and the extent of asymmetry in their interactions. The pertinent rationale is that A's influence attempt on B depends on the existence of a relationship between them and A's success in this potential attempt depends on its bargaining leverage over B, which is reflected by B's extent of dependency on A.

Jonathan Moyer and his colleagues report that China's influence defined in this way has increased both in size and reach around the world in recent years, whereas the influence of the United States has fallen. They construct an index called Formal Bilateral Influence Capacity based on the extent of Chinese (and U.S.) economic, security, and political relations with individual countries and the extent of dependency by the country in question on China (or the United States) created by these relations. The resulting index suggests that Chinese influence exceeded U.S. influence in sixty-one countries in 2020, whereas U.S. influence was greater than Chinese influence in 160 countries.[60] In contrast to the typical analysis, which creates a single composite index of national influence (or power) without paying any attention to how it pertains to specific targets, this project has the virtue of showing variations in Chinese (and U.S.) influence potential across countries and regions. In other words, it applies the concept of influence in a relational way for specific dyads. It thus makes substantial progress in overcoming the current literature's tendency to treat a country's influence abroad in an undifferentiated manner because Beijing's influence obviously varies according to the target state (say, whether it is Cambodia or Japan) and the issue domain (such as economic versus security matters) in question.

Although Moyer and his colleagues show that the number of countries susceptible to Beijing's influence has increased while those subject to potential U.S. influence has decreased (even though, as noted, the United States still leads over China in the number of such countries), it matters who these potential target states are and how influential these target states are in international relations. If China's influence is dominant in Myanmar, Laos, and Cambodia, the U.S. influence is dominant in Singapore and the Philippines, and they are tied in Indonesia, should we conclude that China has greater influence in Southeast Asia?

Although it seems obvious, A may have power or influence over B but not over C, D, or E, thus suggesting a general index of power without designating a specific target country has only limited utility. All else equal,

Washington's sanctions against Myanmar for its violations of human rights are likely to be more effective than, say, similar sanctions directed against Russia or China. This ability to influence is also specific to a particular issue area so that, for example, A may have a great deal of influence over B over the price and supply of oil but not those of grain. Saudi Arabia and Argentina, for example, enjoy different bargaining leverage in these two spheres. Some countries occupy a pivotal position in the relevant issue domain such that their participation in crafting a solution is imperative. The United States and China are both indispensable participants for any collective efforts to tackle problems such as global warming and nuclear proliferation. The matter of issue area is pertinent because it is more revealing about a country's influence when the question at hand touches on its core interests. For example, whether China's Belt and Road Initiative meets resistance or support in Kenya or Sri Lanka is less informative about Beijing's international influence than whether other countries defer to its views on Taiwan, Xinjiang, and the South China Sea disputes because one can reasonably expect Beijing to exert its greatest efforts to prevail over those three issue areas. Any formulaic approach to assessing countries' relative power can miss and even obscure important parts of reality.

This discussion suggests that it is exceedingly difficult, even impossible, to develop a valid indicator of a country's power as or over outcome, one that has also the necessary versatility to be applied across countries and issues areas. We are constantly reminded that power (or influence) is always relational and situational. Moreover, attempts to assess it face challenging methodological issues. Although seemingly simple, Dahl's definition of influence is in fact quite demanding. It requires counterfactual reasoning. How would B have acted in the absence of A's influence attempt? A's influence, after all, is the difference between how B would have acted in the absence of A's attempt to alter its behavior on the one hand, and how B has in fact behaved after A's influence attempt on the other hand. How do we know that B's behavior has been altered by A's influence attempt? How do we know that A has in fact attempted to influence B? Indeed, can B's conduct be altered by A, even without A trying to influence B overtly?

A story tells of a Brooklyn man who goes out of his house at noon every day, shouting and jumping up and down. One day, a neighbor finally approaches him to ask why he is behaving this way. The man replies that he is trying to prevent marauding elephants from invading the neighborhood. The neighbor retorts that there are no elephants in Brooklyn. The man replies, "You see, it works."

Gauging A's influence would be impossible unless we know B's original intention. Was the North Atlantic Treaty Organization (NATO) responsible for deterring a Soviet invasion of Europe? Was Washington instrumental in preserving peace across the Taiwan Strait thus far? We cannot answer in the affirmative unless we know that Moscow and Beijing would have launched their invasion had it not been for the presence of NATO or U.S. deterrence. Counterfactual analysis, however, is inherently difficult to undertake because it requires the analyst to infer B's original intention. Henry Kissinger is quoted saying, "Since deterrence can only be tested negatively, by events that do *not* take place, and since it is never possible to demonstrate why something has not occurred, it became especially difficult to assess whether the existing policy was the best possible policy or a just barely effective one. Perhaps deterrence was even unnecessary because it was impossible to prove whether the adversary ever intended to attack in the first place."[61]

As I discuss in the next chapter, one conception of power does not even require A to undertake a direct, overt attempt to influence B. All that is required is for B to recognize A's possession of powerful resources. Thus, knowing the devastating consequences of a nuclear war, leaders may be leery of escalating a conflict with a counterpart with these weapons without this counterpart making any explicit threat to use them. Another example is countries with massive holdings of the U.S. dollar possibly becoming consciously and even unconsciously more committed to the current international monetary regime because of their vested interest in it. This observation in turn takes us to differentiating bargaining power (A's ability to influence B on a particular issue) from structural power. The latter is more diffuse and includes but is not limited to A's ability to control the "rules of the game." It also pertains to how A can shape B's perceptions of its interests and even its identity.

For now, I explain the difficulties facing empirical attempts to assess a state's power. These difficulties stem in part from the idea of self-selection and the assessment of non-events. People are strategic in the sense that they adjust their behavior based on their anticipation of how others will react. If an encounter is not likely to be rewarding, they will avoid it, such as when I walk away from a fight when facing a stronger antagonist. I realize that I am likely to be pummeled should there be a fight, and my decision to select myself out of this encounter in turn means that the fight never happens. It would be a "non-event." Instances of fighting we observe thus are not a random sample; they are instead a biased sample in the sense that history does not record other occasions when fighting could have happened but did not.

One observable implication of this discussion on self-selection is that countries that start wars usually win them, and these wars usually remain bilateral affairs (that is, they do not expand to involve other countries). This phenomenon can be readily explained because leaders would not have launched a war unless they expect to win, and they choose their victims who are weak and unlikely to receive international assistance.[62] In the context of interstate influence, a country will try to change another's behavior only when it expects to succeed. History therefore overrepresents cases of such success. This tendency has the analytic consequence of inflating a country's influence because history does not report those non-events when it eschews influence attempts in the expectation that they will fail.

Determining influence success or failure is not so easy, however. Win, lose, or draw will have to be assessed in the context of each party's expectations and resource endowments. It would not be surprising for the United States to have its way with Afghanistan, Somalia, Haiti, North Korea, or North Vietnam. It would be more remarkable if these countries, with their much more limited resources, could force Washington to revise or reverse its policy, or to produce a stalemate on the battlefield. We cannot reach a valid inference of the contestants' respective power or influence by simply looking at the outcomes of bilateral contests without considering both tangible and intangible factors about them.

Put differently, the world has both overachievers and underachievers. Even if a larger or more powerful country "wins," it still matters how "big" it wins given the resource disparities between the contestants. The losing contestant's performance can be judged outstanding despite its loss. Here again, counterfactual analysis is necessary to provide us a benchmark for comparing how A is expected to perform versus its actual performance. People who have wagered on the outcomes of athletic contests and horse races are familiar with the idea of point spreads and betting odds that handicappers set. Even when losing a game, a sports team can outperform common expectations.

The story thus far is incomplete and can even be misleading because it overlooks additional complications and nuances. Consider illustrations from the literature on sanctions.[63] Anticipating that the United States would impose sanctions to discourage their nuclear programs, Taiwan and South Korea made preemptive concession by discontinuing these programs. After they have made this adjustment, Washington no longer has a need to threaten or implement sanctions against them. Thus history reports no overt sanction attempt by the United States in these instances, even though Washington's implicit threat to sanction had worked. In this illustration, history underreports those instances where the threat to sanction had worked. At the same time, when threats to sanction are carried out, the target country must be highly resolved because it was evidently not deterred by the prospect of having to pay a heavy price for defying Washington's wishes. So, when history reports the overt and direct application of economic coercion by the United States, these must be the "hardest" cases for it to prevail because, being strategic and anticipatory, the target states (e.g., Iran, North Korea) nevertheless decide to put up resistance against superior resources. The "easy" cases would not have been recorded because the target countries (Taiwan and South Korea in this illustration) have selected themselves out of a sanction encounter.

The general logic presented also applies to insights on deterrence studies, a topic obviously also relevant to discerning a country's influence or power as or over outcome. A situation of general extended deterrence refers to when A announces its intention to protect C from any aggression by B against this protégé, when little evidence points to B's intention or preparation to make such a move. In contrast, immediate extended deterrence involves A making the same declaration after B has started to make moves indicating the seriousness or imminence of its threat to C. Fearon provides an interesting analysis showing that whereas variables such as A's military strength, its alliance ties with C, and its economic interests in C tend to predict the success of its general extended deterrence, the opposite holds for its attempt at immediate extended deterrence.[64] This pattern suggests that those variables just mentioned should contribute to the credibility of A's announced intention to protect C, and thus to discourage B's aggression against C and hence the success of general extended deterrence. If, however, B nevertheless makes a move against C even after learning about A's declared intention to protect C and even in full knowledge of such public information as A's commercial and alliance ties with C, it must be highly resolved and/or it must have private information indicating that it has a good chance of succeeding. Otherwise, it would not have made moves to produce a situation of immediate extended deterrence. Paul Huth and Bruce Russett also report analysis results generally congruent with this reasoning that immediate extended deterrence is likely to fail.[65]

The point of this discussion is of course that we need to consider the relevant situational context before making assertions about a country's ostensible influence. Context is imperative. If China should resort to military coercion against Taiwan, for example, even launching an outright invasion against the island, even when it is fully aware of Washington's support for and commitment to Taiwan, its doing so must mean that it has discounted the U.S. deterrence effort and it must therefore be more resolved or more optimistic about its odds of success (or both).

Even long after an event has occurred, it is sometimes still difficult to reach definitive conclusions about a state's influence or power over outcome. Deterrence is about a policy intended to discourage B from doing something that it has not started doing, whereas compellence is intended to get B to stop doing something that it has already started doing. That it is more difficult for compellence to succeed than deterrence is generally agreed. After all, compellence would cause a loss in B's reputation because the world would be able to witness A having successfully twisted B's arm. But how do we distinguish a situation of deterrence from compellence, and how do we establish the identity of A and B?

Take the example of the 1962 Cuban Missile Crisis, which is generally presented in the United States as a case of John F. Kennedy administration's successfully forcing Moscow to withdraw its missiles from Cuba.[66] This account, however, overlooks a private deal reached between the two countries in which Washington promised to withdraw its missiles from Turkey and to never invade Cuba again in exchange for Moscow's promise to withdraw its missiles from Cuba. The conventional U.S. account also dismisses the Soviet claim that it had introduced missiles to Cuba for defensive purposes, specifically, to deter yet another U.S. attempt to overthrow Fidel Castro's regime after its Bay of Pigs invasion. Moscow proclaimed that having extracted the U.S. pledge not to invade Cuba again, it had fulfilled its mission to protect an ally and it could therefore withdraw its missiles from Cuba. Even though the Cuban Missile Crisis has been the subject of much analysis, we are still not sure who is A and who is B. Was the Soviet Union playing the role of A or was the United States? Was this a case of compellence as Washington would argue, or a case of deterrence from Moscow's perspective? Who prevailed? The historical facts known to analysts without access to privileged information—that the USSR withdrew its missiles from Cuba, and the United States withdrew its missiles from Turkey and never again attempted to invade Cuba—do not help settle the debate.

Finally, to complicate matters further, the declared target of A's influence attempt may not be its true target. For instance, the preventive war waged by the United States against Saddam Hussein did not only have Iraq in mind. This attack publicized Washington's doctrine of regime change, issuing a warning to the other two members of the Axis of Evil, Iran and North Korea, as well as other regimes objectionable to Washington, such as Libya and Syria. Although the U.S. invasion of Afghanistan was a failure according to some criteria, it could have succeeded in deterring other countries from harboring al-Qaeda. Deterrence succeeds when the objectionable behavior does not occur, but we cannot be entirely sure about the causes of such non-events. That C, D, and E may be the audience of A's influence attempt as well as its direct target B naturally reminds one of the Chinese adage of killing a chicken to warn the monkeys. Washington's various diplomatic moves to upgrade its relationship with Taipei clearly has Beijing (a third party in this case) as its intended audience.

CONCLUSION

To what extent do objective indicators typically relied on in academic research in fact correspond with the perceptions and judgments of officials or, for that matter, ordinary people? The standard assumption is that decision-makers as well as the public will rely on the same indicators and draw the same conclusions as scholars. This assumption, though, may not be valid. Dustin Tingley's experimental research investigates people's perceptions of power shifts.[67] He reports that they tend to interpret power shifts differently, seeing other country's gain to be a source of concern but not their own country's gain as a motivation for it to become more revisionist. Moreover, declining states with large power losses are perceived to be more likely to act aggressively than rising states. "Both the asymmetry in how individuals view the threat posed by their country versus the threat from other countries, as well as loss aversion, suggest that a decline in power is more likely to make individuals prefer hostile policies than is a rise in power."[68] This conclusion is obviously relevant to discussion about the psychological tendencies and decision logic motivating studies seeking to connect power transitions to the outbreak of war. Both prospect theory and rationalist analysis would suggest that a declining state is more likely to undertake reckless and aggressive actions than a rising state. These expectations obviously contradict power-transition theory's explanation of systemic wars.

In another interesting study, William Wohlforth concludes that "indicators of numerical capabilities misrepresent not only Russia's prewar power but the system-wide distribution of power."[69] He examines the assessments of Russia's power by the leaders of its allies and adversaries in World War I, discovering important discrepancies among them (leaders allied with Russia assessing it to be stronger than those of its adversaries). Moreover, the COW Project's CINC tends to overestimate Russia's strength by placing it in the same league as Germany. Finally, "the perception of rising Russian power, necessary for the preventive/hegemon war argument, may well have been incorrect" to the extent that it was based on the misperception of an inexorably rising Russia in the long term.[70] Significantly, "in no other country—with the possible exception of Germany—was the assessment of Russian power lower than in Russia herself."[71]

In a review of discourse among Chinese scholars on their country's power, Haixia Qi shows considerable variations in the emphasis given to varying conceptions of power and their components, such as attention to "comprehensive national power" before 2000 and "soft power" after 2008.[72] These scholars also differ in their assessment of China's power and tend to generally give it a lower assessment than their foreign counterparts. This review cautions us that people's assessments of national power, both within a country and across countries, can differ in important ways. Moreover, the criteria and evidence used in this assessment are not fixed but instead likely to change over time. Therefore, it would not be surprising that scholars in different countries reach different conclusions about states' relative power, given how difficult it is for people in the same country to reach consensus about such assessments. As suggested, that officials in charge of foreign affairs will necessarily share scholars' assessment of relative national power also cannot be assumed. Beijing appears to be shifting to a greater emphasis on its own modernization efforts than attempting to influence events abroad such as in Taiwan.[73] This shift relates naturally to its leaders' judgments about the relative efficacy of their efforts to focus on internal development versus external exertion and the priority they assign to each.

Most discussions on power transition proceed with the view that national power is a self-evident concept and therefore does not need explanation or elaboration. They also adopt the view of power as resources without bothering to consider a state's capacity to extract, mobilize, and deploy these resources. They therefore overlook the critical linkage required to convert available resources to effective policy or the idea of power as ability. Finally, the existing literature often overlooks the many difficult empirical issues involved in studying power as outcome. As discussed, the theoretical and methodological challenges to making valid inferences about national power or influence are formidable. Because most analysts working in the tradition of power-transition studies are interested in cross-national comparisons based on quantitative indicators, they do not pay nearly enough attention to the more intangible aspects of national power, such as the quality of a country's leadership, the effectiveness of its strategy, and the cohesiveness of its society. By their nature, these intangible qualities are difficult to measure and compare across countries.[74]

These remarks, however, do not mean that we cannot say something meaningful about the relative influence of states—or their relative power to affect and control events and outcomes in general. In the next chapter, I discuss an affinity between power as resources and power as outcome. That discussion turns from a dominant state's bargaining power with its counterparts in a specific issue area (such as the price and supply of oil or grain) to a more significant and pervasive source of influence, namely, its structural power or the power to decide the rules of the game and to shape the environment in which others will have to operate. This power derives from this state's centrality in the networks of international interactions and thus is structural. Structural power has a profound impact on states' behavior even when A does not undertake any overt or direct attempt to influence B. B's recognition or even just its awareness of A's possession of vital resources is usually enough to influence its behavior. Thus, for example, knowing that it depends heavily on A's market would incline B to consider the ramifications of undertaking a confrontational strategy that could disrupt their trade relationship. This effect on B's behavior exists even without A having to remind B of its trade dependency. When many other countries are in B's situation, A is said to have structural power.

3

PERSISTENCE OF WASHINGTON'S STRUCTURAL POWER IN U.S. GLOBAL DOMINATION

Dyadic comparisons, such as of relative U.S. and Chinese military capabilities across the Taiwan Strait, can be useful for many purposes but do not speak to the core concern of power-transition theory and others like it. Power-transition discourse is not concerned about a country's relative capability in a specific dispute or issue area (discussed in chapter 2) but is instead focused on its global reach and ability to achieve and sustain world domination. This chapter turns to discussing the structural power derived by the United States from its positions in and connections to international security, financial, productive, and knowledge networks.

Karl Marx famously observed that "men make their own history, but they do not make it as they please; they do not make it under self-selected circumstances, but [only] under circumstances existing already, given and transmitted from the past."[1] In the last chapter, I discussed power as outcome, typically defined according to Robert Dahl's formulation to mean A's ability to get B to do something that B would not otherwise do. This conception of power to control outcomes or events, however, is too narrow and even disarmingly misleading because it overlooks more subtle but also more profound and pervasive ways in which B's capacity to shape its environment and destiny can be enabled or constrained.[2] Moreover, the boundary between power as resources and power as outcome is not as clear and sharp as I have presented. B can be influenced, after all, to behave in certain ways by being made aware of, even if only subconsciously, A's possession of certain resources.

Current Western discourse on China's so-called rise, dominated as it is by U.S. commentators and scholars, is often misleadingly alarmist and even dangerously simplistic in exaggerating the prospect of a power transition between China and the United States.[3] This genre of scholarship focuses primarily on China's production or possession of material stocks to the relative neglect of more intangible resources such as soft power.[4] It is also customary practice to use states as the standard accounting units (such as their gross domestic products) to make comparisons, thereby overlooking the global reach of multinational corporations. But even if one is to use states as the appropriate accounting units, it is still relevant to ask whether Britain or the British Empire should be considered because although Imperial Germany had a larger population than Britain in 1914, it had a much smaller population than the British Empire (after all, Australians, Canadians, Indians, and Nepalese fought on Britain's behalf in both world wars). It is, moreover, fundamentally misleading to depict Sino-American competition in strictly dyadic terms because, as mentioned, this approach ignores the importance of alliances. Whereas the United States has many powerful allies, China can hardly count on support from any country of consequence to tip the scale of power in its favor. Although no reasonable person would contest that China has improved its international position in recent decades, the often-heard lament of lost U.S. hegemony remains largely more an illusion than fact.

THE POWER OF STRUCTURAL POWER

More than three decades ago, Susan Strange wrote an influential article challenging the persistent myth that the United States has lost its status as a hegemon.[5] In it, she calls attention to a fundamental distinction between relational (or bargaining) power and structural power.[6] Whether China can influence the income of U.S. soybean farmers or Saudi Arabia can affect the price and supply of oil pertains to relational power. In contrast, structural power refers to an actor's ability to shape and determine the milieu in which others will have to operate. It is distinct from A's conscious, deliberate, and direct attempt to persuade B to act contrary to its initial intention. It is even different from A's ability, derived from the institutions under its control or influence, to set agendas, frame policy issues, and manipulate the proverbial rules of the game in its interactions with B. Structural power determines the circumstances in which people find themselves "entrapped" and their options limited.

Strange defines structural power as "the power to choose and to shape the structures of the global political economy within which other states, their political institutions, their economic enterprises, and (not least) their professional people have to operate."[7] Michael Barnett and Raymond Duvall add that it concerns "what kinds of social beings actors are."[8] It refers to the mutually constitutive relationship between A and B that defines their respective capacities and interests such as that between capital and labor, master and slave, employer and employee, and teacher and student. Given the inherent asymmetries in the respective actors' positions in the relevant social structure, structural power confers advantages and privileges to some to the detriment of others. Moreover, it shapes the relevant parties' self-understanding and subjective interests, inducing them to believe that the existing order of things is natural, legitimate, or inevitable and thus inclining them to accept their role and fate in this order.[9]

Structural power is more subtle and "invisible" and yet also more profound and enduring than bargaining or relational power. It is present even when A does not make any overt, direct, or deliberate attempt to influence or control B. For example, emergent markets' financial stability and economic health are affected by the U.S. appetite for foreign capital. Even though Washington may not have intended or even considered the likely effects of its borrowing activity on the rest of the world, "variations in American demand for capital disproportionately influences global capital cycles."[10] This phenomenon stems more from the structural prominence enjoyed by the United States as the center of global finance than just its wealth and bargaining power.

When the U.S. demand for foreign capital falls, investment money rushes to emergent markets, creating the conditions for asset bubbles and subsequent systemic banking failures. Conversely, when the United States absorbs much of the world's available investment capital, emergent markets will have to pay more to compete for this money and their economic activities are affected by its more limited supply. Moreover, U.S. economic conditions and policies tend to influence the world's capital flows more than global market and credit factors outside the United States. In other words, the United States influences more the rest of the world than vice versa—even though this outcome reflects largely the uncoordinated actions by many market actors inside and outside the United States and occurs without any systematic attempt by U.S. officials to bring it about.

Strange's point is that although the United States might have suffered a relative decline in its control, possession, or production of some kinds of material resources (such as according to the power as resources concept discussed in chapter 2), it continued to sit at the apex of international (structural) power at the time of her writing in 1987. Since then, her conclusions have been supported by other analysts.[11] By virtue of its advantageous, indeed privileged, structural position in the international system, Washington has been able to command an interconnected network of security, financial, productive, and knowledge assets that protects and advances its interests and that by limiting or foreclosing options available to others, makes any challenge to its primacy more difficult for others to mount and succeed. The four dimensions of U.S. structural power mentioned are mutually reinforcing so that "each is held up and supported by the other three."[12] The obstacles facing prospective challengers to U.S. primacy appear as formidable now as in 1987, and in some ways perhaps even more so.

China is starting from a technological position farther behind the United States and thus has farther to travel before it catches up, a situation that distinguishes the contemporary world from previous eras, when the technological capabilities of contending great powers were more comparable. Consider the rivalries between Athens and Sparta, Rome and Carthage, France and the Hapsburgs, Napoleon and his adversaries, and Britain and Germany on the eve of World War I. Although China has significantly improved its position, other countries have not been standing still. Indeed, the speed of technological changes is accelerating, hampering a latecomer's attempt to catch up and even leapfrog an erstwhile leader. Hitler's Germany was able to rearm and pose a military threat to Britain and France in just a few years, a feat that is unimaginable today given the complexity of military technologies, the lead time required to develop new weapons, and the expertise and training needed to manage their production and operation.[13] These remarks do not deny that China has made some significant technological advances and can in some areas even overtake the United States. Much of the prevailing discourse on Thucydides' Trap and power transition, however, overlooks important differences between today's world and previous eras, and therefore the inappropriateness of analogies drawn to compare then with now. They thus tend to exaggerate China's challenge to U.S. primacy.

MILITARY PREPONDERANCE

The four interrelated dimensions of U.S. structural power that Strange discusses start with Washington's near total domination in the security sphere by virtue of its unrivalled control of the global commons,[14] its formidable nuclear arsenal that threatens to nullify China's and Russia's retaliatory capability,[15] its vast network of alliances, and its forward deployment of military assets right up to China's and Russia's borders. No other country can come close to, not to mention match, this ensemble of military superiorities or advantages.

In his well-known article on the near complete dominance of the United States over the world's commons (sea, air, and space), Barry Posen remarks that this domination is the key to Washington's global military position.[16] Not only does this command with its massive network of overseas bases and command structure buttress overwhelming U.S. military superiority, it has also "create[d] barriers to entry into the global military power club that are so high as to seem insurmountable." The United States leverages its advantages in scientific, technological, and economic resources in addition to its highly skilled and trained personnel to make it difficult for any country to challenge, let alone overcome, its command of the commons.[17] Lessons drawn from fighting in the "contested zones," such as Serbia in 1999 and Iraq in 2003, suggest that the defending countries can at best only dampen the U.S. assault and not in any real sense overcome their overall vulnerability.

Only one country today can project its military power abroad and sustain a protracted campaign in a faraway country, as the United States has shown in Afghanistan, Iraq, Vietnam, and Korea. This fact confers tremendous structural power in that Washington has the option of taking war to other countries (i.e., to wage war on their territories), sparing itself the physical destruction that inevitably ensues from fighting on home soil. Other countries, however, do not have this option (excepting possible missile attacks from other nuclear powers or terrorist assaults such as those of 9/11).

Furthermore, whereas the United States has military assets arrayed in China's vicinity, the same cannot be said about the distribution and deployment of China's armed forces, which continue to have "short arms, slow legs" despite their recent modernization. China's limited ability to project its military power abroad and the absence of any countervailing alliance balancing (or threatening to balance) the United States is significant in that it gives Washington the freedom to exercise its power against others individually (especially in the hub-and-spokes system of Washington's bilateral alliances in East Asia),[18] while constraining their options to gang up on it. This is one important manifestation of U.S. structural power. It stems from the nature of the security environment, which other countries recognize and will consider when making their policy choices, even in the absence of any overt attempt by Washington to influence them.

An aspirant to global preeminence must secure dominance in its own region. It needs to pacify or reconcile with its immediate neighbors. China has thus far been unable to do this but the United States, by virtue of its regional hegemony in the Western Hemisphere, has done some time ago. China's acrimonious relationship with Japan presents the key stumbling block to its claim to regional preeminence, and in Barry Buzan's view is a "boon" to the United States, enabling Washington to be the "ring holder" in the region.[19] Moreover, China's tumultuous relations with India, Russia, and Vietnam could be a potential source for its self-encirclement, reminiscent of the backlash by Imperial Germany's neighbors reacting to Berlin's policies before World War I.[20] A significant implication of these remarks is that should China settle its relations with its neighbors on amicable terms for the long term, the development would be detrimental to U.S. influence in the region. "Mechanisms designed to assuage security dilemmas: the deepening of regional economic integration, the development of regional multilateral institutions, and China's participation in both of these processes," as Thomas Christensen notes,[21] would be a loss for U.S. influence in realpolitik terms. Washington's influence and projected power in the Asia Pacific depend to some not inconsiderable extent on China's not getting along with its neighbors. This in turn implies that, paradoxically, it has a vested interest in Beijing's being assertive or aggressive—or allegedly so.

The United States also holds the ring in the Middle East, Europe, and the Western Hemisphere. It has embedded itself in these regions and exercises significant influence in promoting or hindering their prospects for integration. It has interjected itself as an extra-regional actor by successfully constructing and institutionalizing imagined communities of super-regions such as Atlanticism, Asia Pacific, Pan Americanism, and most recently Indo-Pacific (or the Quad, consisting of Japan, India, Australia, and the United States). These moves enable Washington to play a swing strategy whereby it gains leverage in all regions. As Buzan explains, "Because it has the option to delink from, or reduce the priority of its engagement in, any region, the US can use threats and inducements of increasing or decreasing its levels of engagement as a means of playing one region against another."[22] Naturally, the U.S. construction of and embeddedness in these super-regions help Washington both to forestall any attempt by a regional actor to shut it out and to prevent the rise of a potential competitor to its superpower status. No other country, including China, enjoys this positional advantage.

The United States has a uniquely enviable geographic situation. It has only two neighbors, both weak, bordering it and is flanked on its other sides by two oceans. "The stopping power of water"[23] also protects Britain and Japan to some extent. However, they are located near other major powers, such as Germany, France, Russia, India, and China. Naturally, this also means that these countries live in congested neighborhoods. A few of them—Germany, Russia, and China—are hemmed in by other great powers. Geography, then, is an important source of U.S. structural power. This power stems simply from its physical location: Washington does not need to make any deliberate or overt attempt to influence others. The geographic situation characterizing the United States, then, is very different from that facing Germany, Russia, and China. Given the congestion, any increase in any of these countries' power could not but disturb and alarm their neighbors. Washington can count on the natural instincts of China's or Russia's immediate neighbors to mobilize a coalition against them, as was the case for Germany and France in earlier eras. The same is not true of the United States. Canada and Mexico seem doomed to live in its shadow. As the saying goes, "poor Mexico, so close to the United States and so far from God."

In contrast to the United States, China has the most contiguous neighbors in the world. It is surrounded by other great powers or at least great-power contenders: Russia, Japan, and India as well as the United States, which is practically a resident in the western Pacific given its forward deployment of military assets around China's periphery. Among China's neighbors are also middle powers such as Korea and Vietnam, whose economic and military capabilities cannot be easily dismissed. Last is Taiwan, an "unsinkable aircraft carrier" in Douglas MacArthur's words. Setting aside considerations of Chinese nationalism, Taiwan's strategic importance to China is not less than that of Cuba to the United States, which was complicit in various attempts to topple and even assassinate Fidel Castro. Washington launched the 1961 Bay of Pigs invasion against Cuba and was willing to even risk a nuclear war with the Soviet Union in the 1962 missile crisis.[24] This is another instance of U.S strategic advantage. How would Washington feel if Beijing and Cuba were to establish ties comparable to the relationship that the United States has with Taiwan?

The number of neighbors a country has is a significant consideration: boundary or territorial disputes have been by far the most common reason for countries to have military confrontations and fight wars.[25] All else being equal, China has more "opportunity" to get into such disputes. That is, it faces far more security threats from different quarters than the United States. Again, in light of their different geographic realities the United States has a far safer security environment than China.

Given its heavy reliance on sea lanes for the overseas trade required to sustain its economic growth, Beijing is acutely aware of the danger of a U.S.-led naval blockade, described by some as Beijing's Malacca dilemma, referring to its evident vulnerability to the chokepoint presented by the Malacca Strait, which threatens its maritime commerce. Aaron Friedberg observes that China's maritime trade routes can be easily blocked by the United States, and that Beijing could do little or nothing about it.[26] China's navy has become stronger since this observation but is still not capable of challenging or breaking a blockade far from its coastal waters. Indeed, Beijing's most pressing threat is from the sea, not a land invasion similar to the Japanese invasion in the 1930s and 1940s.[27] In contrast, it is difficult to imagine an effective naval blockade against the United States given its unfettered access to two oceans. Germany's and Japan's economic vulnerability to such a blockade and denial of resources was a major factor in the outcome of the two world wars. Ironically, it was also an important motivation behind their instigating these conflicts.[28]

As already mentioned, whereas the United States can always rely on the natural instincts of the other great powers' neighbors to align (or ally) themselves with a distant power to form a countervailing coalition against more nearby threats (such as India, Vietnam, Taiwan, and Japan vis-à-vis a rising China; or Poland, the Czech Republic, Estonia, and Ukraine vis-à-vis a resurgent Russia), its counterparts do not have the same advantage. Who in the Western Hemisphere can China or Russia rally to form an effective coalition against the United States? Venezuela, Cuba, Grenada? To no small extent, Washington obtains tremendous leverage over its allies because of their reliance on it for security protection. Whom else are they to turn to? China may have become the top trading partner for many countries, but the United States remains the most powerful country militarily. That Washington can expect countries surrounding China to be wary of Beijing's increasing power, or to refrain from jumping on its bandwagon, again confers an advantage that Beijing does not have available, at least not yet. This phenomenon presents another example of U.S. structural power, which requires no deliberate effort on Washington's part but relies instead on other countries' natural inclinations. Naturally, most Asia Pacific states would prefer not to choose sides between the United States and China, but any prudent policy to hedge would require them always to keep the United States "in play" as a counterbalance against their nearer neighbor, China.

Some may argue that Washington cannot really count on the instincts and interests of China's neighbors to balance against Beijing's power, thereby justifying a U.S. policy of forward deployment to reassure or reinforce its allies. They may suggest that this has been the main reason for U.S. alliances in the Asia Pacific because without its involvement and support, countries in this region would align with China or at least be intimidated by the prospect of Chinese coercion. This line of reasoning questions the traditional logic that states will naturally align against the implicit threat posed by the superior strength of any neighboring country. It also ignores the fact that U.S. alliances in the region predate a rising

China. Moreover, it overlooks the possibility that Washington's military presence abroad, including its vast alliance networks, can have purposes beyond deterrence against China or Russia. These alternative purposes include keeping its allies from developing any independent military capability and thus containing their military within an alliance framework. In a moment of candor, the first secretary general of the North Atlantic Treaty Organization, Lord Hastings Ismay, famously remarked that the purpose of this alliance is "to keep the Russians out, the Americans in, and the Germans down."[29]

The asymmetry in the military capabilities between the United States and other countries is fundamental and persistent. The overwhelming power of the U.S. military discourages any attempt by other countries to attempt to balance against it (lest they be "picked off" by the United States before a countervailing coalition has a chance to develop, as the world learned from the fate of Saddam Hussein and Muammar Gaddafi). There is a huge difference distinguishing today's world from the European balance-of-power system in a bygone era. The military capabilities separating the United States from the rest of the pack is much greater today. As the demise of the USSR makes clear, an arms race against the United States is practically unwinnable and could result in economic exhaustion.

The United States, then, is truly peerless in the military realm. Commenting on this supremacy, Paul Kennedy remarks that "Nothing has ever existed like this disparity of power, nothing. . . . I have returned to all of the comparative defense spending and military personnel statistics over the past 500 years that I compiled for *The Rise and Fall of the Great Powers*, and no other nation comes close."[30] Stephen Brooks and William Wohlforth concur, remarking that "the overall gap [between the United States and China] in the military realm remains unprecedented in modern international relations."[31] As already mentioned, the U.S. military expenditure in 2019 was greater than the combined total spent by the next eleven highest countries, including China. At one time after the Cold War, these expenditures were nearly as much as the rest of the world combined. Britain was primus inter pares among the great powers at its height, but the United States is in a league by itself today. Thus the extent of U.S. military preponderance is hardly analogous to Britain's in its prime. London's advantage was based on its naval supremacy; it never commanded the most powerful army, which Germany did on the eve of World War I.

FINANCIAL DOMINANCE

Washington's preponderance in the security arena is complemented by its financial power, as suggested by the dollar's continued dominance as the world's reserve currency and the preeminence of American financial institutions in cross-border transactions, advantages that enable Washington to shift the adjustment costs of its fiscal extravagances and monetary expansion onto foreigners, an option unavailable to any other country.

Although they are large by asset size, the international reach and presence of Chinese institutions are still not in the same league as their American and European counterparts in international finance and investment services. These sectors tend to be dominated by the likes of J. P. Morgan Chase, HSBC, Morgan Stanley, Goldman Sachs, Credit Suisse, and UBS. "Chinese banks engage in predominantly domestic activities and are largely nationally contained, so their massive profits are not necessarily at the expense of Western banks (outside of China) nor indicative of Western decline."[32]

Significantly, the centrality of the United States in the global financial network means that whereas it is largely protected from banking crises in the periphery, the reverse does not hold. Any crisis involving U.S. financial institutions (such as that in 2008–2009 caused by subprime mortgage speculation) would have serious global ramifications. But crises elsewhere, such as the Latin American debt defaults in the 1980s and the Asian "financial flu" in the 1990s, did not have the same effect on the United States simply because of the asymmetries in the network linkages characterizing their relations. This is again a consequence of structural power.[33]

The dollar's dominant position gives the United States a huge advantage in attracting capital from abroad. "When US demand [for foreign capital] is high, the American economy attracts as much as two-thirds of net cross-border [capital] flows."[34] This ability enables Washington to defer and reduce its need to undertake necessary domestic adjustments. It has thus been able to perform the magic of consistently getting a quart out of a pint. To paraphrase Susan Strange, for any "normal" country, chronic severe trade and budget deficits would be a sign of serious trouble and weakness. For the United States, however, this phenomenon indicates its extraordinary strength and privilege. Richard Nixon's 1971 decision to delink the dollar from the gold standard was tantamount to unilaterally confiscating or at least greatly devaluing the wealth of foreigners holding dollar assets. If that is not power, what is? Since then, the Federal Reserve has been able to repeatedly prime the pump by "quantitative easing," exercising the power to print money other countries could not afford to refuse except under the direst circumstances.

Given the dollar's premier status and the lack of any plausible alternative, the United States has been the safe-haven destination for flight capital from other countries. Moreover, "The T-bill [U.S. Treasury Bill] market is by far the deepest, most liquid, and safest financial market in the world."[35] The United States is better positioned than any other country to borrow large sums from foreign sources at low interests and over extended periods. If the Great Recession of 2008–2009 did not discourage foreign creditors (foreign creditors instead increased their loans to America), what would? Yet again, this is a manifestation of U.S. structural power.

The 2008–2009 financial crisis, originating from rampant speculation that inflated the U.S. housing bubble, did not significantly transform the existing system. Ironically, it in some ways increased Washington's financial structural power by enhancing its centrality in the global banking network.[36] In contrast, none of the BRICS countries (Brazil, Russia, India, China, and South Africa) gained network importance in its wake.

Given its financial power, the United States has been able to export the inflationary impact of its fiscal and monetary policies to foreign countries whose dollar-denominated assets (including U.S. debts) are consequently depreciated. Moreover, countries with accumulated large foreign-exchange reserves and ownership of U.S. debts (such as China) have become more beholden to the United States. "What defines US financial hegemony is that its problems are *global* ones and that any move by dollar-holding countries to dump dollars and, in doing so, destabilize the system, is likely to do significant damage to their own economies."[37] This expression of U.S. structural power brings to mind the adage "too big to fail" and the saying that "when you owe the bank a little bit of money, the bank owns you but when you owe the bank lots of money, you own the bank." Michael Beckley remarks forthrightly, "foreign governments that hold dollar reserves depend on U.S. prosperity for their continued economic growth and are thus 'entrapped,' unable to disentangle their interests from those of the United States."[38] This too reflects structural power, shaping others' conduct based on their understanding of their self-interests.

The privilege of seigniorage gives the United States unchecked access to the printing press to issue money in exchange for goods and services from other countries, even though this money depreciates over time as a store of value. The dollar's unrivalled supremacy gives Washington an exorbitant privilege in international finance, yet foreigners cannot refuse to accept it in payment except at the high cost of being cut off from international commerce and finance. That is again structural power.

Moreover, given the pivotal importance of the dollar and American financial institutions in the global political economy, Washington enjoys a unique and powerful leverage to undertake economic coercion against other countries (e.g., Cuba, Nicaragua, Iraq, and Iran as well as Russia and China) while limiting or denying the means available to them to protect themselves. The dollar gives the United States unmatched power to control the supply of credit for international commerce and finance. The euro, pound sterling, yen, and renminbi do not command nearly the same importance, and none of them can be expected to displace the dollar's status as the premier international currency, at least not in the foreseeable future.

The United States also commands the largest, most liquid, and most innovative capital markets in the world, giving it another huge advantage over other countries. It also has the power to delist Chinese companies from its stock exchanges or ban public institutions from investing in these companies by imposing various regulatory requirements. Stock exchanges in London, Hong Kong, and Shanghai cannot compete with Wall Street. Relative to their Chinese counterparts, U.S. companies do not need to use China's stock exchanges to gain respectability or raise funds.

Finally, international finance and international security are linked. Access to inexpensive credit enables a country to finance foreign wars and win them more easily.[39]

ECONOMIC EDGE

Strange argues persuasively that a country's share of the world's manufacturing production or its share of global manufactured exports is not what matters most for its economic power. Instead, this power lies in the share of the world's goods and services a country controls, including necessarily those produced or provided by enterprises domiciled in and ultimately accountable to it (even if these enterprises have branches operating abroad where the physical production of goods and provision of services take place). Even this statement is not quite correct. It would under-estimate U.S. economic power, given that Americans are the majority owners not only of large multinational companies located in the United States but also those legally incorporated in other countries as corporate investments and ownership (via acquisitions and mergers) have become globalized.

Sean Starrs puts the matter simply in saying, "Americans own much more of the world than the rest of the world owns the United States" because they "continue to own the dominant share of global wealth at 40% or more."[40] American firms combined to own about 46 percent of all publicly listed shares of the world's top 500 corporations. Chinese firms own 5.9 percent. Moreover, U.S. multinational corporations have dominated other countries' companies in profit-making, and their profit shares have been the largest in most business sectors—eighteen of twenty-five.[41] Cross holdings of corporate assets (when foreigners own a share of large U.S. companies) also means that foreign capitalists now are tied more closely to the well-being and profitability of U.S. corporations, entangling their interests with U.S. interests. This is yet another manifestation of U.S. structural power.

The main point is that traditional accounting practices (such as estimating economic activities inside a country, for example, its gross domestic product) overlook a greatly changed world in which a large and increasing share of these activities involves cross-border transactions by multinational corporations. If we are to view the world from this perspective, U.S. multinational corporations are dominant sector after sector (e.g., aerospace, financial services, software) and have, if anything, increased their edge over their competitors in recent years. Specifically, according to Starrs, U.S. firms dominate in twelve of twenty-five broad business sectors.[42] The United States has economic power because it has the largest domestic market and the most competitive transnational enterprises in the world. Foreign companies must follow U.S. policies and requirements to access this market, and the size of this market has historically provided a strong home base for American companies to compete abroad, not an insignificant factor contributing to U.S. structural power in economics.

Significantly, much of China's exports of manufactures have to date been based on components and technologies imported from foreign sources (estimated to constitute between 40 and 50 percent of the value of these exports) and assembled by foreign companies' subsidiaries located in China. As Brooks and Wohlforth report, "Half of all Chinese exports consist of 'processing trade' (in which parts and components are imported into China for assembly into finished products and are then exported afterward), and the vast majority of these Chinese exports (84% in 2010) are directed not by Chinese firms but by foreign companies (mostly affiliates of MNCs from Organisation for Economic Co-operation and Development countries). In turn, foreign companies are also the source of 29% of Chinese 'ordinary exports'—that is, nonprocessing trade."[43] Thus, production figures alone, without accounting for the ownership of and value-added contributions to the final product, do not tell the most important part of the story about economic competitiveness. Multinational conglomerates with vast overseas operations, many of them of U.S. origin, command and control the most profitable parts of production chain, that is, the design, branding, and marketing of merchandise.

A U.S. company such as Apple can have many, sometimes in the thousands, overseas contractors and subcontractors producing different components for its products, such as iPad and iPhone, that are also assembled abroad. People at the company's headquarters, however, control the most important and lucrative parts of the production chain. Thus, on the one hand, low value-added activities are dispersed among many contractors and subcontractors and, on the other, high value-added activities are concentrated in the company's headquarters—a situation reminiscent of the feudal interaction structure or a hub-and-spokes system described later. This system confers structural power to those occupying a central and thus pivotal position in network relationships.

Significantly, structural power in this case derives from the basic asymmetries built into the production system, causing the many contractors and subcontractors to compete among themselves for business. They are, in other words, usually easily replaceable. In contrast, the activities of the headquarters are not. The fruits of research and development and the connections required for marketing and distribution are protected by high

entry barriers, such as patents protecting a company's intellectual properties or long-standing business, even personal, relations. Entry barriers
are comparatively low for most contractors and subcontractors, however.
This basic asymmetry again points to U.S. structural power, something
that is not and cannot be captured by looking at only production figures
within a country.

Starrs emphasizes this phenomenon:

> In the era of transnational modular production networks, the fact that
> China is the largest exporter of finished smartphones and tablets—with
> the consequent overwhelming trade surplus in these goods—and the fact
> that made in China electronics flood the American market today . . . does
> not at all necessarily imply that Chinese firms are world leaders in elec-
> tronics. Nor does the fact that China exports virtually all iPads and
> iPhones necessarily mean that Chinese firms reap the largest profit from
> the sale of these iPads and iPhones, or electronics more generally. In fact,
> it does not even mean that a Chinese firm is performing final assembly.
> On the contrary, it is a Taiwanese firm, Hon Hai Precision Industry, that
> employs over one million Chinese workers (China's largest private
> employer) to conduct final assembly of electronics such as iPads and
> iPhones in China, but the profit from this final assembly largely goes to
> Taiwanese shareholders, especially to the Taiwanese billionaire founder
> Terry Gou. Even still, the profit that Hon Hai Precision Industry makes
> from the assembly of iPads and iPhones in China is peanuts compared
> with the profit that Apple ultimately makes from owning the proprie-
> tary design and brand.[44]

Chinese companies have become more competitive over time, and
some are now massive enterprises when measured by their business revenues. Although in most business sectors U.S. companies have maintained
and even expanded their lead, Chinese companies have made visible
improvements in banking, construction, and telecommunications thanks
to massive government support and China's large domestic market. U.S.
companies, however, continue to enjoy a powerful position in both the
upstream and downstream operations of businesses, and continue to play
a powerful role in shaping global production and supply chains.

Washington can ask these companies to support economic coercion against foreign countries, such as when in 1982 the Reagan administration ordered Dresser Industries and General Electric to stop supplying equipment for the building of a pipeline exporting Soviet natural gas to European markets (ostensibly in retaliation against the imposition of martial law by Warsaw's communist government). The reach of the U.S. government can extend not only to the subsidiaries of U.S. companies located in foreign countries (such as the Dresser Industries' subsidiary), but also to foreign companies using U.S. technology. Thus the Trump administration tried to impede and disrupt Huawei's telecommunications business by banning the Taiwan Semiconductor Manufacturing Company from supplying key components to this Chinese company in its 5G projects. In December 2018, the United States asked Canada to extradite the daughter of Huawei's founder, Meng Wanzhou, to face charges that she tried to circumvent U.S. sanctions against Iran. Ironically, Washington's basic justification for barring Huawei from its domestic market and for lobbying other countries to do the same is that Beijing can order it to follow and assist its foreign policy objectives and that China would try to use it to apply its laws beyond its domestic jurisdiction—just as the United States did in regard to the building of the Soviet pipeline and the case of Meng Wanzhou just mentioned. During the earlier years of the Cold War, the United States and its allies sought to impose an economic blockade against the USSR and China, banning their companies from doing any business with either country.[45]

What matters most is not how much manufacturing output (whether bicycles, automobiles, or computers) a country has produced, but whether its firms are pioneers of new technologies and leaders in new industrial sectors (such as artificial intelligence, robotics, or genetic engineering). Although the United States has suffered massive and chronic trade deficits in manufacturing, the innovative capacities of U.S. conglomerates enable them to be pioneers and leaders in the most knowledge-intensive industries, especially information technology. Of the world's 154 largest technology companies in 2019, sixty-five were American and twenty were Chinese. Eight of the top ten technology companies were American: Apple, Microsoft, Alphabet, Intel, IBM, Facebook, Cisco Systems, and Oracle, in that order. Only two were not: Korea's Samsung Electronics in second place and China's Tencent Holdings in the ninth.[46]

American media and entertainment companies such as Disney, Netflix, and CNN are also preeminent even though, as noted, aside from pockets of excellence (such as in aerospace, which benefits from large defense contracts), the U.S. manufacturing sector has been in steady decline for some time. Crucially, this decline has been largely confined to the production of goods with low technology content and high labor content. With the advent of robotic technology, the trend to outsource U.S. manufacturing jobs may be reversed in the future (a trend that may be assisted by domestic political pressure and rising labor costs in China and other exporters of manufactured goods).

KNOWLEDGE PRODUCTION AND IDEATIONAL CONTROL

Finally, American universities, research institutions, and mass media companies continue to be peerless in their capacity to make new scientific discoveries, communicate information, provide entertainment, and create and propagate ideas, fads, and fashions (such as through U.S. mass media and education institutions, Hollywood movies, and National Basketball Association games). The ability to shape public opinion and popular tastes abroad can involve mundane matters, from reporting and distributing daily news to promoting, distributing, or selling consumer goods (such as Nike, Starbucks, and McDonalds). All these represent American soft power.

In 2020, the world's largest telecommunications firms were, in descending order, AT&T, China Mobile, Verizon Communications, Vodafone, Nippon Telegraph and Telephone, Softbank, Deutsche Telekom, Telefonica, America Movil, and China Telecom.[47] Measured by their 2016 revenue, the world's leading media companies were, also in descending order, Alphabet, COMCAST, Walt Disney, 21st Century Fox, Facebook, Bertelsmann, Viacom, and CBS Corporation, all American companies. Baidu, a Chinese company, occupied the ninth spot.

Significantly, U.S. education institutions (at both the graduate and undergraduate levels) train most foreign students who on returning to their home countries become leaders in their fields. The United States thus has an unparalleled opportunity to shape the minds and win the hearts of future foreign leaders. This is the power of socialization whereby a country can influence other people's values, interests, and outlook on life. Alastair Johnston explains how this can happen to Chinese elites, both officials and academics, who have worked in international organizations.[48]

The United States also has a unique advantage in recruiting the best and brightest foreign students to become long-term residents and even citizens, thus contributing to a brain drain from their home countries. Although immigration has become a controversial issue in the United States and many European countries, it provides an enduring source of advantage for them over China, which faces an impending decline in its working-age population even as the U.S. labor pool continues to expand due to immigrants.

The popularity of English as lingua franca and of U.S. institutions of higher learning for foreign students also attests to powerful and enduring U.S. advantages in the knowledge dimension of structural power. Scientific publications are written overwhelmingly in English, and the language of instruction for many programs of graduate studies is English. Again, this is not to say that European, Japanese, and Chinese scientists and researchers are not making progress, as shown by their registration of patents, licenses, and copyrights for intellectual properties. Based on thirteen indicators of reputation and research accomplishments, a survey of the "best universities in the world" by *U.S. News and World Report* reports that sixteen of the top twenty are American (Oxford University placing fifth, Cambridge University ninth, University of Toronto eighteenth, the Imperial College of London twentieth).[49]

Another survey of the world's leading research institutions in 2018 put the Chinese Academy of Sciences at number one based on its number of published articles, followed by Harvard University, Germany's Max Planck Society, France's National Center for Scientific Research, Stanford University, the Massachusetts Institute of Technology, the Helmholtz Association of German Research Centers, Cambridge University, Tokyo University, and Peking University, to round out the top ten.[50]

As Strange succinctly puts it, "knowledge is power."[51] The U.S. edge over China in technology is greater than the disparities among great-power contenders in previous eras, meaning that China has a steeper hill to climb before it can catch up. "Without sufficient technological capacity, a large pool of economic resources alone will not enable China to bring the one-superpower world to an end."[52] The quality of a country's human capital is more important than its quantity. Michael Beckley concurs, remarking that although China has produced more engineers than the United States, the average productivity of its engineers does not match that of their U.S. counterparts.[53] He adds whether countries raise their defense budget or import foreign technologies is less important than whether "they develop the economic capacity to produce, maintain, and coordinate complex military systems."[54]

Publicly funded and operated research organizations have played a key role in making scientific discoveries and pioneering new technologies. In a 2019 ranking by Reuter's Ewalt of the world's most innovative research institutions, the U.S. Health and Human Services Department (with its well-known agencies such as the National Institutes of Health, the Centers for Disease Control and Prevention, and the Food and Drug Administration) was given the top spot. Germany's Fraunhofer Society with its many research units and affiliates came in second. France and Japan followed, with China joining the next tier of countries that included Singapore, South Korea, Britain, and Canada.[55] In the evaluation of specific research institutes, those based in the United States have a large presence among the top ten, such as, again, the National Institutes of Health and the Centers for Disease Control and Prevention, as well as the National Aeronautics and Space Administration, the U.S. Department of Veteran Affairs, and the National Atmospheric and Oceanic Administration. Only one Chinese institute, the Chinese Academy of Sciences, was included, in fifth place.

Perhaps the best overall indicator of a country's technological prowess is the royalty and license fees it collects. This indicator shows that "the United States is far and away the leading source of innovative technologies (its $128 billion in receipts of royalty and license fees [in 2010] are four time higher than the next highest state, Japan), whereas China is a huge importer of these technologies while exporting almost nothing (less than $1 billion)."[56]

Again, this discussion should not be interpreted to suggest that U.S. dominance is unassailable. China has become more competitive in science, technology, and commerce, as attested by the rise of its giant e-commerce and internet companies such as Alibaba, Tencent, Huawei, and Baidu. However, China has thus far gone after the lower hanging fruits and not taken on more challenging endeavors, such as building the most advanced engines for submarines and jet fighters. Moreover, relative to their U.S. counterparts, large Chinese companies tend to rely more on the domestic market and have less global reach. Their U.S. counterparts typically enjoy first-mover advantages and are in a more advantageous position to set global technical standards and fend off competition by raising entry barriers. These barriers need not be limited to technical and commercial impediments intended to discourage or disadvantage potential competitors. As noted, they can also be political obstacles, such as Washington's recent lobbying attempts to persuade other countries to ban Huawei's equipment.

Knowledge power includes the ability to fashion and popularize ideas. People respond to the world based on their ideational constructs rather than some objective reality.[57] Memes such as rule-based order have a role in narratives framing China as a challenger to the existing international order. These narratives were popularized after 2018, especially in response to Washington's official designation of China as a revisionist power.[58] They continue to gain dominance among pundits and scholars, crowd out alternative interpretations, and tend to exacerbate the security dilemma.

These ideational constructs themselves reflect power relations among social actors, including people as scholars and researchers. Michel Foucault insists that "there is no power relation without the correlative constitution of a field of knowledge," nor "any knowledge that does not presuppose and constitute at the same time power relations."[59] International relations analysts are embedded in the social structures and power relations they study. Jim George argues that "the process of discursive representation is never a neutral, detached one but is always imbued with the power and authority of the namers and makers of reality—it is always knowledge *as* power."[60] Linus Hagstrom and Bjorn Jerden agree that "knowledge production, including scholarship, plays an important role in promoting collective understandings in which certain ideas are seen as 'legitimate' and others as 'outlandish.' Knowledge production thus becomes deeply entangled in power politics."[61]

According to Stanley Hoffmann, international relations (IR) is an "American social science."[62] In their training of doctoral students and publishing in the most prestigious journals, Americans and those who teach at U.S. institutions dominate. As a recent issue of the *Journal of Global Security Studies* documents,[63] this dominance pervades the international relations discipline and has an oversized influence on the ideas and practices of scholars across the world—with significant attendant biases and blind spots. For example, although more than three-quarters of American IR scholars acknowledge Asia will be the most important region in the world, an examination of the syllabi for introductory PhD seminars shows no readings that draw examples solely from Asia.[64] IR training of graduate students in the United States has increasingly emphasized quantitative methodology and grand theories based on European experiences at the expense of in-depth knowledge about other regions or countries.

Prevailing narratives on an ongoing or impending power transition between the United States and China and their designation of status-quo and revisionist states in world politics demonstrate ideational construction in U.S.-dominated IR scholarship. Dominated as it is by Americans, this discourse shapes public debates, frames policy questions, and mobilizes political support for some courses of action while delegitimating others. In testimony to U.S. soft power, many Chinese scholars and commentators have signed on to the basic premises of these narratives and their associated analytic logic and categories without fully realizing the implications.

Turning to a key aspect of soft power, Chinese values, preferences, and identities do not resonate abroad, where democracy and neoliberalism have sunk deep roots. Thus, Beijing cannot compete effectively with Washington's normative appeal internationally. It will face serious difficulties, indeed resistance, in trying to gain admission to the select club of established powers on that basis and "is unlikely to become the hegemon in the near future" because of this deficit.[65] For the same reason, "China is unlikely to be able to attract powerful followers into a counterhegemonic coalition,"[66] thereby to mount an effective challenge to U.S. primacy. Because people in many countries find U.S. values and preferences more congenial, their views and actions are more likely to be aligned with U.S. interests even without any direct, overt attempt by Washington to influence them.

Even if the United States as the current hegemon declines, the hegemonic order itself (buttressed by the prevailing values, preferences, and identities of the international community) may endure. This view suggests that a power or leadership transition is possible without an order transition.[67] Power or leadership transition is therefore not the same thing as order transition. This view also attests to the power of the liberal ideology that the United States has historically propounded to emphasize democracy and market economics, something that China is unable to match. These remarks do not suggest an absence of objections to capitalist and even democratic institutions. In traditional liberal democracies in the West, including the United States, recent public protests have focused on the injustices and inequalities perpetuated by these institutions. The rejection by Trump's supporters of the outcome of the 2020 U.S. election is but one obvious and dramatic example of an assault on democratic institutions, accompanied by pervasive mistrust of other institutions such as a free and independent press. Institutions of the European Union have also suffered a "democratic deficit" in recent years. At the same time, popular protests have called attention to widening economic disparities and persistent racial injustices in many countries, including the Black Lives Matter movement in the United States.

Signs pointing to widespread skepticism, deep mistrust, and even outright rejection of capitalist and democratic institutions do not mean that such misgivings and alienations will necessarily redound to Beijing's advantage. In fact, although China has done well economically in recent decades, it has not presented an ideational package attractive to the rest of the world. Its diplomacy has stressed the traditional Westphalian principles of sovereignty and non-interference in other countries' domestic affairs, principles many see as outdated. Like its predecessor Japan, Beijing has excelled in economic performance but not in ideational projection. It relies largely on checkbook diplomacy to win foreign popularity.

In summary, a large gap between China and the United States remains, favoring the United States as the leading country not only in extending scientific frontiers and producing cutting-edge technologies but also in informing mass publics and political elites, influencing their attitudes and tastes, shaping their views of realities, defining their self-interests, and even constructing their identities.[68] This last component of structural power—constructing identity—is truly powerful: a country's ability to coopt other people and to get them to identify and cooperate with it of their own volition. Although this assertion may seem grandiose, it has been publicly presented by many leading Americans to justify a policy of engaging China. It is reminiscent of American missionaries' zeal in the 1800s and early 1900s to convert the Chinese people to Christianity, an evangelical impulse, captured in Nebraska's Senator Kenneth Wherry's words, spoken in 1940, that "With God's help, we will lift Shanghai up and up, ever up, until it is just like Kansas City."[69]

ASYMMETRIC NETWORKS AND WEAPONIZING INTERDEPENDENCE

Globalization is now a buzz word. In its simplest form, it means creating denser and deeper relations among people, firms, and countries. It fosters more extensive and entrenched interdependencies, which should in turn further empower the United States given its centrality in many interconnected networks into which more and more people, firms, and countries are drawn.

Some time ago Johan Galtung wrote about the "structure of imperialism."[70] He describes it as a system of relations with a hub-and-spokes arrangement. The center enjoys a pivotal position as the hub, whereas the periphery consists of disparate entities isolated from each other that interact only individually with the center and thus not with each other. This description not only applies to international relations but can also refer to, for example, medieval fiefdoms presided by the lords in their castles over serfs in the countryside. Thus, another name for this system of relations is the feudal interaction structure.

Galtung's analysis points to a key source of the center's structural power. The center enjoys enormous advantages because it occupies the pivotal node with many links, a position from which it can dominate the periphery and engage in a policy of divide and rule. His depiction was made long before network theory became popular, and should resonate with airline travelers in the United States who typically must transit through a few hub cities such as Los Angeles, Houston, Chicago, Denver, or Atlanta to reach their final destinations. It is also reminiscent of a time when telephone calls between two neighboring African countries had to be routed through London or Paris. This phenomenon attests to the fact that relational networks are rarely, if ever, neutral. They tend to instead reflect and support important structural advantages commanded by the center at the expense of the periphery. Moreover, once formed, these asymmetries can be self-reinforcing and become entrenched, thus to endure and become more resistant to change over time. The persistence of this structural dominance is naturally not inevitable. Countervailing forces can erode it in the long term but challenging it successfully in the short and even intermediate term is more difficult.

Galtung's structural network can be used to describe tangible movements or transactions, such as those of people, goods and money, between the center and its periphery. It can also include the transmission of more intangible resources such as authority, deference, influence, and information. Fast forward half a century to today's world, his basic insight about asymmetric networks remains valid.[71] The United States is in a powerful position to leverage its centrality in global financial transactions and internet communications in addition to its alliance arrangements and the international reach of its multinational corporations. This centrality derives from the fact that leading institutions in interbank transfers, data storage and processing, and e-commerce are American, giving it a home-court advantage in information collection about other countries and access denial against its adversaries. Globalization has further enhanced U.S. preponderance.

It again bears repeating that network topography produces power asymmetry and that global economic linkages and information flows have important security consequences. Henry Farrell and Abraham Newman have written about the so-called panopticon (to extract information advantages) and chokepoint (to cut off information and financial flows) effects resulting from international networking.[72] These effects of structural power are reflected in internet communications (the United States has the largest advantage in exercising panopticon influence) and financial messaging (the United States, along with its European allies, can exercise choke-off influence).

For instance, the SWIFT (Society for Worldwide Interbank Financial Telecommunications) system of interbank fund transfers is practically the only game in town, giving the United States and its European allies a unique ability and powerful tool to monitor global financial movements and surveil possible illicit activities. It also gives Washington the ability to cut off, for example, Iran and more recently Russia from the international payment system and thus to effectively blockade these countries economically. The United States has been especially empowered by globalization to "weaponize interdependence."[73] The main nodes of global internet communications, social media, and e-commerce transactions are located inside the United States and are operated or mediated by U.S.-domiciled companies such as Facebook, Google, and Amazon, again giving Washington a unique and powerful advantage for data collection and intelligence analysis.

The liberal international order is a mixed blessing.[74] It presents prospective benefits as well as prospective vulnerabilities. As Farrell and Newman observe, "Focal points of cooperation have become sites of control."[75] The pertinent relationships produce power asymmetries stemming from the hub-and-spoke nature of networks. The uneven ties between nodes enable some to enjoy advantages because of their centrality and saddles others with disadvantages because of their peripheral position.

Significantly, the central nodes are not randomly distributed. Instead, they favor the United States as the pivotal player by virtue of its network centrality. The pertinent networks or commercial arrangements—SWIFT, ICANN (the Internet Corporation for Assigned Names and Numbers), Google, Facebook, Amazon in financial transactions, internet architecture, and e-commerce—may have originated from impersonal market forces or efficiency considerations. Yet they empower the established countries, especially the United States, and have the effect of locking in actors. They tend to be resilient and self-reinforcing and thus to perpetuate unequal relationships, including expanding future options available to the powerful, established actors while preempting or constraining future options available to the less powerful actors and those joining the networks more recently.

Chinese e-commerce and internet companies clearly can have an advantage in "big data" (literally), in part because the population providing these data is large and in part because these companies are less likely to be hindered by privacy concerns. As Farrell and Newman note, Washington's attempts to gain panopticon and chokepoint effects can also present a double-edged sword.[76] For example, the more it engages in economic coercion against other countries, the more it incentivizes its targets and onlookers who fear that they may one day be subjected to the same treatment to develop alternative systems and to switch to doing business without having to rely on the dollar and U.S. banks. One example of such evasive action is the use of crypto currency and blockchain-based payment.

Thus Washington's policies can have diminishing returns over time given that its past and future likely targets can be expected to try to escape from its grip. The same logic suggests that efforts to deny U.S. technologies to Huawei's 5G projects could encourage China to alter its supply chains and accelerate its efforts to build an indigenous capability to produce the necessary components, thus possibly reducing future U.S. leverage. Finally, even West European countries can become concerned with the surreptitious use of unauthorized data on their citizens and the near-monopoly power of U.S. internet behemoths. Thus, in the long run the existence of preponderant U.S. structural power (quite aside from any perception of unwarranted overt exercise of this power) could yield a countervailing reaction. Countries do not want, if possible, to become beholden to another country, especially a powerful one that could turn on them. The pertinent process may resemble the description of punctuated equilibrium offered by paleontologists who study biological evolution, whereby protracted periods of small, incremental, and barely visible changes are followed by large and abrupt transformations.[77]

CONCLUSION

Crucially, the whole is greater than the sum of its parts. The assets the United States enjoys across all four dimensions of structural power confer a significant and persistent advantage that is difficult for China or any other country to overcome in the next few decades. To be clear, China has narrowed the gap that used to characterize its relationship with the United States. Moreover, many Chinese firms have become more competitive internationally and China's military has become a more modern fighting force that is now more capable of denying access by the U.S. air and naval forces right up to the Chinese coastline and inside China's airspace.

The overall structural power of the United States, however, is still largely intact and, as noted, likely to endure for the foreseeable future. Different dimensions of U.S. structural power have a multiplier effect in advancing and sustaining Washington's overall dominance, and their respective institutions tend to become entrenched over time, which does not mean that they are unassailable or cannot erode over the long run. Even though specific aspects of U.S. advantages making up each of the four dimensions of structural power can diminish and even be reversed, the prospect that the entire ensemble will be overtaken seems remote in the short to intermediate run.

As Christopher Layne has argued, that the United States has thus far managed to retain its primacy does not necessarily mean that other countries, including China, have not sought to balance against it.[78] In a unipolar world, by definition, no other country can serve as a counterbalance or as a magnet for a coalition to form against the dominant power. China's rise, however, can set in motion dynamics dormant thus far, thus cautioning us against simply extrapolating from the past to predict the future.

Ironically, and as several scholars suggest,[79] prospective erosion of U.S. structural power is more likely to stem from domestic sources than challenges from abroad. The fractious and contentious nature of its partisan politics and its politicians' tendency to cater to populism are likely to do more harm to its international preeminence by alienating its allies, squandering its assets, and diverting its attention from the pressing need to undertake important reforms.

If this view is correct, it suggests that the emphasis U.S. commentators put on challenges coming from China is misdirected and unwarranted. As power-transition theorists acknowledge, a country's economic growth and its international standing are largely determined by internal factors. American IR scholars and foreign policy officials have an understandable professional bias in focusing on how U.S. policies could or would enable or constrain China's influence even as they overlook the much greater importance that Washington's own conduct and domestic conditions have had or can have on its international influence and stature.

China has also pursued a network strategy. Although it has moved its structural position in the world's trade network closer to that of developed countries, it continues to align itself politically with developing countries, as shown by rollcall votes in the UN General Assembly.

Beijing tries to maximize its brokerage role in these two networks, seeking to exploit its "betweenness centrality."[80] It tries to situate itself as the leader in the global trading network and at the same time, as the champion of the developing world, thus occupying a pivotal intermediary position bridging the world's economic and political divisions and exploring "holes" in the international system.

The main takeaway from this chapter is that U.S. primacy has expanded in recent years. It has done so not despite but rather precisely because of globalization, which has further accentuated and enhanced its network centrality and hence its structural power. Americans who complain about globalization and immigration as a cause of their country's decline are wrong. These factors have in fact been sources of enduring U.S. advantages. Globalization and immigration have benefited the United States disproportionately and augmented Washington's structural power. Donald Trump's policies to reverse these traditional liberal commitments were therefore self-defeating. These policies reflect his and his supporters' view that the United States has been taken advantage of by other countries and that it has not done well under the existing rules of the game. They resonate with many Americans who feel that their economic conditions and social status have declined in recent years, and they overlap with fault lines associated with the intense "culture war" over Americans' values and identities (such as controversies about abortion rights, gender identities, school curriculum, and government mandates). These policies have been motivated primarily by domestic sources.

Recent developments reveal the fragility of professed support for the tenets of liberal international order, not just by the United States but also by other Western countries, which have experienced similar populist movements rejecting open borders to trade and immigrants, including political refugees. It is easy to preach the virtues of liberal international order when it is seen to work to one's advantage. Whether one is a fair-weather supporter of this order is disclosed when one believes that its rules are no longer working in one's favor. Whether one continues to support these rules shows whether one's support is sincere or just lip service. The impetus for deglobalization has come from the United States and the West more generally, not China. In this and other respects mentioned in chapter 1 and elaborated on elsewhere,[81] the United States—not China—has acted more like a revisionist state.

The United States is, in Buzan's view, the "only superpower and there are no other plausible candidates on the horizon for that status for at least a couple of decades."[82] Similarly, in Brooks and Wohlforth's judgment, "any effort by China to rise still further and reach a comparable level to the United States—the superpower level—will be fraught with difficulty and will require a lengthy amount of time."[83] Starrs agrees, remarking that "speculation on China being able to challenge the United States at the technological frontier in the foreseeable future is not credible."[84] Finally, Beckley concludes that "the trends suggest that the United States' economic, technological, and military lead over China will be an enduring feature of international relations, not a passing moment in time, but a deeply embedded condition that will persist well into this century."[85] These colleagues question the suggestion that the United States has lost or is about to lose its hegemonic status. Some also object to the self-serving perspective of hegemonic-stability theory claiming that the United States is an indispensable power providing the world's public goods and with its supposed decline, the world will face a more tumultuous and unstable future—reminiscent of Louis XV's warning, après moi, le déluge.

If these views are correct, what can account for the propagation and popularity of narratives about an ongoing or impending Sino-American power transition and a possible war between them due to this process? Why the persistent worries about the United States having lost or is about to lose its hegemonic status? Why do these accounts have staying power when previous announcements of the United States losing its hegemony have turned out repeatedly to be greatly exaggerated and premature,[86] and when both the logic and evidence behind warnings of a war stemming from power transition are quite dubious when examined closely? Why the hyperbole? What is the subtext of this discourse? What, to put it bluntly, can explain Donald Trump's apparent reelection strategy singling out China as the international bête noire? It seems that although Democrats and Republicans can rarely agree on anything, they have a common strategy of China-bashing in a domestic contest to outbid each other's patriotic credentials.

Charles Kupchan and Peter Trubowitz remarked presciently long before the current turn of worsening Sino-American relations, "Ironically, the only foreign policies that are likely to garner bipartisan support are those that the extremes in each party find appealing—most notably, getting tough with China."[87] They made this observation in the context of bipartisan support for the post-1945 U.S. foreign policy of liberal internationalism having collapsed. They also report, long before anti-globalization mass sentiments became fashionable, that the U.S. public was already disaffected with globalization, 61 percent believing that free trade causes job losses and 56 percent indicating that it lowers wages.[88] China is very much in the crosshairs of this backlash against trade.

Brooks and Wohlforth point to several possible reasons for popular and elite obsessions in the United States about its imminent decline and the rise of China as a competitor even though the pertinent data point largely in the opposite direction.[89] They suggest a tendency to rely on obsolete indicators of national power, a proclivity for dichotomous reasoning, and the misappropriation of historical analogies as obvious candidates for the pervasive and pessimistic views on the United States losing its primacy and being overtaken by China and the ensuing danger of a transitional war. This phenomenon is also in part attributable to domestic political incentives to look for a foreign scapegoat to explain why the average American's life conditions have deteriorated over time and to mobilize public support to justify huge outlays to sustain the military-industrial complex after the demise of the USSR and al-Qaeda. A crusading impulse may also be at play, contravening John Quincy Adams' warning in 1821 that the United States should not go abroad "in search of monsters to slay" or else it would become the "dictatress of the world."[90]

4

DOMESTIC SOURCES OF
FOREIGN POLICY

As it pertains to contemporary Sino-American relations, power-transition theory is seriously wrong in two crucial respects. It is wrong to assign a revisionist role exclusively to a rising power, in this case China. It is also wrong to exaggerate U.S. decline and thus the extent of an ongoing or impending power transition between it and China. My argument is that neither condition postulated by this theory for predicting a transitional war fits the current situation. China is not the revisionist power, or at least not to the same extent as the United States now or when it was a rising power itself, that proponents of this theory typically present it.[1] Moreover, even though China has made significant strides in improving its international power, the United States is not in serious decline, as argued in chapter 3. In fact, it is likely to retain its status as the world's only superpower for at least several decades.

In this chapter, I extend my argument, contending that international power shifts do not in themselves determine war or peace. Their effects are transmitted through and mediated by domestic politics,[2] an important consideration that power-transition theorists have bracketed, or, in other words, omitted given their preference to study the war phenomenon at the systemic or interstate level of analysis. In contrast, I argue that it is important to consider not just developments outside a country such as its shifting power balance relative to another country, but also conditions inside it that can amplify or dampen the effects of foreign developments. As argued earlier, monocausal explanations are rarely sat-isfactory in the study of complex social and political phenomena. His-tory has shown that although power transitions have sometimes been accompanied by war, on other occasions they have occurred peacefully. Therefore, we need to consider additional factors, such as the pertinent countries' domestic politics, that can help explain these different out-comes. Of course, a country's domestic politics can in turn have a blow-back effect in influencing its counterpart's domestic politics. Sometimes, policies and political rhetoric intended for domestic consumption can have an unintended effect on foreigners' perceptions and affect the polit-ical discourse and distribution of power in another country, such as when the United States restricted immigrants of Japanese ancestry and limited the property rights of those already living in the United States.[3]

In his well-known book theorizing international relations, Kenneth Waltz presents three "images," or levels of analysis.[4] He privileges the influence of the first, the effects of the interstate system's structural prop-erties, in shaping states' behavior. According to him, the pressure com-ing from having to operate in an anarchical environment forces all states to behave alike. All will prioritize their physical survival as the paramount concern in this predatory world. All states share this motivation, inclin-ing them all to engage in similar behavior, such as to balance against the strongest country among them. Those that fail to protect themselves will become extinct by being eliminated in the relentless struggle for survival. The first image treats all states as being driven by the same motivation to ensure their survival and therefore, significantly, does not attribute dif-ferent characters to them, such as drawing a distinction between revision-ist and status-quo states. This distinction refers to the second image, the character of states, and therefore corresponds to a different level of anal-ysis than the interstate level that power-transition theory targets.

Waltz's formulation does not address the question of what happens after a state has assured its physical survival or basic security. For instance, unless considering the nightmare scenario of mutual nuclear destruction, it is difficult to imagine another country presenting a threat to the con-tinued existence of the United States as an independent political entity. How would one then expect this country to behave externally? Defensive realism does not seem to provide an answer. It does not tell us whether after assuring its physical survival and basic security, a state will turn to a policy to maintain the existing distribution of power or to expand and seek additional power. Presumably, the nature of its domestic politics and the disposition of its political tradition will offer some clues. Offensive realism contends that such a country will continue to seek more power until it becomes the world's undisputed master or until it is stopped by another country or coalition.[5] But this contention is based more on assertion than analysis given that until the recent U.S. ascendance to become the world's only superpower, in few other instances has a state been so powerful that it did not need to worry about its survival or security. Imperial China is one that comes to mind even though it was also vulnerable to foreign conquest and encroachment during periods of its weakness.[6]

Waltz's second and third images refer respectively to features about a state (or society) and its decision-makers. As mentioned, attention to these features addresses the missing links in the literature on power transition and Thucydides' Trap, whose formulations have thus far overlooked why developments in states' external environments, such as their shifting power balance, should become a source of conflict. By their nature, studies pitched at the systemic or interstate levels of analysis do not tell us about the causal mechanisms converting developments outside a state into its foreign policies. These studies usually postulate the influence of these developments on officials' policy choices and a state's actual conduct by making generic assumptions about their motivations. Yet states and the officials representing them can and have been known to respond differently even when facing similar external opportunities or threats. This acknowledgment in turn brings in Waltz's second and third images, encouraging us to consider how factors introduced by these perspectives can improve our understanding, specifically about how variations at the domestic and individual levels of analysis can mediate influences from the systemic or interstate level and shape a state's formulation and selection of its foreign policy.

In his case studies of revisionist states, Jason Davidson shows that opportunities and constraints abroad interact with a country's domestic political conditions to determine its foreign policy.[7] Relative to developments abroad, he argues, domestic politics are more influential in shaping a country's foreign policy. This conclusion supports Tip O'Neill's remark that all politics is local. Politicians' priority is always to keep power, which in turn means that they must maintain the support of their "selectorate" and in democracies, to win reelection.[8] Those unable to keep their public office find their political influence greatly attenuated.

I discuss in this chapter how the domestic alignment (or realignment) of power, identities, and interests can have an important mediating influence in translating power shifts at the systemic or interstate level into a state's foreign policy. Saying so suggests that the effects of power shifts on a state's foreign policy are indeterminate unless we consider additional factors such as its domestic politics. It is too facile to stipulate that interstate power shifts in and of themselves will raise the danger of war. As reported earlier, many power transitions have ended peacefully. Therefore, additional logic and evidence need to be provided to enable us to differentiate these episodes from others that have led to war.

FRAMING NATIONAL DISCOURSE AND RELATING TO MASS SENTIMENTS

Domestic political entrepreneurs compete to frame international developments and to offer interpretations of their significance. This observation suggests that international developments need to be given meaning by political entrepreneurs and that this meaning must resonate with existing elite and public opinion. Moreover, the competition to offer different frames and interpretations is inseparable from political incentives and agendas. Whose framing and interpretation will prevail in domestic discourse naturally has the effect of steering a state's foreign policy in one direction or another.

For example, this discourse may kindle a people's traditional sense of mission or entitlement or alternatively, inflame its historical grievances. It may arouse a people's alarm over their country's lost power or stature or, conversely, pride and satisfaction from its recovery from setbacks and its restoration to its rightful place in the community of nations. How a country or people reacts to a power shift is thus profoundly political. To paraphrase Alexander Wendt, power transitions are what states make of them.[9] Although on some occasions, power transitions have been accompanied or followed by war, on many others peace has ensued. In the latter cases, power transitions are often treated by the relevant leaders and their respective citizens as non-events or in other words, developments that are hardly worthy of any major concern. Prevailing U.S. narrative suggests that Britain did not view the rise of the United States with serious misgivings, but that it was a different matter when London confronted the prospect of a rising Germany. Some Americans have suggested or implied that China's rise would not concern the United States if it were a democracy; others have argued that the rise of any competitor regardless of its regime type will alarm Washington.[10]

The story of shaping national discourse on power transitions does not start with a blank slate. Political entrepreneurs need to recognize and work with the historical context they inherit if they are to be effective. Memory of a "century of national humiliation" is such an example for the Chinese people.[11] Current events tend to be seen and interpreted through the prism of remembered history ("remembered" because people's memories are selective). Political construction of current events such as China's rise will be more effective if it resonates with the collective memory shared by many citizens that evokes their strong emotions. It is perhaps difficult for the people of established, Western countries to imagine, but economic development has always been connected in the minds of East Asians with national security. From the Qing dynasty in China and the Meiji Restoration in Japan, national rejuvenation has been seen to depend on a modern economy, which is necessary to build a strong military to ward off Western predation. The leaders of these countries were rightfully concerned about their national fate when they saw the rest of the globe being subjugated by Western colonialism and imperialism.

Put differently, national discourse by the Chinese on their country's recent reemergence as an important actor on the international scene cannot be separated from popular recollections of the indignities suffered at the hands of foreign aggressors and China's past status as East Asia's dominant power. This past is an important context and background for current discourse. Similarly, isolationism has a long and distinguished tradition in the history of U.S. foreign policy, and its ideas and principles continue to be important and relevant in debating about the direction and nature of U.S. foreign policy.[12] Political entrepreneurs will have more success when they can take advantage of a people's feelings, even if only latent feelings. It is always easier to fly with tailwinds in your back than headwinds in your face. It is always more expedient for political entrepreneurs to capitalize on or exploit existing mass feelings than to try to challenge or alter them, even if their views reflect unwarranted biases and prejudices.

Donald Trump's popularity reflects his ability to appeal to those white working-class Americans without a college degree and to mobilize these people's grievances that their life conditions have suffered in recent years and that minority groups are threatening their cultural identity and social status. He was also able to take advantage of popular resentments, particularly against China, which is perceived by many Americans to have engaged in unfair and predatory commercial practices that have hurt their incomes and caused the outsourcing of their jobs. Trump's America First rhetoric resonates strongly with a large segment of the American people. He has successfully tapped into their intense feelings even while deepening national division and arousing strong opposition from his detractors. His political base turns out to be resilient in its support despite his many personal flaws and policy mistakes. Many pundits have remarked that his brand of politics has taken over the Republican Party. Their larger point is of course that even though Trump has left office, Trumpism will remain a political force. Even after Joe Biden was sworn in as president, three-quarters of Republicans still believed that Donald Trump won the 2020 election.[13] This social reality in turn means that it will be challenging for the Biden administration to reverse Trump's policies, including his policy toward China, given the likely political opposition from this quarter.

Biden's administration is hamstrung not only by the political right but also the political left. The opposite ends of the U.S. political spectrum have converged on some important issues. Ironically, Donald Trump and Bernie Sanders have some common ground on these issues. They both prefer the United States to undertake more protectionist economic measures and downsize its political and military footprint abroad. This development points to eroding support from the traditional middle of U.S. political spectrum and augurs greater political handicaps facing centrist politicians such as Joe Biden. As Charles Kupchan and Peter Trubowitz show, bipartisan support for liberal internationalism is now a phenomenon of a bygone era in Washington.[14] U.S. leaders today must govern from a smaller political base. Their policy win set contracts in response to the rise of populism from both sides of the aisle.[15]

Anticipating the recent manifestation of populist movements in the West and the Trump phenomenon, Etel Solingen explains that internationalization or globalization produces domestic economic winners and losers but "the effects of [this process] are not restricted to political economy . . .; they are also felt by cultural groups and social movements that perceive internationalization and crude market forces as threatening their values or identities. These movements are receptive to appeals for placing communal 'organic' values, such as nationalism, ahead of all others."[16] Brexit and more broadly, antitrade and anti-immigrant sentiments in the West, including the United States, reflect these populist sentiments.[17] Significantly, the impetus for "economic decoupling" from China has come from the United States and its Western allies, not China.[18] As Trump was being openly critical of the globalization phenomenon, China's Xi Jinping publicly voiced his support for it.[19] In the past, the creation of economic blocs and the pursuit of economic exclusion have caused retaliation and contributed to international tension via the feedback circuit between the competing countries' protectionist and rent-seeking interests.[20]

As remarked earlier, Democrats and Republicans in the United States tend to agree on a policy of getting tough on China. By a margin of 63 to 36 percent, Republicans are more likely than Democrats to say that limiting China's influence and power is a top priority.[21] Notwithstanding this margin of difference between Democratic and Republican respondents, a poll by the Pew Research Center indicates broad national support for confronting China: "Roughly nine-in-ten U.S. adults (89%) consider China a competitor or enemy, rather than a partner. . . . Many also support taking a firmer approach to the bilateral relationship, whether by promoting human rights in China, getting tougher on China economically or limiting Chinese students studying abroad in the United States. More broadly, 48% think limiting China's power and influence should be a top foreign policy priority for the U.S., up from 32% in 2018." Sixty-seven percent of Americans surveyed have a "cold feeling" toward China in a "feeling thermometer," up from just 46 percent in 2018. Those reporting "very cold feelings" have doubled from 23 to 47 percent during the same time span. In view of these figures, it is obvious that a politician will have a difficult time proposing policies that go against the grain of this popular sentiment. The more attractive path is to capitalize on this phenomenon to maximize votes in an election.

We do not have comparable surveys showing popular Chinese views on the United States. Judging from official pronouncements and media coverage, it seems a reasonably safe proposition that mass attitudes in China have also turned sharply negative against the United States. Although China is not a democracy and its leaders should therefore be less sensitive to public opinion than their American counterparts, it would be difficult to argue that popular sentiment is irrelevant to its leaders' calculations. If for nothing else, incumbent officials need to protect themselves from prospective challengers within the elite who could mobilize public opinion against them. As remarked earlier, the mass public in China tends to be more nationalistic than the elite. It tends to be critical of the government for being too soft rather than too hard in its foreign policy, whether toward the United States, Japan, Taiwan, or other countries. As communist ideology has lost much of its allure to the Chinese people, nationalism and economic performance have become more important sources for sustaining the government's legitimacy. This observation pertains especially to Taiwan's status, which is at the top of Chinese leaders' agenda.[22]

However, even though prevailing discourse often refers to Chinese nationalism as a factor influencing Beijing's foreign relations,[23] empirical evidence on the subject is limited. Alastair Johnston's survey results from Beijing question the meme of "rising Chinese nationalism."[24] They show a decline of nationalism on the part of this city's residents since 2009, younger people being less nationalistic than their elders. Nor is the level of Chinese nationalism from this sample evidently higher than that of citizens of most other countries.[25] Americans can be equally nationalistic.[26] Johnston's evidence is certainly illuminating even though it does not tell us the level of nationalism characterizing the Chinese policy elite and its causal impact on Beijing's formulation and selection of its foreign policy. Other survey research suggests that public opinion in China tends to be quite hawkish. For example, Jessica Weiss reports that this opinion generally favors increased defense spending and a harder line of foreign policy.[27] Moreover, younger people are more hawkish than their elders, suggesting patterns that do not quite align with those Johnston reports.

Significantly, Chinese public opinion should not be taken as intransigent or entrenched. Kai Quek and Johnston demonstrate that Chinese people's reaction to their government's foreign policies can be quite contingent on how their leaders frame these policies.[28] For example, they disapprove backing down under U.S. military pressure but are more willing to accept accommodation and even concessions under other circumstances such as UN mediation and when they are reminded of the high economic costs of confrontation (interestingly, they are also less likely to support war against democracies).[29] Similarly, Weiss and Alan Dafoe show that the public may be more inclined to support restraint if this course of action promises future success.[30] Judged from these studies, Chinese leaders' policy space can be expanded considerably depending on how they justify and present their chosen policy to the public, thereby reducing their prospective political vulnerability to a popular backlash from nationalists. They are not without agency to act in ways to lessen domestic audience costs. They thus may be less constrained by popular nationalist sentiments than usually imagined.[31]

Naturally, how their foreign counterparts act can affect Chinese leaders' policy constraints. Quek and Johnston report that U.S. military pressure will have the counterproductive effect of increasing domestic political costs to Chinese leaders who are perceived to have backed down in the face of this pressure.[32] Significantly, the remark that Chinese leaders are not without agency to craft their foreign policy also means that they can arouse or mobilize popular nationalism rather than dampen this sentiment. Ian Chong and Todd Hall remind us that in pre-1914 Germany, nationalism was seen to offer "a bulwark against demands for great political and social reform."[33] Insecure regimes can thus lean on nationalism for legitimacy and to forestall necessary change.

The Chinese do not have a monopoly on nationalism. Amitai Etzioni asks whether America is "becoming a chauvinistic nation."[34] Trump's rhetoric of America First and Make America Great Again have abetted this phenomenon. Content analysis of Trump's speeches shows that *great* and *greatest* are among the most frequently used words and their reference "almost always applies to America." These speeches invariably suggest that the United States "is the greatest nation in the world and should be recognized by others as such. American leaders should recognize their power and not buckle in to the demands or free-riding of others."[35] This message has clearly struck a resonant chord in many Americans.

If the generalizations here are broadly accurate, they point to pessimism about the immediate prospects of reversing the ongoing trend of deteriorating relations between China and the United States. As I have noted, the stars must be aligned in both countries for their leaders to initiate rapprochement. It appears that current public opinions in both countries are not propitious for such an undertaking. It usually takes a major disruptive event or alarming trend to motivate leaders to search for a breakthrough in their existing relations with another country. The windows of opportunity need to be simultaneously open on both sides to initiate a policy to relax tension and for this initiative to be reciprocated.[36] The default is to continue the existing policy because changing it requires political effort and capital.

If this discussion seems too pessimistic, political entrepreneurs can also promote national discourses that turn enemies into friends. Kupchan shows that this process usually begins with a policy of unilateral accommodation by one side of a relationship.[37] If successful, this initiative is followed in the second stage involving reciprocal restraint by both sides. A gradual process then sets in to produce a convergence of elite values and mutual expectations. After this convergence has had time to consolidate, we begin to see social integration and narrative generation, which represent the third and fourth stages of reconciliation. During these later stages is a surge in social and economic exchanges accompanied by each country's mass media presenting and propagating a benign image of the other country. Thus the nature of national discourse is altered and mass attitudes are in turn transformed, as in the Anglo-American rapprochement. This entire process is generated and sustained by political entrepreneurship and is not somehow a natural or inevitable development. It is led by the political elite, a top-down phenomenon that requires an extended time. Thus, although the current deterioration in Sino-American relations seems to have started and become exacerbated rather quickly, it would take a protracted process to reverse it. As noted earlier, it is easy to destroy trust but much more difficult to restore it.

DOMESTIC AMPLIFICATION AND SCARE POLITICS

Politicians can exploit a people's grievances when a national audience is receptive. Countries undergoing the democratizing process, with their fragile institutions and unstable politics, are especially vulnerable to demagogues seeking to exploit frustrations and prejudices. The democratization process is therefore susceptible to being hijacked by such politicians, who often resort to fearmongering and blaming their country's problems on foreigners.[38] Moreover, rival politicians often seek to outbid each other in their hypernationalist rhetoric to gain a partisan edge. Their pursuit of domestic partisan gains can push their country to the brink or even over the edge of a foreign confrontation or war. The ethnic warfare and secessionist movements in former Yugoslavia provide an example. As Edward Mansfield and Jack Snyder suggest, even though established democracies rarely fight each other, this dyadic proposition of the democratic-peace literature does not preclude the tendency for countries in the process of transitioning to democracy to become more susceptible to foreign conflict.[39] Mansfield and Snyder report that "states that make the biggest leap in democratization from total autocracy to extensive mass democracy are about twice as likely to fight wars in the decade after democratization as are states that remain autocracies."[40] Perhaps reflecting this tendency for a democratizing China, Aaron Friedberg remarks that "Ironically, the prospects for a worsening in U.S.-China relations may actually be greater than they would be if China were to remain a stable autocracy."[41] If so, we see here another irony suggested by one of the reasons given for deteriorating Sino-American relations reviewed in chapter 1, specifically, that the problem afflicting this relationship is China's undemocratic political system.

If the danger of a democratizing country's becoming engulfed in foreign disputes and wars is significantly increased, Americans should be more careful about what they wish. A China in the process of becoming more democratic, in the sense that its government's policies becoming more representative of popular sentiments, may in fact be a more nationalistic and even more bellicose China. As the politics of former Yugoslavia and Russia immediately after the USSR's dissolution attest, the democratization process may be hijacked by nationalists, even ultranationalists, who resort to scare politics targeting ethnic and religious minorities, scapegoating domestic dissidents and foreign enemies, and diverting mass attention from problems at home to focus on hostility from abroad.

As a country democratizes, the selectorate to which its leaders must answer to becomes larger and persuading entrenched domestic interests to agree on shifting from an existing foreign policy to a new one becomes more difficult. Ironically, because leaders of an authoritarian system have a smaller selectorate, they are not constrained to the same extent as their democratic counterparts for a foreign deal to be approved by their respective domestic stakeholders. As Robert Putnam remarks, authoritarian leaders tend to therefore have a larger win set, or to be at least perceived to have greater policy space.[42] That is, they are seen as having more discretion to make compromises with foreigners to reach a deal. But precisely because they are less constrained by the need for domestic ratification, authoritarian leaders can be more easily pushed around to make concessions. In contrast, democratic leaders can justify their inability to offer concessions by making credible claims that their hands are tied because any concessions they make would be rejected by their legislature and public opinion.

This situation gives democratic leaders a bargaining advantage. Beijing, for example, has often encountered the tag team of good cop, bad cop (representing the executive and legislative branches of the U.S. government respectively) when dealing with Washington, which has been able to capitalize on the separation of powers in the U.S. system of government such as when explaining why it could not sometimes fulfill promises made by its executive branch to Beijing by appealing to legislative or public sentiments. One such example is when Bill Clinton's administration reneged on its pledge to the Chinese side that it would not issue an entry visa to Taiwan's then President Lee Tenghui to visit his alma mater, Cornell University.

Snyder has studied coalitional politics in interwar Germany and Japan, where industrialists, militarists, and nationalists coalesced to promote an agenda for arms buildup and imperial expansion.[43] Before World War I, Germany's social democrats were also effectively coopted into a grand coalition favoring naval expansion and imperial aggrandizement. The expectation by some that the working class would not fight for king or country turned out to be wrong. The proletariat of the main belligerents flocked to their respective nationalist causes. In this account, when leaders can overcome existing social, economic, and political cleavages, this development does not necessarily mean that the outcome will always favor international peace or stability. National unity may have the reverse effect or, to be more accurate, this development's effect on a country's foreign policy remains indeterminate until additional factors are taken into account.

The opposite story of social discord and political disunity has been told about interwar Britain and France.[44] These democracies failed to take effective policies in the face of rising German threat. A lack of elite cohesion, social unity, and ineffective and vulnerable governments combined to cause underbalancing this threat. Indeed, some elements of British and French society were more concerned about the threat coming from their respective proletariat than from Germany. The main lesson is that international developments (in this case, the rising threat from Germany) cannot be expected to necessarily produce appropriate and timely policy responses. Domestic dysfunctions often impede or distort such responses. Moreover, the default choice is to continue the existing policy. It is usually more difficult to put together a winning coalition to overturn the status quo than to continue the same policy or to make minor adjustments to it. This view echoes my earlier observation that it will take considerable political capital and effort for leaders in both China and the United States to change the present state of their relations. It appears that at the moment neither side has the necessary incentive or political space to do so.

As noted, in today's China the ideological appeal of communism has waned. But nationalism continues to be a powerful force that unifies people from all social strata and different political leanings. Nationalism "sells," and the belief is pervasive that foreign countries, especially the United States, are trying to block or obstruct China's rise and to frustrate its legitimate aspirations to return to its former status as a great power. This sense of annoyance, resentment, and even outrage can be a palpable source of national grievance and anger. It can engender a strong sense of status immobility despite a country's objective achievements as Steven Ward describes in the case of interwar Japan, or a feeling of status denial discussed in studies on contemporary Russia and China by Andrej Krickovic, Chang Zhang, Deborah Larson, and Alexei Shevchenko.[45]

Ward stresses the interactions between domestic politics and foreign developments such as U.S. anti-Asian legislations that reverberated in domestic Japanese politics in the interwar years.[46] Domestic Japanese politics reflected a sense of humiliation compounded by overt racism and a refusal by the established Western countries to recognize the principle of sovereign and racial equality at the Paris Peace Conference after World War I. These actions signaled to the Japanese people that admission to the club of elite powers was closed to their country. In recent years, Russia and Turkey have also been excluded from European institutions based on perceived "civilizational" reasons often presented as these countries' inadequate commitments to democracy. As the burgeoning literature on international status suggests,[47] states do not fight over international order or even relative power as much as they contest over demand for recognition. Because recognition and status are inherently intangible qualities and therefore not as easily divided as money and territory, disputes over them are more difficult to resolve.[48]

Anger and even outrage can result from a sense of injustice and hypocrisy in others' treatment of one's country and have a powerful effect on politics, such as the impact of U.S. policies to deny immigrants of Japanese ancestry (as well as other people of Asian descent, including the Chinese, as documented in the Chinese-Exclusion Act of 1882) and limit their property rights in the United States. This example shows how one country's actions or policies, often motivated by its domestic politics, can reverberate to exacerbate popular indignation and backlash politics in another country. It illustrates the feedback loop that can cause events outside a country to affect its domestic politics, which can in turn produce policies that exacerbate tension. National discourse in interwar Japan was affected by this perceived indignity and humiliation inflicted by the United States, changing its content and direction to the benefit of ultranationalists. The latter's arguments and cause appeared to have been vindicated by foreigners' attitudes and actions. These same foreign developments have the concomitant effect of delegitimating the more moderate political elements. Thus developments abroad can have a powerful effect in redistributing domestic political power and realigning public support in favor of the more radical politicians.

Similar episodes have happened in recent Sino-American relations, such as when the United States bombed the Chinese embassy in Belgrade and when a U.S. intelligence aircraft EP-3 collided with a Chinese jet fighter near China's Hainan Island, causing the latter to crash and the death of its pilot. Both occasions provoked popular outrage and mass protests in China, fueling nationalistic feelings there. Although the leaders of both countries were able to defuse the consequent tension and work out a settlement by resorting to the ambiguous language of "apology diplomacy,"[49] the dynamics show how easily such incidents can escalate.[50]

These incidents are catalysts or triggers, as mentioned in the introduction, that can set off a larger confrontation resulting from a combination of pre-existing conditions such as enduring rivalry, an armament race, and recurrent militarized disputes.

Although Washington insisted that the bombing of the Chinese embassy in Belgrade was an accident, disbelief inside China was widespread and it was even evident in some reports from international media,[51] suggesting that it was a deliberate attack. This episode also reflects attribution theory, whereby one's own objectionable behavior is explained away by pointing to circumstantial constraints or unintentional consequences whereas the other's tends to be seen as a reflection of its inherent bad faith or character flaw.[52] Few Americans ponder to ask how they would react if their embassy were bombed by the Chinese air force resulting in American fatalities (even if Beijing claims that this attack was an innocent mistake), or if a U.S. fighter jet were lost due to a collision with a Chinese spy plane off Florida's Key West.

Antiforeign nationalism is more powerful in China than popular demands for democracy, suggesting that the West's demands for democratic reform will resonate less well with the Chinese people than Beijing's nationalistic appeals. Given the nature of mass attitudes in China, which should be common knowledge to Western analysts and officials, the question is whether Western demands for China to institute democracy are sincere or primarily intended for domestic consumption. After all, Western countries have not hesitated to support authoritarian governments in the past or to continue to support them today (such as looking the other way when the military overthrew a popularly elected government in Egypt to establish authoritarian rule, or when Saudi Crown Prince Mohammed bin Salman authorized the murder of a *Washington Post* journalist). These remarks return us to the topic addressed in chapter 1, namely, what is the main reason for the deteriorating relationship between the United States and China. Is it China's authoritarian government, its abuse of human rights, its foreign coercion, or its rising power? When a country's material interests and its professed values converge to suggest the same course of action, it is difficult to tell whether its policy is motivated primarily by realpolitik or commitment to its values. When its interests and values diverge, however, its conduct is more informative about how sincere and committed it is to its professed values when pursuing them will harm its material interests.

NATIONAL HUBRIS AND THE STRUGGLE FOR RECOGNITION

The Chinese government's patriotic campaigns and propaganda are based on a receptive audience. China's rise is seen as restoring the country's dignity and rightful status and as eradicating its past humiliations at the hands of foreign imperialists. These feelings are difficult for some countries, such as the United States, to appreciate because they have not been victimized by foreign predation and occupation in recent memory (for the United States since the British burned the Capitol in the War of 1812), or have suffered a precipitous fall in their country's international status (as in the case of both China and Russia). Many Americans can still remember the days of racial segregation when "for colored" signs dotted public facilities, but few probably know about signs posted outside public parks administered by foreign authorities in Shanghai that barred Chinese and dogs from admission.[53]

As mentioned earlier, several recent studies show that countries struggle to recover dignity from past wrongs and to strive for status and recognition more than to pursue power. These studies therefore disagree with power-transition theorists' claim that the two leading states at the apex of the international hierarchy go to war over which one of them should decide the rules of international order. They also provide an answer to a question raised earlier: why do countries such as China and the United States engage in power pursuits even after their physical safety and security have been assured?

On the other side of the ledger showing a sense of national humiliation and grievance, one can observe a feeling of national entitlement and exceptionalism, a people's supreme confidence in their country's superiority and manifest destiny. A loss of status and power, even if only relative, can be hard to swallow, and another country's improvement in status and power is likely to be attributed to its guile or theft rather than one's own underperformance. The U.S. reaction to China's recent rise sometimes resembles a situation that professors have encountered: when an A student notices the improvement of a classmate's grade D to B, the A student perceives the improvement as a threat and complains that the classmate is busting the grade curve.

Randall Schweller observes that the Bush doctrine of preventive war makes the United States "the true revisionist power" and asks his readers to "imagine another globally dominant power, say China or Russia, [had] acted on its beliefs that: (1) its mission is to rid the world of evil by spreading what it claims are its universal values; (2) its security requires waging preventive wars; and (3) international norms, rules, and law apply to everyone else but not to itself because world order requires that it acts differently from all other states. Would we not consider that to be a revisionist power?"[54]

One may hypothesize that the more powerful a country is, the more likely its foreign policies reflect its domestic politics and its people's inherent dispositions. Foreign countries lack the necessary capabilities to restrain the United States, which is therefore more able to act on its natural impulses and popular inclinations. More than any other country, the United States tends to show this propensity. Despite a tradition supporting U.S. isolationism, a stronger strain since its rise to global primacy has been its missionary zeal to change other countries in its own image. Growing power and inflated hubris have gone hand in hand. Although the lesson of Vietnam and presumably the experiences in Afghanistan and Iraq have aroused doubts about the wisdom of Washington's proclivity to intervene abroad, that the United States must maintain its dominance in international relations and prevent the rise of any peer competitor remains deeply ingrained in popular ethos and official dogma.[55] The National Security Report of the George W. Bush administration commits the United States to keep its global primacy: "Our forces will be strong enough to dissuade potential adversaries from pursuing a military build-up in hopes of surpassing, or equaling, the power of the United States."[56] The Pew Research Center survey cited earlier attests to the public's overwhelming support to check China's rising power.

Ironically, even though the United States and China have many differences, they also have one important similarity. Both countries believe in their uniqueness and exceptionalism. Both exude supreme confidence, conceit, and self-righteousness, and both display no small degree of ethnocentrism and hubris. The Chinese no less than the Americans have a sense of entitlement and a belief in their country's manifest destiny. When people holding these self-images or featuring these traits clash, they are less likely to compromise.

One major characteristic distinguishes the two countries' foreign policies, however. Beijing has thus far refrained from exporting its model of governance and economic development, whereas Washington has done the opposite.[57] Many American liberals and conservatives alike have advocated that the United States should stand up for "its values," even though Americans disagree sharply about these values, as shown in controversies about abortion rights, gender identities, school prayers, affirmative action, measures to protect the integrity of elections, and the government's authority to require face masks and vaccination during a pandemic. This advocacy also raises the question whether it is a good idea to start a contest over competing values or an ideological conflict,[58] even though the United States undoubtedly enjoys much more popular support abroad for its professed values and ideology than China does. It is more difficult to resolve differences in values and ideology, which tend to stand in the way of more pragmatic politics. One important distinction between the current situation and the Cold War is that China is not seeking ideological converts or military allies abroad. Eschewing formal alliances, Beijing resorts more often to various forms of soft balancing, including leveraging existing international institutions.[59]

Although the United States is clearly seeking to promote a coalition to contain China (such as the Quadrilateral Security Dialogue), today's East Asia does not feature the bifurcated alignment patterns of the Cold War years. Countries in the region are generally leery of having to choose between Washington and Beijing. In Yuen Foong Khong's view, "All things considered, it will prove extremely difficult today for the United States to corral a serious Asian coalition to check China's power."[60] Moreover, as Adam Liff and John Ikenberry note, "traditional, full-scale security dilemma-induced arms races do not appear to be occurring—at least not yet."[61] Whether the dynamics of armament race described in Richardson's classic model will emerge in the future bears careful monitoring.[62] Another difference between today's world and that during the Cold War is that China is much more deeply embedded in the international economy than the USSR was.

WHO BENEFITS AND WHO IS HURT?

This embeddedness has strong implications because it affects the relative power and interest of domestic groups. It is a truism that a country's foreign policy produces domestic winners and losers. The decision to open China's economy to the world has undoubtedly benefited the coastal provinces more than the interior provinces. Foreign investments and operations have tended to favor the more developed parts of China. An economic policy of autarchy or self-reliance would be more advantageous to the less developed parts, at least relative to practicing market economics, which, in the absence of strong government intervention, tends to make the rich richer and the poor poorer. Socioeconomic inequities have widened in China since the Maoist years.

Various domestic interests can be expected to form political coalitions seeking to promote or block policies seen to benefit or hurt them. The iron-and-rye coalition in pre-1914 Germany, consisting of conservative Junkers, industrialists, and militarists, played an important, even decisive, role in Berlin's push for naval expansion and colonial acquisition. This agenda for weltpolitik, as some historians have suggested, was also motivated in part by an attempt by the Kaiser's conservative stalwarts to coopt and control Germany's social democrats. The general contours of this situation were repeated in interwar Japan, where various nationalist, industrialist, and military groups logrolled to push for imperial aggrandizement.[63] Rent-seeking and ideological concordance among these interest groups combined to motivate an aggressive and expansionist foreign policy.

Thus, domestic coalitions operate as transmission belts between internal and external conditions.[64] Solingen's main insight is that inward-looking interest groups and the coalitions they form tend to be less averse to war and external conflict than outward-looking groups or coalitions that have a vested interest in foreign trade and investment and thus a stable, open, and peaceful external environment required to sustain commerce. A corollary of these tendencies is that politicians craft their political appeal according to their domestic constituents' economic interest and cultural identity, especially those who feel threatened by downward social mobility. Those "advancing inward-looking models logroll across constituencies adversely affected by openness, including proponents of state entrepreneurship, nationalism, 'self-sufficiency,' and military-industrial complexes."[65]

Naturally, the extent to which inward- or outward-looking coalitions are likely to prevail depends on not just the domestic context but also the regional and global context. To the extent that other states in the region or world act in a way that accords with a particular domestic coalition's proclivities, a synergism or positive feedback loop means that this coalition is more likely to prevail domestically and become entrenched. Thus Germany's iron-and-rye coalition was successful in part because its outlook and interests were concordant with and thus reinforced by some other European powers' inward-looking orientations, especially Austria-Hungary and Russia. Similarly, racist policies against the Japanese (and Asians in general) by the United States were backed by countries such as Britain and Australia. These policies conferred political credibility and legitimacy to nationalist groups in Japan that advocated a hardline external policy. The 1930 Smoot-Hawley Act enacted by the U.S. Congress reverberated as other countries responded with similar protectionist measures, exacerbating the Great Depression. Anti-globalization populism in today's West can encourage and reinforce groups with a similar outlook in other countries.

Washington's policies to "decouple economically" from China raises the question of which Chinese groups are likely to be hurt by it and which to be empowered by it. The more hawkish and inward-looking interest groups tend to be the beneficiaries of such policies. This said, the anti-globalization phenomenon has thus far been primarily a Western phenomenon, meaning that in other regions of the world, especially East Asia where China is most deeply engaged in commercial relations with its neighbors, outward-looking internationalist coalitions that prioritize economic performance over security competition continue to be dominant in domestic politics. This is an important consideration distinguishing the landscape of pre-1914 Europe from today's East Asia, even though many have observed that some countries (especially Britain and Germany) eventually became antagonists in the Great War despite their close economic relationship.

Who are likely to be helped or hurt in a more protectionist world with increased political and military tension? For instance, are reductions in trade caused by increased U.S. tariffs more likely to hurt the interests of certain sectors and regions in China than others? Would sanctions against cotton produced in Xinjiang by the United States do more harm than good in affecting the living conditions of people living there? Or are these sanctions and others targeting officials in Hong Kong likely to be symbolic actions with little material consequences, even adverse consequences for the people they are supposed to help? Once instituted, would it be difficult to reverse them because this reversal is likely to be perceived as a sign of weakness or ineffectiveness? Sanctions, like wars, are easier to start than end. They are also often undertaken for symbolic reasons to appease domestic and foreign public opinion and as a substitute for rather than a prelude to more tangible actions.

Coastal China with its more frequent and intense contact with the outside world tends to be more cosmopolitan and less politically conservative than the interior regions. Because major Chinese exporters to the United States are concentrated in coastal China, U.S. sanctions tend to be more damaging to them. These segments also tend to represent the strongest advocates of maintaining economic and political ties with the rest of the world, including the United States. Wealthier individuals in China's coastal provinces are more likely to send their children to study in the United States and have properties there. In other words, they are likely to have a greater vested interest in cordial or at least stable relations between China and the United States. Washington's sanctions and other forms of coercive statecraft, however, are likely to undercut their political position as well as undermine their economic interests, and to bolster other interest groups that are economically more inward-looking and politically more conservative.

Like the United States, China is not a monolith. But unlike the United States, a democracy where voters' sentiments matter, it is not so clear whether those sectors and industries targeted by U.S. tariffs or sanctions will blame their government and, if so, how effectively they may lobby Beijing to change its policy. Tariffs and sanctions that Washington imposes may have the opposite effect of arousing nationalism and stiffen opposition to the United States. Johan Galtung remarked some time ago that foreign economic coercion is likely to create a boomerang effect whereby people in the country being sanctioned rally around the flag and become more resolved to resist this coercion rather than blaming their government for their plight.[66]

This tendency is not inevitable. Although we do not have specific information on the political impact of U.S. tariffs inside China, we do have some information on the impact of Chinese retaliatory tariffs on U.S. politics. Beijing's strategy targeted the Trump administration's important political constituents, such as mid-Western soybean exporters. Using a variety of evidence based on campaign communications, voters' online search patterns, and opinion survey, Sung Eun Kim and Yotam Margalit show that Americans tend to blame their government and Republicans for their economic malaise stemming from China's retaliation. "We found strong evidence that Chinese tariffs systematically targeted U.S. goods that had production in Republican-supporting counties, particularly when located in closely contested Congressional districts. This apparent strategy was successful: targeted areas were more likely to turn against Republican candidates."[67]

Beijing has deliberately targeted politically important or economically sensitive sectors on other occasions, such as when it singled out banana exports from the Philippines and pineapples from Taiwan. It has also applied pressure on Taiwan's tourism industry by discouraging its citizens from visiting the island. China enjoys a bargaining leverage because of its counterparts' heavy and asymmetric reliance on it in these sectors. Despite reports that China sought to pressure Japan by stopping its supply of rare earth (an important ingredient for a variety of consumer goods and weapons systems) after a collision of vessels from these two countries and Japan's arrest of the Chinese captain involved in this incident, the claim cannot be substantiated.[68]

How effective are sanctions likely to be? As alluded to, the prospective costs to a target country depend on the degree of concentration and hence the degree of dependency of the sanctioned product on the sanctioning country as well as on whether substitute markets are available. The higher this concentration or dependency, and the more difficulty in accessing alternative markets, the greater the vulnerability of and expected costs to the industry being sanctioned. A recent spat between Australia and China illustrates these dynamics in operation. About 30 percent of Australia's exports went to China, and an array of them have come under Beijing's sanction pressure, including barley, lobster, and wine. Beijing has also discouraged Chinese students seeking education in Australia, a major source of Australia's foreign revenue. Conversely, to the extent that other countries' exporters, such as American grain and wine producers and New Zealand's lobster fishermen, stand ready to step in as alternative suppliers,[69] they reduce the cost of sanctions to China.

The same logic applies to denial of critical imports to an industry, such as the U.S. refusal to supply important components to the Chinese telecom company Huawei. Naturally, in addition to calculating the economic costs that commercial tariffs, technological embargo, or trade boycotts can impose on a target country's industry, one needs to consider the political clout of the relevant businesses in the target country's domestic politics. Some economic sectors have an outsized political influence and can have more lobbying power than others. For instance, pineapple growers in Taiwan are an important constituent of the pro-independence Democratic Progressive Party. Similarly, soybean, grain, and pork farmers in the mid-Western states are a critical part of Trump's political base and thus his reelection strategy.

Several points embedded in this discussion bear emphasis. First, most broad-gauged sanctions, causing a shortage of daily necessities including fuel, food, and medical supplies, tend to hurt the masses of the country being sanctioned rather than its elite. This has been the general experience in countries such as Haiti and Iraq where the civilian population bears the brunt of economic deprivation. Recent U.S. sanctions denying favorable commercial treatment to Hong Kong are likely to have the same effect, hurting the people they are supposed to protect.

Second, we cannot assume that just because sanctions can have a costly impact on those affected, they will naturally lobby their government to relent by stopping the objectionable behavior that brought on the sanction. Those who suffer most economically from foreign sanction may not be in the best position to influence their government's policy. Theorizing on collective action and selective incentives, Mancur Olson taught us that concentrated interests are more likely to organize themselves politically than diffused interests and that the former are more likely to succeed in lobbying favorable government treatment.[70] Whereas the extent of economic pain inflicted on an industry or group would be relevant, it is also germane to consider whether it has the political wherewithal to affect government policy. This consideration in turn depends on whether this industry or group is an important part of the selectorate, whose support is important to incumbent leaders to maintain their power. Ironically for Beijing, from the perspective of communist orthodoxy, large transnational companies and Wall Street financiers have been more disposed to counsel a pragmatic and nonconfrontational approach to deal with China, whereas U.S. representatives of labor interests, the proletariat, have been more vocal in demanding a get-tough policy on China. This remark in turn directs attention to which groups are more important constituents to competing elites in a counterpart country, such as Democratic versus Republican politicians.

Third, the U.S. political system provides more points of access by foreigners to influence its policy processes because these processes are more decentralized and involve multiple participants. Further, these participants are more accessible to lobbyists representing domestic and foreign interests. In contrast, China's policy processes tend to be more centralized and their participants more inaccessible to groups from civil society, not to mention lobbyists representing foreign interests. Thus it is far more uncertain that groups or industries hurt by foreign sanctions can effectively mobilize to pressure Beijing to change its policy responsible for their hardships due to foreign sanctions.

Fourth, policies seeking to affect people's interests are more likely to succeed than those trying to change their identity. Partisan division in the United States reflects not only differences in sectoral or geographic interests, but also differences in cultural and political identities. As mentioned earlier, existing institutions tend to magnify the power of Middle America (pejoratively described as flyover country), where many voters feel that their cultural identity and social status have been threatened by ongoing trends of globalization and multiculturalism. A survey by the Pew Research Center shows unsurprisingly that older, rural, less educated, white Americans who identify with the Republican Party tend to have more hostile feelings toward China.

Fifth, from the perspective of the sanctioning country, the aggregate or average impact of its economic coercion on the entire target country is less important than its marginal impact on specific industries, groups, or regions, as suggested by earlier references to pineapple growers in southern Taiwan and soybean farmers in the U.S. Midwest. Sanctions that focus on politically salient targets or closely contested election districts are more likely to be effective. Political saliency confers publicity and thus a value in political advertisement. As Kim and Margalit suggest, influence attempts targeting swing voters in closely contested election districts are more likely to bear fruit.[71] It is difficult to flip a voter's preference or support from one party to another, especially if they are strongly committed partisans. Changing the minds of those who are less committed would be easier, however, and the result of political contests can be altered when some of undecided voters sit out an election. Similar reasoning inclines U.S. presidential candidates to focus their resources on the dozen or so swing states rather than diverting these resources to states that they are already likely to win or have little chance of winning even if they tried (such as California and New York for Republicans, and Louisiana and Oklahoma for Democrats).

Sixth, high-profile sanctions targeting specific individuals, such as Chinese officials in charge of affairs in Xinjiang and Hong Kong, can create considerable inconveniences for those concerned but are not likely to alter Beijing's policies. These symbolic actions are intended more for domestic consumption rather than undertaken in any serious expectation of influencing Beijing's policies. To the extent that such symbolic actions are seen to be a substitute for more concrete and consequential policies, they represent "cheap talk" or "hot air" in James Fearon's bargaining theory.[72] In this connection, it is important and relevant to point again to his observation that the costlier an action or announcement is to the party undertaking it, the more credible it will be to its intended target. Moreover, when symbolic sanctions are undertaken against China and Russia to support "our values," they are less likely to succeed because relative to specific economic demands they are vague about what specifically the target country must do to lift them, or the bar is set so high as to make it nearly impossible for the target country to meet. Washington's announcement that it will not send officials to the 2022 Beijing Winter Olympics (but will nevertheless permit American athletes to participate) is an example. In this instance, the professed reason for the U.S. boycott is Beijing's alleged genocidal policies in Xinjiang. Yet if Beijing is truly guilty of genocide, is this symbolic protest the appropriate response? It seems far too weak for the serious crime being lodged against China and thus inadvertently attests to Washington's weak commitment to human rights.

This discussion also applies to China because Beijing has taken retaliatory steps to sanction individuals, both public officials and private citizens, in the United States and European Union, banning them from entering China or doing business there. These actions are unlikely to change these counterparts' foreign policies and have the effect of inflaming an already acrimonious situation. They are symbolic. Significantly, once nationalism is aroused, it is difficult to put the genie back in the bottle. Official endorsement of public boycott of foreign companies perceived to have undertaken unfriendly actions against China (such as when they embargo cotton grown in Xinjiang) can start a chain reaction that may be difficult to reverse.

Seventh, the seriousness of the party undertaking a sanction can be gauged by the relative emphasis the country places on its imports from or exports to the target country. Import duties or tariffs can be a disguised attempt at protectionism, and thus the real purpose behind them can be to promote domestic producers who face competition from foreigners. Export bans, however, are a different matter because they deny sales to one's own exporters and therefore hurt their profits and market shares abroad. U.S. sanctions against Huawei clearly protect the U.S. domestic market. However, more ominously from Beijing's perspective, they also signal a more determined attempt at technological embargo because this move blocks sales by U.S. companies to Huawei and therefore indicates Washington's willingness to bear serious economic costs.

Finally, sanctions are a double-edged sword. They can impose economic pain on the target country but also encourage it to undertake mitigation efforts such as fostering its self-sufficiency to minimize its vulnerability to future economic coercion. They can even affect onlookers who are motivated to take precautions to avoid a similar fate. Once a particular political narrative gains dominance in domestic discourse and its advocates become empowered, it becomes more difficult to dislodge them. Path dependency argues that once a country launches a certain action, it affects future choices by closing off some options while opening others. Armament races, for example, enhanced the domestic influence and standing of militarists and industrialists in a log-rolling coalition in pre-1914 Germany. Once entrenched, it became more diffi-cult to overcome this coalition's power grip and its effects on Berlin's subsequent policies. Naturally, sanctions are double-edged also because they impose costs on the sanctioning country, such as tariffs on Chinese goods exacerbating U.S. inflation and boycott of Russia's energy exports causing hardship for European economies.

BLOWBACK EFFECTS OF LIBERAL
INTERNATIONAL ORDER

Resistance to the liberal international order is a powerful example of the foreign-domestic connections discussed in this chapter. This order has had serious domestic economic and political consequences, and its redistrib-utive effects have in turn created a strong backlash. Even though scholars working in the tradition of power-transition theory are animated by the dynamics of interstate power shifts, they invoke a ruled-based interna-tional order as the reason states compete. According to them, leading states struggle for power to decide the nature of this order. China's rise is concerning because it threatens the current rule-based liberal order. I argue, however, that the main challenge to this order has come from the West, stemming from elite and mass discontent with its redistributive consequences.

The United States, joined by its West European partners, fostered the so-called liberal international order after 1945. This system has been described as a constitutional pact, one that is "open, integrated, and rule-based."[73] John Ikenberry argues that its institutions create a win-win sit-uation for all concerned because it helps sustain U.S. power while restraining its exercise of its enormous power. In his view, it is an order easy for China to join and difficult for it to resist. He also argues that although China may one day overtake the United States, it will be diffi-cult for China to overtake the entire West. By constructing a rule-based order, the United States can help integrate China in this order and shape its future behavior. Naturally, a rule-based order binds not only the less powerful countries but also the leading country to the same set of rules.

Why should a hegemon want to forfeit the opportunity to maximize its current gains by limiting its discretion and constraining its exercise of power in exchange for some vague hope of restraining other countries' misbehavior and taming the power of a prospective rising state at some indefinite future time? Moreover, why should we expect a deliberately constructed order, one based on rules and institutions, to work better at preserving international peace and stability than a behavioral order such as one based on the logic and dynamics of balance of power?[74] Many scholars working in the power-transition tradition are realists who would typically emphasize the importance of power in international relations and the need for a balance of power to maintain peace and stability. When discussing a rising China, however, they shift to liberal institutionalist arguments, invoking the need for rule-based behavior and calling attention to the danger that a more balanced distribution of power can pose (by undermining the hegemon's dominance) to peace and stability. They try to wriggle out of this analytic bind by proclaiming two kinds of states: one that is satisfied and committed to the existing international order, and one that is dissatisfied and bent on overthrowing it. Rather than undertaking empirical analysis, however, they settle matters by definitional fiat by stipulating that a hegemon is necessarily satisfied with the current state of affairs and that a rising power must be dissatisfied.

How binding are the international order's rules on the hegemon and how much do institutions constrain it? It is easy for this country to profess its commitment to the liberal international order when the rules and institutions are working in its favor and sustaining its power. But what happens when they no longer serve this purpose? The crux, as Schweller notes, is that the order's rules and institutions need to be autonomous and thus capable of restraining the hegemon's wanton use of its power when this becomes necessary.[75] After all, it is the relatively weak countries that need these rules and institutions to protect them; the strong can rely on their power. The test of the effectiveness of rules and institutions comes when they collide with the hegemon's important interests. Will a declining hegemon continue to be committed to the pertinent rules and institutions? Or will it try to alter and even dismantle these rules and institutions?

When a hegemon grows even stronger, will it also be motivated to change the rules and institutions so that it can further advance its interests and secure its preferences? As Schweller remarks, "binding institutions either work best when they are needed least or simply do not work at all."[76] These rules and institutions are backed up by the hegemon's power and typically serve its interests, as power-transition theorists acknowledge.

"Indeed, one would be hard put to find any solid evidence throughout the entire Cold War period of institutions restraining the arbitrary use of American power."[77] Recent events support this observation. Washington's European allies complained that their pleas to extend the U.S. troop presence in Afghanistan were ignored, and France complained bitterly about "unacceptable behaviour among partners and allies" when Australia ditched its agreement to purchase French submarines in favor of those provided by the United States.[78] Paris then recalled its ambassadors to Washington and Canberra over its foreign minister's allegation of "lying, duplicity, a major breach of trust and contempt."[79]

It is not clear why a dominant power should be tied permanently to a fixed international order. People's views on legitimate and appropriate norms are always evolving and international rules and institutions are always in flux, being negotiated and renegotiated. Ideas such as crimes against peace and humanity, decolonization and racial equality, preventive war, regime change, and responsibility to protect were introduced after 1945. Would one seriously consider calling those advocating these new principles revisionists? Few commentators and scholars in the West have used this label to describe those countries and groups seeking to introduce such changes to the existing international order. In addition to being sufficiently autonomous and strong to restrain the hegemon, a viable order must be sufficiently flexible to adjust to changing reality such as those stemming from interstate power shifts.

The liberal international order created after World War II began as a bounded system. It was limited both geographically and ideologically, comprising primarily established democracies with a capitalist economy located in the North Atlantic region.[80] It "was neither liberal nor international. It was a bounded order that was limited mainly to the West and was realist in all its key dimensions."[81] It was also an order backed by U.S. power, and one that did not stop Washington from abandoning its ostensible rules when they clashed with its interests. As Schweller notes, "The empirical record strongly suggests that international institutions have not checked the use of American power, which, in the most dramatic decisions since 1945, has been repeatedly exercised unilaterally—often without prior consultation with or even advance warning of its allies."[82] He continues, "In any case, leading states can never be bound by institutions. A hegemon may choose to exhibit restraint, and then again it may not. In these matters, however, institutions are guarantors of nothing."[83] The restraining influence of rules and institutions rests entirely on a hegemon's voluntary compliance. Who was powerful enough to stop the United States from invading Iraq when it insisted on its right to wage a preventive war without UN authorization?

After the Cold War ended and U.S. power reached another peak, American leaders did not take Ikenberry's advice: they did not try to forge a new constitutional order, inviting a defeated Russia and a still relatively weak China to join other stakeholders to create a consensual set of rules for the sake the world's future peace and stability. The United States and its allies have instead pushed to expand their influence globally, seeking to introduce democracy and capitalism to other parts of the world. The globalization project, involving increasing economic exchanges such as cross-border investment and production, became part of this process. The process also included the transformation of former socialist countries' planned economies to market-oriented and internationally open economies and, on the political front, the transformation of previously one-party or authoritarian political systems to those with multiparty competition and regular (although not necessarily always open or fair) elections. The promotion of various color revolutions and regime changes and the fight against international terrorism and efforts to install democracy on alien soils such as Afghanistan and Iraq made up another part of this campaign.

This order has promoted freer trade and investment across borders, and China has been one of its chief beneficiaries. Beijing has embraced the economics of this order, and Xi Jinping was quoted at the Davos Economic Forum that China is committed to the globalization process. Power-transition theorists claim that a rising China intends to displace the United States as the world's hegemon and to overturn the existing international order, whereas the United States as the established power wants only to maintain it and its existing position in it. The previous paragraph argues instead that the U.S.-led West has gone on the offense after the Soviet Union's demise in a campaign to expand what used to be a regionally and ideologically bounded order. It has not been playing defense, as is presented in conventional Western discourse. The public rationale for engaging China, namely, to alter the character of its political system and to convert its people's values and identities, reflects this effort to extend the liberal international order. The doctrines of regime change and preventive war also suggest an offensive motivation. Lenin's famous dictum (кто кого) asks the fundamental question of who, whom? Power-transition theory misrepresents which side is playing the offense and which side the defense. The established power or the rising power?

Many people acknowledge that U.S. policies, joined by its NATO partners, toward Afghanistan and Iraq have failed. Western interventions in Libya, Somalia, and Syria have brought more chaos and turmoil than order and stability. As John Mearsheimer notes, these interventions have aroused nationalism in the targeted countries and encountered fierce resistance.[84] At the same time, globalization has widened economic inequities in developed economies, causing disadvantaged sectors and groups to suffer income and job losses. It has also engendered social frustration and political resentment against ruling elites. Donald Trump was the chief political beneficiary of this boomerang effect and the associated culture war caused by the perception of many white Americans without a college degree that not only their economic and social status but also their cultural heritage and identity are threatened in an increasingly diverse, multicultural America. Adverse reaction to open-border policies accepting the free movement of people, goods, and money has been evident in both Europe and the United States. A sentiment against immigrants and refugees has developed, for example (in part for racial reasons, as the recent and much more positive reception of refugees from Ukraine attests). Nationalists have prevailed over integrationists, shown most vividly in Britain's exit from the European Union. Other manifestations have come from protest movements against big government, including demonstrations against lockdowns, mandates to wear face masks, and resistance to vaccination during the COVID-19 pandemic.

Thus, by trying to extend what used to be a bounded order to a global one, the United States and its allies have inadvertently committed the mistake of overreach. In Mearsheimer's words, "the liberal international order is crumbling," and it "contained the seeds of its own ruin" because of its boomerang effects on the West's own domestic politics and economics.[85] Further, the recent phenomenon of deglobalization and the declared U.S. intention to "economically decouple" from China have originated from the West and not China. Its impetus has come from the West, especially as evidenced by Trump's rhetoric and action to disengage from multilateral diplomacy, withdraw from international economic arrangements, and restrict the admission of refugees such as his ban on immigrants from Muslim-majority countries and his project to build a wall along the border of the United States with Mexico.

In an earlier era, the Concert of Europe failed due to political changes within the relevant great powers. By almost all accounts, this institution helped keep European peace and stability between 1816 and 1848. After it broke down, more wars and militarized disputes followed from 1849 to 1870. The breakdown of this institution was not because its autocratic members—Prussia, Russia, and Austria-Hungary—had wanted to abandon it. In fact, they continued to support it to preserve their conservative regimes and sustain the continent's political status quo. The institution failed because its liberal members deliberately undermined it. Britain and France withdrew to appease their domestic publics, which were undergoing democratization. As Kupchan remarks, "Britain had in effect become a revisionist power, seeking to extend its geopolitical influence and export its liberal ideology."[86] An established power, in this case the most powerful one, can be a revisionist seeking to change the prevailing order and its revisionism originates from its domestic politics. Thus the source demanding such change does not need to be rising upstart. The democratization process can have important international reverberations.

CONCLUSION

States compete not necessarily for more power or tangible material resources. They also contest for intangible or psychological rewards such as status, recognition, and respect. Besides material goods, people also crave for status, recognition, and respect. They react angrily when they feel that their dignity has been compromised and their legitimate aspirations for their country's standing have been denied or frustrated by other countries. Interestingly, when deciding which candidate or party to support, people are more likely to be influenced by their cultural identities and values than their material interests.

Ned Lebow argues that the desire for status, prestige, or *gloire* has been a much more important source for warfare than the pursuit of security concerns.[87] He reports that the quest for standing was present as a primary or secondary motivation in sixty-two of the ninety-four wars involving great powers since 1648. His analysis contributes to understanding the enigma presented earlier, namely, why states continue to spend on their military and recruit allies long after their physical survival and security are assured. This chapter introduces an additional, not necessarily mutually exclusive, explanation, namely, the domestic power and incentives of entrenched interests along with states' pursuit of psychological or emotional gratification.

This chapter argues that when people feel that their country has been disrespected or humiliated, or that their political and cultural identities have been threatened, these feelings present a potent force that dispose them to confront each other internationally. Popular sentiments can be especially powerful in domestic politics when they are led and mobilized by elites motivated by a partisan agenda to exploit mass grievances and hijack the nationalist cause. Foreigners' sanctions can of course affect the material interests of their intended targets but, more important, they challenge a people's sense of identity and their belief about their country's place and entitlement in the world. Feelings of national pride and resentments of being disrespected are inherently intangible qualities that are more difficult for leaders to manage or control. Unlike resources that can be more easily divided, such feelings are more likely to inflame public opinion and engender a strong negative sense of being mistreated. Once the genie has been aroused, putting it back in the bottle is difficult.

It is difficult in part because such mass feelings can help politicians score political points and keep them in power. Hard-liners have a vested interest in sustaining hostility directed against a foreign enemy or ethnic minority. In times of tension, national discourse typically gravitates in their favor, empowering them at the expense of the more moderate elements. Politicians and officials often try to outbid one another in demonstrating their patriotic or nationalist credential. This development can start a process that leads to a further deterioration in relations with foreign countries. Thus efforts at foreign coercion can have a blowback effect, getting both sides in a dispute to climb onto an escalator of mutual recrimination and retaliation that will be difficult for them to get off because of domestic partisan considerations. Public opinion and political opposition in both countries can tie the hands of those who want to deescalate, trapping these countries in a perpetual standoff. These processes are the transmission mechanisms that enable international developments, which include a shifting power balance, to have domestic consequences, which can in turn cause blowback in the domestic politics and foreign policies of a counterpart state.

5

TAIWAN AS A POSSIBLE CATALYST FOR SINO-AMERICAN CONFLICT

Contrary to power-transition theory, the second most powerful country in the world rarely chooses to fight the most powerful one. Both are more likely to pick on secondary powers or former great powers in serious decline. As discussed in the context of self-selection, countries that initiate war tend to pick vulnerable targets that are, in their view, unlikely to receive international help and thus most wars remain bilateral affairs. Large wars involving many countries rarely result from a direct conflict between the two most powerful states. As Michael Swaine and Ashley Tellis observe, "Most systemic wars . . . come about as a result of catalytic interventions by the existing hegemon on behalf of some other victims—interventions undertaken mainly for balance of power considerations—and rarely because the rising state directly attacks the existing hegemon to begin with."[1]

Large wars typically happen because great powers are drawn into them by alliance commitments and their concern with how a local dispute involving their ally could affect their reputation for resolve and the international balance of power if they failed to act. This process of chain ganging, whereby great powers become embroiled in what was initially a local crisis because of their formal or informal alliance ties,[2] is the key transmission mechanism for a conflict to escalate and spread.

Both world wars originated from disputes involving associates of great powers, such as Serbia and Austria, who were respectively Russia's and Germany's junior partners in 1914. Britain entered World War I because it was allied with France, which was in turn allied with Russia, and the United States became embroiled in part because of its close ties with Britain. Similarly, the proximate cause for World War II was Germany's invasion of Poland, a country that Britain and France had pledged to defend. Thus it is not quite correct to describe the two world wars as a direct challenge mounted by Germany against Britain, as often presented by power-transition theory.

These conflicts occurred not because Berlin had wanted to fight London but because Berlin was unable to keep London on the sideline. Germany's diplomacy in the lead-up to both wars had undoubtedly antagonized Britain, but it was fundamentally geared to secure British neutrality in a possible future conflict. That Britain nevertheless fought against Germany testifies to Berlin's failed diplomacy rather than its eagerness or set agenda to challenge London. Adolf Hitler averred, "Everything I undertake is directed against the Russians; if the West is too stupid and blind to grasp this, then I shall be compelled to come to an agreement with the Russians, beat the West, and then after their defeat turn against the Soviet Union with all my forces."[3] On another occasion, he declared, "Originally I wanted to work together with Britain. But Britain has rejected me again and again. It is true, there is nothing worse than a family quarrel, and racially the English are in a way our relatives. . . . It's a pity that we have to be locked in this death struggle, while our real enemies in the East can sit back and wait until Europe is exhausted. That is why I do not wish to destroy Britain and never shall."[4]

China and the United States are separated by an ocean. They do not have any direct territorial dispute, which is the most common reason for states to have a conflict. It is also hard to argue that these countries can come to blows because, in line with power-transition theory, they want to be the one to decide the nature of international order. This order can hardly be imposed unilaterally by any country, even a dominant power. Contest over regional hegemony seems a plausible reason for these countries to collide. After all, the United States had fought two world wars to prevent Germany from gaining this position in Europe and, in World War II, also to stop Japan's bid for regional hegemony in East Asia. The Cold War can also be interpreted as a U.S. effort to check the USSR from securing its dominance in Europe. However, as shown by the history of the Cold War, containment or blocking policies do not suddenly develop into a hot war. A trigger typically sets off a conflagration, such as the assassination of Archduke Ferdinand in 1914. Significantly, other crises had arisen in the Balkans before this incident but war was averted each time. Sarajevo was a *streetcar*—a metaphor that points to those chronic hot splots that can present recurrent threats to peace. Given the constellation of dangerous factors encouraging escalation and contagion, other similar incidents could also have provided the catalyst to set off the war.[5]

Taiwan is the most obvious place for a military confrontation between China and the United States. Beijing has repeated many times that this island's status is a "core interest," and that it will not accept foreign interference in its project of national reunification to return the island to Chinese sovereignty. In line with my earlier argument about human agency, this chapter reflects on how macro trends intersect with the decision processes of the relevant parties. It focuses on how their interactions can produce a Sino-American conflict. It therefore seeks to fill in the details on how such a conflict can develop during a time of shifting power balance, which is but just one variable in the broader policy context facing decision-makers. An important flaw of the typical account given by power-transition theory is that should there be a war between China and the United States, it would not be due to Beijing's revisionism and desire to challenge Washington and to replace the United States as the world's hegemon. Instead, analogous to relations between Germany and Britain before the world wars, it is much more accurate to say that should such a conflict occur, it would be because Beijing's diplomacy has failed to persuade Washington to stay out of China's unfinished civil war. In various communiqués, the United States has acknowledged the Chinese position that Taiwan is part of China and a domestic matter for the Chinese people to settle. Indeed, Washington had insisted for many years before it switched its diplomatic recognition from Taipei to Beijing that the government in Taipei represented the entirety of China even though it no longer had control over the mainland.

ONGOING TRENDS INVOLVING TAIWAN

I do not repeat here Taiwan's recent history except to say that shortly after the outbreak of the Korean War, President Harry Truman ordered the U.S.

Seventh Fleet to intervene in the Taiwan Strait. This action prevented the Communists from invading the island. It saved the Nationalists, who had been driven from the Chinese mainland, in their last island refuge. The United States recognized this Nationalist regime as the legitimate government representing China (including the mainland) until President Jimmy Carter reversed this decision and announced that Washington would extend diplomatic recognition to Beijing in December 1978.

Shortly after Carter switched U.S. diplomatic recognition, Congress passed the Taiwan Relations Act, pledging continued U.S. political and military support (such as arms transfers) for Taiwan. This support has been indispensable for the island's continued existence as an independent political entity in fact though not in name. Despite Beijing's vow to reunite the island with the mainland, the standoff between the two regimes has persisted. It has been a continued source of tension in Sino-American relations since Truman's order.

Since formal diplomatic relations were established between China and the United States, the hallmark of Washington's policy toward Taiwan has been characterized by "strategic ambiguity."[6] In essence, this policy refuses to formally commit the United States to any definite course of action. It suggests that the United States is opposed to any military attempt by Beijing to seize the island. At the same time, it signals that Washington is opposed to any move by Taipei to declare its de jure independence, a move that could cause Beijing to start a war to prevent it. This policy is supposed to present dual deterrence against Beijing's use of force and Taipei's declaration of formal independence.[7] It is supposed to preserve peace by freezing the political status quo for an indefinite future. It has succeeded in this objective thus far. Its effectiveness, though, is threatened by ongoing trends.

These trends pertain to, on the one hand, China's military modernization shifting the power balance across the Taiwan Strait and, on the other, changes in public opinion and mass identity in Taiwan enhancing political support for the island's independence.[8] The Pentagon's 2020 report to Congress concludes that although significant gaps and shortcomings remain, the Chinese military has made significant progress in the past two decades. This report identifies several areas where China has overtaken the United States, such as in shipbuilding, land-based conventional ballistic and cruise missiles, and integrated air defense systems.[9] In recent years, China's navy has undertaken a massive expansion program, having launched two aircraft carriers and is in the process of commissioning a third. China has also reformed its armed forces and updated its military doctrine and organization to be better prepared to undertake joint combat operations. Although analysts continue to differ on the feasibility and the likely success of a Chinese military attempt to coerce or seize Taiwan, they generally agree that the military balance is evolving rapidly in a direction unfavorable to Taiwan.[10] This threat would likely involve a naval blockade rather than amphibious landing reminiscent of the Normandy invasion by the allies in World War II. Stephen Biddle and Ivan Oelrich argue that "Taiwan . . . faces a serious threat of A2/AD [Anti-Access/Area Denial] blockade in coming decades, and one that the United States cannot easily lift."[11] Fareed Zakaria writes that "the Pentagon has reportedly enacted 18 war games against China over Taiwan, and China has prevailed in every one."[12]

China was until recently unable to prevent unhampered U.S. air and naval access almost right up to its coastline. In March 1996, it was forced to watch when President Bill Clinton ordered two U.S. carrier groups to the Taiwan Strait; open sources differ on whether these vessels sailed through the Taiwan Strait on this occasion.[13] The Nimitz group did transit it earlier in December 1995; more recently, in early 2022, the USS *Ralph Johnson* in February and USS *Sampson* in April also made a transit through the Taiwan Strait. The 1996 demonstration of U.S. military power and its support for Taiwan originated from a change of Washington's decision and an apparent contradiction to its earlier pledges to Beijing, when it issued a visa to Taiwan's pro-independence president, Lee Teng-hui, to visit the United States. The events of March 1996 have been widely mentioned by China's netizens and remembered as a national embarrassment and humiliation. Since that time, China's navy has undergone rapid modernization and expansion, and its land-based missiles now pose a threat to U.S. aircraft carriers. Thus Beijing has been able to extend the defense of its shorelines further out to the sea. It has also enhanced its amphibious and logistic capabilities to support a possible invasion of Taiwan. Many observers have written about the volatile nature of relations across the Taiwan Strait, with several of them urging a reexamination of U.S. policy toward Taiwan.[14]

As the military balance changes, Beijing is also losing its patience and its citizens are becoming more strident in demanding a tough policy toward Taiwan. According to a survey by the *Global Times*, 70 percent of Chinese support strongly the use of force to reunify Taiwan with the mainland, and 37 percent believe that it would be best if war occurred in the next three to five years.[15] China has welcomed investments and business operations from Taiwan, commercial relations that have blossomed and yielded significant profits for Taiwan's firms. Beijing has also extended various preferential treatments to Taiwan's visitors, students, and investors to win over their hearts and minds. Nevertheless, even though Taiwan's economy has become intertwined with the mainland's and even though this relationship is characterized by Taiwan's significant asymmetric dependency on the mainland, this soft approach has not produced positive results for Beijing.[16]

If anything, recent trends in public opinion show that more and more of Taiwan's people have come to identify themselves as Taiwanese rather than Chinese, and that the cause of securing eventual political independence has the voters' overwhelming support.[17] This support is especially strong among young people. Ongoing generational change suggests that with the passage of time, popular support for the island's independence will only grow. This social reality naturally affects the incentives of Taiwan's politicians, who naturally wish to win elections. It also constrains the policy space available to officials who need domestic ratification to reach an agreement with the mainland. These officials need to engage in a delicate balancing act to ensure continued commercial access to the mainland to sustain the island's economic health and at the same time, to secure U.S. military support to protect its political survival. Given deteriorating relations between Beijing and Washington, this dilemma is likely to only intensify despite official government statements routinely demanding Beijing to relax its political and military pressure on the island.

Significantly, public opinion polls show that although a large majority of Taiwan's people have a Taiwanese rather than a Chinese identity and prefer eventual political independence, most also are pragmatic in not wanting to change the status quo and risk a confrontation with China. Their preference for independence tends to be conditional on their views on how likely China is to resort to force in that event and how likely the United States is to intervene on behalf of Taiwan. Those who strongly advocate independence tend to also be more convinced that China will not use force and that if it did the United States would come to Taiwan's aid. These patterns suggest that public opinion tends to depend on context and the possible presence of motivated bias. This opinion is also subject to changes over time and, as mentioned, has moved increasingly toward an independent Taiwanese identity and reluctance and even resistance to reunify with China.

An example of shifting public opinion due to recent events can be seen in the results of a March 2022 survey conducted by Taiwan's Institute for National Defense and Security Research, an affiliate of its Ministry of Defense. They show a significant drop in the number of people believing that the United States would or could come to Taiwan's defense if China attacked. More specifically, 14 percent of the respondents said the United States would do so, and 26 percent said it would be a possibility, a total of 40 percent of the survey's respondents. In contrast, an earlier survey undertaken by the same institute in September 2021 showed that 57 percent had believed that there "would be" or "could be" U.S. military involvement to help Taiwan. The rather significant shift of 17 percent on this question has come in a short amount of time, the cause of which the source attributes to the war between Russia and Ukraine.[18]

As mentioned, the majority of Taiwan's voters support independence if this goal can be accomplished without provoking China to attack. In view of this threat, they are also pragmatic in favoring maintenance of the status quo for now and even for an indefinite future. From Beijing's perspective, this means that its threat to use military force has been the main reason deterring Taiwan's independence, thus explaining its reluctance to renounce the possible use of force. Moreover, a militarily stronger China is more likely to keep the United States at bay. If the United States were not concerned about China's reaction, it would be less inclined to restrain Taipei and perhaps even be more disposed to support its secession from China. Washington's support for Taipei was certainly stronger when China was militarily weaker. The logic of this situation suggests that appeals by Taipei and Washington for Beijing to renounce the use of force is unlikely to persuade Chinese leaders. Whereas much has been written about U.S. deterrence to prevent China's threat to Taiwan, less attention has been paid to China's deterrence concerns vis-à-vis Taiwan and the United States.

Why can China not just "let it go"? Why does it insist on reunifying with Taiwan? First of course is the role of human emotions, as mentioned earlier. Second is geostrategy.[19] Why should Beijing care less about Taiwan than Washington about Cuba when Havana was allied with Moscow? Last are domestic political considerations. In 1962, the United States went to the brink of nuclear war to evict Soviet missiles from Cuba, even though some of Kennedy's advisors had thought that the missiles did not pose a security threat to the United States. They were, however, concerned that the missiles posed a threat to the presidency and the Democrats' electoral chances in the forthcoming congressional elections. The prospect that the president might even be impeached if he failed to act against the missiles had come up in conversation between the Kennedy brothers.[20] Taiwan is important to China for these reasons rather than for its relevance in tipping the global balance of power in a Sino-American struggle for world domination.

As noted, just like their counterparts in Taipei and Washington, Beijing's leaders also have domestic concerns. Nationalism has always been a potent force in Chinese politics and with China's increasing economic and military capabilities, more people are demanding that the government adopt an assertive foreign policy. The government is often criticized for not being tough enough toward Taiwan and the United States. Hsin-Hsin Pan and her colleagues report that their Chinese respondents favor an early resolution of the Taiwan issue, preferring negotiation over the use of force.[21] Elina Sinkkonen, however, finds overwhelming support for military action should Taiwan declare independence.[22] As in Taiwan, then, public opinion on the mainland is not fixed but tends to instead reflect the state of China's relations with Taiwan and the United States. Some evidence indicates, though, that the public is becoming more impatient to resolve the Taiwan issue and that support is increasing for the use of force to resolve it.[23] Several Chinese leaders, including Xi Jinping in a speech on January 2, 2019, have also expressed impatience, indicating that the Taiwan issue "should not be passed down from generation to generation" without a resolution.[24]

Of course, public opinion can constrain leaders' policy discretion but as mentioned previously, these leaders may be able to steer and shape public opinion. The government resorts sometimes to playing the nationalist card when it wants to mobilize public support to oppose foreign pressure or to push back on perceived insults from foreigners. Rather than calming the sense of national indignation and outrage, China's media sometimes tend to abet such feelings. The danger is that, once mass anger is aroused, it will be difficult for officials to contain and control it. Significantly, antiforeign sentiments can quickly become a conduit for the public to vent its frustration and even to show displeasure with unpopular government policies or abusive practices. Therefore, when the government allows and even mobilizes mass protests, it runs the risk that they may get out of hand and the government itself may become their target.[25] Parenthetically, authorities in democracies can also encourage mass demonstrations, such as when Trump incited his supporters to storm the Capitol on January 6, 2021, albeit in this case the target was his own government.

In short, an emerging confluence of developments augurs a dangerous time ahead. We have not yet reached a situation reminiscent of the height of the Cold War, when two contesting sides have little economic interaction but intense military and ideological competition. However, relations between Washington and Beijing are more tense now than at any time since the 1970s, and signs point to increasing investment in military capabilities and decreasing economic interdependence. The eye of this gathering storm is Taiwan, whose contested status is more likely to trigger a Sino-American military showdown than any other issue.[26] Rising Chinese nationalism and military capabilities, shifting Taiwanese identities, and a palpable U.S. impulse to use Taiwan as a lever to irritate and even provoke China are a dangerous combination conducive to conflict escalation and contagion.

Despite occasional frictions and even minor crises, however, the Taiwan Strait has remained peaceful for four decades. The main stabilizing force has been the amicable, even cooperative, relationship between Beijing and Washington. Both sides have been willing to subordinate the Taiwan issue to sustaining their symbiotic relationship. Beijing has also been willing to delay because it has lacked a military capability to take over the island forcibly and because the Kuomintang, which has been generally more opposed to the island's independence, has given it some hope for a peaceful compromise. Beijing has pursued the soft approach, using economic carrots to sway Taiwan's public and especially business opinion in favor of reunification. These hopes have evidently been dashed, and conditions are now shifting against a political resolution to avoid the risk of a military confrontation.

Significantly, Sino-American relations no longer provide the stabilizing ballast to steady the situation but are heading instead in the opposite direction. Taipei now is emboldened to believe that Washington has its back and is therefore more willing to take more provocative policies. Washington's officials and politicians, just like their counterparts in Taipei, are also expressing a stance of getting tough on China, in part also because of domestic partisan politics. The same motivation is evident in China, where popular nationalism inclines officials to stand firm. Moreover, judging by media narratives, Beijing appears to have become more confident that its improved capabilities now empower it to push back more forcefully against Washington and to enable it to coerce Taiwan more effectively than before. Having failed in its soft approach, Beijing is now likely to try a harder one.

Significantly, a harder Chinese approach does not necessarily stem exclusively from its increased military capability and its leaders' confidence in this capability. Among the recent and ongoing developments is closer Washington-Taipei ties. U.S. officials are increasingly departing from practices followed since formal diplomatic relations were established with China, and more U.S. politicians and pundits are advocating a tougher policy stance toward China and stronger support for Taiwan. The justification for this stance is China's recent assertiveness and aggressiveness and its increasing threat to Taiwan. What this argument does not usually try to determine is whether China's assertiveness and aggressiveness may be also a response to what Beijing perceives to be revisionist moves by Taipei and Washington to alter the status quo. A process of reciprocal causality is unfolding such that all three parties believe that they are responding to the others' policies and their responses in turn precipitate the others' responses. Closer relations between Washington and Taipei and their respective words and deeds tend to suggest to Beijing an intention to move the status quo closer to an independent Taiwan. This perception inclines Beijing to increase its deterrence efforts. Recent increased U.S. arms sales to Taiwan and the meetings of their officials in formal settings are clearly provocative to Beijing and thus call for greater efforts on its part to arrest this trend by military threats if necessary. Whether an actor is revisionist depends on the point of reference being used, and the parties concerned use different benchmarks when accusing their counterparts of being revisionist. From Beijing's perspective, it has been trying to restore the status quo ante ever since the United States intervened in June 1950, protecting the Kuomintang government that had fled the mainland and installed itself on the island.

The Taiwan standoff presents a greater danger of military escalation today than any other time since then. It could trigger a Sino-American confrontation. Wars among great powers have often started from a local dispute. The parties involved sometimes find themselves trapped by their own rhetoric and are reluctant to back down for fear of losing their international reputation or domestic credibility.

ASSESSING POWER AS ABILITY AND RESOLVE

Having sketched the general context that is evolving to make the Taiwan Strait the most likely catalyst for a Sino-American clash, we now move beyond power as resources in characterizing the shifting balance of military capabilities across the Taiwan Strait and turn to other factors that are more pertinent to power as ability and power as (control over) outcome.

As argued earlier, ownership or possession of resources can be a misleading indicator of a country's actual capacity to influence an outcome, which can be attenuated or compensated by other factors. One well-known factor is the "loss-of-strength gradient."[27] The physical distance separating a crisis from a country's home territory matters. The greater this distance, the greater its projection of power is diminished. Thus, should there be a military confrontation over Taiwan, the United States will be disadvantaged by this consideration whereas, other things being equal, China will have more of a home court advantage even though other factors may offset the relative U.S. disadvantage because it has nearby allies and bases, such as in Guam, South Korea, and Japan (acknowledging that whether Washington is able to use its assets in Korea and Japan in a Taiwan contingency is not a certainty). The Taiwan Strait is a contested zone in which the United States does not command its usual undisputed military superiority. Christopher Layne argues for attention to how U.S. and Chinese military power stack up regionally in East Asia rather than globally.[28]

The "stopping power of water" favors Taiwan and the United States.[29] To plan and undertake an amphibious attack is challenging even in the best of circumstances. This difficulty is attested by the Normandy invasion in World War II, and by the disastrous failures when the Spanish

Armada attempted to invade England in 1588 and the Mongols sought to conquer Japan in 1274 and 1281. Unless the invader controls the air and sea, its flotilla is subject to attack while in transit. Even in normal circumstances, the defensive side enjoys an advantage over the offensive side.

Beyond factors that may enhance or hamper the respective parties' ability to use their resources is the consideration of their relative stake in a dispute and their commitment to their cause. The distance of a potential flashpoint from a country's homeland can be a proxy of its likely resolve and stake. Ceteris paribus, the closer is a dispute to a country's homeland, the greater will be its resolve to stand firm and the larger will be its stake in this dispute's outcome. Accordingly, the U.S. advantage in capabilities is offset by China's likely greater commitment to its cause. Oriana Mastro, however, takes the opposite view, that China does not doubt Washington's resolve but instead questions its capability.[30] China was much weaker when it fought the United States in Korea. Beijing nonetheless decided to resist because, relative to the United States, it had a larger stake given Korea's strategic importance for its security. Despite Washington's repeated assurances to both Saigon and Kabul, it abandoned them because it in the end considered these fights to involve only its peripheral interests.

No matter what Washington says or does, it will find it difficult to convince Beijing that it has a larger stake than Beijing does in the defense of Taiwan and is more resolved to defend it than Beijing is committed to reunify China. Whereas the United States has many interests and concerns all over the world, China has put the question of Taiwan at the very top of its national priorities. It is far less clear, even doubtful, that the United States gives the same importance to Taiwan. Washington was willing to switch its diplomatic recognition from Taipei to Beijing when it wanted Beijing's help to oppose the Soviet Union and to end the Vietnam War. The Vietnam conflict also suggests that Washington's commitment to an ally can be severely shaken when it is not able to prevail militarily in a reasonably short time. As casualties mount and domestic opposition increases, its resolve may weaken, as suggested by its other experiences in Afghanistan, Iraq, Korea, and Somalia (recall the Blackhawk Down incident). Moreover, even though the United States commands tremendous military assets and destructive power, it faces severe constraints in using this capability given domestic and international opinion.

This discussion also raises the question of national unity and social cohesion. As just implied, the United States failed in Vietnam not because it did not have the military means to prevail and not because it was defeated on the battlefield. Instead, it failed because of domestic opposition to the war. This proposition in turn raises the question which side of a potential conflict over Taiwan is more likely to face internal dissension, especially when the conflict becomes protracted and its costs begin to mount. Power as ability and power as outcome depend on not only the ownership of resources, but also intangible qualities such as a people's dedication to their cause and their willingness to endure privations and make sacrifices.

Officials in Washington face varying constraints by public opinion when they consider military intervention abroad. A 2019 survey by the Chicago Council on Global Affairs reported that 59 percent of its respondents opposed using U.S. troops if China invades Taiwan and that 55 percent were similarly opposed in the event of a military conflict between China and Japan over their disputed islands in the East China Sea.[31] A more recent survey in 2020 conducted by the Center for Strategic and International Studies reported that 54 percent of its American respondents saw China as presenting the greatest challenge to the United States, but only 22 percent viewed Russia in this role.[32] Both U.S. opinion leaders and Americans generally expressed a willingness in this poll to take on significant risks to work with allies and partners even if it damages relations with China. On a scale of 1 (least) to 10 (most), the mean for U.S. opinion leaders to defend Taiwan if it comes under threat from China was 7.93 versus 6.69 for the public at large. Thus it appears that Americans have recently become more supportive of assisting Taiwan.

Public opinion is subject to change, reflecting the development of international events and how policy elites choose to frame them. American views of China have become decidedly more negative recently. At the same time, public support for the pursuit of liberal internationalism, a hallmark of post-1945 U.S. foreign policy, has also eroded over the long term. Peter Harris and Peter Trubowitz make the important point that domestic politics can impose a loss in the amount of U.S. "useable power" on the world stage even though U.S. power (as resources) has not waned. In their view, "the US political system has become a weak foundation upon which to build any ambitious foreign-policy superstructure."[33]

Offsetting the U.S. advantage in power as resources, China appears to have an edge in more intangible qualities. Put simply, China has a larger stake in the future of Taiwan than the United States and Beijing's commitment to national reunification is presumed to be greater than that of Washington to defend an informal ally whose fate does not directly affect its core national interest. The United States can undoubtedly impose more destruction and casualties on its opponent, but its counterpart can compensate this phenomenon by having a higher threshold to accept pain and hardship and to fight longer and harder. This willingness is the key to explaining why powerful countries sometimes lose wars to weaker adversaries.

The costs of war include more than lives lost and properties destroyed. They encompass care for veterans and wounded soldiers and the money that could have been spent on other worthwhile social projects. They also pertain to a country's reputation. Vietnam and Afghanistan were costly to the United States in part because Washington's reputation as a reliable ally was seriously damaged. Switching diplomatic recognition from Taipei to Beijing had a similar, albeit obviously much more attenuated, effect. It raised questions about whether a foreign country should take Washington's commitments seriously. Trump's America First policy has had a similar effect in arousing doubts around the world about U.S. steadfastness. Naturally, the more often a country's leaders declare their support for another country and the more authoritative the person making this declaration, the more credible its professed commitment should be. This declaration communicates to the international audience a country's intention, reflecting what James Fearon calls "tying hands" to make threats or promises more credible.[34] In making repeated public announcements about this intention, leaders tie their hands so that should they fail to carry it out, they will suffer a reputation loss domestically and internationally. They will be subject to criticisms and even face political challenges that can cause them to lose popularity or their office. Thus, by deliberately exposing themselves to these adverse consequences, tying hands is supposed to enhance the credibility of a declared policy intention so that foreigners will not dismiss their words as cheap talk or hot air. This proposition implies that leaders of democracies should be more able to communicate their intentions credibly because relative to their authoritarian counterparts, they are more likely to suffer the consequences of being held accountable should they renege on their announced commitment.

EXTENDED DETERRENCE AND
STRATEGIC AMBIGUITY

Still, matters are not so simple. Naturally, whether President Joe Biden says publicly that the United States will come to Taiwan's aid carries more weight than statements by a Florida senator who may be angling for publicity and partisan gain. Moreover, a country's historical record and its power standing in the world are pertinent. Do leaders who renege on their policy promises in fact pay a political price? Does empirical evidence support the claim of audience cost? Michael Tomz reports this evidence based on survey experiments involving U.S. subjects.[35] Xiaojun Li and Dingding Chen also show it in their research involving Chinese subjects.[36] But analyses of actual historical episodes show that U.S. leaders usually paid only a minor political price, if any, for empty threats.[37] If we can rely on this historical evidence, then tying hands does not provide the necessary assurance that those making these public declarations of support for an ally are necessarily sincere by deliberately exposing themselves to serious political fallout (the so-called audience cost should they fail to carry out the promised policy course). Moreover, even if sincere, such leaders may be constrained by circumstances that prevent them from honoring their pledge, a phenomenon Robert Putnam calls "involuntary defection."[38] When this phenomenon is likely, declarations may not be taken seriously.

In late 2021 and early 2022, Biden tried to deter Vladimir Putin from making an aggressive move against Ukraine. Biden warned that dire consequences would follow such action and yet made it clear that direct military intervention by the United States is not in the cards. Obviously, a country should demonstrate that it is willing to take on serious costs and run great risks so that its deterrence threat is made more credible. This remark in turn raises the question that by taking direct military intervention off the table, whether the United States is in fact signaling it cares less about Ukraine than, say, an ally, a member of the North Atlantic Treaty Organization, that it will defend with its own troops. This episode also reminds us of the possible presence of indirect audiences. For example, what inferences will Beijing draw from the Ukraine situation to update its assessment of a possible showdown over Taiwan?

Fearon presents another course of action a leader may adopt to make foreign counterparts take a state's declared intention seriously. He speaks of "sunk cost" as another (not mutually exclusive) approach to "tying hands."[39] By sunk costs, he has in mind tangible military or diplomatic preparations, such as signing a mutual defense treaty with an ally, deploying troops on the ally's front lines, establishing military bases there, and forming a unified command for the two countries' combined forces. By making these investments, a country is providing credible information about its future intention to defend an ally. Significantly, sinking costs involves taking on ex ante costs. It calls for investments before a crisis happens. In contrast, tying hands involves potential ex post costs. In other words, tying hands entails a price only when a purported commitment is exposed as an empty threat. If this commitment is not challenged, an insincere leader will have gotten away with the bluff. Even if this leader's bluff is called, the research mentioned earlier suggests that the political cost may be quite minor, even insignificant. Thus, signaling by sinking costs seems to indicate a more serious and thus credible commitment than just verbal declarations (or tying hands).

So what? The more powerful a country, the more likely it is to bluff. Less powerful countries are reluctant to call its bluff even when they suspect one. They are reluctant because should they be wrong, they would pay a heavy price. Conversely, calling the bluff of a less powerful country has less adverse consequences even if it turns out to be the wrong decision. In other words, a powerful country has more incentive to bluff because it can reasonably expect to get away with it. It can also more afford to pay the reputation costs for breaking promises and making empty threats, because these costs are offset by its overwhelming power. Foreign audiences will have to reckon with this reality even if they have doubts about this country's real intentions.

As suggested earlier, a failure to keep promises or carry out threats may reflect daunting domestic constraints rather than an intention to lie or mislead. Leaders of democracies naturally face stronger domestic constraints than their authoritarian counterparts. Veto groups are more numerous in democracies, where leaders need to satisfy a larger and more diverse selectorate and may therefore be less able to follow through on their announced policy intentions. The consequent "involuntary defection" suggests that even though democracies' leaders are hypothesized to be more subject to domestic audience costs, incentivizing them to keep their promises and follow through on their threats, they may still be less able to honor their announced intentions even if they want to do so.

Extended deterrence to protect an ally is inherently less believable than a threat to fight back if one's own homeland is attacked. Accordingly, threats of extended deterrence require more effort to make them believable. This means that Washington needs to try harder to convince Beijing that it cares more about Taiwan's fate than Beijing does. In terms of sinking costs and tying hands, South Korea is the closest parallel to Taiwan. Beijing's leaders can be expected to ask what these two cases have in common and how they are different in regard to Washington's attempts at extended deterrence. In the case of South Korea, the United States has formally declared its willingness to intervene on Seoul's behalf if it is attacked. It has also made substantial tangible investments such as signing a security treaty with Seoul and establishing military bases and deploying troops in South Korea. That is, it has undertaken both tying hands and sinking costs in communicating the seriousness of its commitment to defend South Korea. What about Taiwan? The United States withdrew its military installations from the island and unilaterally abrogated its security treaty with the island when it derecognized Taipei in deference to Beijing. This situation may change in the future. As reported earlier, Washington has initiated high-level official contacts with Taipei in an obvious break from precedents followed in the years since establishing formal diplomatic relations with Beijing. It has not, however, stationed any combat troops or joined any formal defense arrangements with Taipei, at least not publicly. Therefore, from Beijing's perspective, U.S. commitment to Taiwan's defense is clearly not as strong as it is to South Korea.

Moreover, Washington's declared policy of strategic ambiguity is puzzling. As Fearon explains, a commitment to deter a prospective attack involves a binary choice of all or nothing. For instance, when trying to prevent an assault on my daughter, I will threaten a prospective attacker that I will definitely fight him if he touches her. To say in this situation that I may fight him undermines my credibility. Beijing will naturally ask how a sincerely committed defender can be expected to act relative to one who is equivocating. It will assume that the deliberate ambiguity in U.S. policy means that Washington is not fully committed to Taiwan's defense under all foreseeable circumstances. By refusing to specify clearly and publicly the conditions under which it will intervene on Taiwan's behalf, the United States obviously wants to keep its options open rather than to tie its hands.

This inference, however, does not deny the possibility of a good reason for the United States to be ambiguous. Washington would be rightly concerned with the moral hazard of giving a definite guarantee to defend Taiwan, which would have the perverse effect of incentivizing Taipei to announce formal independence and thereby to precipitate a Chinese attack that the United States seeks to prevent in the first place. Moreover, to the extent that Taipei can expect Washington to come to its aid, it will be less inclined to increase its own defense efforts. That is, Taipei may take a free ride on a prospective U.S. security guarantee. (In the blame game after the Taliban's victory, the Biden administration argued that the Afghan government's failure to fight for itself was the chief reason for its collapse.) Naturally, were Washington to suggest by its words and deeds that it would stand aside should China attack Taiwan, Beijing would likely be encouraged to use force against Taipei—something Washington also wants to prevent. These competing considerations thus inherently give rise to tension. This tension was clear in British diplomacy before World War I. London did not want to clearly and definitely commit to support France out of concern that Paris might use this commitment to pursue its own agenda and even to provoke Germany. Britain's deterrence threat against Germany suffered as a result, inclining Berlin to entertain the ultimately false hope until the very last days before war broke out that London could and would remain neutral.[40]

Given the history of its relations with Washington, Beijing would not be unreasonable to conclude that Taiwan's importance to the United States is derivative, this is, secondary. Washington's policy on Taiwan is about its policy on China. In this view, Taiwan is important to the United States because it is important to China, and that the United States has been willing to sacrifice Taiwan's interests when reconciling with China is a priority, such as when Washington derecognized Taipei in favor of Beijing. Taiwan is therefore of instrumental value to Washington, providing the United States with a constant thorn to irritate Beijing and a lever to pressure it. To put it bluntly, this perspective suggests that Washington has more to gain from an unsettled Taiwanese status than from a resolved one.

Taiwan is worth more to the United States as a bargaining chip if the current state of unsettled affairs continues indefinitely. North Korea provides a parallel that gives Beijing leverage to seek concessions from Washington and Seoul for its cooperation.

Why should China put up with this situation of protracted stalemate? Washington's policy of strategic ambiguity perpetuates rather than resolves the current situation. It is a policy of dual deterrence, seeking to prevent China from attacking Taiwan and Taiwan from declaring formal independence.[41] Beijing's leaders may naturally wonder whether it is designed precisely to foster Taipei's de facto independence. By threatening to intervene against a Chinese attack on Taiwan, Washington has intended to enable (and achieved) Taipei's continued existence as a separate political entity and to frustrate indefinitely China's national priority of reunification. The threat of U.S. intervention has, moreover, encouraged the increasingly popular sentiment in Taiwan for de jure independence. Beijing's leaders have been waiting for nearly seventy-five years. How long can their patience be expected to last, especially now their military capabilities have increased and their soft approach attempting to court the support of Taiwan's people has seemingly failed to win them over to the cause of national reunification?

As mentioned, conditional or qualified threats to fight are inherently not believable. Washington's policy of strategic ambiguity, however, gives it flexibility at the expense of credibility. "Who started it" will always be contested, which in turn leaves open any option for the United States to choose after a crisis has occurred. Washington is free to assign the responsibility for this crisis to either Beijing or Taipei, thereby retaining the discretion to act in whichever way it chooses. In contrast, a flat-out declaration that A will defend C regardless of circumstances is more believable to B because A has deliberately denied itself any escape to evade its commitment to C.

The upshot of this discussion is that the current situation is dangerous not only because a confluence of trends seems to be constraining the policy space, or win set, for all involved parties, but also because of the likelihood of misjudgment due to Washington's policy of strategic ambiguity. Errors of misjudgment can of course be compounded by motivated bias and partisan incentives to seek domestic political gains, as discussed in chapter 4. The possibility of misjudgment remains even though, in my view, given their frequent communication and extensive experience from past crises, the parties should know well each other's concerns and intentions. This knowledge, however, does not necessarily mean that war is impossible or even unlikely, as shown by the recurrent violent encounters between Israel and its Arab neighbors, India and Pakistan, and North and South Korea (involving parties that should know their counterparts very well because of cultural affinity or extensive past experiences of interaction, or both). States sometimes cause deliberate confusion. At least on three occasions, President Biden answered "yes" publicly when asked whether the United States would intervene if Taiwan were attacked—only to have the White House walk back his words the next day, declaring that there has not been a change in U.S. policy.

Debate is ongoing whether the United States ought to change its policy toward Taiwan from strategic ambiguity to strategic clarity, declaring publicly its commitment to defend the island against a Chinese attack.[42] The main impetus to advocating a policy change has clearly been China's increasing military capabilities (as discussed, the claim that Beijing has acted more assertively or aggressively in recent years being much more open to debate). To offset the change in Chinese capabilities, the United States could try to augment its capabilities or to demonstrate its increased resolve. The proposed change to strategic clarity is of course intended to demonstrate U.S. resolve. But, as discussed, this change also presents a moral hazard that could encourage Taipei to use the U.S. commitment to serve its own agenda of declaring de jure independence (or to invest less in its military capabilities in the expectation that the United States would defend it), thus provoking a Chinese attack that the U.S. policy is intended to deter in the first place. It is not clear whether those who advocate that the United States should clearly and publicly commit itself to Taiwan's defense have in mind primarily the proposed policy's effect on deterring Beijing, reassuring Taipei, or influencing domestic audiences in the United States. Naturally, this change means locking in U.S. policy, a move toward self-binding (or tying hands) that reduces Washington's discretion and increases its costs to reverse its policy in the future. Perhaps the intention behind the proposed policy change is to initiate and publicize a debate that is, in and of itself, intended to signal to Beijing the shifting views of Washington's policy establishment.

It has been argued that Washington's current policy of strategic ambiguity inclines both Beijing and Taipei to engage in "salami tactics" to probe where the actual U.S. "red line" lies. Of course, a counterargument can be made that once Washington declares its red line, the new policy could encourage both Beijing and Taipei to make moves toward this line but not beyond it, moves they might not have considered previously. Moreover, having declared the line, the reputation cost to Washington would be more severe if it were to fail to honor its commitment. One example is when Barack Obama declined to carry out his threat when Bashar al-Assad used chemical weapons in Syria's civil war. Naturally, a public declaration by the United States to defend Taiwan would be seen by Beijing as a provocation and a violation of Washington's previous acknowledgment and commitment to Beijing that Taiwan is a part of China. A public declaration of U.S. commitment to defend Taiwan not only engages U.S. reputation but also challenges China's. Thomas Schelling reminds us that in addition to considering one's own credibility, it is "equally important . . . to help to decouple an adversary's prestige and reputation from a dispute; if we cannot afford to back down we must hope that he can, and if necessary, help him [to do so]."[43] A change of U.S. policy to strategic clarity could tie the hands of leaders in both Washington and Beijing.

Thus reputation and audience costs are also pertinent for China. With nationalism seemingly on the rise, Chinese leaders face the prospect of domestic censure and the loss of power if they are perceived to be soft on the core national issue of Taiwan. This potential cost is not limited to democracies, where voters and political opponents can hold a leader making false promises or empty threats to account. Recall that Nikita Khrushchev was ousted from office by his domestic detractors after the Cuban missile crisis. Although China had sparked crises over the Taiwan Strait but then decided to pull back on several occasions, it was ruled by Mao Tse-tung and Deng Xiaoping, dominant leaders at that time. Mao had the power and authority to decide China's foreign policy unilaterally, such as when he welcomed Richard Nixon to Beijing in 1972 and offered to set aside the Taiwan issue to secure Sino-American rapprochement. It is not clear that China's current leaders, including Xi Jinping, have the same stature and authority to make such deals. They are not in the same position as their predecessors, who were veterans from the Chinese Communist Party's formative years, to switch on and off a Taiwan crisis so easily.

Having initiated crises and then terminated them when the United States threatened to intervene, Chinese leaders have already suffered a reputation or audience cost. By pulling back in prior episodes, Beijing has shown that it lacked the capability or the resolve, or both, to confront Washington. It therefore seems reasonable to expect it to be more reluctant and cautious about initiating another confrontation. I have mentioned that Chinese officials had to put up with Clinton's 1996 deployment of two U.S. carrier groups in Taiwan's vicinity because they were unable to do anything about it. I also have introduced the idea of self-selection, referring to an actor's strategic anticipation such that it will only put itself in a situation that it believes will produce a rewarding outcome for it. In other words, one would not knowingly put oneself in a situation that will end in heavy reputation or audience costs.

What does this reasoning imply? With past crisis outcomes over Taiwan as the background, if Beijing were to initiate another crisis, it would likely be more confident that it would not be repeating its mistakes and incurring additional reputation or audience costs. Indeed, these costs would be more severe the next time Beijing pulled back from a confrontation it instigated because such costs are cumulative. Moreover, China is supposed to have become stronger since the earlier episodes. The logical inference is that, given another crisis over the Taiwan Strait, Chinese leaders must have concluded that they have a greater chance of succeeding or they are simply more determined to have their way.[44]

On the eve of World War I, Russian leaders became more resistant to yielding to German pressure because they had already done so on previous occasions. They were concerned that to do so again would escalate their reputation or audience cost and result in an irreversible setback for them, especially their position in the Balkans. They therefore decided to stand firm against Germany's final demands in 1914, contributing to the outbreak of war.[45] They did so even though they realized that their country was still weaker than Germany and even though they expected that in a few years' time Russia would have significantly improved its strategic position.

WHAT CAN DECISION THEORIES TELL US?

Prospect theory teaches us that people are more disposed to take risks when they attempt to reverse or prevent a loss than when they seek to make gains.[46] Whether people see a loss or gain depends on their point of reference. Significantly, people have different ideas about whether they and their counterparts are grappling with a situation of prospective gain or loss. From Taiwan's perspective, a Chinese takeover would mean a loss of Taiwanese autonomy. From the U.S. perspective, it would mean the loss of a de facto ally. Conversely, Washington would see this as a gain for China, given that Beijing would have expanded its territory and extended its influence over a part of the world that has so far escaped its control.

Beijing is unlikely to share the same framing of the situation. Taiwan has been a loss for it since Truman's order in 1950 for the U.S. naval intervention to prevent a Chinese takeover of the island. Had it not been for this intervention, Beijing would have completed its mission of unifying the mainland and Taiwan under the communist government. From Beijing's perspective, the Taiwan issue is a matter of recovering sovereignty and territory that rightly belong to China. The U.S. media and academic discourse often observes that Taiwan has not been governed by Beijing since the founding of the communist government in 1949, implying that China is the aggressor in seeking to change the status quo. One rarely hears the same narrative about the Jewish people's wish to return to their ancestral homeland, even though they had not ruled this territory for centuries.

People who face setbacks and losses are typically more reluctant to adjust their reference point to a new reality, an adjustment that would require them to acknowledge and accept a setback or loss, something that can be psychologically uncomfortable and difficult for them to do. Conversely, people who have made gains are more likely to adjust quickly their reference point. The discrepancy in the timing of these adjustments is one cause for contentious international relations, such as when a rising power demands recognition for its newly gained power while an established power continues to feel entitled despite its relative decline. In regard to Taiwan's status, the reference point for the Chinese people is not the current situation but instead that when the Kuomintang government fled to Taiwan after its defeat on the mainland. The allies who won World War II had agreed that this island, which was a Japanese colony during the war, should be returned to China (Japan had acquired Taiwan as a result of the Treaty of Shimonoseki in 1895 after it defeated the Qing dynasty).

Recent and ongoing trends in Taiwan, as already discussed, suggest that the prospect for reunification is fading for Beijing. When ongoing trends suggest a deteriorating situation and the prospect of a permanent and irreversible loss, an actor's inclination to take risks increases. Motivated bias may further exaggerate this actor's belief in its ability to reverse loss. The resulting psychological impulses can thus contribute to an elevated danger of war or confrontation.

Discrepant reference points and a failure to adjust them to new realities can thus be a cause for disagreements and disputes. This situation can be complicated because even politicians and officials belonging to the same state may adopt different reference points, creating the impression of moving goalposts. Thus, an administration can change its predecessor's policies, causing confusion about what should be the benchmark for reaching an agreement with a foreign counterpart. For example, reflecting more the Kuomintang's traditional view that there is one China and Taiwan is part of it, Taiwan's President Ma Ying-jeou was inclined to agree with Beijing on the so-called 1992 Consensus declaring this principle. His successor Tsai In-wen, representing the pro-independence Democratic Progressive Party, however, was not willing to accept this premise as the baseline for negotiating with Beijing.[47]

As mentioned, sometimes different parts of the same state may present different reference points to the outside world. Thus, although the executive branch of the U.S. government has acknowledged Beijing as the legitimate government of China and Taiwan as part of China, the legislative branch has offered a different view, such as when it enacted the Taiwan Relations Act and other legislation more sympathetic to Taiwan. This may be a deliberate ploy to maximize a state's diplomatic flexibility or discretion, or a reflection of discordance in the democratic process. These interpretations need not be mutually exclusive.

This discussion suggests that all three parties involved in the Taiwan Strait dispute are likely to feel that they are in the domain of prospective loss and, as suggested by prospect theory, be disposed to take more risks. Rationalist theory based on cost-benefit analysis cautions them against taking these risks. Such an analysis can tell Beijing's leaders that even if it is successful in a military takeover of the island, a large segment of Taiwan's political economy would be destroyed and the prospective support of Taiwan's people lost, turning its endeavor into a pyrrhic victory. An outright military attempt by Beijing to take over the island would therefore be a last resort, only to be considered after Beijing had exhausted all other options. Much of the existing literature tends to focus on how the balance of military forces (including the threat of U.S. intervention) can influence Beijing's willingness or incentive to start a war. It tends to overlook the issue of Beijing's self-deterrence or self-restraint due to the prospect that even if it should succeed in a military attempt to coerce or occupy Taiwan, the victory might be hollow.

Similarly, even if somehow Taiwan, with U.S. assistance, were to avoid a direct military attack from China after declaring de jure independence, it would face severe economic and political fallout. This possibility would make its current situation comparatively more attractive. Moreover, its continued autonomy would depend on perpetual U.S. military protection. This outcome would also be a pyrrhic victory for Taiwan, and one that applies equally to the United States. Britain's defeat of Argentina in Argentina's quest to take over the Falklands/Malvinas offers a lesson. The so-called victory committed Britain to defend indefinitely these faraway, sparsely populated islands with little economic or military value, a commitment it had rather preferred not to take on before the Argentinians invaded the islands.

Bueno Aires' misjudgment when it decided to invade, thinking that London would not respond to a fait accompli, was a serious one. Instead, British prime minister Margaret Thatcher insisted on recovering the islands even though they had little economic or military value. The Argentinian generals did not take into account the domestic motivations of and pressures on Britain's politicians and officials, much less their emotional attachment to the islands. Domestic lobbies and partisan competition to ride a nationalist surge inclined British leaders to adopt a "get tough" policy relying on the military to retake the islands from Argentinian control. A British cabinet member is said to have confided to a reporter, saying, "To be frank, I don't see how she [Margaret Thatcher] can survive [politically] if she shrinks from a military showdown."[48] Before the war, British backbenchers had frustrated every attempt by Whitehall to work out a compromise, claiming that their own government was undermining British sovereignty and selling out the islanders' right to self-determination. The trouble with rationalist cost-benefit theorizing is that it assumes a unitary actor when in fact domestic politics can incline leaders with partisan interests to adopt policies that are suboptimal for their country but beneficial to their personal political fortunes. Moreover, such analysis tends to not adequately emphasize the emotional basis for conflicts.

On the other side of the Atlantic, Argentinian officials faced even more serious peril, politically and even personally, if they were to "sell out" their country's patrimony. They reportedly feared a "lynching" by their citizens if they were to succumb to a humiliating settlement over the Falklands/Malvinas.[49] Motivated in part by domestic politics to launch an invasion, the junta became locked in a bellicose course of action even in the face of military defeat and political dismissal. Even though cooler heads making a rational cost-benefit analysis would have cautioned against a reckless move entailing great risks and elusive returns, both sides of the conflict pushed ahead and are now stuck in a stalemate worse than the situation facing them before the 1982 war.

The islanders (the Kelpers) had played an influential role in the lead-up to war. Before 1982, they had welcomed various gestures of economic assistance and political concession from Argentina, which is much more closely located to them than Britain. They had, however, always declined to extend the reciprocity Buenos Aires had expected of them, namely, some form of accommodation recognizing Argentinian sovereignty. They had wanted to have their cake and eat it too: having access to Argentina and its economic assets yet retaining their political affiliation with Britain. The talks between Buenos Aires and London, involving the Kelpers as a party at the table, dragged on for years without a resolution, which led the Argentinians to feel that they had been strung along. They became increasingly frustrated and "came increasingly to believe, and not without reason that they were behaving like the proverbial donkey, tricked into pulling the cart by a carrot on a stick dangled before him."[50] The parallel to the situation across the Taiwan Strait is clear.

CONCLUSION

States do not fight about power transitions.[51] They fight over issues or, more specifically, grievances over issues. Cost-benefit analysis tells us about how cool-headed people with a rational perspective and long-term view would have acted. The problem is that states are not monolithic,

unitary actors. Instead, subnational players within each state are motivated by different interests and agendas to push or pull foreign policy in a
direction that best serves them. Domestic partisan politics can abet the
danger of war. Moreover, people can succumb to various forms of motivated bias. Sometimes, in making political choices, actors are swayed
by the ideal situation they prefer rather than by the feasible alternatives
that exist. In their quest for the ideal, they often end up in a worse place
than their current situation.

The stars must be aligned for all the relevant parties for a peaceful resolution to their dispute to be found. The window for settlement must be
open for all of them, which suggests that their political clocks must be in
sync and their prevailing domestic political conditions must enlarge rather
than constrain the respective political leaders' policy space or win set.
Obviously, when the number of concerned parties increases from two to
three, as in this case involving Beijing, Taipei, and Washington (disregard-
ing for the moment various stakeholders in each state), the odds for
the stars to become aligned get smaller compared to a strictly bilateral
dispute.

Significantly, current trends in all three principal parties to the dispute
over Taiwan's status indicate that the window for a peaceful settlement
appears to be closing. The respective leaders face political headwinds in
any effort to reach a compromise based on mutual accommodation.
Indeed, they face strong political disincentives to reach out to their counterparts lest they be accused by their respective domestic constituents for
being weak in dealing with their opposite numbers. Rather than trying
to reassure their counterparts, the leaders of each side have taken actions
that the other side will see as provocative. They have been pulling at the
opposite ends of a rope that makes the knot more difficult to untie. As
mentioned before, once leaders get on an escalator that dials up tension,
they often find it difficult to jump off from it for fear that such a reversal
would be interpreted as a sign of weakness by their adversary and an indication of betrayal by their associates.

As mentioned in chapter 2, in assessing the outcome of an influence
encounter, we should consider the context. In a guerrilla war, the insur-
gents win if they do not lose. In the current context, that Taiwan has been
able to maintain its de facto autonomy is clearly a win for it. Perpetuating
this situation frustrates Beijing's goal of national reunification. Taiwan is

an independent state in fact if not in name. Moreover, the United States has thus far managed to sustain this situation without causing China to attack Taiwan, even as it has used the Taiwan issue as leverage over China. Sustaining the current situation of denying Taiwan to China while preventing a Chinese attack is ideal for Washington.

This framing naturally raises the question of why Beijing would accept the current situation in perpetuity, especially given that ongoing trends are making its goal of national reunification more difficult to reach. Even though China's military capabilities have increased, Taiwan's evolving public opinion and deteriorating Sino-American relations point to this greater difficulty. As Taiwan's people become more supportive of de jure independence, Beijing is likely to feel the need to apply greater military pressure to offset this unfavorable trend. Public opinion in Taiwan suggests that Beijing's threat to use force is the main reason restraining Taipei's pursuit of formal independence. Popular support for formal independence is also conditional on Taiwan people's perception of likely U.S. reaction. Beijing thus sees the United States playing a pivotal role. Whereas Washington has previously restrained Taiwan's pro-independence politicians, such as Chen Shui-bian, its recent words and deeds may encourage them, which would in turn require Beijing to undertake more vigorous deterrence efforts. In the context of rising Sino-American tension, Taiwan has become more important in Washington's policy to contain China. Thus, perhaps paradoxically, a crisis over Taiwan could unfold not because of a more optimistic China but because of a more pessimistic one.

Significantly, leaders in Taipei are not unaware that Taiwan is a pawn in U.S. policy on China. They certainly recognize that on several occasions Washington has signaled that it would abandon Taipei for reasons of domestic politics or foreign grand strategy. U.S. withdrawal from South Vietnam and Afghanistan are still fresh in memory. Taipei is fully aware that despite Washington's rhetoric on self-determination and democracy, it is opposed to Taiwan's pursuit of formal independence out of a concern that such a move could provoke China to attack. At the same time, Taipei remembers that Washington had stopped Taiwan's nuclear program in the 1970s and again in the 1980s, leaving it without the means to defend itself except by relying on the United States. Yet, as John Mearsheimer notes, "there is a reasonable chance that American policy makers will eventually conclude that it makes good strategic sense to abandon Taiwan and allow China to coerce it into accepting unification."[52] He continues, "of course, in the near term, the United States will protect Taiwan and treat it as a strategic asset. But how long that relationship lasts is an open question." Taiwan could easily turn into a strategic liability in American eyes. Surely some voices among American scholars question a policy of continued U.S. support for Taiwan.[53]

Wars do not happen out of the blue. Behind every conflict is a history. A serious problem afflicting many studies on the relationship between power transition and war occurrence is their oversight of this legacy. The onset of war is just the final step in a usually long pathway. This outcome is not somehow predetermined. It is conditional on numerous contingencies in a long process involving multiple domestic and foreign actors and in the final analysis is a result of human choices. Contrary to the suggestion of power-transition scholars, international relations are rarely dyadic, pitting the world's two most powerful countries against each other. Large conflagrations tend to start from local disputes and evolve through alliance commitments to become large-scale warfare.

Local crises often function as a catalyst that draws in third parties in a larger conflict. The occurrence or recurrence of many local crises should not come as a surprise because they usually reflect enduring rivalries.[54] This chapter discusses Taiwan, which is most likely to get the United States involved in a confrontation with China. Other long-standing disputes include the tumultuous relations between North and South Korea, India and Pakistan, Israel and Syria, Iran and Saudi Arabia, and Ukraine and Russia. By focusing on these relations, we can gain a better analytic grip on how chronic tension can provide the fuse for larger conflicts involving extra-regional powers.

As mentioned already, wars can rarely be explained by a single cause. Instead, a constellation of factors in combination usually elevates its danger, power transition being just one such possible factor. This constellation has in the past included the tension and mistrust set off by armament races and the bipolarization of states taking sides in opposing alliances. Although in the years immediately after the end of the Cold War these contributors had dissipated, they are now making a comeback. Armament expenditures have been rising for China, the United States, and other major powers. These states are beginning to align themselves in a manner reminiscent of the Cold War years. Members of the European

Union have joined the United States and Canada in sanctioning Russia and China. A new coalition, the Quad—Australia, India, Japan, and the United States—is becoming institutionalized. At the same time, Beijing and Moscow are moving closer in political alignment, military collaboration, and economic cooperation. These recent signs pointing to increasing armament competition and bifurcated alignment are worrisome because they are important conditions that facilitate the onset of war.

Finally, we should remind ourselves again that it is individual leaders' policy choices that are ultimately responsible for wars. The decision to go to war usually reflects a situation in which domestic and foreign circumstances increasingly constrain the menu for choices as leaders see it, inclining them to take the gamble that is called war. At the same time, leaders may be motivated by anger, arrogance, and hubris to adopt bellicose policies. Their judgments, instincts, and personalities matter. Do they have the experience, the fortitude, and the disposition to reach out to their opposite numbers to ease international tension and reduce the danger of war? Or do they further inflame the situation by their rhetoric and action? We know that human emotions such as antipathy, fear, and pride can influence decision-making. The rich and nuanced account told by Thucydides about the Peloponnesian War is full of such insights. We need more social psychological studies on human emotions, which too often undermine expectations derived from rational cost-benefit analysis.

CONCLUSION

This chapter recapitulates my arguments, focusing on major problems in the current literature before turning to a review of recent and current U.S. and Chinese policies and their effects in contributing to ongoing tension. I wrap up with several policy suggestions that could contribute to easing this tension.

THE PROBLEMS WITH CONVENTIONAL NARRATIVES

Complaints about the character of China's government or its human rights record as a source of current Sino-American discord lose their credibility in the context of Washington's having been a much stronger supporter of Taiwan when the island was a garrison state under one-party authoritarian rule. As Taiwan democratized, Washington's support for it weakened, that is, until recently, when it again became useful as leverage over Beijing. Washington and Beijing were also on friendlier terms during the 1970s and 1980s when China was more authoritarian. Realists are generally more honest intellectually, suggesting that national interest as defined by a country's power position is the strongest and basic motivation behind foreign policy. John Mearsheimer acknowledges forthrightly that the

United States was itself an expansionist and aggressive state during its years of ascendance and expects China to follow its footsteps.[1] Similarly, as already mentioned, Graham Allison warns that Americans should be careful in wishing the Chinese to be more like them. Imagine if Xi Jinping were to imitate Theodore Roosevelt, who threatened to go to war against Britain, Spain, and Germany and launched military interventions against U.S. neighbors nine times in the seven years of his presidency.[2]

Power-transition theory is wrong, however, in explaining war as the result of a rising revisionist state seeking to overthrow the international order established by the current but declining hegemon.[3] Judging from a battery of empirical indicators, the United States rather than China has behaved more like a revisionist power in recent years.[4] Characterizing China as such is inaccurate whether comparing its current conduct with its recent past or with U.S. conduct and this characterization is based as well on questionable logical grounds. Why would a rising state want to upend the international order that has enabled its ascent? Why would it not let the ongoing trend be its friend, allowing it to make further possible gains without running the risk of a war? Even though a rising power may have gained a greater ability to alter the existing order more to its liking, it now also has a larger stake in the order and a greater incentive to not rock the boat. Conversely, a declining but still dominant power is more likely to be motivated to change the rules of the game to arrest its decline and still has the greatest capability to undertake such change.

It is also not clear why on empirical grounds Imperial Germany and Imperial Japan are said to be revisionist states. In what ways have their conduct and policy agenda been different from those of other great powers such as Britain, France, Russia, and the United States (or, for that matter, other polities in earlier eras such as the Netherlands, Portugal, Venice, Rome, and Athens, which were once dominant actors in interstate relations) so that they warrant this designation? What have they done or aspired to that the British, French, Russians, and Americans have not? As alluded to previously, if revisionism is defined as a country's increased power to alter the existing interstate distribution of power, all these states qualify as such because they were all once upstarts that later became powerful. Even an incumbent hegemon can be revisionist, according to this definition, when its power increases further, such as when the United States acquired a unipolar status after the Soviet Union's dissolution.

The view that shifting bilateral power balance is the fundamental factor affecting Sino-American relations implies that even if China were to become more democratic, abandon its communist ideology, and pursue more moderate foreign policies, bilateral tension would remain. References to these differences tend to distract and distort, to hide the real cause of discord. China's increased power in and of itself would pose the biggest threat to U.S. interests and primacy in the international political economy. Short of China's agreeing to eschew further growth, which narrows the power disparity between it and the United States, the question becomes whether and in what ways the United States can live with a stronger China, and what costs it is willing to bear to prevent China from becoming stronger.

But the story does not end there. The conundrum deepens when we realize that relations between Beijing and Washington were intensely hostile even when China was much weaker than today, such as during the 1950s and 1960s. Indeed, and ironically, even if China's power were to wane and it becomes weaker and more accommodating to U.S. interests, this occurrence does not necessarily mean that better bilateral relations would follow. Beijing would only have to look at the Soviet Union's experience. Mikhail Gorbachev's unilateral concessions to the West did not ease U.S. pressure for even more concessions. Even though Moscow withdrew the Red Army from eastern Europe, dissolved the Warsaw Pact and the Soviet Union itself, abolished communism as the official ideology and dismantled its planned economy, accepted the reunification of Germany within the North Atlantic Treaty Organization (NATO), and facilitated the establishment of U.S. military bases in Central Asia to fight terrorism, relations between it and Washington have not turned amicable or trusting. From Beijing's perspective, what would it have to do to accommodate Washington? What concessions would reassure Washington rather than embolden it to ask for more concessions? Indeed, it is possible for gestures of conciliation to be mistaken as signs of weakness, thus inviting further pressure from the other side to pile on.[5]

Many Chinese commentators agree that their country's rising power and stature have motivated Washington to pursue more energetic policies to block its further ascent. Realists such as Mearsheimer agree with this view, that the rise of any country would necessarily arouse U.S. concern.[6] Moreover, any rising power would likely become more demanding and aggressive. In Mearsheimer's view, Beijing would follow the precedent Washington set with its expansionist policies when it was a rising power. This view accords analytic primacy to the interstate balance of power and distinctly secondary considerations to factors such as a regime's character and its leaders' personalities.

In this sense, it echoes scholars who have written about the increased danger of war when a rising latecomer catches up to an established dominant power. Power-transition theory points to both world wars as the result of Germany's challenge to British primacy.[7] In a similar vein, Allison warns about Thucydides' Trap, alleging that Athens' rise and Sparta's consequent fear caused the Peloponnesian War.[8] He reports that in sixteen historical episodes when a rising state caught up to a ruling state, twelve ended in a violent confrontation. Both formulations are structural in the sense that they see the dynamics of interstate power shifts to constrain and even overwhelm human beings' ability to control their destiny. Accordingly, leaders are often trapped by circumstances, and history repeats itself when war is a recurrent phenomenon in the context of power transitions.

These formulations often overlook the histories of established powers when they were themselves a rising power and fail to ask how these countries became dominant in the first place. Did they not engage in expansionist policies such as in a quest for overseas colonies and wage war on erstwhile dominant powers that had declined (e.g., Spain, the Ottoman Empire, and Qing China)? Critics have raised various objections about the selection of cases and the analytic logic used to support prevailing Western narratives.[9] Rising states are less likely to confront the incumbent dominant state than to pick on declining or secondary powers.

Prevailing formulations of wars of power transition therefore reflect social and political construction rather than an impartial analysis of international relations. Although few people would deny that China has made significant progress in improving its position and status in the world, the question about the extent of power shift between it and the United States would remain. Is there an ongoing or impending power transition to support the view that China is poised to displace the United States as the world's premier power? Although the production or possession of tangible assets such as territory, weapons, and foreign reserves are not unimportant, they do not in themselves translate directly to influence in a country's external relations. Indeed, it behooves us to consider multiple forms of influence beyond equating it with a direct and overt exertion by A to alter B's behavior.[10]

Moreover, peaceful power transitions are numerous. The only instance in modern history when one country replaced another as the undisputed leader of the world's political economy was the transition from Britain to the United States, and in this case the expectation of war was disconfirmed. Beyond the world's two most powerful countries, many more instances of peaceful power transition have occurred, such as in recent decades when Germany overtook Russia and China overtook Japan. Power transition is not the only factor that elevates the danger of war. Whether countries involved in such a transition have a similar cultural heritage and common political institutions, trade and invest heavily in each other, are caught up in competing alliances and armament races, and are located in close physical proximity to one another are among the pertinent considerations. None of these other variables, however, is decisive in its own right. At the same time, they may even suggest spurious explanations, such as when shared cultural heritage, common political institutions, and extensive commercial relations did not prevent war. These factors may increase the probability of maintaining peace but are clearly insufficient in and of themselves to prevent war.

Equally important, perceptions of an ongoing or impending power transition rather than the reality of this transition are what matters for policymaking. Do leaders see this process unfolding and, if so, why do they sometimes become alarmed and undertake policies that raise mistrust and abet tension? As already mentioned, existing research has largely failed to address the link connecting power shifts at the interstate level of analysis to leaders' perceptions and reactions at the individual or group level of decision-making. Surely, in many past transitions, leaders have not acted with fear or alarm and these occasions have passed peacefully, such as when Germany overtook Russia, Japan overtook Germany, and China overtook Japan. Of course, sometimes leaders disagree in their assessments of their own country's power and that of other countries. On the eve of World War I, for example, the Germans assessed Russia to be stronger than the Russians' own assessment.

How do we know a power transition is happening? Presumably, such a recognition calls for an understanding of what constitutes national power in an age of globalization. Measurements of the output of smokestack industries or the size of a country's population and its infantry are more likely to mislead than inform. Nor can economic production within a country's boundaries be taken to indicate its power because this measure fails to account for the role of multinational corporations in cross-border production processes. China's exports reflect to a large extent the technology, parts, capital, and even management imported from foreign sources, its own workforce often being involved mainly in the assembly of final products to be exported (the value of which is inflated because it does not discount the imported resources).

The fundamental reality is that the most important and profitable parts of cross-border production chains remain the upstream and downstream activities involving product design, branding, and marketing—not the actual assembly work. A country's ability to promote technological innovations and develop pioneering industries points to a far more accurate picture of national power than its physical size. Indeed, global leaders from past eras, whether Portugal, the Netherlands, or Britain, were usually dwarfed by their larger neighbors.

Most studies of national power focus on individual states. This approach has two problems. Systemic wars are usually fought and won by coalitions. Whether Imperial and Nazi Germany had overtaken Britain before both world wars can be debated. Whether Germany's alliances were stronger than the opposing coalitions is less subject to debate. Both contests were highly lopsided, leaving little doubt about their eventual outcome. In today's world, it is fundamentally misleading to present China and the United States in a one-on-one comparison of national power for the simple reason that the United States can count much more confidently on its traditional allies to support it in a possible conflict with China. Which countries will side with China in a possible conflict with the United States, and how much difference will they make in the balance of opposing forces? This perspective in turn puts into serious doubt China's ability to displace the United States and its coalition from the pinnacle of international hierarchy, at least for the foreseeable future.

Relying on states as the basic units of accounting also overlooks the globalization process which has extended a leading country's power beyond its physical boundaries. Significantly, this tendency gives short shrift to the influence conferred on this state by its centrality in networks of interlocking relations, whether financial, economic, military, or technological. For example, the preeminence of U.S. financial institutions in international banking and the primacy of the dollar in international transactions give Washington powerful levers for influence that China and other countries do not have. Those who suggest that the United States is in danger of losing its hegemonic status usually fail to recognize the enduring advantages provided by its structural power in the world. In this view, national power is not something that can be measured in discrete units of tangible assets but needs instead to be seen holistically as inherent in a country's position in the global political economy.

The existing literature is simplistic in assuming that possession of material stocks is tantamount to having national power. This tendency does not address the extent to which officials can effectively extract and use their country's resources for policy purposes. Even though they are outmatched in physical size and material stockpile, the Israelis and North Vietnamese have prevailed over their larger adversaries in part because they are better able to mobilize the resources available to them and to put these resources to effective use. A country's policy capacity matters.[11] Despite its many advantages, the United States has performed relatively poorly in containing the COVID-19 pandemic because of its lack of leadership, social trust, and policy capacity.[12] It leads the world in the number of deaths caused by this virus. Naturally, these ideas pertain to intangible qualities that are much more elusive to capture than counting stockpiles of material assets. Yet overlooking these qualities misses a large part of national power.

WHAT ESTABLISHED POWERS DO ALSO MATTERS

It has been said that Britain has no permanent friends or enemies, only permanent interests. The same aphorism applies to the United States. As Mearsheimer suggests, an enduring goal of Washington's foreign policy has been to prevent another country from accomplishing what it itself has succeeded in doing, namely, to establish a regional hegemony.

In earlier eras, London had alternated its support between France and Prussia/Germany, always seeking to tip the balance in favor of the weaker of the two to prevent the stronger from claiming regional hegemony in Europe. The United States fought the two world wars for the same reason, preventing Germany from claiming hegemony in Europe, and then again in the Cold War, preventing the Soviet Union from the same. In East Asia, the United States has switched its support back and forth between China and Japan, always shifting to the weaker of the two to prevent the other from establishing regional hegemony. It practices the same policy of divide and rule and a regional stalemate between Iraq and Iran, and again between Iran and Saudi Arabia in the Middle East. It continues to support Pakistan as well, to keep it in play as a counterweight to India, and India in turn as a counterweight to China.

Although I criticize power-transition theory and the metaphor of Thucydides' Trap for multiple reasons, their proponents are right in pointing to the shifting power balance as the fundamental factor affecting relations between China and the United States. This acknowledgment does not, however, mean that power balance is the only factor in affecting international relations because, as already noted on several occasions, many power transitions have occurred without war following in their wake. In the case of deteriorating Sino-American relations, shifting power balance offers a more persuasive explanation than other reasons that one often hears. Beijing's record on human rights, its treatment of domestic dissidence, its communist ideology, its economic model, and its basic stance on Taiwan or sovereignty disputes in the South China Sea did not prevent the United States and China from reaching rapprochement and even undertaking cooperation on various previous occasions. Again, Beijing's attitudes and actions on these matters have either not changed or changed in a direction that Washington should welcome. Instead, its growing strength has become concerning to Washington, which feels that it needs to take countermeasures to preserve its primacy.

Power-transition theorists offer us only a partial story of why states sometimes escalate their conflict and even go to war. China's rise, or for that matter the rise of other latecomers such as Russia/the Soviet Union, Prussia/Germany, and Japan, are pertinent to this story. The story, though, needs to be supplemented with a deeper historical and geographic understanding and especially the motivation or rationale for the actions of the dominant power. The one told by power-transition theorists focuses its attention on the ostensibly ambitious and impatient rising upstart but does not attend to the incumbent hegemon's fears, desires, and policies.

This said, it is helpful to repeat that power-transition theory points correctly to the central role played by power or more exactly, the shifting distribution of power, in influencing international relations. Other variables are distinctly secondary. A government's professed ideology, a country's cultural affinity or racial composition, and its democratic or authoritarian institutions are secondary factors influencing an incumbent hegemon's policy toward a rising power. This proposition in turn suggests that even if China were a democracy, its rise would still be a concern for the United States and likely to induce a similar response from Washington to block or contain its increasing power. In the 1970s and 1980s, Japan's rise raised alarm in Washington and caused it to take steps to limit Japan's economic prowess and reach, even though in this case the United States was dealing with a fellow democracy, military ally, and economic partner. Popular books of that period had titles such as *Japan as Number One: Lessons for America, Trading Places: How We Are Giving Our Future to Japan and How to Reclaim It*, and even *The Coming War with Japan*.[13] Of course, Britain did accommodate the United States as a rising power but the world then was characterized by multipolarity and London faced multiple challengers, especially from nearby Germany.

Prevailing U.S. discourse on China's rise, based as often it is on power-transition theory, has two serious flaws. First, it exaggerates this phenomenon because it understates enduring U.S. advantages over China. In fact, as documented in chapter 3, the United States continues to enjoy a large lead that will be difficult for China to surmount in the next two or three decades, if ever. Second, it is too dogmatic in insisting that rising powers necessarily have a revisionist agenda and that an established, dominant power is inevitably committed to the defense of the existing international order. Recent U.S. policies show that an incumbent hegemon can seek to alter, even upend, the existing rules, norms, and institutions of this order. The United States rather than China has acted more like a revisionist power.[14] Getting these two critical aspects of the theory wrong means that power-transition theory is in jeopardy of misattributing the causes of a war should it occur. Indeed, this theory risks the danger of fostering a self-fulfilling prophecy, elevating the danger of a war even when the factual basis for this conflict as postulated by it does not exist.

As Ned Lebow and Benjamin Valentino observe, "Should war come between the United States and China in the future it will not be a result of a power transition. The greater risk is that conflict will result from the misperception that such a transition is imminent, and the miscalculation by decision-makers in the United States (or China) that China will soon be in a position to do what no state has done before—unilaterally dictate the rules of the international system. Power transition theory would be made self-fulfilling—generating its own corroboration where history has failed to oblige."[15]

John Ikenberry argues that the liberal international order can endure even if the United States, the leading state that has fostered and sustained this order, should someday decline.[16] In his view, this order's consensual rules will continue to be self-binding for the major stakeholders, including the rising power that has become integrated into it. The key to this proposition is the cooptation and incorporation of this and other latecomers. Is the club of great powers open to newcomers or do these newcomers face significant barriers to entry? Do the newcomers have a say in updating the order's rules and institutions? As mentioned earlier, Japan faced racial discrimination when it sought to join. The UN Security Council today is a poor reflection of the distribution of power in today's international system. Some countries, such as Britain and France, hold on to their seats even though they have fallen from the front ranks, whereas other countries with larger economies or populations, such as Japan, Germany, and India, are excluded. The discrepancy between a state's achievements and the recognition it receives from others, such as a Security Council seat, is addressed by the theory of relative deprivation.[17] Considerable empirical research points to the anger and frustration that can stem from a large discrepancy between a state's achievements and the recognition accorded to it as a major source of international conflict.[18] More recently, Jonathan Renshon shows persuasively that states suffering a status deficit are more likely to initiate militarized disputes or wars and that they usually win these contests.[19]

A rising state's perception that it has been denied its rightful place in the world tends to be the fundamental reason for its resentment and dissatisfaction.[20] Power-transition theory captures this feeling when it tries to explain why such a state is dissatisfied. This theory, however, refers only to the rising state's demand for recognition; it does not look at the other side of the ledger, namely, the established powers' reaction to the demand. Why do established powers sometimes refuse to extend recognition and accept newcomers as equals? A variety of political, bureaucratic, and psychological reasons are possible, as are ideological and even racial-ethnic ones. It is not rare for declining states to retrench. Countries that have done so have been able to recover their previous rank.[21]

Whether a rising power feels that it is accepted by the established powers is a critical but understudied topic. Power-transition theory's depiction of a dissatisfied rising power is incomplete because it does not pay enough attention to the sources of the dissatisfaction. As Robert Powell remarks, "If the distribution of benefits mirrors the distribution of power, no state can credibly threaten to use force to change the status quo and the risk of war is smallest. If, however, there is a sufficiently large disparity between the distribution of power and benefits, the status quo may be threatened regardless of what the underlying distribution of power is."[22] Status denial to rising powers can thus be a factor even though these states' ambitions, usually the reason for war given by power-transition theory, can also be relevant.

THE BIDEN ADMINISTRATION'S POLICIES

President Joe Biden began his administration by rescinding many of his predecessor's policies, including returning the United States to the Paris climate accord and the World Health Organization. He has not, however, lifted U.S. tariffs on Chinese imports (averaging about 19 percent of these imports' value), even though he argued during his campaign that they were hurting Americans and the U.S. economy. Indeed, he has thus far maintained these tariffs even though inflation in the United States has risen to the highest level in more than forty years. Nor has he reversed actions Beijing perceives as the start of a technological war. Although still in its early days, the Biden administration has not walked back President Donald Trump's unilateral steps that violated the understanding that Washington would refrain from high-level official contact with Taipei. If anything, the Biden administration has continued contacts started by the

Trump administration. Moreover, high-ranking U.S. officials such as Biden's secretary of state, Antony Blinken, continue to use what to Beijing must appear to be inflammatory language, agreeing with Trump's secretary of state Mike Pompeo's designation of China's treatment of Uighurs as "genocide" and its use of "concentration camps" to deny rights to this minority.[23] This rhetoric departs from the customary meaning of the two terms and adds fuel to an already tense situation.

Although the Biden administration has signaled its intention to pursue multilateral diplomacy, it has publicly professed that its aim is to rally its traditional allies to put collective pressure on Beijing.[24] This point is not lost on Beijing, which sees that Biden has changed the ways of but not necessarily the end of U.S. policy to block China's ascent. Moreover, Biden's call to stand up for "our values" sounds to Beijing like a renewal of Washington's policy to remake the world in America's image.[25] This call could turn the current Sino-American competition into an ideological struggle and have other negative ramifications.[26] It may sound more ominous to Beijing than Trump's America First policy in that the latter appears to be more understandable and even more congenial to Chinese officials, reflecting a more go-it-alone approach based on cost-benefit transactions rather than an inclination to export or spread U.S. ideology and its values. Biden's criticisms of China's performance on human rights are received in Beijing with considerable skepticism, given that their timing almost coincided with Washington's decision to refrain from condemning or sanctioning Saudi Arabia for its Crown Prince Mohammed bin Salman's direct involvement in and approval of the murder of a U.S. permanent resident, Jamal Khashoggi, a columnist for the *Washington Post*, in Saudi Arabia's Istanbul consulate.[27]

As already mentioned, China's values and identities have not resonated with the elites and masses of most other countries. Beijing, however, has thus far refrained from undertaking a direct, vigorous campaign to propagate its ideology despite establishing Confucius Institutes abroad. A disinterest in proselytizing and waging an ideological campaign has been a hallmark of its recent diplomacy, differentiating it from Moscow's conduct during the Cold War. Another equally important difference is the intense economic interdependence between China and the United States. "Standing firm on our values" and "decoupling economically" from China are dangerous because they suggest the removal of two important ballasts that have steadied Sino-American relations. They also tend to reflect more domestic than foreign policy considerations. Americans have disagreed strongly among themselves over political and cultural values, and some have questioned the performance of their democratic institutions, especially concerning the integrity of the 2020 presidential election and the storming of the Capitol by Trump's supporters in January 2021. It seems obvious but contests over values are more difficult to resolve because they invoke strong emotions and stress moral judgments. They are, in James Fearon's terminology, about inherently indivisible matters and broach no compromise.[28] Just as in domestic politics, they tend to result in demonizing the opposition and calling for total victory in a struggle between good and evil in international relations. Classical realists have warned about these tendencies, especially the pitfalls of moral crusades.[29]

The Biden administration's policy toward China is different in two important ways from the Trump administration. First, it emphasizes working with U.S. allies to bring collective pressure to bear on Beijing. For example, it rallied its European allies as well as Canada and Japan in demanding that China be more transparent in disclosing the origin of the COVID-19 virus. It has also rallied its allies to boycott cotton produced in Xinjiang and to sanction Chinese officials for suppressing political opposition in Hong Kong. These efforts are an important departure from the Trump administration's tendency to act with unilateral assertiveness. Biden's revival of the Quad is another example of emphasizing multilateral diplomacy. These events suggest that the world is beginning to coalesce into a more bipolar alignment. This said, many European governments have openly questioned the extent to which Washington is committed to multilateralism after its withdrawal from Afghanistan without consulting its NATO allies and even the Afghan government.

Signs also indicate that Russia and China are becoming more aligned strategically. After meeting with his Chinese counterpart in Beijing in March 2021, Russia's Foreign Minister Sergei Lavrov criticized the United States for the "destructive nature" of its intentions to "undermine the UN-centered international legal architecture relying on military-political alliances of the Cold War era and creating new closed alliances in the same vein."[30] During an interview with China's state-run Xinhua News, he emphasized that "China is a truly strategic partner of Russia and a like-minded country, and their mutually trusting and respectful dialogue should serve as an example to other countries," noting that "the formation of a truly multipolar and democratic world, [is] unfortunately being hindered by Western countries, particularly the United States. In response, Russia and China are promoting a constructive and unifying agenda and hope that the international governance system would be fair and democratic." In the wake of Russia's invasion of Ukraine, Western countries have imposed severe sanctions on Moscow, increasing China's value to Russia as an alternate source of economic support. Although Beijing has not yet provided substantial aid to Russia, it has refrained from openly criticizing Russia's aggression. The increasing bipolarization of states' alignment patterns is important because, as suggested in earlier chapters, it is one of the key factors elevating international tension.

Second, the Biden administration endorses strongly a rule-based international system. U.S. secretary of state Antony Blinken publicly berated a high-level Chinese delegation at a March 2021 meeting in Alaska, saying that Beijing's actions "threaten the rules-based order that maintains global stability" and arguing that this is "why they're not merely [China's] internal matters."[31] China's top diplomat Yang Jiechi gave a lengthy rebuttal, questioning in effect which and whose rules Blinken was speaking about and who should judge alleged transgressions. He was possibly recalling President Barack Obama's statement that "America should write the rules. America should call the shots. Other countries should play by the rules that America and our partners set, and not the other way around."[32] Specifically, Yang argued that China would only follow "the United Nations–centered international system and the international order underpinned by international law, not what is advocated by a small number of countries of the so-called rules-based international order."[33]

After a U.S.-Japan joint statement, China's Foreign Ministry spokesperson Zhao Lijian responded in a similar vein, stressing that "there is only one system in the world, and it is the UN-centered international order; there is only one set of rules, and it is the basic norms governing international relations with the UN Charter as its cornerstone."[34] He also emphasized China's sovereignty over Taiwan, Hong Kong, Xinjiang, the South China Sea, and the disputed Diaoyu/Senkaku Islands while accusing "the two countries [the United States and Japan] [of] colluding to meddle in China's internal affairs and malign China."

Another joint U.S.-Japan statement, issued after President Biden and Prime Minister Yoshihide Suga met in Washington in April 2021, stated that they shared "a vision for a free and open Indo-Pacific" and called for "the peaceful resolution of cross-[Taiwan]Strait issues." Responding to this statement, an editorial in *China Daily* warned that "Neither Washington nor Tokyo can pretend that they do not know China's clear-cut stance over issues concerning its core interests. . . . The new US administration . . . has succeeded in displaying the US' hostility toward China. . . . Yet the administration needs to answer the inevitable questions: Where is its anti-China policy heading? Is it prepared to shoulder the dire consequences of decoupling with the Chinese economy or even a full-blown conflict over a regional flashpoint, such as Taiwan or the South China Sea?"[35]

The *China Daily* editorial just mentioned claims that the United States and Japan are quite aware of China's core national interests. Top Chinese and U.S. officials probably understand their counterparts quite well, but the danger of war remains. How can I reconcile these seemingly contradictory views? Although I do not have any direct evidence, U.S. officials are in my opinion correct that Beijing's eventual goal is to oust U.S. influence from China's immediate neighborhood, even though they would be in this case criticizing Beijing for something that the United States itself had done in pursuing the Monroe Doctrine. Chinese officials are also right in their belief that the United States has sought to change China's political system and contain its international influence, blocking its ascent to become a peer.[36] Given that the military balance across the Taiwan Strait is expected to shift even more in favor of Beijing and that Taiwan's economy is already deeply integrated with China's, why is Taipei holding out in reaching a deal with Beijing given that its bargaining power can be expected to erode further in the future? "Time," as Mearsheimer succinctly observes, "is not on Taiwan's side."[37] In addition to its politicians' consideration of public opinion, the other obvious reason is that Taipei thinks Washington has its back. Again, all three parties understand the key role Washington plays. Beijing would not be wrong to believe that the United States presents the major stumbling block to its goal of national reunification. Without U.S. support, Taipei would be far more easily coerced to accept compromises on Beijing's terms. Moreover, despite

Chinese media hype, Beijing realizes (correctly) that China is still considerably weaker than the United States; Washington knows this too.

This said, Washington could underestimate Beijing's determination to stand its ground. Washington could also overestimate its own staying power in a protracted struggle with China. Conversely, Beijing could misjudge the extent to which its behavior has had and will have seriously negative ramifications in other countries, causing them to become more suspicious of its agenda. The danger of confrontation rises when both sides practice diplomatic and military brinksmanship and miscalculate the other side's resolve. Thus, even though both sides probably have a rather accurate assessment of their counterparts' capabilities and an understanding of these counterparts' general intentions, the danger of war remains. Human emotions and domestic politics can also get in the way of making a rational decision. Also significant is the role of "private information,"[38] that is, information only privy to the actor. Thus we still see recurrent wars involving belligerents that have great familiarity with each other, such as Israel and Syria, and India and Pakistan.

Diplomatic honesty pays.[39] Diplomats are less likely to make empty threats or false promises than we usually assume. This is because when they are exposed as dishonest or insincere, their reputation suffers.[40] Hypocrisy is said to be the compliment vice pays to virtue. It is not without cost, however; specifically, the extent to which others are willing to extend trust again. This consideration is naturally pertinent to the debate about whether the United States should abandon its policy of strategic ambiguity about defending Taiwan against a Chinese attack.

It is easy to talk about human rights when concern about their abuse coincides with realpolitik. A true test of whether a country cares about human rights is when its professed commitment to this value clashes with realpolitik. In this situation, one is better able to tell which of these motivations receives a higher priority, and whether expressions of lofty ideals are just excuses or a camouflage for policies undertaken for realpolitik reasons, exposing a country's true color as a fair-weather supporter of human rights. Washington's reactions to Khashoggi's murder and to the Rwanda genocide, as well as its inaction or underreaction in other human rights episodes involving Haiti, Myanmar, Somalia, Darfur, and Central America, are revealing in this light. Its opposition to the International

Criminal Court's investigators looking into possible war crimes committed by Americans in Afghanistan and its support of Israel's annexation of Arab land also undermine its avowed values and principles. Although Washington criticizes China's conduct in Beijing's maritime disputes and routinely invokes the principle of freedom of navigation, it has declined to join the UN Convention on the Law of the Sea (UNCLOS, which China has ratified). How a country treats its own ethnic, racial, or religious minorities is similarly informative. As mentioned already, if it mistreats its own citizens, the sincerity of its commitment to foreigners' human rights comes into doubt.

Washington faces a delicate balancing act in its approach to China. On the one hand, it portrays a rising China that poses a serious threat to the rule-based international system. On the other, it presents a China that is not strong enough to defy multilateral pressure and that thus can still be contained. It appeals to rule-based international relations but is at the same time leery of accepting an order centered on the United Nations, where it is frequently outvoted. Thus, even in its early days, the Biden administration faced internal contradictions in its China policies.

Washington cannot advocate a rule-based international system while criticizing and defying the United Nations and even withdrawing from its affiliates when it finds itself in the minority (such as refusing to pay its dues to the United Nations and withdrawing from the World Health Organization, the UN Educational, Scientific and Cultural Organization, and the UN Human Rights Council). The United States cannot condemn other countries for committing war crimes and advocate that their alleged perpetuators be brought to face justice at the International Criminal Court when it refuses to join this institution and rejects its authority to investigate the possible transgressions of U.S. citizens. It cannot proclaim freedom of navigation while refusing to join UNCLOS. It cannot urge China to accept the International Arbitration Tribunal's jurisdiction over Beijing's sovereignty claims in the South China Sea while rejecting the International Court of Justice's ruling that it broke international law when it mined Nicaragua's ports. It cannot ask China to accept arms control while insisting on its right to sell weapons to Taiwan and terminating agreements it has signed. (The Biden administration has agreed with Russia to extend the Strategic Arms Reduction Treaty for five years; Trump pulled out of the Open Skies Treaty, the Intermediate-Range Nuclear

Forces Treaty, the Arms Trade Treaty, and the multilateral nuclear deal with Iran; and George W. Bush abrogated the Anti-Ballistic Missile Treaty with Moscow.) In short, it is difficult for Washington to urge others to observe international rules and accords but recoils from complying with them itself.

CHINESE POLICIES UNDER XI JINPING

One often hears that Xi Jinping has amassed vast personal power and consolidated his political position to dictate Chinese foreign policy, which in the view of many foreign observers has become more assertive and aggressive in recent years. Offensive realism claims that as a country becomes stronger, it is likely to also become more aggressive in undertaking expansionist policies. Does this proposition also apply to the United States after it became the world's only superpower after the Soviet Union's demise? Whether these countries have acted more assertively or aggressively naturally requires systematic evidence to show how much their conduct has changed over time and how it compares with that of their counterparts.

Since its reforms of the late 1970s, China has prioritized modernizing its economy. In pursuing this goal, it has sought assistance from foreign markets, technology, and capital. For such assistance, it needs a stable, peaceful international environment and especially a cordial relationship with the United States. It wants to avoid any external conflict that may distract its attention or divert its resources from economic modernization. Most Sinologists subscribe to this view. Michael Swaine and Ashley Tellis refer to it as Beijing's "calculative strategy," and expect this policy to continue at least until 2015 to 2020, with military modernization being subordinated to the higher priority given to economic moderization.[41] This strategy is premised on the recognition of China's continued weakness in overall national power and its dependence on conducive foreign conditions to sustain its growth. According to this view, Beijing will be self-restrained from undertaking coercive policies that could endanger the provision of foreign factors contributing to its economic modernization and even risk the formation of a coalition against it.

This strategy corresponds with Deng Xiaoping's advice that China should "hide its brilliance and bide its time." Avery Goldstein characterizes this policy orientation as follows:

> [Beijing's] grand strategy aims to engineer China's rise to great power status within the constraints of a unipolar international system that the United States dominates. It is designed to sustain the conditions necessary for continuing China's program of economic and military modernization, as well as to minimize the risk that others, most importantly the peerless United States, will view the ongoing increases in China's capabilities as an unacceptably dangerous threat that must be parried or perhaps even forestalled. China's grand strategy, in short, aims to increase the country's international clout without triggering a counterbalancing reaction.[42]

What could have caused Beijing to abandon its calculative strategy if the view of an increasingly assertive and aggressive China is correct? Two possibilities come to mind. They are not mutually exclusive. First, Beijing's leaders may have come to believe that China has become strong enough that it can now throw its weight around with only limited repercussions. Second, they may have come to realize that no matter what they do, foreign opposition to their country's rise and quest for its legitimate status in the world is implacable. Even though China has joined multilateral diplomacy in a constructive role and abandoned its former rhetoric in support of revolutionary change to overthrow incumbent bourgeois elites, it still faces rejection by the established powers. This view implies that playing nice no longer pays because it does not invite reciprocity. It may even suggest that as China has become stronger, it will face greater pressure from the West and especially the United States to contain it.

I disagree with both explanations mainly because I question the premise that China's recent foreign policy has become more assertive and aggressive, that it is done biding its time.[43] This premise does not give enough emphasis to the continuities in Beijing's foreign policy, such as regarding its sovereignty disagreements over Taiwan, with India, and in its maritime disputes, or to the possibility that it is reacting to other countries' actions. If anything, China's orientation in foreign policy has evolved over time so that it is now more aligned with the expectations of a responsible stakeholder than in the first three decades of the People's

Republic. As explained earlier, I do not see its behavior in recent years to be more assertive or aggressive than that of the United States, which has engaged in coercive diplomacy much more frequently and on a much larger scale. Consider the incidence of U.S. military attack on other countries after 1945 and especially after the Soviet Union collapsed, its promoting color revolution and regime change abroad, and its abandoning multilateral accords and institutions. In contrast, China has not been implicated or involved in any assassination of foreigners, the use of drones to kill suspected enemies abroad (with collateral civilian casualties), the organization of plots to overthrow foreign governments, the abandonment of international agreements or withdrawal from international organizations, and since 1979, any military assault on another country (it had in March 1988 a skirmish with Vietnamese forces in the Union Banks region of the Spratly Islands). In terms of both scale and magnitude, it is not clear that Washington has acted with more restraint than Beijing. We need to specify the benchmark for assessing China's aggressiveness, that is, relative to when and whom? Instead of repeating them as mantra, we should also be more specific about which norms and rules we have in mind when we speak of an international order based on them.

Like the United States, China is trying to balance its messaging to the rest of the world. On the one hand, it wants to demonstrate that its rise is inevitable. Therefore, it is futile for other countries to block its ascent. On the other hand, it wants to suggest that its rise is beneficial to other countries. Therefore, the situation will be a win-win for both China and its partners. Whereas for the United States the promotion of its liberal values provides it a competitive edge over China, Beijing's strong calling card is the possibility that it could present a counterpoise to Washington's overwhelming power. Its implicit appeal invokes the realist logic that states should always balance against the stronger or the strongest among them, lest they be left to fend for themselves in a world where the dominant state can exercise its power without being restrained by the prospect of counterpower. Although continuing to try to expand its foreign economic connections through its Belt and Road Initiative, Beijing has come to realize that relying on exporting to foreign markets can be a vulnerability and that a strategy of export-dependent growth has limits. It has therefore rolled out the dual-circulation approach, calling for balanced growth with an emphasis on both domestic consumption and foreign exports.

STRATEGIC RESTRAINT TO AVOID ESCALATION

Barry Buzan remarks that China's rise has been facilitated by two fortuitous developments: the collapse of the USSR and a relatively open and stable global economy.[44] I add two other lucky breaks for Beijing: the 9/11 terrorist attack on the United States and the 2008–2009 financial crisis. The campaign against al-Qaeda and Osama bin Laden diverted U.S. attention and energy from China and inclined Washington to be more solicitous in recruiting Beijing to join it in the war on international terrorism. Had it not been for this development, Beijing would have become the focus of U.S. strategic headlight that much earlier. Similarly, the global financial crisis brought on by the U.S. housing bubble gave China another round of breathing space. As Obama remarked, "if we hadn't been going through a financial crisis, my posture toward China would have been more explicitly contentious around trade issues."[45] It took the Trump presidency to openly confront China. Trump's failed reelection bid removed him from power although, as remarked earlier, in many ways the Biden administration has continued his policy on China and will be hamstrung by Trump's legacy domestically and internationally. The ongoing pandemic could yet intervene in unpredictable ways to alter the course of Sino-American relations. As well, Russia's invasion of Ukraine could give China another break to the extent that the United States will be distracted by that conflict, with its resources (including policy attention) diverted to Europe rather than allocated to China's neighborhood as conceived in Washington's plan to pivot to Asia.

Some believe that states fight wars for power or security; others believe that wars happen because of pride, arrogance, or fear. Scholars also have varying opinions about whether states stumbled into some wars or entered them with their eyes wide open. Athanassios Platias and Vasilis Trigkas, for example, dismiss the idea that the Peloponnesian War was a result of inadvertent escalation.[46] They attribute it instead to premeditated strategic choices. Some see World War I as a blunder attributable to misjudgments, organizational rigidity, or loss of control over the momentum of events. Others see it as a conflict deliberately sought and consciously accepted. As Kier Lieber writes, "German leaders understood the reality of their strategic circumstances—the balance of power, power trends, and the reality of modern warfare—and decided that the prospect of attaining European hegemony was worth the risk of a long and costly war."[47] Certainly, the adjective *inadvertent* does not apply to recent U.S.

military actions, such as in Afghanistan, Iraq, Libya, Serbia, and Syria. Washington made these decisions consciously and deliberately. On Sino-American relations, some think that a clash is inevitable.[48] Others consider this danger to be small, exaggerated, or indeterminate and therefore manageable by prudent statecraft.[49]

Beijing has made it abundantly clear that Taiwan's status impinges on China's core national interest. Despite its strategic ambiguity in the past, Washington has recently initiated diplomatic contacts with Taiwan suggesting that it may abandon this posture. China and the United States have maintained close and frequent contact in different issue domains both officially and unofficially. That they have lowers the possibility that their leaders are poorly informed about the other side's concerns and interests, suggesting instead that they probably know each other quite well. As Alastair Johnston says, "there is evidence that the very top levels of both sides actually have a better understanding of each other's interests and red lines than is implied in public debates."[50] If this is true, the recent escalation of tension in their relations is likely to reflect deliberate calculation and an accurate diagnosis of the other side's motivations and intentions rather than a regrettable misunderstanding or failure to communicate.

I have suggested that, from the perspective of rational cost-benefit analysis, both China and the United States have more to lose than to gain by going to war, even if a cold one. Certainly, whatever additional increment of security or influence Beijing hopes to gain by launching a hegemonic bid, even just for East Asia, is not worth the risks and costs that the backlash it could expect to encounter. Why would it expect to be materially better off by launching such a bid rather than letting the current growth trajectory continue to unfold?

Conversely, even if Beijing gains hegemony in East Asia (a huge if), Washington's hegemony will remain secure in the Western Hemisphere. It will still be dominant in Europe and the Middle East—unless it equates its security with retaining its worldwide dominance and denying the emergence of any regional hegemon. Would the risks and costs it will bear to block the rise of Chinese influence enhance its security and well-being? Or could this policy have the opposite effect of compromising these desiderata and even accelerate its relative decline—without possibly in the end changing the eventual outcome that China will still attain regional preeminence despite its opposition? Would each country's desire to be the top dog in East Asia be so strong that both judge this stake to be worth a nuclear confrontation? Prudent officials would not want to put their country on a collision course with such an eventuality.

The trouble is that states are not unitary, rational actors. Partisan politics, bureaucratic incentives, and organizational inertia can take over, especially if they are aided and abetted by similar processes occurring in counterpart countries. As described in the steps-to-war model, each step on the escalation ladder produces feedback that leads to a further step.[51] These reciprocal moves accumulate to create a combustive brew of armament competition, alliance formation, military display, recurrent crises, economic closure, hardball diplomacy, and rhetorical escalation. Even though rationalist theory makes it clear that wars are inefficient and that the contending parties should always prefer a settlement to going to war, wars nevertheless happen.[52]

Certain things are more within leaders' control than others. Strategic restraint is among them. To avoid escalating tension, leaders can minimize using the tools of power politics, such as arms racing, alliance formation, military display, and diplomatic confrontation. They can also refrain from actions that impinge on the other side's core security interests. Strategic restraint entails due recognition of the other country's sensitivities and predicaments, such as avoiding actions that infringe on its traditional sphere of influence and heighten its leaders' constraints related to domestic partisan politics and public opinion. Further, strategic restraint requires eschewing opportunistic behavior, accepting limits to the use of military force, and complying with treaty obligations and international agreements. These policies are easier to preach than practice. Moreover, even though leaders can communicate their intentions and make these intentions more credible to their counterparts,[53] we obviously cannot be completely sure that they or their successors will honor their commitments. International relations are inherently uncertain and indeterminate to some extent. This said, how a state acts in part depends on how it is treated by its counterpart—that is, agency matters.

CONCLUSION

This agency is influenced and constrained by environmental conditions. East Asia is seeing an emergent bifurcation whereby the United States continues to be the most powerful country militarily, but China has become the most important commercial partner for most countries. Sino-American relations are embedded in this evolving context.

Since the early 1950s, the United States and its East Asian partners have had an implicit grand bargain.[54] The Yoshida Doctrine set the precedent whereby the United States would offer military protection to Japan and grant it access to the U.S. market in return for Japan's political and military subordination. South Korea and other newly industrializing economies such as Taiwan also signed on to this bargain. They were followed by other late industrializing countries, including China, which, however, did not submit to various forms of formal political and military subordination—such as becoming a junior partner in a defense alliance, forming a joint military command, providing military bases to U.S. forces—but nevertheless showed substantial political deference and refrained from challenging U.S. influence in regions Washington considers to be vital to its interests, such as Europe, the Middle East, and the Western Hemisphere. China joined the United States as a junior partner in a joint effort to contain the USSR and supported the U.S. eviction of Iraqi forces from Kuwait and the war on terrorism. More recently, it also played a facilitative role in negotiations to curtail Iran's and North Korea's nuclear programs.

In exchange for access to the U.S. market, Beijing has recycled its export earnings by purchasing large amounts of U.S. debt, thereby helping Washington sustain its fiscal extravagance and monetary expansion as well as accepting the inflationary burden exported by the United States and the depreciation of U.S. currency that Beijing has accumulated. This part of the tacit bargain has also been characteristic of other countries, such as Japan and Saudi Arabia, which have also recycled their dollar revenues in return for political and military protection and access to the U.S. market. Although Japan and South Korea had only minimal foreign direct investment and foreign ownership of production when they joined this bargain, China opened itself to foreign investors and producers whose presence has loomed much larger than in these other countries.

This grand bargain, however, is becoming obsolete. The U.S. market is not as alluring and its capital and technology are not as important as before. The dollar as a store of value has also lost considerable luster. Moreover, with the collapse of the Soviet Union, the demise of al-Qaeda, and China's and Vietnam's turn to a market economy, the need for U.S. military protection has become more open to debate—unless the threat from a rising China gains traction to justify more U.S. military spending, the forward deployment of U.S. forces and, of course, the value of U.S. military protection.

China's increasing economic importance to its neighbors has diminished that of the United States and, indirectly, Washington's role as a military protector due to the perceived pacifying influence of greater economic intercourse on Beijing's conduct. China has increasingly steered its trade surpluses to finance its Belt and Road Initiative and has now more doubts about the wisdom of accumulating U.S. debt. In the meantime, the United States has been attempting to renegotiate the terms of the grand bargain, asking its formal and informal allies to contribute more to their own defense and to accept more protectionist measures favoring U.S. companies even while continuing their political and military subordination to Washington. It is in a sense trying to sell the same horse twice.

This situation obviously affects the potential costs of a U.S. policy to confront China as well as its prospective success. Conventional wisdom says that East Asian countries would rather not have to choose between Beijing and Washington, and that the wisest course for them is to hedge their policy, to practice various forms of soft balancing,[55] to enmesh both China and the United States in a web of multilateral institutions,[56] and to equivocate between them to extract the greatest amount of concessions from each and to get them to restrain each other from aggressive behavior. This phenomenon suggests, ironically, that the U.S. policy of engaging China has largely succeeded because it has now enmeshed China in a web of multilateral diplomatic and economic relations.

China is today deeply and widely embedded in international economic relations and participates actively in many multilateral institutions. It has therefore become more difficult for Washington to isolate China and to mobilize other countries to join a coalition to oppose Beijing. Indeed, positive-sum developments enhancing regional and global stability can be construed as a zero-sum loss for the United States. As Thomas Christensen observes, "seemingly everything that increases China's appeal to its neighbors and reassures them about China's intentions appears threatening to U.S. interests in a zero-sum competition."[57] Demand for U.S. military protection depends on Chinese misbehavior that alarms its neighbors. Conversely, the cost of defying the United States declines as

China emerges as an incipient counterpoise, protecting those that resist Washington's pressures from its wrath or, more plausibly, causing Washington to restrain itself should its arm-twisting policies redound to Beijing's benefit. To the extent that economic interdependence and multilateral diplomacy have assuaged fears of Chinese aggression and promoted trust in China, they also have made Washington's military protection less indispensable. It thus becomes more difficult for it to reconcile talking the liberal talk while walking the realist walk.

ACKNOWLEDGMENTS

I thank the three anonymous reviewers for their helpful comments and suggestions and Stephen Wesley for his expert stewardship of the review process. I am also grateful to the University of Colorado for a research award for retired faculty.

NOTES

INTRODUCTION

1. Irving L. Janis, *Groupthink: Psychological Studies of Policy Decisions and Fiascoes* (Boston: Houghton Mifflin, 1982).

2. Ariel Edwards-Levy, "Polls Find Most Republicans Say 2020 Election Was Stolen and Roughly One-Quarter Embrace QAnon Conspiracies," CNN, May 28, 2021, https://www.cnn.com/2021/05/28/politics/poll-qanon-election-conspiracies/index.html; and Amitai Etzioni, "Capitalism Needs to Be Re-encapsulated," *Society* 58, no. 1 (2021): 1–15.

3. Bentley Allan, Srdjan Vucetic, and Ted Hopf, "The Distribution of Identity and the Future of International Order: China's Hegemonic Prospects," *International Organization* 72, no. 4 (2018): 839–69.

4. Joseph S. Nye Jr., *Bound to Lead: The Changing Nature of American Power* (New York: Basic Books, 1990); Nye, *The Paradox of American Power* (New York: Oxford University Press, 2002); and Nye, *Soft Power: The Means to Success in World Politics* (New York: Public Affairs, 2004).

5. Andrew J. Bacevich, *American Empire: The Realities and Consequences of U.S. Diplomacy* (Cambridge, MA: Harvard University Press, 2002), 90.

6. Steven Ward, *Status and the Challenge of Rising Powers* (Cambridge: Cambridge University Press, 2017).

7. Graham T. Allison, "The Thucydides Trap: Are the U.S. and China Headed for War?," *The Atlantic*, September 24, 2015, https://www.theatlantic.com/international/archive/2015/09/united-states-china-war-thucydides-trap/406756/; and Allison, *Destined for War: Can America and China Escape Thucydides's Trap?* (Boston: Houghton Mifflin Harcourt, 2017).

8. A. F. K. Organski, *World Politics* (New York: Knopf, 1958); Organski and Jacek Kugler, *The War Ledger* (Chicago: University of Chicago Press, 1980); and Robert Gilpin, *War and Change in World Politics* (Cambridge: Cambridge University Press, 1981).

9. Yicai Global, "China 'Lacks the Gene' to Fall into Thucydides Trap, Says Xi Jinping," September 20, 2017, https://yicaichina.medium.com/china-lacks-the-gene-to-fall-into -the-thucydides-trap-says-xi-jinping-ccade48ac392.

10. Xi Jinping, "Work Together to Build a Community of Shared Future for Mankind," Xin-huanet, January 19, 2017, http://www.xinhuanet.com/english/2017-01/19/c_135994707 .htm.

11. James D. Fearon, "Rationalist Explanations for War," *International Organization* 49, no. 3 (1995): 379–414; and Robert Powell, "War as a Commitment Problem," *International Organization* 60, no. 1 (2006): 169–203.

12. Steve Chan, *Trust and Distrust in Sino-American Relations: Challenge and Opportunity* (Amherst, NY: Cambria Press, 2017).

13. John J. Mearsheimer, "China's Unpeaceful Rise," *Current History* 105, no. 690 (2006): 160–62; and Sebatian Rosato, "The Inscrutable Intentions of Great Powers," *International Security* 39, no. 3 (2015): 48–88.

14. Sebatian Rosato, "Why the United States and China Are on a Collision Course," Policy Brief (Cambridge, MA: Belfour Center for Science and International Affairs, Harvard Kennedy School, 2015), https://www.belfercenter.org/publication/why-united-states -and-china-are-collision-course.

15. Kori Schake, *Safe Passage: The Transition from British to American Hegemony* (Cambridge, MA: Harvard University Press, 2017).

16. Kenneth Bourne, *Britain and the Balance of Power in North America, 1815–1908* (Berkeley: University of California Press, 1967); and Christopher Layne, "Kant or Cant: The Myth of the Democratic Peace," *International Security* 19, no. 2 (1994): 5–49.

17. Samuel P. Huntington, *The Clash of Civilizations and the Remaking of the World Order* (New York: Simon & Schuster, 1996).

18. Thomas J. Christensen, "Posing Problems without Catching Up: China's Rise and Challenges for U.S. Security Policy," *International Security* 25, no. 4 (2001): 5–40.

19. Dale C. Copeland, *The Origins of Major War* (Ithaca, NY: Cornell University Press, 2000); and Stephen Van Evera, *Causes of War: Power and the Roots of Conflict* (Ithaca, NY: Cornell University Press, 1999).

20. William Burr and Jeffrey Richelson, "Whether to 'Strangle the Baby in the Cradle': The United States and the Chinese Nuclear Program, 1960–64," *International Security* 25, no. 3 (2000–2001): 54–99.

21. Bob Woodward and Robert Costa, *Peril* (New York: Simon & Schuster, 2021).

22. Kyle Morris, "Milley Secretly Called Chinese Officials Out of Fear Trump Would 'Attack' in Final Days: Book Claim," Fox News, September 14, 2021, https://www .foxnews.com/politics/milley-secretly-called-chinese-officials-out-of-fear-trump -would-attack-in-final-days-book-claims.

23. Samuel R. Bell and Jesse C. Johnson, "Shifting Power, Commitment Problems, and Preventive War," *International Studies Quarterly* 59, no. 1 (2015): 124–32; Copeland, *Origins of Major War*; Jack S. Levy, "Declining Power and the Preventive Motivation for War," *World Politics* 60, no. 1 (1987): 82–107; Levy, "Preventive War and Democratic Politics," *International Studies Quarterly* 52, no. 1 (2008): 1–24; Karl P. Mueller et al.,

Striking First: Preemptive and Preventive Attack in U.S. National Security Policy (Santa Monica, CA: RAND, 2006); Scott A. Silverstone, *Preventive War and American Democracy* (London: Routledge, 2007); Marc Trachtenberg, "Preventive War and U.S. Foreign Policy," *Security Studies* 16 no. 1 (2007): 1–31; and Van Evera, *Causes of War*.

24. Dan Reiter, "Exploding the Powder Keg Myth: Preemptive Wars Almost Never Happen," *International Security* 20, no. 2 (1995): 5–34.

25. Allen Buchanan, *Institutionalizing the Just War* (Oxford: Oxford University Press, 2018), 71.

26. Ivo H. Daalder and James M. Lindsay, *America Unbound: The Bush Revolution in Foreign Policy* (New York: Wiley, 2005); and John J. Mearsheimer and Stephen M. Walt, "An Unnecessary War," *Foreign Policy* 134 (January/February 2003): 50–59.

27. Charles A. Kupchan, *How Enemies Become Friends: The Sources of Stable Peace* (Princeton, NJ: Princeton University Press, 2010), 407.

28. R. Ned Lebow and Daniel P. Tompkins, "The Thucydides Claptrap," *Washington Monthly*, June 28, 2016, https://washingtonmonthly.com/2016/06/28/thucydides-claptrap; and Lebow and Benjamin Valentino, "Lost in Transition: A Critical Analysis of Power Transition Theory," *International Relations* 23, no. 3 (2009): 389–410.

29. Michael D. Swaine and Ashley L. Tellis, *Interpreting China's Grand Strategy: Past, Present, and Future* (Santa Monica, CA: RAND, 2000), 227.

30. Organski and Kugler, *War Ledger*.

31. Douglas Lemke, *Regions of War and Peace* (Cambridge: Cambridge University Press, 2002).

32. Organski and Kugler, *War Ledger*.

33. Swaine and Tellis, *Interpreting China's Grand Strategy*, 227.

34. Lebow and Valentino, "Lost in Transition."

35. Steve Chan, "More Than One Trap: Problematic Interpretations and Overlooked Lessons from Thucydides," *Journal of Chinese Political Science* 24, no. 1 (2019): 11–24; and Chan, *Thucydides's Trap? Historical Interpretation, Logic of Inquiry, and the Future of Sino-American Relations* (Ann Arbor: University of Michigan Press, 2020).

36. Jervis and Gaddis quoted in Aaron Friedberg, "The Future of U.S.-China Relations: Is Conflict Inevitable?," *International Security* 30, no. 2 (2005): 11.

37. William R. Thompson, "A Streetcar Named Sarajevo: Catalysts, Multiple Causation Chains, and Rivalry Structures," *International Studies Quarterly* 47, no. 3 (2003): 453–74.

38. Charles F. Doran, *Systems in Crisis: New Imperatives of High Politics at Century's End* (Cambridge: Cambridge University Press, 1991); and Doran and Wes Parsons, "War and the Cycle of Relative Power," *American Political Science Review* 74, no. 4 (1980): 947–65.

39. Robert Jervis, "Thinking Systematically about China," *International Security* 31, no. 2 (2006): 206–208.

40. John A. Vasquez, "Whether and How Global Leadership Transitions Will Result in War: Some Long-Term Predictions from Steps-to-War Explanation," in *Systemic Transitions: Past, Present, and Future*, ed. William R. Thompson (New York: Palgrave Macmillan, 2009), 133 (italics in original).

41. Paul D. Senese and John A. Vasquez, *The Steps to War: An Empirical Study* (Princeton, NJ: Princeton University Press, 2008).

42. Michael Beckley, "The Myth of Entangling Alliances," *International Security* 39, no. 4 (2015): 7–48; Thomas J. Christensen and Jack Snyder, "Chain Gangs and Passed Bucks: Predicting Alliance Patterns in Multipolarity," *International Organization* 44, no. 2 (1992): 137–68; and Dominic Tierney, "Does Chain-Ganging Cause the Outbreak of War?," *International Studies Quarterly* 55, no. 2 (2011): 285–304.

43. Athanassios Platias and Vasilis Trigkas, "Unravelling the Thucydides' Trap: Inadvertent or War of Choice?," *Chinese Journal of International Politics* 14, no. 2 (2021): 187–217.

44. Victor D. Cha, "Powerplay: Origins of the U.S. Alliance System in Asia," *International Organization* 34, no. 3 (2009–2010): 158–96.

45. David Welch, "Can the United States and China Avoid a Thucydides Trap?," E-International Relations, 2015, https://www.e-ir.info/2015/04/06/can-the-united-states-and-china-avoid-a-hucydides-trap/.

46. Vasquez, "Whether and How Global Leadership," 135.

47. Vasquez, "Whether and How Global Leadership," 147.

48. Ward, *Status and the Challenge.*

49. Michelle Murray, "Identity, Insecurity, and Great Power Politics: The Tragedy of German Naval Ambition before First World War," *Security Studies* 19, no. 4 (2010): 656–88; Murray, *The Struggle for Recognition in International Relations: Status, Revisionism, and Rising Powers* (New York: Oxford University Press, 2019); and Jack Snyder, *Myths of Empire: Domestic Politics and International Ambition* (Ithaca, NY: Cornell University Press, 1993).

50. Gilpin, *War and Change.*

51. Paul Wolfowitz, "Bridging Centuries: Fin de Siècle All Over Again," *Wall Street Journal*, June 10, 1997, https://www.wsj.com/articles/SB865919411252495500.

52. Lewis F. Richardson, *Arms and Insecurity* (Pittsburgh, PA: Boxwood Press, 1960).

53. John J. Mearsheimer, "The Gathering Storm: China's Challenge to US Power in Asia," *Chinese Journal of International Politics* 3, no. 4 (2010): 381–96; and Mearsheimer, "China's Unpeaceful Rise."

54. Jonathan Kirshner, "Offensive Realism, Thucydides Trap, and the Tragedy of Unforced Errors: Classical Realism and US-China Relations," *China International Strategy Review* 1 (2019): 62.

55. John J. Mearsheimer, *The Tragedy of Great Power Politics* (New York: Norton, 2001).

56. Robert Jervis, "Unipolarity: A Structural Perspective," *World Politics* 61, no. 1 (2009): 188–213.

57. Kupchan, *How Enemies Become Friends*, 10.

58. Barry Buzan and Michael Cox, "China and the US: Comparable Cases of 'Peaceful Rise'?," *Chinese Journal of International Politics* 6, no. 2 (2013): 109–32; Yongping Feng, "The Peaceful Transition of Power from the UK to the US," *Chinese Journal of International Politics* 1, no. 1 (2006): 83–108; and Reinhard Wolf, "Rising Powers, Status Ambitions, and the Need to Reassure: What China Could Learn from Imperial Germany's Failures," *Chinese Journal of International Politics* 7, no. 2 (2014): 185–219.

59. Chan, *Thucydides's Trap?*; and T. V. Paul, ed., *Accommodating Rising Powers: Past, Present, and Future* (Cambridge: Cambridge University Press, 2016).

60. Mearsheimer, "China's Unpeaceful Rise."

61. Colin Elman, "Extending Offensive Realism: The Louisiana Purchase and America's Rise to Regional Hegemony," *American Political Science Review* 98, no. 4 (2004): 563–76.

62. T. V. Paul, "The Accommodation of Rising Powers in World Politics," in *Accommodating Rising Powers: Past, Present, and Future*, ed. T. V. Paul (Cambridge: Cambridge University Press, 2016), 4.

63. Philip H. Gordon, *Losing the Long Game: The False Promise of Regime Change in the Middle East* (New York: St. Martin's, 2020).

64. David C. Kang, *China Rising: Peace, Power, and Order in East Asia* (New York: Columbia University Press, 2007); Kang, "Hierarchy and Legitimacy in International Systems: The Tribute System in Early Modern East Asia," *Security Studies* 19, no. 4 (2010): 591–622; Kang, *East Asia before the West: Five Centuries of Trade and Tribute* (New York: Columbia University Press, 2012); and Kang, "International Order in Historical East Asia: Tribute and Hierarchy beyond Sinocentrism and Eurocentrism," *International Organization* 74, no. 1 (2020): 65–93.

65. Bourne, *Britain and the Balance*; and Aaron L. Friedberg, *The Weary Titan: The Experience of Relative Decline, 1895–1905* (Princeton, NJ: Princeton University Press, 1988).

66. David Treisman, "Rational Appeasement," *International Organization* 58, no. 2 (2004): 344–73.

67. Kurt M. Campbell and Jake Sullivan, "Competition without Catastrophe: How America Can Both Challenge and Coexist with China," *Foreign Affairs*, September-October 2020, https://www.foreignaffairs.com/articles/china/competition-with-china-without-catastrophe; and Charles A. Kupchan and Peter L. Trubowitz, "A China Strategy to Reunite America's Allies," Project Syndicate, January 4, 2021, https://www.project-syndicate.org/commentary/biden-china-strategy-to-reunite-us-allies-by-charles-a-kupchan-and-peter-trubowitz-1-2021-01.

68. John A. Vasquez, "When Are Power Transitions Dangerous? An Appraisal and Reformulation of Power Transition Theory," in *Parity and War: Evaluations and Extensions of the War Ledger*, ed. Jacek Kugler and Douglas Lemke (Ann Arbor: University of Michigan Press, 1996), 35–56; and Vasquez, "Whether and How."

69. Jervis, "Unipolarity: A Structural Perspective."

70. Stephen G. Brooks and William C. Wohlforth, *America Abroad: The United States' Global Role in the 21st Century* (New York: Oxford University Press, 2016).

71. A. F. K. Organski and Jacek Kugler, "The Costs of Major Wars: The Phoenix Factor," *American Political Science Review* 71, no. 4 (1977): 1347–66.

72. Allison, "Thucydides Trap"; and Allison, *Destined for War*.

73. Organski and Kugler, *War Ledger*; Ronald L. Tammen, Jacek Kugler, and Douglas Lemke, "Foundations of Power Transition Theory," in *Oxford Encyclopedia of Empirical International Relations*, ed. William R. Thompson (Oxford: Oxford University Press, 2017), https://oxfordre.com/politics/view/10.1093/acrefore/9780190228637.001.0001

/acrefore-9780190228637-e-296; and Ronald L. Tammen et al., *Power Transitions: Strategies for the 21st Century* (New York: Chatham House, 2000).

74. Steve Chan, "Why Thucydides' Trap Misinforms Sino-American Relations," *Vestnik RUDN, International Relations* 21, no. 2 (2021): 234–42.

75. Platias and Trigkas, "Unravelling the Thucydides' Trap," 18 (italics in the original).

76. Quoted in Platias and Trigkas, "Unravelling the Thucydides' Trap," 11.

77. James Lee, "Did Thucydides Believe in Thucydides' Trap?: The History of the Peloponnesian War and Its Relevance to US-China Relations," *Journal of Chinese Political Science* 24, no. 1 (2019): 67–86.

78. Yuen Foong Khong, "The American Tributary System," *Chinese Journal of International Politics* 6, no. 1 (2013): 18.

79. Swaine and Tellis, *Interpreting China's Grand Strategy*, 228.

80. Gilpin, *War and Change.*

81. Francis Fukuyama, "The Pandemic and the Political Order: It Takes a State," *Foreign Affairs*, July/August 2020, https://www.foreignaffairs.com/articles/world/2020-06-09/pandemic-and-political-order.

82. Worldometer, "Coronavirus: Reported Cases and Deaths by Country or Territory," https://www.worldometers.info/coronavirus/#countries.

83. Peter B. Evans, *Embedded Autonomy: States and Industrial Transformation* (Princeton, NJ: Princeton University Press, 1995); and Evans, Dietrich Rueschemeyer, and Theda Skocpol, eds., *Bringing the State Back In* (Cambridge: Cambridge University Press, 1985).

84. Sean Starrs, "American Economic Power Hasn't Declined—It Globalized! Summoning the Data and Taking Globalization Seriously," *International Studies Quarterly* 57, no. 4 (2013): 817–30.

85. George Modelski and William R. Thompson, *Leading Sectors and World Powers: The Coevolution of Global Politics and Economics* (Columbia: University of South Carolina Press, 1996); Rafael Reuveny and William R. Thompson, *Growth, Trade, and Systemic Leadership* (Ann Arbor: University of Michigan Press, 2004); and Ashley J. Tellis, Janice Bially, Christopher Layne, and Melissa McPherson, *Measuring National Power in the Postindustrial Age* (Santa Monica, CA: RAND, 2000).

86. Michael Beckley, "The Power of Nations: Measuring What Matters," *International Security* 43, no. 2 (2018): 7–44; and Carsten Rauch, "Challenging the Power Consensus: GDP, CINC, and Power Transition," *Security Studies* 26, no. 4 (2017): 642–64.

87. Marina Arbetman and Jacek Kugler, eds., *Political Capacity and Economic Behavior* (Boulder, CO: Westview, 1997); and Kugler and Ronald L. Tammen, eds., *The Performance of Nations* (Lanham, MD: Rowman & Littlefield, 2012).

88. Jacek Kugler and William Domke, "Comparing the Strengths of Nations," *Comparative Political Studies* 19, no. 1 (1986): 39–69; and Organski and Kugler, *War Ledger.*

89. Brian Resnick, "Please, Trump: Keep Telling Your Supporters the Covid-19 Vaccines Work," *Vox*, March 18, 2021, http://maristpoll.marist.edu/wp-content/uploads/2021/03/NPR_PBS-NewsHour_Marist-Poll_USA-NOS-and-Tables_202103091124.pdf#page=3.

90. Michele Gelfand, Joshua C. Jackson, Xinyue Pan, Dana Nau, Dylan Pieper, Emmy Denison, Munqith Dagher, Paul A. M. Van Lange, Chi-Yue Chiu, and Mo Wang, "The

Relationship between Cultural Tightness-Looseness and COVID-19 Cases and Deaths: A Global Analysis," *Lancet Planetary Health* 5, no. 3 (2021): E135-E144, https://www.thelancet.com/journals/lanplh/article/PIIS2542-5196(20)30301-6/fulltext.

91. Charles A. Kupchan and Peter L. Trubowitz, "Dead Center: The Demise of Liberal Internationalism in the United States," *International Security* 32, no. 2 (2007): 7–44; and Kupchan and Trubowitz, "The Illusion of Liberal Internationalism's Revival," *International Security* 35, no. 1 (2010): 95–109.

92. Peter Harris and Peter L. Trubowitz, "The Politics of Power Projection: The Pivot to Asia, Its Failure, and the Future of American Primacy," *Chinese Journal of International Politics* 14, no. 2 (2021): 187–217.

93. Charles A. Kupchan and Peter L. Trubowitz, "The Home Front: Why an Internationalist Foreign Policy Needs a Stronger Domestic Foundation," *Foreign Affairs*, May–June 2021, https://www.foreignaffairs.com/articles/united-states/2021-04-20/foreign-policy-home-front.

94. Edwards-Levy, "Polls Find Most Republicans."

95. Monmouth University Polling Institute, "Doubt in American System Increases" (West Long Branch, NJ: Monmouth University, November 12, 2021), https://www.monmouth.edu/polling-institute/reports/monmouthpoll_us_111521/.

96. Randall L. Schweller, *Unanswered Threats: Political Constraints on the Balance of Power* (Princeton, NJ: Princeton University Press, 2006).

97. Donald Kagan, *The Outbreak of the Peloponnesian War* (Ithaca, NY: Cornell University Press, 1969), 192.

98. Joseph S. Nye Jr., "The Rise and Fall of American Hegemony: From Wilson to Trump," *International Affairs* 95, no. 1 (2019): 63–80.

99. Amitai Etzioni, "Is America Becoming a Chauvinistic Nation?," *National Interest*, March 20, 2021, https://nationalinterest.org/feature/america-becoming-chauvinistic-nation-180660; and Fareed Zakaria, "On Domestic Front, Biden Is All Ambition. Why Not Foreign Policy?," *Washington Post*, February 11, 2021, https://fareedzakaria.com/columns/2021/2/11/on-the-domestic-front-biden-is-all-ambition-why-not-on-foreign-policy.

100. Kupchan and Trubowitz, "China Strategy."

101. Edward D. Mansfield and Jack Snyder, "Democratic Transitions, Institutional Strength, and War," *International Organization* 56, no. 2 (2002): 297–337; and Mansfield and Snyder, *Electing to Fight: Why Emerging Democracies Go to War* (Cambridge, MA: MIT Press, 2005).

102. Allison, *Destined for War*, 89.

103. Mearsheimer, *Tragedy of Great Power Politics*, 238.

104. Michael C. Desch, "America's Liberal Illiberalism: The Ideological Origins of Overreaction in U.S. Foreign Policy," *International Security* 32, no. 3 (2007–2008): 7–43.

105. Peter B. Evans, Harold K. Jacobson, and Robert D. Putnam, eds., *Double-Edged Diplomacy: International Bargaining and Domestic Politics* (Berkeley: University of California Press, 1993); and Robert D. Putnam, "Diplomacy and Domestic Politics: The Logic of Two-Level Games," *International Organization* 42, no. 3 (1988): 427–60.

106. Bruce Bueno de Mesquita and Alastair Smith, *The Dictator's Handbook: Why Bad Behavior Is Almost Always Good Politics* (New York: PublicAffairs, 2012); and Bueno de Mesquita, Alastair Smith, Randolph M. Siverson, and James D. Morrow, *The Logic of Political Survival* (Cambridge, MA: The MIT Press, 2003).

107. Howard Raiffa, *The Art and Science of Negotiation* (Cambridge, MA: Harvard University Press, 1982), 166.

108. Miroslav Nincic, *The Logic of Positive Engagement* (Ithaca, NY: Cornell University Press, 2011).

109. Kupchan, *How Enemies Become Friends*.

110. For example, Allison, "Thycidides Trap"; and Allison, *Destined to War*.

111. Steve Chan, "Thucydides's Trap?," H-Diplo/ISSF Roundtable Discussion 12-2, November 9, 2020, https://networks.h-net.org/node/28443/discussions/6721850/h-diploissf-roundtable-12-2-thucydides%E2%80%99s-trap-historical; Chan, "China and Thucydides's Trap," in *China's Challenges and International Order Transition: Beyond the "Thucydides Trap,"* ed. Kai He and Huiyun Feng (Ann Arbor: University of Michigan Press, 2020), 52–71; and Chan, *Thucydides's Trap?*

112. Peter H. Gries and Yiming Jing, "Are the U.S. and China Fated to Fight? How Narratives of 'Power Transition' Shape Great Power War or Peace," *Cambridge Review of International Affairs* 32, no. 4 (2019): 456–82.

113. Chan, *Thucydides's Trap?*

114. Paul A. Rahe, "Sparta Ascendant, Athens Rising: Alliance, Ambivalence, Rivalry, and War in a Tripolar World," in *Disruptive Strategies: The Military Campaigns of Ascendant Powers and Their Rivals*, ed. David Beekwy (Stanford, CA: Hoover Institution Press 2021), 13–42.

115. Yuen Foong Khong, *Analogies at War: Korea, Munich, Dien Bien Phu, and the Vietnam Decisions of 1965* (Princeton, NJ: Princeton University Press, 1992).

116. Platias and Trigkas, "Unravelling the Thucydides' Trap."

117. Paul K. MacDonald and Joseph M. Parent, "Graceful Decline? The Surprising Success of Great Power Retrenchment," *International Security* 35, no. 4 (2011): 42.

118. Ja Ian Chong and Todd H. Hall, "The Lessons of 1914 for East Asia Today: Missing the Trees for the Forest," *International Security* 39, no. 1 (2014): 15.

119. Etel Solingen, "Domestic Coalitions, Internationalization, and War: Then and Now," *International Security* 39, no. 1 (2014): 45.

120. Solingen, "Domestic Coalitions," 69.

121. Chan, *Thucydides's Trap?*

122. Ayse Zarakol, "Use of Historical Analogies in IR Theory," H-Diplo/ISSF Roundtable Discussion 12–2, November 9, 2020, https://networks.h-net.org/node/28443/discussions/6721850/h-diploissf-roundtable-12-2-thucydides%E2%80%99s-trap-historical.

123. Laurie M. Bagby, "The Use and Misuse of Thucydides in International Relations," *International Organization* 48, no. 1 (1994): 131–53; and Jonathan Kirshner, "The Tragedy of Offensive Realism: Classical Realism and the Rise of China," *European Journal of International Relations* 18, no. 1 (2012): 53–75.

124. Bagby, "Use and Misuse," 153.

125. Kirshner, "Tragedy of Offensive Realism"; and R. Ned Lebow, "Thucydides and Deterrence," *Security Studies* 16, no. 2 (2007): 163–88.

126. R. Ned Lebow, *Why Nations Fight: Past and Future Motivations for War* (Cambridge: Cambridge University Press, 2010); Lebow and Tompkins, "Thucydides Claptrap"; and Lebow and Valentino, "Lost in Transition."

127. Janis, *Groupthink*; and Robert Jervis, *Perception and Misperception in International Politics* (Princeton, NJ: Princeton University Press, 1976).

128. Daniel Kahneman and Amos Tversky, "Prospect Theory: An Analysis of Decision under Risk," *Econometrica* 47, no. 2 (1979): 263–92.

129. William A. Boettcher III, *Presidential Risk Behavior in Foreign Policy: Prudence or Peril?* (New York: Palgrave, 2005); Kai He and Huiyun Feng, *Prospect Theory and Foreign Policy Analysis in the Asia Pacific: Rational Leaders and Risky Behavior* (New York: Routledge, 2012); Jack S. Levy, "Loss Aversion, Framing and Bargaining: The Implications of Prospect Theory for International Conflict," *International Political Science Review* 17, no. 2 (1996): 177–93; and Rose McDermott, *Risk-Taking in International Relations: Prospect Theory in American Foreign Policy* (Ann Arbor: University of Michigan Press, 1998).

130. Dustin Tingley, "Rising Power on the Mind," *International Organization* 71, no. S1 (2017): S165–88.

131. Quoted in Lebow and Valentino, "Lost in Transition," 389.

132. Linus Hagstrom, "'Power Shift' in East Asia? A Critical Reappraisal of Narratives on the Diaoyu/Senkaku Islands Incident in 2010," *Chinese Journal of International Politics* 5, no. 3 (2012): 267–97; and Mingjiang Li, "China's Non-Confrontational Assertiveness in the South China Sea," East Asia Forum, June 14, 2012, https://www.eastasiaforum.org/2012/06/14/china-s-non-confronational-assertiveness-in-the-south-china-sea.

133. Andrew Chubb, "PRC Assertiveness in the South China Sea: Measuring Continuity and Change, 1970–2015," *International Security* 45, no. 3 (2020–2021): 79–121; Bjorn Jerden, "The Assertive China Narrative: Why It Is Wrong and How So Many Still Bought into It," *Chinese Journal of International Politics* 7, no. 1 (2014): 47–88; Alastair I. Johnston, "How New and Assertive Is China's New Assertiveness?," *International Security* 37, no. 4 (2013): 7–48; Tongfi Kim, Andrew Taffer, and Ketian Zhang, "Is China a Cautious Bully?," *International Security* 45, no. 2 (2020): 187–93; and Ketian Zhang, "Cautious Bully: Reputation, Resolve, and Beijing's Use of Coercion in the South China Sea," *International Security* 44, no. 1 (2019): 117–59.

134. Johnston, "How New and Assertive," 47.

135. Robert Powell, *In the Shadow of Power: States and Strategies in International Politics* (Princeton, NJ: Princeton University Press, 1999).

136. Fearon, "Rationalist Explanations."

137. Powell, *Shadow of Power*.

138. Ted R. Gurr, *Why Men Rebel?* (Princeton, NJ: Princeton University Press, 1970).

139. For example, Organski and Kugler, *War Ledger*; and Gilpin, *War and Change*.

140. Evelyn Goh, *The Struggle for Order: Hegemony, Hierarchy, and Transition in the Cold-War East Asia* (Oxford: Oxford University Press, 2013); and Goh, "Contesting Hegemonic Order: China in East Asia," *Security Studies* 28, no. 3 (2019): 614–44.

141.   Kirshner, "Tragedy of Offensive Realism."

142.   Paul Kennedy, *The Rise and Fall of Great Powers* (New York: Vintage Books, 1987).

143.   Swaine and Tellis, *Interpreting China's Grand Strategy*, 228.

144.   Brooks and Wohlforth, *America Abroad*; Charles A. Kupchan, *Isolationism: A History of America's Efforts to Shield Itself from the World* (Oxford: Oxford University Press, 2020); and Joshua I. R. Shifrinson and Michael Beckley, "Correspondence: Debating China's Rise and U.S. Decline," *International Security* 37, no. 3 (2012–2013): 172–81.

145.   Kirshner, "Tragedy of Offensive Realism."

146.   Elman, "Extending."

147.   Copeland, *Origins of Major War*; and Van Evera, *Causes of War*.

148.   Stephen Van Evera, "The Cult of Offensive and the Origins of the First World War," *International Security* 9, no. 1 (1984): 84.

149.   Quoted in Van Evera, *Causes of War*, 77.

150.   Quoted in R. Ned Lebow, *Between Peace and War: The Nature of International Crisis* (Baltimore: Johns Hopkins University Press, 1981), 229 (italics in the original).

151.   Fritz Fischer, *The War of Illusions* (New York: Norton, 1975), quoted in Copeland, *Origins of Major War*, 71.

152.   Quoted in Van Evera, *Causes of War*, 77–78, 96–97.

153.   Quoted in Margaret MacMillan, *The War That Ended Peace* (New York: Random House, 2013), 38.

154.   Yongping Feng, "The Peaceful Transition of Power from the UK to the US," *Chinese Journal of International Politics* 1, no. 1 (2006): 107.

155.   Randall L. Schweller, "Democratic Structure and Preventive War: Are Democracies More Pacific?," *World Politics* 44, no. 2 (1992): 235–69.

156.   Burr and Richelson, "Whether 'to Strangle the Baby'."

157.   Ben Westcott, "US Military Considered Using Nuclear Weapons Against China in 1958 Taiwan Strait Crisis, Leaked Documents Show," CNN, May 24, 2021, https://www.cnn.com/2021/05/24/china/us-china-taiwan-1958-nuclear-intl-hnk/index.html.

158.   Jack S. Levy, "Preventive War and Democratic Politics," *International Studies Quarterly* 52, no. 1 (2008): 1–24.

1. POWER SHIFT EXPLAINS BETTER WORSENING SINO-AMERICAN RELATIONS

1.   Kishore Mahbubani, "Was Trump Right or Wrong on China? Biden's Answer Will Shape the Future," *GlobalAsia*, March 2021, https://globalasia.org/v16no1/cover/was-trump-right-or-wrong-on-china-bidens-answer-will-shape-the-future_kishore-mahbubani.

2.   Rising Power Initiative, "RPI Policy Alert: Rising Powers React to Contentious U.S.-China Relations: A Roundup" (Washington, DC: George Washington University, March 2021), https://www.risingpowersinitiative.org/publication/rising-powers-react-to-contentious-u-s-china-relations-a-roundup/.

3. YouTube, "It Is Not Up to the U.S. Alone to Evaluate Its Democracy: Yang Jiechi," May 19, 2021, https://www.youtube.com/watch?v=ETOfymWVShM.

4. Xinhuanet, "China Welcomes Helpful Suggestions, but Won't Accept Sanctimonious Preaching: Xi," July 1, 2021, http://www.xinhuanet.com/english/special/2021–07/01/c _1310037332.htm.

5. Kurt M. Campbell and Ely Ratner, "The China Reckoning: How Beijing Defied American Expectations," *Foreign Affairs* 97, no. 2 (2018): 60–70; Campbell and Jake Sullivan, "Competition without Catastrophe: How America Can Both Challenge and Coexist with China," *Foreign Affairs*, September-October 2020, https://www.foreignaffairs.com /articles/china/competition-with-china-without-catastrophe; Robert Kagan, "The Illusion of 'Managing' China," *Washington Post*, May 15, 2005, https://www.washingtonpost .com/wp-dyn/content/article/2005/05/13/AR2005051301405.html; David M. Lampton, "Reconsidering U.S.-China Relations: From Improbable Normalization to Precipitous Deterioration," *Asia Policy* 14, no. 2 (2019): 43–60; and Anne F. Thurston, *Engaging China: Fifty Years of Sino-American Relations* (New York: Columbia University Press, 2021).

6. For example, Nina Silove, "The Pivot before the Pivot: U.S. Strategy to Preserve the Power Balance in Asia," *International Security* 40, no. 4 (2016): 45–88; and Fareed Zakaria, "The New China Scare: Why America Shouldn't Panic about Its Latest Challenger," *Foreign Affairs* 99, no. 1 (2020): 52–69.

7. Silove, "Pivot before the Pivot."

8. Arman Grigoryan, "Selective Wilsonianism: Material Interests and the West's Support for Democracy," *International Security* 44, no. 4 (2020): 158.

9. Graham T. Allison, *Destined for War: Can America and China Escape Thucydides's Trap?* (Boston: Houghton Mifflin Harcourt, 2017).

10. Allison, *Destined for War*, 90.

11. Allison, *Destined for War*, 89.

12. Amitai Etzioni, "The Challenging Results of China's New Anti-Poverty Campaign: It's Not as Simple as Critics Might Have You Believe," *The Diplomat*, March 11, 2021, https://thediplomat.com/2021/03/the-challenging-results-of-chinas-new-anti-poverty -campaign/.

13. Thomas J. Christensen, "Fostering Stability or Creating a Monster? China's Rise and U.S. Policy toward East Asia," *International Security* 31, no. 1 (2006): 106.

14. Michael D. Swaine and Ashley L. Tellis, *Interpreting China's Grand Strategy: Past, Present, and Future* (Santa Monica, CA: RAND, 2000), 196.

15. Alastair I. Johnston, "China in a World of Orders," *International Security* 44, no. 2 (2019): 37–38.

16. Johnston, "World of Orders," 41.

17. M. E. Sarotte, "China's Fear of Contagion: Tiananmen Square and the Power of European Example," *International Security* 37, no. 2 (2012): 156–82.

18. Mahbubani, "Was Trump Right or Wrong?"

19. Silove, "Pivot before the Pivot."

20. Jasmine Wright, "Biden Commits to 'Free, Open, Secure' Indo-Pacific in Rare Op-ed with 'Quad' Members," CNN, March 14, 2021, https://www.cnn.com/2021/03/14/politics /biden-modi-morrison-suga-quad-op-ed/index.html.

21. Raymond D. Gastil, *Freedom in the World: Political Rights and Civil Liberties, 1978* (New York: Freedom House, 1978), 10, https://freedomhouse.org/sites/default/files/2020-02/Freedom_in_the_World_1978_complete_book.pdf.

22. Freedom House, "Countries and Territories," 2021, https://freedomhouse.org/countries/freedom-world/scores.

23. Jane Ferguson, "As Peace Talks with the Taliban Stall, Deadline to Withdraw U.S. Troops from Afghanistan Looms," PBS, February 20, 2021, https://www.pbs.org/newshour/show/as-peace-talks-with-the-taliban-stall-deadline-to-withdraw-u-s-troops-from-afghanistan-looms.

24. Barry Buzan and Michael Cox, "China and the US: Comparable Cases of 'Peaceful Rise'?," *Chinese Journal of International Politics* 6, no. 2 (2013): 118.

25. Richard C. Bush, *Untying the Knot: Making Peace in the Taiwan Strait* (Washington, DC: Brookings Institution Press, 2005); and Bush, *Uncharted Strait: The Future of China-Taiwan Relations* (Washington, DC: Brookings Institution Press, 2013).

26. *The Economic Times*, "China Slams US for Delisting Xinjiang's East Turkestan Islamic Movement as Terrorist Outfit," November 6, 2020, https://economictimes.indiatimes.com/news/defence/china-slams-us-for-delisting-xinjiangs-east-turkestan-islamic-movement-as-terrorist-outfit/articleshow/79083396.cms.

27. James Griffiths, "These Uighurs Were Locked Up by the US in Guantanamo. Now They're Being Used as an Excuse for China's Crackdown in Xinjiang," May 15, 2021, https://www.cnn.com/2021/05/15/china/china-xinjiang-guantanamo-uyghurs-intl-hnk/index.html.

28. Bill Bostock, "Secretary of State Antony Blinken Says He Stands by Mike Pompeo's Designation That China Committed Genocide against the Uighurs," Yahoo!News, January 28, 2021, https://news.yahoo.com/secretary-state-antony-blinken-says-110049095.html.

29. *The Economist*, " 'Genocide' Is the Wrong Word for the Horrors of Xinjiang: To Confront Evil, the First Step Is to Describe It Accurately," February 13, 2021, https://www.economist.com/leaders/2021/02/13/genocide-is-the-wrong-word-for-the-horrors-of-xinjiang; and Amitai Etzioni, "Will the Biden Administration Embrace Trump's Extreme Anti-China Rhetoric? The New Administration Will Have to Sidestep yet Another Trump Landmine," *The Diplomat*, February 1, 2021, https://thediplomat.com/2021/02/will-the-biden-administration-embrace-trumps-extreme-anti-china-rhetoric/.

30. Samantha Power, "Bystander to Genocide," *The Atlantic*, September 2001, https://www.theatlantic.com/magazine/archive/2001/09/bystanders-to-genocide/304571/.

31. Jonathan Weisman and Reid J. Epstein, "G.O.P. Declares Jan. 6 Attack 'Legitimate Political Discourse,' " *Washington Post*, February 4, 2022, https://www.nytimes.com/2022/02/04/us/politics/republicans-jan-6-cheney-censure.html.

32. Jonathan Masters, "Trump's Threat to Use the Military against Protestors: What to Know" (New York: Council on Foreign Relations, June 5, 2020), https://www.cfr.org/in-brief/trumps-threat-use-military-against-protesters-what-know; Michael Martin and Tinbete Ermyas, "Former Pentagon Chief Esper Says Trump Asked About Shooting Protestors," NPR, May 9, 2022, https//www.npr.org/2022/05/09/1097517470/trump-esper

-book-defense-secretary; and NPR, "Trump Calls Governors Weak, Urging Them to 'Dominate' to Quell Violence," June 1, 2020, https://www.npr.org/2020/06/01/867063007 /trump-calls-governors-weak-and-urges-them-to-dominate-violent-protesters.

33. Amitai Etzioni, "Challenging Results;" and Etzioni, "Capitalism Needs to Be Re-encapsulated," *Society* 58, no. 1 (2021): 1-15.

34. Johan Galtung, "Violence, Peace, and Peace Research," *Journal of Peace Research* 6, no. 3 (1969): 167–91.

35. Steve Chan, *Trust and Distrust in Sino-American Relations: Challenge and Opportunity* (Amherst, NY: Cambria Press, 2017).

36. Feng Liu, "China's Security Strategy toward East Asia," *Chinese Journal of International Politics* 9, no. 2 (2016): 177.

37. Human Rights Watch (HRW), "US Sanctions International Criminal Court Prosecutor: Trump Administration's Action Tries to Block World's Worst Crimes," September 2, 2020, https://www.hrw.org/news/2020/09/02/us-sanctions-international-criminal -court-prosecutor; and HRW, "US Sanctions on the International Criminal Court: Questions and Answers," December 14, 2020, https://www.hrw.org/news/2020/12/14 /us-sanctions-international-criminal-court.

38. Deutsche Welle, "US Lifts Trump Sanctions on International Criminal Court Officials," April 3, 2021, https://www.dw.com/en/us-lifts-trump-sanctions-on-international-criminal -court-officials/a-57089520.

39. Graham T. Allison, "Of Course China, Like All Great Powers, Will Ignore an International Legal Verdict" (Cambridge, MA: Belfer Center, Harvard Kennedy School, July 11, 2016), https://www.belfercenter.org/publication/course-china-all-great-powers-will -ignore-international-legal-verdict.

40. Alan Wachman, *Why Taiwan? Geostrategic Rationales for China's Territorial Integrity* (Stanford, CA: Stanford University Press, 2007).

41. M. Taylor Fravel, "Regime Insecurity and International Cooperation: Explaining China's Compromises in Territorial Disputes," *International Security* 30, no. 2 (2005): 81.

42. Ministry of Foreign Affairs, People's Republic of China, "Set Aside Dispute and Pursue Joint Development," Diplomatic History, Events and Issues, November 2000, https://www.fmprc.gov.cn/mfa_eng/ziliao_665539/3602_665543/3604_665547/200011 /t20001117_697808.html.

43. John A. Vasquez, *The War Puzzle* (New York: Cambridge University Press, 1993); Vasquez, *The War Puzzle Revisited* (Cambridge: Cambridge University Press, 2009); and Vasquez and Marie T. Henehan. *Territory, War, and Peace* (New York: Routledge, 2011).

44. Fravel, "Regime Insecurity;" M. Taylor Fravel, *Strong Border, Secure Nation: Cooperation and Order in China's Territorial Disputes* (Princeton, NJ: Princeton University Press, 2008); and Albert B. Wolf, "Correspondence: Structural Sources of China's Territorial Compromises," *International Security* 31, no. 2 (2006): 206–208.

45. M. Taylor Fravel, "Power Shifts and Escalation: Explaining China's Use of Force in Territorial Disputes," *International Security* 32, no. 3 (2007–2008): 44–83; and Ketian Zhang, "Cautious Bully: Reputation, Resolve, and Beijing's Use of Coercion in the South China Sea," *International Security* 44, no. 1 (2019): 117–59.

46. Bjorn Jerden, "The Assertive China Narrative: Why It Is Wrong and How So Many Still Bought into It," *Chinese Journal of International Politics* 7, no. 1 (2014): 47–88; and Alastair I. Johnston, "How New and Assertive Is China's New Assertiveness?," *International Security* 37, no. 4 (2013): 7–48.

47. Monica D. Toft, "Why Is America Addicted to Foreign Interventions?," *National Interest*, December 10, 2017, https://nationalinterest.org/feature/why-america-addicted -foreign-interventions-23582.

48. Quoted in David C. Kang, "Thought Games about China," *Journal of East Asian Studies* 20, no. 2 (2020): 140.

49. Quoted in Chengxin Pan, *Knowledge, Desire and Power in Global Politics: Western Representations of China's Rise* (Cheltenham, UK: Edward Elgar, 2012), 101.

50. Stephen G. Brooks and William C. Wohlforth, *America Abroad: The United States' Global Role in the 21st Century* (New York: Oxford University Press, 2016); Andrea Gilli and Mauro Gilli, "Why China Has Not Caught Up Yet: Military-Technological Superiority and the Limits of Imitation, Reverse Engineering, and Cyber Espionage," *International Security* 43, no. 3 (2019): 141–89; and Barry R. Posen, "Command of the Commons: The Military Foundation of U.S. Hegemony," *International Security* 28, no. 1 (2003): 5–46.

51. Diego Lopes da Silva, Nan Tian, and Alexandra Marksteiner, "Trends in World Military Expenditure, 2020," SIPRI Fact Sheet (Solna: Stockholm International Peace Research Institute, 2021).

52. Indra de Soysa and Paul Midford, "Enter the Dragon! An Empirical Analysis of Chinese versus US Arms Transfers to Autocrats and Violators of Human Rights," *International Studies Quarterly* 56, no. 4 (2012): 843–56.

53. For example, Kenneth N. Waltz, *Theory of International Politics* (Reading, MA: Addison-Wesley, 1979).

54. For example, John J. Mearsheimer, *The Tragedy of Great Power Politics* (New York: Norton, 2001).

55. Steve Chan, "Power Shift, Problem Shift, and Policy Shift: Americans' Reactions to Global China's Rise," unpublished manuscript.

56. Steve Chan, *Thucydides's Trap? Historical Interpretation, Logic of Inquiry, and the Future of Sino-American Relations* (Ann Arbor: University of Michigan Press, 2020); and Chan et al., *Contesting Revisionism: China, the United States, and the Transformation of International Order* (Oxford: Oxford University Press, 2021).

57. R. B. J. Walker, *Inside/Outside: International Relations as Political Theory* (Cambridge: Cambridge University Press, 1995), 6.

58. Daniel W. Drezner, "Perception, Misperception, and Sensitivity: Chinese Economic Power and Preferences after the 2008 Financial Crisis," in *Strategic Adjustment and the Rise of China*, ed. Robert S. Ross and Oystein Tunsjo (Ithaca, NY: Cornell University Press, 2017), 82.

59. Drezner, "Perception," 91.

60. J. Lawrence Broz, Zhiwen Zhang, and Gaoyang Wang, "Explaining Foreign Support for China's Global Economic Leadership," *International Organization* 74, no. 3 (2020): 432.

61. Zakaria, "New China Scare," 58.

62. Zakaria, "New China Scare," 57.

63. Broz, Zhang, and Wang, "Explaining Foreign Support," 433.

64. Ha-Joon Chung, *Kicking Away the Ladder: Development Strategy in Historical Perspective* (London: Anthem Press, 2002).

65. Kristen Hopewell, "Strategic Narratives in Global Trade Politics: American Hegemony, Free Trade, and the Hidden Hand of the State," *Chinese Journal of International Politics* 14, no. 1 (2021): 51–86.

66. Hopewell, "Strategic Narratives," 73.

67. Hopewell, "Strategic Narratives," 86.

68. Jennifer Lind and Daryl G. Press, "Markets and Mercantilism? How China Secures Its Energy Supplies," *International Organization* 42, no. 4 (2018): 203 (italics in the original).

69. Johnston, "World of Orders," 42.

70. Taiwan Documents Project, "Shanghai Communiqué: Joint Communique of the United States of America and the People's Republic of China," February 28, 1972, http://www.taiwandocuments.org/communique01.htm.

71. Quoted in Patrick Tyler, *A Great Wall, Six Presidents and China: An Investigative History* (New York: Perseus, 1999), 225.

72. Reuters, "Timeline: U.S. Arms Sales to Taiwan in 2020 Total $5 Billion Amid China Tensions," December 7, 2020, https://www.reuters.com/article/us-taiwan-security-usa-timeline/timeline-u-s-arms-sales-to-taiwan-in-2020-total-5-billion-amid-china-tensions idUSKBN28I0BF.

73. Chiang Yi-ching and Stacy Hsu, "U.S. Tweet Signals Level of Engagement with Taiwan Seen under Trump," Central News Agency, February 11, 2021, https://www.globalsecurity.org/wmd/library/news/taiwan/2021/taiwan-210211-cna02.htm.

74. Ben Blanchard, "U.S. Should Recognise Taiwan, Former Top Diplomat Pompeo Says," Reuters, March 4, 2022, https://www.reuters.com/world/asia-pacific/us-should-recognise-taiwan-former-top-diplomat-pompeo-says-2022-03-04/.

75. Dov H. Levin, *Meddling in the Ballot Box: The Causes and Effects of Partisan Electoral Interventions* (Oxford: Oxford University Press, 2020).

76. Alastair I. Johnston and Robert S. Ross, conclusion to *Engaging China: The Management of an Emergent Power*, ed. Alastair I. Johnston and Robert S. Ross (London: Routledge, 1999), 291–92.

77. Evan S. Medeiros, *China's International Behavior: Activism, Opportunism, and Diversification* (Santa Monica, CA: RAND Corporation, 2009), xx.

78. Georg Struver, "China's Partnership Diplomacy: International Alignment Based on Interest or Ideology," *Chinese Journal of International Politics* 10, no. 1 (2017): 31–65.

79. Jennifer Lind, "Asia's Other Revisionist Power: Why U.S. Grand Strategy Unnerves China," *Foreign Affairs* 96, no. 2 (2017): 74–82.

80. Stuart Lau, "German Minister and US Envoy Clash Over Huawei's Possible Participation in Germany's 5G Network," *South China Morning Post*, November 26, 2019, https://www.scmp.com/news/world/europe/article/3039320/german-minister-and-us-envoy-clash-over-huaweis-possible.

81. Jeffrey T. Richelson, ed., "The Snowden Affair: Web Resources the Latest Firestorm over the National Security Agency," *National Security Archive Electronic Briefing Book* (Washington, DC: National Security Archive, George Washington University, September 4, 2013), https://nsarchive2.gwu.edu/NSAEBB/NSAEBB436/.

82. Jon R. Lindsay, "The Impact of China on Cybersecurity: Fiction and Friction," *International Security* 39, no. 3 (2014–2015): 27.

83. John Pomfret, "China Finds Bugs on Jet Equipped in U.S.," *Washington Post*, January 19, 2002, https://www.washingtonpost.com/archive/politics/2002/01/19/china-finds-bugs -on-jet-equipped-in-us/65089140-2afe-42e0-a377-ec8d4e5034ef/.

84. Nicole Perlroth, *This Is How They Tell Me the World Ends: The Cyber-Weapons Arms Race* (New York: Bloomsbury, 2020).

85. Lindsay, "Impact of China," 44.

86. Nectar Gan, "China Pushes Back on U.S. Claims That Coronavirus Originated from Wuhan Lab," CNN, May 4, 2020, https://www.cnn.com/2020/05/04/asia/china-us -coronavirus-spat-intl-hnk/index.html.

87. Gan, "China Pushes Back."

88. Geneva Sands, Kylie Atwood, Stephen Collinson, and Kevin Bohn, "US Government Report Assesses China Intentionally Concealed Severity of Coronavirus," CNN, May 4, 2020, https://www.cnn.com/2020/05/03/politics/mike-pompeo-china-coronavirus-supplies /index.html.

89. Gan, "China Pushes Back."

90. Kevin Stankiewicz, " 'They Owe Trillions'—Steve Bannon Says China Must Be Held Accountable for Coronavirus Spread," CNBC, April 30, 2020, https://www.cnbc .com/2020/04/30/steve-bannon-china-must-be-held-accountable-for-coronavirus -spread.html. For the ramifications of this claim, see Jessica C. Weiss, "Can the U.S. Sue China for Covid-19 Damages? Not Really. Here's How This Could Quickly Backfire," *Washington Post*, April 29, 2020, https://www.washingtonpost.com /politics/2020/04/29/can-us-sue-china-covid-19-damages-not-really-this-could-quickly -backfire/.

91. Eileen A. J. Connelly, "Blinken Dodges Question on Punishing China for Covid-19 Pandemic," *New York Post*, March 28, 2021, https://nypost.com/2021/03/28/blinken -dodges-on-punishing-china-for-covid-19-pandemic/.

92. Jacqueline Howard, "Coronavirus Likely Spread to People from an Animal—But Needs More Study, New WHO Report Says," CNN, March 30, 2021, https://www.cnn.com/2021 /03/30/health/who-coronavirus-origin-report/index.html.

93. Carolyn Crist, "Investigation into Coronavirus Origins," WebMD, May 28, 2021, https://www.webmd.com/lung/news/20210527/biden-orders-investigation-into-corona virus-origins.

94. *The Guardian*, "US Intelligence Couldn't Resolve Debate over Covid Origins—Official Report," August 27, 2021, https://www.theguardian.com/us-news/2021/aug/27/coronavirus -origin-us-intelligence.

95. John J. Mearsheimer and Stephen M. Walt. "An Unnecessary War," *Foreign Policy*, 134 (January/February 2003): 50–59.

96. John J. Mearsheimer, *Why Leaders Lie: The Truth about Lying in International Politics* (Oxford: Oxford University Press, 2011), 46–49; and John M. Schuster, "The Deception Dividend: FDR's Undeclared War," *International Security* 34, no. 3 (2010): 133–65.

97. Rising Power Initiative, "Rising Powers React."

98. Anna Chernova, Zahra Ullah, and Rob Picheta, "Russia Reacts Angrily after Biden Calls Putin a 'Killer,'" CNN, March 18, 2021, https://www.cnn.com/2021/03/18/europe/biden-putin-killer-comment-russia-reaction-intl/index.html.

99. David C. Kang, *China Rising: Peace, Power, and Order in East Asia* (New York: Columbia University Press, 2007), 87.

100. Immanuel Kant, "Perpetual Peace: A Philosophical Note," 1795, https://www.gutenberg.org/files/50922/50922-h/50922-h.htm#tnote.

101. G. John Ikenberry, *After Victory: Institutions, Strategic Restraint, and the Rebuilding of Order after Major Wars* (Princeton, NJ: Princeton University Press, 2001).

102. Bruce M. Russett and John R. Oneal, *Triangulating Peace: Democracy, Interdependence and International Organizations* (New York: Norton, 2001).

103. China Global Television Network, "Full Text of Xi Jinping Keynote at the World Economic Forum," January 17, 2017, https://america.cgtn.com/2017/01/17/full-text-of-xi-jinping-keynote-at-the-world-economic-forum; and Annabelle Timsit, "Xi Jinping Sends Warning to the US at Davos," World Economic Forum, January 25, 2021, https://qz.com/1962084/read-xi-jinpings-speech-at-the-2021-davos-forum/.

104. Graham T. Allison, "The Myth of Liberal Order: From Historical Accident to Conventional Wisdom," *Foreign Affairs* 97, no. 4 (2018): 124–33; Charles L. Glaser, "A Flawed Framework: Why the Liberal International Concept Is Misguided," *International Security* 43, no. 4 (2019): 51–87; Joseph S. Nye Jr., "The Rise and Fall of American Hegemony: From Wilson to Trump," *International Affairs* 95, no. 1 (2019): 63–80; and Randall L. Schweller, "The Problem of International Order Revisited: A Review Essay," *International Security* 26, no. 1 (2001): 161–86.

105. Zakaria, "New China Scare," 62.

106. Zakaria, "New China Scare," 64.

107. Fareed Zakaria, "Opinion: Is Biden Normalizing Trump's Foreign Policy?," *Washington Post*, September 16, 2021, https://www.washingtonpost.com/opinions/2021/09/16/is-biden-normalizing-trumps-foreign-policy/.

108. Barry Buzan, *The United States and the Great Powers: World Politics in the Twenty-First Century* (Cambridge: Polity Press, 2004); Steve Chan, Richard W. X. Hu, and Kai He, "Discerning States' Revisionist and Status-Quo Orientations: Comparing China and the U.S.," *European Journal of International Relations* 27, no. 2 (2019): 613–40; Steve Chan et al., *Contesting Revisionism*; and Erik Voeten, "Resisting the Lonely Superpower: Responses of States in the United Nations to U.S. Dominance," *Journal of Politics* 66, no. 3 (2004): 729–54.

109. Consumer News and Business Channel, "Trump: NAFTA Worst Trade Deal in History," June 28, 2016, https://www.cnbc.com/video/2016/06/28/trump-nafta-worst-trade-deal-in-history.html.

110. Such as their distributive effects as pointed out by David A. Lake, Lisa L. Martin, and Thomas Risse, "Challenges to Liberal Order: Reflections on *International Organization*," *International Organization* 75, no. 2 (2021): 248.

111. Chan et al., *Contesting Revisionism*.

112. Ido Oren, *Our Enemies and US: America's Rivalries and the Making of Political Science* (Ithaca, NY: Cornell University Press, 2003).

113. Chan, Hu, and He, "Discerning States' Revisionist"; and Voeten, "Resisting the Lonely Superpower."

114. Johnston, "World of Orders," 12.

115. Randall L. Schweller, "Opposite but Compatible Nationalisms: A Neoclassical Realist Approach to the Future of US-China Relations," *Chinese Journal of International Politics* 11, no. 1 (2018): 39, 41.

116. Jisi Wang, "The Plot against China? How Beijing Sees the New Washington Consensus," *Foreign Affairs* 100, no. 4 (2021): 48–57.

117. Jonathan Kirshner, "Handle Him with Care: The Importance of Getting Thucydides Right," *Security Studies*, 28, no. 1 (2019): 1–24; and Kirshner, "Offensive Realism, Thucydides Trap, and the Tragedy of Unforced Errors: Classical Realism and US-China Relations," *China International Strategy Review* 1 (2019): 51–63.

118. John J. Mearsheimer, "China's Unpeaceful Rise," *Current History* 105, no. 690 (2006): 160–62.

119. Mearsheimer, *Tragedy*.

120. James D. Fearon, "Rationalist Explanations for War," *International Organization* 49, no. 3 (1995): 379–414; and Robert Powell, "War as a Commitment Problem," *International Organization* 60, no. 1 (2006): 169–203.

121. Charles A. Kupchan, *How Enemies Become Friends: The Sources of Stable Peace* (Princeton, NJ: Princeton University Press, 2010), 397.

122. Christopher Layne, "The Waning of U.S. Hegemony—Myth or Reality? A Review Essay," *International Security* 34, no. 1 (2009): 147–72; and John J. Mearsheimer, "Bound to Fail: The Rise and Fall of the Liberal International Order," *International Security* 43, no. 4 (2019): 7–50.

123. Andrej Krickovic, "The Symbiotic China-Russia Partnership: Cautious Riser and Desperate Challenger," *Chinese Journal of International Politics* 10, no. 3 (2017): 299–329; and Krickovic and Chang Zhang, "Fears of Falling Short versus Anxieties of Decline: Explaining Russia and China's Approach to Status-Seeking," *Chinese Journal of International Politics* 13, no. 2 (2020): 219–51.

124. On the Kantian tripod and the literature on democratic peace, see Russett and Oneal, *Triangulating Peace*.

2. CONCEPTUAL AND MEASUREMENT PROBLEMS IN STUDYING POWER

1. Stephen G. Brooks, "Dueling Realisms," *International Organization* 51, no. 3 (1997): 445–77; Jonathan Kirshner, "The Tragedy of Offensive Realism: Classical Realism and

the Rise of China," *European Journal of International Relations* 18, no. 1 (2012): 53–75; John J. Mearsheimer, *The Tragedy of Great Power Politics* (New York: Norton, 2001); Hans J. Morgenthau, *Politics among Nations: The Struggle for Power and Peace* (New York: Knopf, 1960); John A. Vasquez, "The Realist Paradigm and Degenerative versus Progressive Research Programs: An Appraisal of Neotraditional Research on Waltz's Balancing Proposition," *American Political Science Review* 91, no. 4 (1997): 899–912; and Kenneth N. Waltz, *Theory of International Politics* (Reading, MA: Addison-Wesley, 1979).

2. Graham T. Allison, *Destined for War: Can America and China Escape Thucydides's Trap?* (Boston: Houghton Mifflin Harcourt, 2017); Robert Gilpin, *War and Change in World Politics* (Cambridge: Cambridge University Press, 1981); and A. F. K. Organski and Jacek Kugler, *The War Ledger* (Chicago: University of Chicago Press, 1980).

3. David A. Baldwin, "Power Analysis and World Politics: New Trends Versus Old Tendencies," *World Politics* 31, no 2 (1979): 161–94; Baldwin, *Power and International Politics: A Conceptual Approach* (Princeton, NJ: Princeton University Press, 2016); Ray S. Cline, *The Power of Nations in the 1990s: A Strategic Assessment* (Lanham, MD: University Press of America, 2002); Jeffrey Hart, "Three Approaches to the Measurement of Power in International Relations," *International Organization* 30, no. 2 (1976): 289–305; Jacek Kugler and Marina Arbetman, "Choosing among Measures of Power: A Review of the Empirical Record," in *Power in World Politics*, ed. Richard J. Stoll and Michael D. Ward (Boulder, CO: Lynne Rienner, 1989), 49–78; Richard L. Merritt and Dina A. Zinnes, "Validity of Power Indices," *International Interactions* 14, no. 2 (1988): 141–51; Merritt and Zinnes, "Alternative Indexes of National Power," in *Power in World Politics*, ed. Richard J. Stoll and Michael D. Ward (Boulder, CO: Lynne Rienner, 1989), 11–28; Lewis W. Snider, "Identifying the Elements of State Power: Where Do We Begin?," *Comparative Political Studies* 20, no. 3 (1987): 314–56; Charles S. Taber, "Power Capability Indexes in the Third World," in *Power in World Politics*, ed. Richard J. Stoll and Michael D. Ward (Boulder, CO: Lynne Rienner, 1989), 29–48; Ashley J. Tellis, "Overview: Assessing National Power," in *Foundations of National Power in the Asia-Pacific*, ed. Ashley J. Tellis, Alison Szalwinski, and Michael Willis (Seattle: National Bureau of Asian Research, 2015), 2–21, https://www.nbr.org/wp-content/uploads/pdfs/publications /sa15_overview_telllis.pdf; and Dennis H. Wrong, *Power: Its Forms, Bases, and Uses* (New Brunswick, NJ: Transaction, 1995).

4. Joseph S. Nye Jr., *Bound to Lead: The Changing Nature of American Power* (New York: Basic Books, 1990); Nye, *The Paradox of American Power* (New York: Oxford University Press, 2002); and Nye, *Soft Power: The Means to Success in World Politics* (New York: Public Affairs, 2004).

5. Raymond Boudon and Francois Bourricaud, *A Critical Dictionary of Sociology* (London: Routledge, 1989).

6. Tellis, "Overview: Assessing National Power."

7. Tellis, "Overview: Assessing National Power," 5.

8. J. David Singer, Stuart Bremer, and John Stuckey, "Capability Distribution, Uncertainty, and Major Power War, 1820–1965," in *Peace, War, and Numbers*, ed. Bruce M. Russett (Beverly Hills, CA: SAGE, 1968), 19–48.

9.   Statistics Times, "Comparing United States and China by Economy," 2019, http://statisticstimes.com/economy/united-states-vs-china-economy.php.

10. Michael Beckley, "The Power of Nations: Measuring What Matters," *International Security* 43, no. 2 (2018): 22.

11. Beckley, "Power of Nations," 11. See also Caleb Pomeroy and Michael Beckley, "Correspondence: Measuring Power in International Relations," *International Security* 44, no. 1 (2019): 197–200.

12. Beckley, "Power of Nations," 28.

13. Michael Beckley, "Economic Development and Military Effectiveness," *Journal of Strategic Studies* 34, no. 1 (2010): 54.

14. Beckley, "Power of Nations," 42.

15. Tellis, "Overview: Assessing National Power," 5.

16. International Strategic Analysis, "The ISA 2022 Country Power Ranking," https://www.isa-world.com/news/?tx_ttnews%5BbackPid%5D=1&tx_ttnews%5Btt_news%5D=595&cHash=d37d2e848d6b79811749a619c74abebc.

17. R. Ned Lebow and Benjamin Valentino, "Lost in Transition: A Critical Analysis of Power Transition Theory," *International Relations* 23, no. 3 (2009): 389–410.

18. Lebow and Valentino, "Lost in Transition," 397–398, 400, 406.

19. Organski and Kugler, *War Ledger*.

20. Carsten Rauch, "Challenging the Power Consensus: GDP, CINC, and Power Transition," *Security Studies* 26, no. 4 (2017): 642–64.

21. David A. Lake, "Economic Openness and Great Power Competition: Lessons for China and the United States," *Chinese Journal of International Politics* 11, no. 3 (2018): 259.

22. As reported by Rauch, "Challenging the Power Consensus," 654. The Maddison project refers to Angus Maddison, "Historical Statistics of the World Economy: 1–2006 AD," 2010, http://www.ggdc.net/maddison/Historical_Statistics/horizontal-file_02-2010.xls.

23. Edie Purdie, "Tracking GDP in PPP Terms Shows Rapid Rise of China and India," *Data Blog* (World Bank ICP blog), October 19, 2019, https://blogs.worldbank.org/opendata/tracking-gdp-ppp-terms-shows-rapid-rise-china-and-india.

24. Rauch, "Challenging the Power Consensus," 654.

25. Rauch, "Challenging the Power Consensus," 655.

26. Organski and Kugler, *War Ledger*.

27. Joshua I. R. Shifrinson and Michael Beckley, "Correspondence: Debating China's Rise and U.S. Decline," *International Security* 37, no. 3 (2012–2013): 172–81.

28. Sean Starrs, "American Economic Power Hasn't Declined—It Globalized! Summoning the Data and Taking Globalization Seriously," *International Studies Quarterly* 57, no. 4 (2013): 817–30.

29. Kristen Hopewell, "Strategic Narratives in Global Trade Politics: American Hegemony, Free Trade, and the Hidden Hand of the State," *Chinese Journal of International Politics* 14, no. 1 (2021): 77.

30. George Modelski and William R. Thompson, *Leading Sectors and World Powers: The Coevolution of Global Politics and Economics* (Columbia: University of South Carolina Press, 1996).

31. Kishore Mahbubani, *Has China Won? The Chinese Challenge to American Primacy* (New York: Hachette, 2020); and Tian Zhu, *Catching Up to America: Culture, Institutions, and the Rise of China* (Cambridge: Cambridge University Press, 2021), 43.

32. Michael D. Swaine and Ashley L. Tellis, *Interpreting China's Grand Strategy: Past, Present, and Future* (Santa Monica, CA: RAND, 2000), 227.

33. Organski and Kugler, *War Ledger*.

34. Jacek Kugler and Marina Arbetman, "Relative Policy Capacity: Political Extraction and Political Reach," in *Political Capacity and Economic Behavior*, ed. Marina Arbetman and Jacek Kugler (Boulder, CO: Westview, 1997), 11–45; and Kugler and William Domke, "Comparing the Strengths of Nations," *Comparative Political Studies* 19, no. 1 (1986): 39–69.

35. Marina Arbetman-Rabinowitz and Kristin Johnson, "Oil . . . Path to Prosperity or Poverty," in *The Performance of Nations*, ed. Jacek Kugler and Ronald L. Tammen (Lanham, MD: Rowman & Littlefield, 2012), 138–59.

36. Andrew Mack, "Why Big Nations Lose Small Wars: The Politics of Asymmetric Conflict," *World Politics* 27, no. 2 (1975): 175–200; and Frank Wayman, J. David Singer, and Gary Goertz, "Capabilities, Allocations, and Success in Militarized Disputes and Wars, 1816–1976," *International Studies Quarterly* 27, no. 4 (1983): 497–515.

37. Beckley, "Economic Development and Military Effectiveness," 75.

38. Boudon and Bourricaud, *Critical Dictionary*.

39. Tellis, "Overview: Assessing National Power," 5.

40. Organski and Kugler, *War Ledger*.

41. Kugler and Domke, "Comparing the Strength of Nations," 43.

42. Arbetman and Kugler, *Relative Policy Capacity*.

43. Organski and Kugler, *War Ledger*.

44. Jacek Kugler, Ronald L. Tammen, and John Thomas, "How Political Performance Impacts Conflict and Growth," in *The Performance of Nations*, ed. Kugler and Tammen (Lanham, MD: Rowman & Littlefield, 2012), 85.

45. Marina Arbetman-Rabinowitz et al., "Political Performance," in *The Performance of Nations*, ed. Jacek Kugler and Ronald L. Tammen (Lanham, MD: Rowman & Littlefield, 2012), 32.

46. Robert D. Putnam, *Bowling Alone: The Collapse and Revival of American Society* (New York: Simon & Schuster, 2000).

47. Peter B. Evans, *Embedded Autonomy: States and Industrial Transformation* (Princeton, NJ: Princeton University Press, 1995).

48. Jacek Kugler and Ronald L. Tammen, eds., *The Performance of Nations* (Lanham, MD: Rowman & Littlefield, 2012).

49. Mark Abdollahian, Kyungkook Kang, and John Thomas, "The Politics of Economic Growth," in *The Performance of Nations*, ed. Jacek Kugler and Ronald L. Tammen (Lanham, MD: Rowman & Littlefield, 2012), 56–78.

50. Arbetman-Rabinowitz et al., "Political Performance," 43.

51. Kimberly Amadeo, "U.S. National Debt by Year," *The Balance*, February 3, 2022, https://www.thebalance.com/national-debt-by-year-compared-to-gdp-and-major-events-3306287.

52.   Fareed Zakaria, "The Divided States of America," YouTube, February 10, 2021, https://www.youtube.com/watch?v=7szHDdPdEfs, 8:52.

53.   Kugler, Tammen, and Thomas, "How Political Performance," 94.

54.   Tellis, "Overview: Assessing National Power," 6.

55.   For example, James C. Coleman, *The Mathematics of Collective Action* (Chicago: Aldine, 1973); and Jeffrey Hart, "Three Approaches to the Measurement of Power in International Relations," *International Organization* 30, no. 2 (1976): 289–305.

56.   Robert Dahl, "The Concept of Power," *Behavioral Science* 2, no. 3 (1957): 201–15.

57.   Robert O. Keohane and Joseph S. Nye Jr., *Power and Interdependence* (Boston: Little, Brown, 1977), 12, 13.

58.   Keohane and Nye, *Power and Interdependence*, 13.

59.   Jonathan D. Moyer, Collin J. Meisel, Austin S. Matthews, David K. Bohl, and Mathew J. Burrows, *China-US Competition: Measuring Global Influence* (Washington, DC: Scowcroft Center, Atlantic Council and Frederick Pardee Center for International Futures, University of Denver, 2021), https://www.atlanticcouncil.org/wp-content/uploads/2021/06/China-US-Competition-Report-2021.pdf.

60.   Moyer et al., *China-US Competition*, 12.

61.   Quoted in Vesna Danilovic, "Conceptual and Selection Bias Issues in Deterrence," *Journal of Conflict Resolution* 45, no. 1 (2001): 97 (italics in the original).

62.   Scott S. Gartner and Randolph M. Siverson, "War Expansion and War Outcome," *Journal of Conflict Resolution* 40, no. 1 (1996): 4–15.

63.   Daniel W. Drezner, *The Sanctions Paradox: Economic Statecraft and International Relations* (Cambridge: Cambridge University Press, 1999).

64.   James D. Fearon, "Signaling versus the Balance of Power and Interests: An Empirical Test of a Crisis Bargaining Model," *Journal of Conflict Resolution* 38, no. 2 (1994): 236–69.

65.   Paul K. Huth and Bruce M. Russett, "General Deterrence Between Enduring Rivals: Testing Three Competing Models," *American Political Science Review* 87, no. 1 (1993): 61–73.

66.   Graham T. Allison and Philip Zelikow, *Essence of Decision: Explaining the Cuban Missile Crisis*, 2nd ed. (New York: Longman, 1999).

67.   Dustin Tingley, "Rising Power on the Mind," *International Organization* 71, no. S1 (2017): S165–88.

68.   Tingley, "Rising Power," S169.

69.   William C. Wohlforth, "The Perception of Power: Russia in the Pre-1914 Balance," *World Politics* 39, no. 3 (1987): 354.

70.   Wohlforth, "Perception of Power," 381.

71.   Wohlforth, "Perception of Power," 365.

72.   Haixia Qi, "Disputing Chinese Views on Power," *Chinese Journal of International Politics* 10, no. 2 (2017): 211–39.

73.   Qiang Xin, "Having Much in Common? Changes and Continuity in Beijing's Taiwan Policy," *Pacific Review* 33, no. 6 (2021): 926–45.

74.   For an example, see Ashley J. Tellis et al., *Measuring National Power in the Postindustrial Age* (Santa Monica, CA: RAND, 2000).

3. PERSISTENCE OF WASHINGTON'S STRUCTURAL POWER IN U.S. GLOBAL DOMINATION

1.   Karl Marx, "Eighteenth of Brumaire of Louis Napoleon" (first published 1852; New York: International Publishers, 1963), https://archive.org/details/eighteenthbrumai017766mbp.

2.   Michael Barnett and Raymond Duvall, "Power in International Politics," *International Organization* 59, no 1 (2005): 471–506.

3.   Graham T. Allison, *Destined for War: Can America and China Escape Thucydides's Trap?* (Boston: Houghton Mifflin Harcourt, 2017); and Aaron L. Friedberg, *A Contest for Supremacy: China, America, and the Struggle for Mastery in Asia* (New York: Norton, 2011).

4.   Joseph S. Nye Jr., *Bound to Lead: The Changing Nature of American Power* (New York: Basic Books, 1990); Nye, *The Paradox of American Power* (New York: Oxford University Press, 2002); and Nye, *Soft Power: The Means to Success in World Politics* (New York: Public Affairs, 2004).

5.   Susan Strange, "The Persistent Myth of Lost Hegemony," *International Organization* 41, no. 4 (1987): 551–74.

6.   On this distinction, see also Robert O. Keohane and Joseph S. Nye Jr., *Power and Interdependence* (Boston: Little, Brown, 1977).

7.   Strange, "Persistent Myth of Lost Hegemony," 565.

8.   Barnett and Duvall, "Power in International Politics," 52–53.

9.   Steven Lukes, *Power: A Radical View* (Houndmills, UK: MacMillan, 1975), 24.

10. Sarah B. Danzman, Thomas Oatley, and William K. Winecoff, "All Crises Are Global: Capital Cycles in an Imbalanced International Political Economy," *International Studies Quarterly* 6, no. 1 (2017): 911.

11. Michael Beckley, "China's Century? Why America's Edge Will Endure," *International Security* 36, no. 3 (2011–2012): 41–78; Stephen G. Brooks and William C. Wohlforth, *America Abroad: The United States' Global Role in the 21st Century* (New York: Oxford University Press, 2016); and Carla Norrlof and William C. Wohlforth, "*Raison de l'Hégémonie* (The Hegemon's Interest): Theory of the Costs and Benefits of Hegemony," *Security Studies* 28, no. 3 (2019): 422–50.

12. Strange, "Persistent Myth of Lost Hegemony," 565.

13. Stephen G. Brooks and William C. Wohlforth, "The Rise and Fall of the Great Powers in the Twenty-First Century: China's Rise and the Fate of America's Global Position," *International Security* 40, no. 3 (2016): 7–53; Andrea Gilli and Mauro Gilli, "Why China Has Not Caught Up Yet: Military-Technological Superiority and the Limits of Imitation, Reverse Engineering, and Cyber Espionage," *International Security* 43, no. 3 (2019): 141–89; and Michael C. Horowitz, Shahryar Pasandideh, Andrea Gilli, and Mauro Gilli, "Correspondence: Military-Technological Imitation and Rising Powers," *International Security* 44, no. 2 (2019): 185–92.

14. Brooks and Wohlforth, "Rise and Fall of the Great Powers;" and Barry R. Posen, "Command of the Commons: The Military Foundation of U.S. Hegemony," *International Security* 28, no. 1 (2003): 5–46.

15. Keir A. Lieber and Daryl G. Press, "The End of MAD: The Nuclear Dimension of U.S. Primacy," *International Security* 30, no. 4 (2006): 7–44.

16. Posen, "Command of Commons," 8–9.

17. Posen, "Command of Commons," 21.

18. Victor D. Cha, *Alignment despite Antagonism: The United States-Korea-Japan Triangle* (Stanford, CA: Stanford University Press, 1999); and Christopher Hemmer and Peter J. Katzenstein, "Why Is There No NATO in Asia? Collective Identity, Regionalism, and the Origins of Multilateralism," *International Organization* 56, no. 3 (2002): 575–607. For a different view, see Yasuhiro Izumikawa, "Network Connections and the Emergence of the Hub-and-Spokes Alliance System in East Asia," *International Security* 45, no. 2 (2020): 7–50.

19. Barry Buzan, "China in International Society: Is 'Peaceful Rise' Possible?," *Chinese Journal of International Politics* 3, no. 1 (2010): 5–36.

20. Reinhard Wolf, "Rising Powers, Status Ambitions, and the Need to Reassure: What China Could Learn from Imperial Germany's Failures," *Chinese Journal of International Politics* 7, no. 2 (2014): 185–219.

21. Thomas J. Christensen, "Fostering Stability or Creating a Monster? China's Rise and U.S. Policy toward East Asia," *International Security* 31, no. 1 (2006): 101.

22. Barry Buzan, *The United States and the Great Powers: World Politics in the Twenty-First Century* (Cambridge: Polity Press, 2004), 105.

23. John J. Mearsheimer, *The Tragedy of Great Power Politics* (New York: Norton, 2001).

24. Graham T. Allison and Philip Zelikow. *Essence of Decision: Explaining the Cuban Missile Crisis*, 2nd ed. (New York: Longman, 1999).

25. John A. Vasquez, *The War Puzzle* (Cambridge: Cambridge University Press, 1993); and Vasquez, *The War Puzzle Revisited* (Cambridge: Cambridge University Press, 2009).

26. Aaron L. Friedberg, *A Contest for Supremacy: China, America, and the Struggle for Mastery in Asia* (New York: Norton, 2011), 228.

27. Fiona S. Cunningham, "The Maritime Rung on the Escalation Ladder: Naval Blockade in a US-China Conflict," *Security Studies* 29, no. 4 (2020): 730–68.

28. Michael A. Barnhart, *Japan Prepares for Total War: The Search for Economic Security, 1919–1945* (Ithaca, NY: Cornell University Press, 1987).

29. Victor D. Hanson, "Lord Ismay, What Has Happened to the Prescient Post-WWII Dictum 'Russians Out, Americans In, Germans Down'?," *National Review*, July 5, 2017, https://www.nationalreview.com/2017/07/nato-russians-out-americans-germans-down -updated-reversed/.

30. Quoted in G. John Ikenberry, Michael Mastanduno, and William C. Wohlforth, "Introduction: Unipolarity, State Behavior, and Systemic Consequences," *World Politics* 61, no. 1 (2009): 10.

31. Brooks and Wohlforth, "Rise and Fall of the Great Powers," 22.

32. Sean Starrs, "American Economic Power Hasn't Declined—It Globalized! Summoning the Data and Taking Globalization Seriously," *International Studies Quarterly* 57, no. 4 (2013): 823.

33. Thomas Oatley et al., "The Political Economy of Global Finance: A Network Model," *Perspectives on Politics* 11, no. 1 (2013): 133–53.

34. Danzman, Oatley, and Winecoff, "All Crises Are Global," 920.

35. Starrs, "American Economic Power," 828.

36. William K. Winecoff, "Structural Power and the Global Financial Crisis: A Network Analytical Approach," *Business and Politics* 17 (2015): 495–525.

37. Richard Saull, "Rethinking Hegemony: Uneven Development, Historic Blocs, and the World Economic Crisis," *International Studies Quarterly* 56, no. 2 (2012): 326 (italics in the original).

38. Beckley, "China's Century?," 49.

39. Patrick E. Shea, "Financing Victory: Sovereign Credit, Democracy, and War," *Journal of Conflict Resolution* 58, no. 5 (2014): 771–85; and Michael Tomz, *Reputation and International Cooperation: Sovereign Debt across Three Centuries* (Princeton, NJ.: Princeton University Press, 2007).

40. Starrs, "American Economic Power," 827.

41. Starrs, "American Economic Power," 820–24.

42. Starrs, "American Economic Power."

43. Brooks and Wohlforth, *America Abroad*, 23.

44. Starrs, "American Economic Power," 819.

45. Michael Mastanduno, *Economic Containment: Cocom and the Politics of East-West Trade* (Ithaca, NY: Cornell University Press, 1992).

46. Jonathan Ponciano, "The Largest Technology Companies in 2019: Apple Reigns as Smartphones Slip and Cloud Services Thrive," *Forbes*, May 15, 2019, https://www.forbes.com/sites/jonathanponciano/2019/05/15/worlds-largest-tech-companies-2019/.

47. Nathan Reiff, "10 Biggest Telecommunications Companies," Investopedia, January 13, 2021, https://www.investopedia.com/articles/markets/030216/worlds-top-10-telecommunications-companies.asp.

48. Alastair I. Johnston, *Social States: China in International Institutions, 1980–2000* (Princeton, NJ: Princeton University Press, 2008).

49. U.S. News and World Report, "2021 Best Global Universities Rankings," 2021, https://www.usnews.com/education/best-global-universities/rankings.

50. Nature Index, "The Top 10 Research Institutions for 2018," June 20, 2019, https://www.natureindex.com/news-blog/ten-global-institutions-universities-twenty-nineteen-annual-tables.

51. Strange, "Persistent Myth of Lost Hegemony," 569.

52. Brooks and Wohlforth, "Rise and Fall of the Great Powers," 42.

53. Beckley, "China's Century?"

54. Beckley, "China's Century?," 75.

55. David M. Ewalt, "The World's Most Innovative Research Institutions 2019," Reuters, September 18, 2019, https://www.reuters.com/innovation/most-innovative-institutions-2019.

56. Brooks and Wohlforth, *America Abroad*, 28.

57. Antonio Gramsci, *Selections from the Prison Notebooks of Antonio Gramsci* (New York: International Publishers, 1971).

58. Adam Breuer and Alastair I. Johnston, "Memes, Narratives and the Emergent US-China Security Dilemma," *Cambridge Review of International Affairs* 32, no. 4 (2019): 429–55.

59. Quoted in Chengxin Pan, *Knowledge, Desire and Power in Global Politics: Western Representations of China's Rise* (Cheltenham, UK: Edward Elgar, 2012), 17.

60. Quoted in Pan, *Knowledge, Desire and Power*, 17 (italics in the original).

61. Linus Hagstrom and Bjorn Jerden, "East Asia's Power Shift: The Flaws and Hazards of the Debate and How to Avoid Them," *Asian Perspective* 38, no. 3 (2014): 352.

62. Stanley Hoffmann, "An American Social Science," *Daedalus* 106, no. 3 (1977): 41–60.

63. Jeff D. Colgan, "American Perspectives and Blind Spots on World Politics," *Journal of Global Security Studies* 4, no. 3 (2019): 300–309.

64. David C. Kang and Alex Yu Ting Lin, "US Bias in the Study of Asian Security: Using Europe to Study Asia," *Journal of Global Security Studies* 4, no. 3 (2019): 393–401.

65. Bentley Allan, Srdjan Vucetic, and Ted Hopf, "The Distribution of Identity and the Future of International Order: China's Hegemonic Prospects," *International Organization* 72, no. 4 (2018): 839.

66. Allan, Vucetic, and Hopf, "Distribution of Identity," 841.

67. Steve Chan et al., *Contesting Revisionism: China, the United States, and the Transformation of International Order* (Oxford: Oxford University Press, 2021).

68. David Rousseau, *Identifying Threats and Threatening Identities: The Social Construction of Realism and Liberalism* (Stanford, CA: Stanford University Press, 2006).

69. Quoted in Joel Carillet, "Hidden Treasures: Shanghai Just Like Kansas City?," Wandering Educators, September 25, 2008, https://www.wanderingeducators.com/best /traveling/hidden-treasures-shanghai-just-kansas-city.html.

70. Johan Galtung, "A Structural Theory of Imperialism," *Journal of Peace Research* 3 (1971): 81–117.

71. Erik Weibel, "Dependency Revisited: International Markets, Business Cycles, and Social Spending in the Developing World," *International Organization* 60, no. 2 (2006): 433–69.

72. Henry Farrell and Abraham L. Newman, "Weaponized Interdependence: How Global Economic Networks Shape State Coercion," *International Security* 44, no. 1 (2019): 42–79.

73. Farell and Newman, "Weaponized Interdependence."

74. G. John Ikenberry, *After Victory: Institutions, Strategic Restraint, and the Rebuilding of Order after Major Wars* (Princeton, NJ: Princeton University Press, 2001); Ikenberry, "The Rise of China and the Future of the West: Can the Liberal System Survive?," *Foreign Affairs* 87, no. 1 (2008): 23–37; Ikenberry, "The Future of the Liberal World Order: Internationalism after America," *Foreign Affairs* 90, no. 3 (2011): 56–68; Ikenberry, *Liberal Leviathan: The Origins, Crisis, and Transformation of the American World Order* (Princeton, NJ: Princeton University Press, 2012); Ikenberry, "The Plot Against American Foreign Policy: Can the Liberal Order Survive?," *Foreign Affairs* 96, no. 3 (2017): 2–9; Ikenberry, "The Rise, Character, and Evolution of International Order," in

International Politics and Institutions in Time, ed. Orfeo Fioretos (Oxford: Oxford University Press, 2017), 59–75; and Ikenberry, "The End of Liberal International Order?," *International Affairs* 94, no. 1 (2018): 7–23.

75. Farrell and Newman, "Weaponized Interdependence," 47.

76. Farrell and Newman, "Weaponized Interdependence."

77. Frank Baumgartner and Bryan D. Jones, *Agendas and Instability in American Politics* (Chicago: University of Chicago Press, 1993); and Claudio Cioffi-Revilla, "The Political Uncertainty of Interstate Rivalries: A Punctuated Equilibrium Model," in *The Dynamics of Enduring Rivalries,* ed. Paul Diehl (Chicago: University of Chicago Press, 1998), 64–97.

78. Christopher Layne, *The Peace of Illusions: American Grand Strategy from 1940 to the Present* (Ithaca, NY: Cornell University Press, 2006).

79. For example, Peter Harris and Peter L. Trubowitz, "The Politics of Power Projection: The Pivot to Asia, Its Failure, and the Future of American Primacy," *Chinese Journal of International Politics* 14, no. 2 (2021): 187–217; Ikenberry, "The End of Liberal International Order?"; Charles A. Kupchan and Peter L. Trubowitz, "Dead Center: The Demise of Liberal Internationalism in the United States," *International Security* 32, no. 2 (2007): 7–44; Kupchan and Trubowitz, "The Illusion of Liberal Internationalism's Revival," *International Security* 35, no. 1 (2010): 95–109; and Joseph S. Nye Jr., "The Rise and Fall of American Hegemony: From Wilson to Trump," *International Affairs* 95, no. 1 (2019): 63–80.

80. Xun Pang, Linda Liu, and Stephanie Ma, "China's Network Strategy for Seeking Great Power Status," *Chinese Journal of International Politics* 10, no. 1 (2017): 1–29.

81. Steve Chan, Richard W. X. Hu, and Kai He, "Discerning States' Revisionist and Status-Quo Orientations: Comparing China and the U.S.," *European Journal of International Relations* 27, no. 2 (2019): 613–40; and Chan et al., *Contesting Revisionism.*

82. Buzan, *United States and the Great Powers,* 69.

83. Brooks and Wohlforth, "Rise and Fall of the Great Powers," 43.

84. Starrs, "American Economic Power," 821.

85. Beckley, "China's Century?," 77.

86. Bruce M. Russett, "The Mysterious Case of Vanishing Hegemony: Or, Is Mark Twain Really Dead?," *International Organization* 39, no. 2 (1985): 207–31.

87. Kupchan and Trubowitz, "Illusion of Liberal Internationalism," 107.

88. Kupchan and Trubowitz, "Illusion of Liberal Internationalism," 108.

89. Brooks and Wohlforth, *America Abroad,* 63–64.

90. Quoted in Jacob G. Hornberger, "America: The Dictatress of the World," Mises Wire, October 9, 2017, https://mises.org/wire/america-dictatress-world.

4. DOMESTIC SOURCES OF FOREIGN POLICY

1. Steve Chan et al., *Contesting Revisionism: China, the United States, and the Transformation of International Order* (Oxford: Oxford University Press, 2021); and Steve Chan, Richard W. X. Hu, and Kai He, "Discerning States' Revisionist and Status-Quo

Orientations: Comparing China and the U.S.," *European Journal of International Relations* 27, no. 2 (2019): 613–40.

2.   Jack Snyder, *Myths of Empire: Domestic Politics and International Ambition* (Ithaca, NY: Cornell University Press, 1993); Etel Solingen, *Regional Orders at Century's Dawn: Global and Domestic Influences on Grand Strategy* (Princeton, NJ: Princeton University Press, 1998); Solingen, "Pax Asiatica versus Bella Levantina: The Foundations of War and Peace in East Asia and the Middle East," *American Political Science Review* 101, no. 4 (2007): 757–80; Solingen, "Domestic Coalitions, Internationalization, and War: Then and Now," *International Security* 39, no. 1 (2014): 44–70; and Arthur A. Stein and Richard Rosecrance, eds., *The Domestic Bases of Grand Strategy* (Ithaca, NY: Cornell University Press, 1993).

3.   Zoltan I. Buzas, "The Color of Threat: Race, Threat Perception, and the Demise of the Anglo-Japanese Alliance, 1902–1923," *Security Studies* 22, no. 4 (2013): 573–606; and Steven Ward, *Status and the Challenge of Rising Powers* (Cambridge: Cambridge University Press, 2017).

4.   Kenneth N. Waltz, *Theory of International Politics* (Reading, MA: Addison-Wesley, 1979).

5.   John J. Mearsheimer, *The Tragedy of Great Power Politics* (New York: Norton, 2001).

6.   David C. Kang, *China Rising: Peace, Power, and Order in East Asia* (New York: Columbia University Press, 2007); Kang, "Hierarchy and Legitimacy in International Systems: The Tribute System in Early Modern East Asia," *Security Studies* 19, no. 4 (2010): 591–622; Kang, *East Asia Before the West: Five Centuries of Trade and Tribute* (New York: Columbia University Press, 2012); Kang, "Thought Games about China." *Journal of East Asian Studies* 20, no. 2 (2020): 135–50; Yuan-kang Wang, *Harmony and War: Confucian Culture and Chinese Power Politics* (New York: Columbia University Press, 2010); and Wang, "The Durability of a Unipolar System: Lessons from East Asian History," *Security Studies* 29, no. 5 (2020): 832–63.

7.   Jason W. Davidson, *The Origins of Revisionist and Status-Quo States* (London: Palgrave Macmillan, 2006).

8.   Bruce Bueno de Mesquita et al., *The Logic of Political Survival* (Cambridge, MA: MIT Press, 2003).

9.   Alexander Wendt, "Anarchy Is What States Make of It: The Social Construction of Power Politics," *International Organization* 46, no. 2 (1992): 391–425.

10. Aaron L. Friedberg, *A Contest for Supremacy: China, America, and the Struggle for Mastery in Asia* (New York: Norton, 2011); and John J. Mearsheimer, "The Gathering Storm: China's Challenge to US Power in Asia," *Chinese Journal of International Politics*. 3, no. 4 (2010): 381–96.

11. Zheng Wang, *Never Forget National Humiliation: Historical Memory in Chinese Politics and Foreign Relations* (New York: Columbia University Press, 2012).

12. Charles A. Kupchan, *Isolationism: A History of America's Efforts to Shield Itself from the World* (Oxford: Oxford University Press, 2020).

13. Fareed Zakaria, "The Divided States of America," YouTube, February 10, 2021, https://www.youtube.com/watch?v=7szHDdPdEfs.

14. Charles A. Kupchan and Peter L. Trubowitz, "Dead Center: The Demise of Liberal Internationalism in the United States," *International Security* 32, no. 2 (2007): 7–44; and Kupchan and Trubowitz, "The Illusion of Liberal Internationalism's Revival," *International Security* 35, no. 1 (2010): 95–109.

15. Robert D. Putnam, "Diplomacy and Domestic Politics: The Logic of Two-Level Games," *International Organization* 42, no. 3 (1988): 427–60.

16. Solingen, "Domestic Coalitions, Internationalization, and War."

17. For discussions on the deglobalization phenomenon, see David A. Lake, Lisa L. Martin, and Thomas Risse, "Challenges to Liberal Order: Reflections on *International Organization*," *International Organization* 75, no. 2 (2021): 225–57; and T. V. Paul and Markus Kornprobst, eds., "Deglobalization and the International Order," special issue, *International Affairs* 97, no. 5 (September 2021).

18. Steve Chan, "Challenging the Liberal Order: The U.S. Hegemon as a Revisionist Power," *International Affairs* 97, no. 5 (2021): 1335–52.

19. China Global Television Network, "Full Text of Xi Jinping Keynote at the World Economic Forum," January 17, 2017, https://america.cgtn.com/2017/01/17/full-text-of-xi-jinping-keynote-at-the-world-economic forum; and Annabelle Timsit, "Xi Jinping Sends Warning to the US at Davos," World Economic Forum, January 25, 2021, https://qz.com/1962084/read-xi-jinpings-speech-at-the-2021-davos-forum/.

20. David A. Lake, "Economic Openness and Great Power Competition: Lessons for China and the United States," *Chinese Journal of International Politics* 11, no. 3 (2018): 237–70.

21. Laura Silver, Kat Devlin, and Christine Huang, "Most Americans Support Tough Stance toward China on Human Rights, Economic Issues," Pew Research Center, March 4, 2021, https://www.pewresearch.org/global/2021/03/04/most-americans-support-tough-stance-toward-china-on-human-rights-economic-issues/.

22. Susan L. Shirk, *China, Fragile Superpower: How China's Internal Politics Could Derail its Peaceful Rise* (Oxford: Oxford University Press, 2007).

23. Peter H. Gries, *China's New Nationalism: Pride, Politics, and Diplomacy* (Berkeley: University of California Press, 2012).

24. Alastair I. Johnston, "Is Chinese Nationalism Rising? Evidence from Beijing," *International Security* 41, no. 3 (2016–2017): 7–43.

25. Johnston, "Is Chinese Nationalism Rising?," 36.

26. Randall L. Schweller, "Opposite but Compatible Nationalisms: A Neoclassical Realist Approach to the Future of US-China Relations," *Chinese Journal of International Politics* 11, no. 1 (2018): 23–48.

27. Jessica C. Weiss, "How Hawkish Is the Chinese Public? Another Look at 'Rising Nationalism' and Chinese Foreign Policy," *Journal of Contemporary China* 28, no. 119 (2019): 679–95.

28. Kai Quek and Alastair I. Johnston, "Can China Back Down? Crisis De-escalation in the Shadow of Popular Opposition," *International Security* 42, no. 3 (2017–2018): 7–36.

29. Mark S. Bell and Kai Quek, "Authoritarian Public Opinion and the Democratic Peace," *International Organization* 72, no. 1 (2018): 227–42.

30. Jessica C. Weiss and Alan Dafoe, "Authoritarian Audiences, Rhetoric, and Propaganda in International Crises: Evidence from China," *International Studies Quarterly* 63, no. 4 (2019): 963–73.

31. Ja Ian Chong, "Popular Narratives versus Chinese History: Implications for Understanding an Emergent China," *European Journal of International Relations* 20, no. 4 (2014): 939–64.

32. Quek and Johnston, "Can China Back Down?"

33. Ja Ian Chong and Todd H. Hall, "The Lessons of 1914 for East Asia Today: Missing the Trees for the Forest," *International Security* 39, no. 1 (2014): 27.

34. Amitai Etzioni, "Is America Becoming a Chauvinistic Nation?," *National Interest*, March 20, 2021, https://nationalinterest.org/feature/america-becoming-chauvinistic -nation-180660.

35. R. Ned Lebow, *The Rise and Fall of Political Orders* (Cambridge: Cambridge University Press, 2018), 213.

36. Miroslav Nincic, *The Logic of Positive Engagement* (Ithaca, NY: Cornell University Press, 2011).

37. Charles A. Kupchan, *How Enemies Become Friends: The Sources of Stable Peace* (Princeton, NJ: Princeton University Press, 2010).

38. Michael Colaresi, *Scare Politics: The Politics of International Rivalry* (Syracuse, NY: Syracuse University Press, 2005).

39. Edward D. Mansfield and Jack Snyder, "Democratization and the Danger of War," *International Security* 20, no. 1 (1995): 5–38; Mansfield and Snyder, "Democratic Transitions, Institutional Strength, and War," *International Organization* 56, no. 2 (2002): 297–337; and Mansfield and Snyder, *Electing to Fight: Why Emerging Democracies Go to War* (Cambridge, MA: MIT Press, 2005).

40. Mansfield and Snyder, "Democratization and the Danger," 6.

41. Aaron Friedberg, "The Future of U.S.-China Relations: Is Conflict Inevitable?," *International Security* 30, no. 2 (2005): 31.

42. Putnam, "Diplomacy and Domestic Politics."

43. Snyder, *Myths of Empire*.

44. Randall L. Schweller, *Unanswered Threats: Political Constraints on the Balance of Power* (Princeton, NJ: Princeton University Press, 2006).

45. Ward, *Status and the Challenge*; Andrej Krickovic, "The Symbiotic China-Russia Partnership: Cautious Riser and Desperate Challenger," *Chinese Journal of International Politics* 10, no. 3 (2017): 299–329; Krickovic and Chang Zhang, "Fears of Falling Short versus Anxieties of Decline: Explaining Russia and China's Approach to Status-Seeking," *Chinese Journal of International Politics* 13, no. 2 (2020): 219–51; Deborah W. Larson and Alexei Shevchenko, "Status Seekers: Chinese and Russian Responses to U.S. Primacy," *International Security* 34, no. 4 (2010): 63–95; and Larson and Shevchenko, *Quest for Status: Chinese and Russian Foreign Policy* (New Haven, CT: Yale University Press, 2019).

46. Ward, *Status and the Challenge*.

47. Larson and Shevchenko, "Status Seekers"; Larson and Shevchenko, *Quest for Status*; Michelle Murray, "Identity, Insecurity, and Great Power Politics: The Tragedy of German Naval Ambition before the First World War," *Security Studies* 19, no. 4 (2010): 656–88; Murray, *The Struggle for Recognition in International Relations: Status, Revisionism, and Rising Powers* (New York: Oxford University Press, 2019); T. V. Paul, "The Accommodation of Rising Powers in World Politics," in *Accommodating Rising Powers: Past, Present, and Future*, ed. T. V. Paul (Cambridge: Cambridge University Press, 2016), 3–32; Xiaoyu Pu, *Rebranding China: Contested Status Signaling in the Changing Global Order* (Stanford, CA: Stanford University Press, 2019); Jonathan Renshon, "Status Deficits and War," *International Organization* 70, no. 3 (2016): 513–50; Renshon, *Fighting for Status: Hierarchy and Conflict in World Politics* (Princeton, NJ: Princeton University Press, 2017); Ward, *Status and the Challenge*; and Reinhard Wolf, "Rising Powers, Status Ambitions, and the Need to Reassure: What China Could Learn from Imperial Germany's Failures," *Chinese Journal of International Politics* 7, no. 2 (2014): 185–219.

48. James D. Fearon, "Rationalist Explanations for War," *International Organization* 49, no. 3 (1995): 379–414.

49. Gries, *China's New Nationalism*.

50. Jessica C. Weiss, *Powerful Patriots: Nationalist Protest in China's Foreign Relations* (Oxford: Oxford University Press, 2014).

51. *The Guardian*, "Truth Behind America's Raid on Belgrade," November 28, 1999, https://www.theguardian.com/theobserver/1999/nov/28/focus.news1; and *The Guardian*, "NATO Bombed Chinese Deliberately," October 17, 1999, https://www.theguardian.com/world/1999/oct/17/balkans.

52. Jonathan Mercer, *Reputation and International Politics* (Ithaca, NY: Cornell University Press, 1996).

53. Robert A. Bickers and Jeffrey N. Wasserstrom, "Shanghai's 'Dogs and Chinese Not Admitted' Sign: Legend, History and Contemporary Symbol," *China Quarterly* 142 (2009): 444–66.

54. Randall L. Schweller, "Rising Powers and Revisionism in Emerging World Orders," *Russia in Global Affairs*, 2015, http://eng.globalaffairs.ru/valday/Rising-Powers-and-Revisionism-in-Emerging-International-Orders-17730.

55. Christopher Layne, *The Peace of Illusions: American Grand Strategy from 1940 to the Present* (Ithaca, NY: Cornell University Press, 2006); Layne, "Preventing the China–U.S. Cold War from Turning Hot," *Chinese Journal of International Politics* 13, no. 3 (2020): 343–85; Peter D. Feaver et al., "Correspondence: The Establishment and U.S. Grand Strategy," *International Security* 42, no. 2 (2019): 197–204; and Patrick Porter, "Why America's Grand Strategy Has Not Changed: Power, Habit, and U.S. Foreign Policy Establishment," *International Security* 42, no. 4 (2018): 9–46.

56. The White House, *The National Security Strategy of the United States of America* (Washington: U.S. State Department, 2002), https://2009-2017.state.gov/documents/organization/63562.pdf.

57. Jennifer Lind, "Asia's Other Revisionist Power: Why U.S. Grand Strategy Unnerves China," *Foreign Affairs* 96, no. 2 (2017): 74–82.

58. Thomas Pepinsky and Jessica C. Weiss, "The Clash of Systems? Washington Should Avoid Ideological Competition with Beijing," *Foreign Affairs*, June 11, 2021, https://www .foreignaffairs.com/articles/united-states/2021-06-11/clash-systems.

59. Kai He et al., "Rethinking Revisionism in World Politics," *Chinese Journal of International Politics* 14, no. 2 (2021): 159–86; Scott L. Kastner, Margaret M. Pearson, and Chard Rector, *China's Strategic Multilateralism: Investing in Global Governance* (Cambridge: Cambridge University Press, 2018); and T. V. Paul, *Restraining Great Powers: Soft Balancing from Empires to the Global Era* (New Haven, CT: Yale University Press, 2018).

60. Yuen Foong Khong, "Primacy or World Order? The United States and China's Rise—A Review Essay," *International Security* 38, no. 3 (2013–2014): 170.

61. Adam P. Liff and G. John Ikenberry, "Racing Toward Tragedy? China's Rise, Military Competition in the Asia Pacific, and the Security Dilemma," *International Security* 39, no. 2 (2014): 88. See also Ronan Tse-min Fu et al., "Correspondence: Looking for Asia's Security Dilemma," *International Security* 40, no. 2 (2015): 181–204.

62. Lewis F. Richardson, *Arms and Insecurity* (Pittsburgh, PA: Boxwood Press, 1960).

63. Snyder, *Myths of Empire*.

64. Solingen, "Domestic Coalitions, Internationalization, and War."

65. Solingen, "Domestic Coalitions, Internationalization, and War," 47.

66. Johan Galtung, "On the Effects of International Sanctions: With Examples from the Case of Rhodesia," *World Politics* 19, no. 3 (1967): 378–416.

67. Sung Eun Kim and Yotam Margalit, "The Tariffs as Electoral Weapons: The Political Geography of US-China Trade War," *International Organization* 75, no. 1 (2021): 1.

68. Linus Hagstrom, "'Power Shift' in East Asia? A Critical Reappraisal of Narratives on the Diaoyu/Senkaku Islands Incident in 2010," *Chinese Journal of International Politics* 5, no. 3 (2012): 267–97; and Alastair I. Johnson, "How New and Assertive Is China's New Assertiveness?," *International Security* 37, no. 4 (2013): 7–48.

69. Gareth Evans, "What Asia Wants from the Biden Administration," *GlobalAsia*, March 2021, https://globalasia.org/v16no1/cover/what-asia-wants-from-the-biden -administration_gareth-evans.

70. Mancur Olson Jr., *The Logic of Collective Action* (Cambridge, MA: Harvard University Press, 1965); and Olson, *The Rise and Decline of Nations: Economic Growth, Stagflation, and Social Rigidities* (New Haven, CT: Yale University Press, 1982).

71. Kim and Margalit, "Tariffs as Electoral Weapons."

72. James D. Fearon, "Signaling Foreign Policy Interests: Tying Hands versus Sinking Costs," *Journal of Conflict Resolution* 41, no. 1 (1997): 68–90.

73. G. John Ikenberry, "The Rise of China and the Future of the West: Can the Liberal System Survive?," *Foreign Affairs* 87, no. 1 (2008): 24.

74. Randall L. Schweller, "The Problem of International Order Revisited: A Review Essay," *International Security* 26, no. 1 (2001): 161–86. A behavior-based order can reflect spontaneous and uncoordinated actions by the pertinent actors stemming from their

natural instincts. Examples include those dynamics based on the logic of balance of power promoting peace and stability, the predispositions of democratic and interdependent states forging a Kantian peace, and the influence of the "invisible hand" in guiding economic markets.

75. Schweller, "International Order Revisited."

76. Schweller, "International Order Revisited," 163.

77. Schweller, "International Order Revisited," 179.

78. News18, "'Unacceptable Behaviour Among Allies': Snubbed over Submarines Deal, France Recalls Envoys from Oz, US," September 19, 2021, https://www.news18.com /news/world/france-recalls-ambassadors-to-australia-us-in-escalating-row-4216139 .html.

79. Jennifer Hauser and Ivana Kottasova, "Australia Had 'Deep and Grave' Concerns about French Submarines' Capabilities, PM Says," CNN, September 19, 2021, https://www.cnn .com/2021/09/19/australia/aukus-australia-submarine-deal-concerns intl/index.html.

80. Joseph S. Nye Jr., "The Rise and Fall of American Hegemony: From Wilson to Trump," *International Affairs* 95, no. 1 (2019): 63–80.

81. John J. Mearsheimer, "Bound to Fail: The Rise and Fall of the Liberal International Order," *International Security* 43, no. 4 (2019): 8. See also Fareed Zakaria, "The New China Scare: Why America Shouldn't Panic About Its Latest Challenger," *Foreign Affairs* 99, no. 1 (2020): 62.

82. Schweller, "International Order Revisited," 164.

83. Schweller, "International Order Revisited," 182.

84. Mearsheimer, "Bound to Fail."

85. Mearheimer, "Bound to Fail," 30.

86. Charles A. Kupchan, *How Enemies Become Friends: The Sources of Stable Peace.* (Princeton, NJ: Princeton University Press, 2010), 24.

87. R. Ned Lebow, *Why Nations Fight: Past and Future Motivations for War* (Cambridge: Cambridge University Press, 2010), 18.

5. TAIWAN AS A POSSIBLE CATALYST FOR SINO-AMERICAN CONFLICT

1. Michael D. Swaine and Ashley L. Tellis, *Interpreting China's Grand Strategy: Past, Present, and Future* (Santa Monica, CA: RAND, 2000), 227.

2. Thomas J. Christensen and Jack Snyder, "Chain Gangs and Passed Bucks: Predicting Alliance Patterns in Multipolarity," *International Organization* 44, no. 2 (1992): 137–68.

3. Quoted in Dale C. Copeland, *The Origins of Major War* (Ithaca, NY: Cornell University Press, 2000), 135.

4. Trumbull Higgins, *Hitler and Russia: The Third Reich in a Two-Front War, 1937–1943* (New York: Macmillan, 1966), 55.

5. William R. Thompson, "A Streetcar Named Sarajevo: Catalysts, Multiple Causation Chains, and Rivalry Structures," *International Studies Quarterly* 47, no. 3 (2003): 453–74.

6. Richard C. Bush, *Untying the Knot: Making Peace in the Taiwan Strait* (Washington, DC: Brookings Institution Press, 2005); and Bush, *Uncharted Strait: The Future of China-Taiwan Relations* (Washington, DC: Brookings Institution Press, 2013).

7. Timothy W. Crawford, *Pivotal Deterrence: Third-Party Statecraft and the Pursuit of Peace* (Ithaca, NY: Cornell University Press, 2003).

8. Steve Chan, "In the Eye of the Storm: Taiwan, China, and the U.S. in Challenging Times," in *Taiwan's Political Economy*, ed. Cal M. Clark, Karl Ho, and Alex C. Tan (New York: Nova Science Publishers, 2021), 61–78.

9. Office of the Secretary of Defense, *Military and Security Developments Involving the People's Republic of China 2020, Annual Report to Congress* (Washington: U.S. Department of Defense, 2020), ii, https://media.defense.gov/2020/Sep/01/2002488689/-1/-1/1/2020-DOD-CHINA-MILITARY-POWER-REPORT-FINAL.PDF.

10. Michael Beckley, "The Emergent Balance in East Asia: How China's Neighbors Can Check Chinese Naval Expansion," *International Security* 42, no. 2 (2017): 78–119; Stephen Biddle and Ivan Oelrich, "Future Warfare in the Western Pacific: Chinese Antiaccess/Area Denial, U.S. AirSea Battle, and Command of the Commons in East Asia," *International Security* 41, no. 1 (2016): 7–48; Andrew S. Erickson et al., "Correspondence: How Good Are China's Antiaccess/Area-Denial Capabilities?," *International Security* 41, no. 4 (2017): 202–13; Michael A. Glosny, "Strangulation from the Sea? A PRC Submarine Blockade of Taiwan," *International Security* 28, no. 4 (2004): 125–60; Lyle Goldstein and William Murray, "Undersea Dragons: China's Maturing Submarine Force," *International Security* 28, no. 4 (2004): 161–96; Oriana S. Mastro, "The Taiwan Temptation: Why Beijing Might Resort to Force," *Foreign Affairs* 100, no. 4 (2021): 58–67; John L. Mearsheimer, "Taiwan's Dire Straits," *National Interest* 130 (March-April 2014): 29–39; Evan B. Montgomery, "Contested Primacy in the Western Pacific: China's Rise and the Future of U.S. Power Projection," *International Security* 38, no. 4 (2014): 115–49; Michael O'Hanlon, "Why China Cannot Conquer Taiwan," *International Security* 25, no. 2 (2000): 51–86; O'Hanlon, Lyle Goldstein, and William Murray, "Correspondence: Damn the Torpedoes: Debating Possible U.S. Navy Losses in a Taiwan Scenario," *International Security* 29, no. 2 (2004): 202–206; Robert S. Ross, "Navigating the Taiwan Strait: Deterrence, Escalation Dominance, and US-China Relations," *International Security* 27, no. 2 (2002): 48–85; and Travis Sharp, John S. Meyers, and Michael Beckley, "Correspondence: Will East Asia Balance against Beijing?" *International Security* 43, no. 3 (2018–2019): 194–97.

11. Biddle and Oelrich, "Future Warfare," 42.

12. Fareed Zakaria, "The New China Scare: Why America Shouldn't Panic About Its Latest Challenger," *Foreign Affairs* 99, no. 1 (2020): 68.

13. Douglas Porch, "The Taiwan Strait Crisis of 1996," *Naval War College Review* 52, no. 3 (1999): 1–34; Robert S. Ross, "The 1995–96 Taiwan Strait Confrontation: Coercion, Credibility, and the Use of Force," *International Security* 25, no. 2 (2000), 110; GlobalSecurity.org, "Taiwan Strait: 21 July 1995 to 23 March 1966," n.d., https://www.globalsecurity.org/military/ops/taiwan_strait.htm; and Vasilas Trigkas, "Aircraft Carriers in the Taiwan Strait," *The Diplomat*, 2014, https://thediplomat.com/2014/12/aircraft-carriers-in-the-taiwan-strait/.

14. Richard D. Fisher Jr., "'One China' and the Military Balance on the Taiwan Strait," in *The "One China" Dilemma*, ed. Peter C. Y. Chow (New York: Palgrave Macmillan, 2008), 217–56; Bruce Gilley, "Not So Dire Straits: How the Finlandization of Taiwan Benefits U.S. Security," *Foreign Affairs* 89, no. 1 (2010): 44–56, 58–60; Charles L. Glaser, "A U.S.-China Grand Bargain: The Hard Choice between Military Competition and Accommodation," *International Security* 39, no. 4 (2015): 49–90; Derek Grossman et al., "Correspondence: Stability or Volatility across the Taiwan Strait?," *International Security* 41, no. 2 (2016): 192–197; Scott L. Kastner, *Political Conflict and Economic Interdependence across the Taiwan Strait and Beyond* (Stanford, CA: Stanford University Press, 2009); Kastner, "Is the Taiwan Strait Still a Flash Point? Rethinking the Prospects for Armed Conflict between China and Taiwan," *International Security* 40, no. 3 (2015–2016): 54–92; Kastner and Chard Rector, "National Unification and Mistrust: Bargaining Power and the Prospects for a PRC/Taiwan Agreement," *Security Studies* 17, no. 1 (2008): 39–71; George Liao, "Military Balance Across Taiwan Strait Slipping Toward China: Development of Chinese Landing Ships Significantly Enhancing Invasion Capability," *Taiwan News*, July 14, 2020, https://www.taiwannews.com.tw/en/news/3966391; Mastro, "Taiwan Temptation"; Alan D. Romberg, *Rein in at the Brink of the Precipice: American Policy toward Taiwan and U.S.-PRC Relations* (Washington, DC: Stimson Center, 2003); Phillip C. Sanders and Scott L. Kastner, "Bridge Over Troubled Water? Envisioning a China-Taiwan Peace Agreement," *International Security* 33, no. 4 (2009): 87–114; and David Shambaugh, "A Matter of Time: Taiwan's Eroding Military Advantage," *Washington Quarterly* 23, no. 2 (2000): 119–33.

15. Mastro, "Taiwan Temptation."

16. Qiang Xin, "Selective Engagement: Mainland China's Dual Track Taiwan Policy," *Journal of Contemporary China* 29, no. 124 (2020): 535–52; and Xin, "Having Much in Common? Changes and Continuity in Beijing's Taiwan Policy," *Pacific Review* 33, no. 6 (2021): 926–45.

17. Brett V. Benson and Emerson M. S. Niou, "Public Opinion, Foreign Policy, and the Security Balance in the Taiwan Strait," *Security Studies* 14, no. 2 (2005): 274–89; John F. S. Hsieh and Emerson M. S. Niou, "Measuring Taiwan Public Opinion on Taiwanese Independence," *China Quarterly* 181, no. 1 (2005): 158–68; Syaru S. Lin, *Taiwan's China Dilemma: Contested Identities and Multiple Interests in Taiwan's Cross-Strait Economic Policy* (Stanford, CA: Stanford University Press, 2016); Frank C. S. Liu, "Taiwanese Voters' Political Identification Profile, 2013–2014: Becoming One China or Creating a New Country?," *Asian Survey* 56, no. 5 (2016): 931–57; Shelley Rigger, *Why Taiwan Matters: Small Island, Global Powerhouse* (Lanham, MD: Rowman & Littlefield, 2011); T. Y. Wang, "Changing Boundaries: The Development of the Taiwan Voters' Identity," in *The Taiwan Voter*, ed. Christopher H. Achen and T. Y. Wang (Ann Arbor: University of Michigan Press, 2017), 45–70; Wang, "Strategic Ambiguity or Strategic Clarity? US Policy toward the Taiwan Issue," *Taiwan Insight*, June 7, 2021, https://taiwaninsight.org/2021/06/07/strategic-ambiguity-or-strategic-clarity-us-policy-towards-the-taiwan-issue/; Wang and I-Chou Liu, "Contending Identities in Taiwan: Implications for Cross-Strait Relations," *Asian Survey* 44, no. 4 (2004): 568–90; Yu-Shan Wu, "Heading

Towards Troubled Waters? The Impact of Taiwan's 2016 Elections on Cross-Strait Relations," *American Journal of Chinese Studies* 23, no. 1 (2016): 59–75; and Zhong Yang, "Explaining National Identity Shift in Taiwan," *Journal of Contemporary China* 25, no. 99 (2016): 336–52.

18. Matt Yu and Shi Hsiu-chuan, "Public Less Confident in U.S. Coming to Taiwan's Defense: Survey," Central News Agency, April 30, 2022, https//focustaiwan.tw/politics /202204300009.

19. Steve Chan, *China's Troubled Waters: Maritime Disputes in Theoretical Perspective* (Cambridge: Cambridge University Press, 2016); and Alan Wachman, *Why Taiwan? Geostrategic Rationales for China's Territorial Integrity* (Stanford, CA: Stanford University Press, 2007).

20. Graham T. Allison, *Essence of Decision: Explaining the Cuban Missile Crisis* (New York: HarperCollins, 1971), 188, 194–95.

21. Hsin-Hsin Pan, Wen-Chin Wu, and Yu-Tzung Chang, "How Chinese Citizens Perceive Cross-Strait Relations: Survey Results from Ten Major Cities in China," *Journal of Contemporary China* 26, no. 106 (2017): 616–31.

22. Elina Sinkkonen, "Nationalism, Patriotism, and Foreign Policy Attitudes among Chinese University Students," *China Quarterly* 216 (2013): 1045–63.

23. Peter Gries and Tao Wang, "Taiwan's Perilous Futures: Chinese Nationalism, the 2020 Presidential Elections, and U.S.-China Tensions Spell Trouble for Cross-Strait Relations," *World Affairs* 183, no. 1 (2020): 40–61.

24. Richard C. Bush, "Eight Things to Notice in Xi Jinping's New Year Speech on Taiwan," *Order from Chaos* (Brookings Institution blog), January 7, 2019, https://www.brookings .edu/blog/order-from-chaos/2019/01/07/8-key-things-to-notice-from-xi-jinpings-new -year-speech-on-taiwan/.

25. Jessica C. Weiss, *Powerful Patriots: Nationalist Protest in China's Foreign Relations* (Oxford: Oxford University Press, 2014).

26. Chan, "Eye of the Storm."

27. Kenneth E. Boulding, *Conflict and Defense: A General Theory* (New York: Harper, 1962).

28. Christopher Layne, "Preventing the China-U.S. Cold War from Turning Hot," *Chinese Journal of International Politics* 13, no. 3 (2020): 343–85.

29. John J. Mearsheimer, *The Tragedy of Great Power Politics* (New York: Norton, 2001).

30. Mastro, "Taiwan Temptation."

31. Dina Smeltz et al., *Rejecting Retreat: Americans Support US Engagement in Global Affairs* (Chicago: Chicago Council on Global Affairs, 2019), 20, https://www.thechic agocouncil.org/sites/default/files/2020–11/report_ccs19_rejecting-retreat_20190909 .pdf.

32. Center for Strategic and International Studies, "Mapping the Future of U.S. China Policy: Views of U.S. Thought Leaders, the U.S. Public, and U.S. Allies and Partners," 2020, https://chinasurvey.csis.org/analysis/.

33. Peter Harris and Peter L. Trubowitz, "The Politics of Power Projection: The Pivot to Asia, Its Failure, and the Future of American Primacy," *Chinese Journal of International Politics* 14, no. 2 (2021): 187.

34. James D. Fearon, "Signaling Foreign Policy Interests: Tying Hands versus Sinking Costs," *Journal of Conflict Resolution* 41, no. 1 (1997): 68–90.

35. Michael Tomz, "Domestic Audience Costs in International Relations: An Experimental Approach," *International Organization* 61, no. 4 (2007): 821–40.

36. Xiaojun Li and Dingding Chen, "Public Opinion, International Reputation, and Audience Costs in an Authoritarian Regime," *Conflict Management and Peace Science* 38, no. 5 (2020): 543–60.

37. Jack Snyder and Erica D. Borghard, "The Cost of Empty Threats: A Penny, Not a Pound," *American Political Science Review* 105, no. 3 (2011): 437–56; and Marc Trachtenberg, "Audience Costs: An Historical Analysis," *Security Studies* 21, no. 1 (2012): 3–42.

38. Robert D. Putnam, "Diplomacy and Domestic Politics: The Logic of Two-Level Games," *International Organization* 42, no. 3 (1988): 427–60.

39. Fearon, "Signaling Foreign Policy Interests."

40. Ja Ian Chong and Todd H. Hall, "The Lessons of 1914 for East Asia Today: Missing the Trees for the Forest," *International Security* 39, no. 1 (2014): 15.

41. Crawford, *Pivotal Deterrence.*

42. Georgetown University Initiative for U.S.-China Dialogue on Global Issues, "America's Taiwan Policy: Debating Strategic Ambiguity and the Future of Asian Security," October 2, 2020, https://uschinadialogue.georgetown.edu/events/america-s-taiwan -policy-debating-strategic-ambiguity-and-the-future-of-asian-security; Bonnie S. Glaser et al., "Dire Straits: Should American Support for Taiwan Be Ambiguous?," *Foreign Affairs,* September 24, 2020, https://www.foreignaffairs.com/articles/united-states/2020 -09-24/dire-straits; Richard Haass and David Sacks, "American Support for Taiwan Must be Unambiguous," *Foreign Affairs,* September 20, 2020, https://www.foreignaffairs .com/articles/united-states/american-support-taiwan-must-be-unambiguous; Patrick Hulme, "Taiwan, 'Strategic Clarity' and the War Powers: A U.S. Commitment to Taiwan Requires Congressional Buy-In," *Lawfare* (blog), December 4, 2020, https://www .lawfareblog.com/taiwan-strategic-clarity-and-war-powers-us-commitment-taiwan -requires-congressional-buy; Wang, "Strategic Ambiguity or Strategic Clarity?"; and Andy Zelleke, " 'Strategic Clarity' Won't Solve the United States' Taiwan Dilemma: An Open Commitment to Defend Taiwan Won't Mean Much Unless the U.S. Has the Certain Capacity to Do So," *The Diplomat,* October 2, 2020, https://thediplomat.com /2020/10/strategic-clarity-wont-solve-the-united-states-taiwan-dilemma/.

43. Thomas Schelling, *Arms and Influence* (New Haven, CT: Yale University Press), 125.

44. Steve Chan, "Prognosticating About Extended Deterrence in the Taiwan Strait: Implications from Strategic Selection," *World Affairs* 168, no. 1 (2005): 13–25; and Chan, "Extended Deterrence in the Taiwan Strait: Discerning Resolve and Commitment," *American Journal of Chinese Studies* 21, no. 2 (2014): 83–93.

45. Jack S. Levy and William Mulligan, "Shifting Power, Preventive Logic, and the Response of the Target: Germany, Russia, and the First World War," *Journal of Strategic Studies* 40, no. 5 (2017): 731–69.

46. William A. Boettcher III, *Presidential Risk Behavior in Foreign Policy: Prudence or Peril?* (New York: Palgrave, 2005); Kai He and Huiyun Feng, *Prospect Theory and Foreign*

Policy Analysis in the Asia Pacific: Rational Leaders and Risky Behavior (New York: Routledge, 2012); Daniel Kahneman and Amos Tversky, "Prospect Theory: An Analysis of Decision under Risk," *Econometrica* 47, no. 2 (1979): 263–92; Jack S. Levy, "Loss Aversion, Framing and Bargaining: The Implications of Prospect Theory for International Conflict," *International Political Science Review* 17, no. 2 (1996): 177–93; and Rose McDermott, *Risk-Taking in International Relations: Prospect Theory in American Foreign Policy* (Ann Arbor: University of Michigan Press, 1998).

47. Ives-Heng Lim, "The Future Instability of Cross-Strait Relations: Prospect Theory and Ma Ying-Jeou's Paradoxical Legacy," *Asian Security* 14, no. 3 (2017): 318–33.

48. R. Ned Lebow, "Miscalculation in the South Atlantic: The Origins of the Falklands War," in *Psychology and Deterrence*, ed. Robert Jervis, R. Ned Lebow, and Janice G. Stein (Baltimore: Johns Hopkins University Press, 1985), 117.

49. Virginia Gamba, *The Falklands/Malvinas War: A Model for North-South Crisis Prevention* (London: Allen & Unwin, 1987), 155.

50. Lebow, "Miscalculation in the South Atlantic," 104.

51. John A. Vasquez, "Whether and How Global Leadership Transitions Will Result in War: Some Long-Term Predictions from Steps-to-War Explanation," in *Systemic Transitions: Past, Present, and Future*, ed. William R. Thompson (New York: Palgrave Macmillan, 2009), 131–60.

52. Mearsheimer, "Taiwan's Dire Straits," 36.

53. Gilley, "Not So Dire Straits"; and Glaser, "U.S.-China Grand Bargain."

54. Paul F. Diehl, ed., *The Dynamics of Enduring Rivalries* (Urbana: University of Illinois Press, 1998); Diehl and Gary Goertz, *War and Peace in International Rivalry* (Ann Arbor: University of Michigan Press, 2000); and Goertz and Diehl, "Enduring Rivalries: Theoretical Constructs and Empirical Patterns," *International Studies Quarterly* 37, no. 2 (1993): 147–71.

CONCLUSION

1. John J. Mearsheimer, *The Tragedy of Great Power Politics* (New York: Norton, 2001); and Mearsheimer, "China's Unpeaceful Rise," *Current History* 105, no, 690 (2006): 160–62.

2. Graham T. Allison, *Destined for War: Can America and China Escape Thucydides's Trap?* (Boston: Houghton Mifflin Harcourt, 2017), 90.

3. See, for example, A. F. K. Organski and Jacek Kugler, *The War Ledger* (Chicago: University of Chicago Press, 1980).

4. Steve Chan, Weixing Hu, and Kai He, *Contesting Revisionism: China, the United States, and the Transformation of International Order* (Oxford: Oxford University Press, 2021); and Chan et al., "Discerning States' Revisionist and Status-Quo Orientations: Comparing China and the U.S.," *European Journal of International Relations* 27, no. 2 (2019): 613–40.

5. Ole R. Holsti, "The Belief System and National Images: A Case Study," *Journal of Conflict Resolution* 6, no. 3 (1962): 244–52.

6.   Mearsheimer, "China's Unpeaceful Rise."

7.   Organski and Kugler, *War Ledger.*

8.   Allison, *Destined for War.*

9.   For example, Steve Chan, *China, the U.S., and the Power-Transition Theory: A Critique* (London: Routledge, 2008); and Chan, *Thucydides's Trap? Historical Interpretation, Logic of Inquiry, and the Future of Sino-American Relations* (Ann Arbor: University of Michigan Press, 2020).

10.   Michael Barnett and Raymond Duvall, "Power in International Politics," *International Organization* 59, no 1 (2005): 471–506.

11.   Marina Arbetman and Jacek Kugler, eds., *Political Capacity and Economic Behavior* (Boulder, CO: Westview, 1997); and Jacek Kugler and Ronald L. Tammen, eds., *The Performance of Nations* (Lanham, MD: Rowman & Littlefield, 2012).

12.   Francis Fukuyama, "The Pandemic and the Political Order: It Takes a State," *Foreign Affairs*, July/August 2020, https://www.foreignaffairs.com/articles/world/2020-06-09/pandemic-and-political-order.

13.   George Friedman and Meredith LeBard, *The Coming War with Japan* (New York: St. Martin's, 1991); Clyde V. Prestowitz Jr., *Trading Places: How We Are Giving Our Future to Japan and How to Reclaim It* (New York: Basic Books, 1990); and Ezra F. Vogel, *Japan as Number One: Lessons for America* (Cambridge, MA: Harvard University Press, 1979).

14.   Chan et al., *Contesting Revisionism.*

15.   R. Ned Lebow and Benjamin Valentino, "Lost in Transition: A Critical Analysis of Power Transition Theory," *International Relations* 23, no. 3 (2009): 410.

16.   G. John Ikenberry, *After Victory: Institutions, Strategic Restraint, and the Rebuilding of Order after Major Wars* (Princeton, NJ: Princeton University Press, 2001).

17.   Ted R. Gurr, *Why Men Rebel?* (Princeton, NJ: Princeton University Press, 1970).

18.   Maurice A. East, "Status Discrepancy and Violence in the International System," in *The Analysis of International Politics*, ed. James N. Rosenau, Vincent Davis, and Maurice A. East, 299–319 (New York: Free Press, 1972); Charles S. Gochman, "Status, Capabilities, and Major Power Conflict," in *The Correlates of War II: Testing Some Realpolitik Models*, ed. J. David Singer, 83–123 (New York: Free Press, 1980); Manus I. Midlarsky, *On War: International Violence in the International System* (New York: Free Press, 1975); Zeev Maoz, *Networks of Nations: The Evolution, Structure, and Impact of International Networks, 1816–2001* (Cambridge: Cambridge University Press, 2010); James L. Ray, "Status Inconsistency and War Involvement among European States, 1816–1970," *Peace Science Society Papers* 23 (1974): 69–80; Thomas J. Volgy and Stacey Mayhall, "Status Inconsistency and International War: Exploring the Effects of Systemic Change," *International Studies Quarterly* 39, no. 1 (1995): 67–84; and Michael D. Wallace, *War and Rank Among States* (Lexington, KY: Heath, 1973).

19.   Jonathan Renshon, "Status Deficits and War," *International Organization* 70, no. 3 (2016): 513–50; and Renshon, *Fighting for Status: Hierarchy and Conflict in World Politics* (Princeton, NJ: Princeton University Press, 2017).

20.   Chan, *Thucydides's Trap?*

21. Paul K. MacDonald and Joseph M. Parent, "Graceful Decline? The Surprising Success of Great Power Retrenchment," *International Security* 35, no. 4 (2011): 7–44; MacDonald and Parent, "The Road to Recovery: How Once Great Powers Became Great Again," *Washington Quarterly* 41, no. 3 (2018): 21–39; and MacDonald and Parent, *Twilight of Titans: Great Power Decline and Retrenchment* (Ithaca, NY: Cornell University Press, 2018).

22. Robert Powell, *In the Shadow of Power: States and Strategies in International Politics* (Princeton, NJ: Princeton University Press, 1999), 199.

23. Bill Bostock, "Secretary of State Antony Blinken Says He Stands by Mike Pompeo's Designation that China Committed Genocide against the Uighurs," Yahoo!News, January 28, 2021, https://news.yahoo.com/secretary-state-antony-blinken-says-110049095.html.

24. Kurt M. Campbell and Jake Sullivan, "Competition without Catastrophe: How America Can Both Challenge and Coexist with China," *Foreign Affairs*, September-October 2020, https://www.foreignaffairs.com/articles/china/competition-with-china -without-catastrophe.

25. Charles A. Kupchan and Peter L. Trubowitz, "A China Strategy to Reunite America's Allies," Project Syndicate, January 4, 2021, https://www.project-syndicate.org /commentary/biden-china-strategy-to-reunite-us-allies-by-charles-a-kupchan-and -peter-trubowitz-1-2021-01.

26. Christopher Layne, "Preventing the China-U.S. Cold War from Turning Hot," *Chinese Journal of International Politics* 13, no. 3 (2020): 343–85; and Thomas Pepinsky and Jessica C. Weiss, "The Clash of Systems? Washington Should Avoid Ideological Competition with Beijing," *Foreign Affairs*, June 11, 2021, https://www.foreignaffairs.com /articles/united-states/2021-06-11/clash-systems.

27. Jason Slotkin, "Report on Khashoggi Killing Prompts Calls for Penalties against Crown Prince," NPR, February 27, 2021, https://www.npr.org/2021/02/27/972141908/report-on -khashoggi-killing-prompts-calls-for-penalties-against-crown-prince.

28. James D. Fearon, "Rationalist Explanations for War," *International Organization* 49 no. 3 (1995): 379–414.

29. Jonathan Kirshner, "The Tragedy of Offensive Realism: Classical Realism and the Rise of China," *European Journal of International Relations* 18, no. 1 (2012): 53–75; and Kirshner, "Offensive Realism, Thucydides Trap, and the Tragedy of Unforced Errors: Classical Realism and US-China Relations," *China International Strategy Review* 1 (2019): 51–63.

30. Quoted in Rising Powers Initiative, "RPI Policy Alert: Rising Powers React to Contentious U.S.-China Relations: A Roundup," George Washington University, March 2021, https://www.risingpowersinitiative.org/publication/rising-powers-react-to-contentious -u-s-china-relations-a-roundup/.

31. Rising Power Initiative, "RPI Policy Alert."

32. Voice of America News, "Obama: US, Not China, Should Set Pacific Trade Rules," May 3, 2016, https://www.voanews.com/a/obama-united-states-pacific-trade-rules /3313875.html.

33. Rising Power Initiative, "RPI Policy Alert."

34. Rising Power Initiative, "RPI Policy Alert."

35. Rising Power Initiative, "RPI Policy Alert: Rising Powers React to Biden-Suga Summit," George Washington University, April 2021, https://www.risingpowersinitiative .org/publication/rising-powers-react-to-biden-suga-summit/.

36. Jisi Wang, "The Plot Against China? How Beijing Sees the New Washington Consensus," *Foreign Affairs* 100, no. 4 (2021): 48–57; Xuetong Yan, "The Instability of China-US Relations," *Chinese Journal of International Politics* 3, no. 3 (2010): 263–92; and the White House, "The National Security Strategy of the United States of America" (Washington: U.S. State Department, 2002), https://2009-2017.state.gov/documents/organization /63562.pdf. For a response to Yan, see Alastair I. Johnston, "Stability and Instability in Sino-US Relations: A Response to Yan Xuetong's Superficial Friendship Theory," *Chinese Journal of International Politics* 4, no. 1 (2011): 5–29.

37. John J. Mearsheimer, "Taiwan's Dire Straits," *National Interest* 130 (March-April 2014), 29.

38. Fearon, "Rationalist Explanations for War."

39. Anne E. Sartori, "The Might of the Pen: A Reputation Theory of Communication in International Disputes," *International Organization* 56, no. 1 (2002): 121–49; and Sartori, *Deterrence by Diplomacy* (Princeton, NJ: Princeton University Press, 2005).

40. Steve Chan, *Trust and Distrust in Sino-American Relations: Challenge and Opportunity* (Amherst, NY: Cambria Press, 2017).

41. Michael D. Swaine and Ashley L. Tellis, *Interpreting China's Grand Strategy: Past, Present, and Future* (Santa Monica, CA: RAND, 2000).

42. Avery Goldstein, *Rising to the Challenge: China's Grand Strategy and International Security* (Stanford, CA: Stanford University Press, 2005), 12.

43. Kurt M. Campbell and Mira Rapp-Hooper, "China Is Done Biding Its Time: The End of Beijing's Foreign Policy Restraint?," *Foreign Affairs*, July 15, 2020, https://www .foreignaffairs.com/articles/china/2020-07-15/china-done-biding-its-time.

44. Barry Buzan, "China in International Society: Is 'Peaceful Rise' Possible?," *Chinese Journal of International Politics* 3, no. 1 (2010): 5–36.

45. Quoted in Peter Harris and Peter L. Trubowitz, "The Politics of Power Projection: The Pivot to Asia, Its Failure, and the Future of American Primacy," *Chinese Journal of International Politics* 14, no. 2 (2021): 206.

46. Athanassios Platias and Vasilis Trigkas, "Unravelling the Thucydides' Trap: Inadvertent or War of Choice?," *Chinese Journal of International Politics* 14, no. 2 (2021): 187–217.

47. Keir A. Lieber, "The New History of World War I and What It Means for International Relations Theory," *International Security* 32, no. 2 (2007): 193.

48. John J. Mearsheimer, "China's Unpeaceful Rise," *Current History* 105, no, 690 (2006): 160–62; Mearsheimer, "The Gathering Storm: China's Challenge to US Power in Asia," *Chinese Journal of International Politics* 3, no. 4 (2010): 381–96; and Sebastian Rosato, "The Inscrutable Intentions of Great Powers," *International Security* 39, no. 3 (2015): 48–88.

49. Kirshner, "Offensive Realism;" MacDonald and Parent, "Graceful Decline?"; and Yuan Yang, "Escape from both the 'Thucydides Trap' and the 'Churchill Trap': Finding a

Third Type of Great Power Relations Under the Bipolar System," *Chinese Journal of International Politics* 11, no. 2 (2018): 193–235.

50. Johnston, "Stability and Instability," 28.

51. Paul D. Senese and John A. Vasquez, *The Steps to War: An Empirical Study* (Princeton, NJ: Princeton University Press, 2008).

52. Fearon, "Rationalist Explanations for War."

53. James D. Fearon, "Signaling Foreign Policy Interests: Tying Hands versus Sinking Costs," *Journal of Conflict Resolution* 41, no. 1 (1997): 68–90; and Brandon K. Yoder, "Hedging for Better Bets: Power Shifts, Credible Signals, and Preventive Conflict," *Journal of Conflict Resolution* 63, no. 4 (2019): 923–49.

54. Steve Chan, *Looking for Balance: China, the United States, and Power Balancing in East Asia* (Stanford, CA: Stanford University Press, 2012).

55. T. V. Paul, *Restraining Great Powers: Soft Balancing from Empires to the Global Era* (New Haven, CT: Yale University Press, 2018).

56. Evelyn Goh, "Great Powers and Hierarchical Order in Southeast Asia: Analyzing Regional Security Strategy," *International Security* 32, no. 3 (2007–2008): 113–57.

57. Thomas J. Christensen, "Fostering Stability or Creating a Monster? China's Rise and U.S. Policy Toward East Asia," *International Security* 31, no. 1 (2006): 101–102.

BIBLIOGRAPHY

Abdollahian, Mark, Kyungkook Kang, and John Thomas. "The Politics of Economic Growth." In *The Performance of Nations*, ed. Jacek Kugler and Ronald L. Tammen, 56–78. Lanham, MD: Rowman & Littlefield, 2012.

Allan, Bentley, Srdjan Vucetic, and Ted Hopf. "The Distribution of Identity and the Future of International Order: China's Hegemonic Prospects." *International Organization* 72, no. 4 (2018): 839–69.

Allison, Graham T. *Destined for War: Can America and China Escape Thucydides's Trap?* Boston: Houghton Mifflin Harcourt, 2017.

——. *Essence of Decision: Explaining the Cuban Missile Crisis.* New York: HarperCollins, 1971.

——. "The Myth of Liberal Order: From Historical Accident to Conventional Wisdom." *Foreign Affairs* 97, no. 4 (2018): 124–33.

——. "Of Course China, Like All Great Powers, Will Ignore an International Legal Verdict." Cambridge, MA: Belfer Center, Harvard Kennedy School, July 11, 2016. https://www.belfercenter.org/publication/course-china-all-great-powers-will-ignore-international-legal-verdict.

——. "The Thucydides Trap: Are the U.S. and China Headed for War?" *The Atlantic*, September 24, 2015. https://www.theatlantic.com/international/archive/2015/09/united-states-china-war-thucydides-trap/406756/.

Allison, Graham, and Philip Zelikow. *Essence of Decision: Explaining the Cuban Missile Crisis.* 2nd ed. New York: Longman, 1999.

Amadeo, Kimberly. "U.S. National Debt by Year." *The Balance*, February 3, 2022. https://www.thebalance.com/national-debt-by-year-compared-to-gdp-and-major-events-3306287.

Arbetman, Marina, and Jacek Kugler, eds. *Political Capacity and Economic Behavior.* Boulder, CO: Westview, 1997.

Arbetman-Rabinowitz, Marina, and Kristin Johnson. "Oil . . . Path to Prosperity or Poverty." In *The Performance of Nations*, ed. Jacek Kugler and Ronald L. Tammen, 138–59. Lanham, MD: Rowman & Littlefield, 2012.

Arbetman-Rabinowitz, Marina, Jacek Kugler, Mark Abdollahian, Kyungkook Kang, Hal T. Nelson, and Ronald L. Tammen. "Political Performance." In *The Performance of Nations*, ed. Jacek Kugler and Ronald L. Tammen, 19–54. Lanham, MD: Rowman & Littlefield, 2012.

Bacevich, Andrew J. *American Empire: The Realities and Consequences of U.S. Diplomacy.* Cambridge, MA: Harvard University Press, 2002.

Bagby, Laurie M. "The Use and Misuse of Thucydides in International Relations." *International Organization* 48, no. 1 (1994): 131–53.

Baldwin, David A. "Power Analysis and World Politics: New Trends versus Old Tendencies." *World Politics* 31, no 2 (1979): 161–94.

——. *Power and International Politics: A Conceptual Approach.* Princeton, NJ: Princeton University Press, 2016.

Barnett, Michael, and Raymond Duvall. "Power in International Politics." *International Organization* 59, no 1 (2005): 471–506.

Barnhart, Michael A. *Japan Prepares for Total War: The Search for Economic Security, 1919–1945.* Ithaca, NY: Cornell University Press, 1987.

Baumgartner, Frank, and Bryan D. Jones. *Agendas and Instability in American Politics.* Chicago: University of Chicago Press, 1993.

Beckley, Michael. "China's Century? Why America's Edge Will Endure." *International Security* 36, no. 3 (2011–2012): 41–78.

——. "Economic Development and Military Effectiveness." *Journal of Strategic Studies* 34, no. 1 (2010): 43–79.

——. "The Emergent Balance in East Asia: How China's Neighbors Can Check Chinese Naval Expansion." *International Security* 42, no. 2 (2017): 78–119.

——. "The Myth of Entangling Alliances." *International Security* 39, no. 4 (2015): 7–48.

——. "The Power of Nations: Measuring What Matters." *International Security* 43, no. 2 (2018): 7–44.

Bell, Mark S., and Kai Quek. "Authoritarian Public Opinion and the Democratic Peace." *International Organization* 72, no. 1 (2018): 227–42.

Bell, Sam R., and Jesse C. Johnson. "Shifting Power, Commitment Problems, and Preventive War." *International Studies Quarterly* 59, no. 1 (2015): 124–32.

Benson, Brett V., and Emerson M. S. Niou. "Public Opinion, Foreign Policy, and the Security Balance in the Taiwan Strait." *Security Studies* 14, no. 2 (2005): 274–89.

Bickers, Robert A., and Jeffrey N. Wasserstrom. "Shanghai's 'Dogs and Chinese Not Admitted' Sign: Legend, History and Contemporary Symbol." *China Quarterly* 142 (2009): 444–66.

Biddle, Stephen, and Ivan Oelrich. "Future Warfare in the Western Pacific: Chinese Antiaccess/Area Denial, U.S. AirSea Battle, and Command of the Commons in East Asia." *International Security* 41, no. 1 (2016): 7–48.

Blanchard, Ben. "U.S. Should Recognise Taiwan, Former Top Diplomat Pompeo Says." Reuters, March 4, 2022. https://www.reuters.com/world/asia-pacific/us-should-recognise-taiwan-former-top-diplomat-pompeo-says-2022-03-04/.

Boettcher, William A., III. *Presidential Risk Behavior in Foreign Policy: Prudence or Peril?* New York: Palgrave, 2005.

Bostock, Bill. "Secretary of State Antony Blinken Says He Stands by Mike Pompeo's Designation That China Committed Genocide Against the Uighurs." Yahoo!News, January 28, 2021. https://news.yahoo.com/secretary-state-antony-blinken-says-110049095.html.

Boudon, Raymond, and Francois Bourricaud. *A Critical Dictionary of Sociology.* London: Routledge, 1989.

Boulding, Kenneth E. *Conflict and Defense: A General Theory.* New York: Harper, 1962.

Bourne, Kenneth. *Britain and the Balance of Power in North America, 1815–1908.* Berkeley: University of California Press, 1967.

Breuer, Adam, and Alastair I. Johnston. "Memes, Narratives, and the Emergent US-China Security Dilemma." *Cambridge Review of International Affairs* 32, no. 4 (2019): 429–55.

Brooks, Stephen G. "Dueling Realisms." *International Organization* 51, no. 3 (1997): 445–77.

Brooks, Stephen G., and William C. Wohlforth. *America Abroad: The United States' Global Role in the 21st Century.* New York: Oxford University Press, 2016.

——. "The Rise and Fall of the Great Powers in the Twenty-First Century: China's Rise and the Fate of America's Global Position." *International Security* 40, no. 3 (2016): 7–53.

Broz, J. Lawrence, Zhiwen Zhang, and Gaoyang Wang. "Explaining Foreign Support for China's Global Economic Leadership." *International Organization* 74, no. 3 (2020): 417–52.

Buchanan, Allen. *Institutionalizing the Just War.* Oxford: Oxford University Press, 2018.

Bueno de Mesquita, Bruce, and Alastair Smith. *The Dictator's Handbook: Why Bad Behavior Is Almost Always Good Politics.* New York: PublicAffairs, 2012.

Bueno de Mesquita, Bruce, Alastair Smith, Randolph M. Siverson, and James D. Morrow. *The Logic of Political Survival.* Cambridge, MA: The MIT Press, 2003.

Burr, William, and Jeffrey Richelson. "Whether to 'Strangle the Baby in the Cradle': The United States and the Chinese Nuclear Program, 1960–64." *International Security* 25, no. 3 (2000–2001): 54–99.

Bush, Richard C. "Eight Things to Notice in Xi Jinping's New Year Speech on Taiwan." *Order from Chaos* (Brookings Institution blog), January 7, 2019. https://www.brookings.edu/blog/order-from-chaos/2019/01/07/8-key-things-to-notice-from-xi-jinpings-new-year-speech-on-taiwan/.

——. *Uncharted Strait: The Future of China-Taiwan Relations.* Washington, DC: Brookings Institution Press, 2013.

——. *Untying the Knot: Making Peace in the Taiwan Strait.* Washington, DC: Brookings Institution Press, 2005.

Buzan, Barry. "China in International Society: Is 'Peaceful Rise' Possible?" *Chinese Journal of International Politics* 3, no. 1 (2010): 5–36.

——. *The United States and the Great Powers: World Politics in the Twenty-First Century.* Cambridge: Polity Press, 2004.

Buzan, Barry, and Michael Cox. "China and the US: Comparable Cases of 'Peaceful Rise'?" *Chinese Journal of International Politics* 6, no. 2 (2013): 109–32.

Buzas, Zoltan I. "The Color of Threat: Race, Threat Perception, and the Demise of the Anglo-Japanese Alliance, 1902–1923." *Security Studies* 22, no. 4 (2013): 573–606.

Campbell, Kurt M., and Mira Rapp-Hooper. "China Is Done Biding Its Time: The End of Beijing's Foreign Policy Restraint?" *Foreign Affairs*, July 15, 2020. https://www.foreignaffairs .com/articles/china/2020-07-15/china-done-biding-its-time.

Campbell, Kurt M., and Ely Ratner. "The China Reckoning: How Beijing Defied American Expectations." *Foreign Affairs* 97, no. 2 (2018): 60–70.

Campbell, Kurt M., and Jake Sullivan. "Competition without Catastrophe: How America Can Both Challenge and Coexist with China." *Foreign Affairs*, September-October 2020. https:// www.foreignaffairs.com/articles/china/competition-with-china-without-catastrophe.

Carillet, Joel. "Hidden Treasures: Shanghai Just Like Kansas City?" Wandering Educators, September 25, 2008. https://www.wanderingeducators.com/best/traveling/hidden-treasures -shanghai-just-kansas-city.html.

Center for Strategic and International Studies. "Mapping the Future of U.S. China Policy: Views of U.S. Thought Leaders, the U.S. Public, and U.S. Allies and Partners." 2020. https:// chinasurvey.csis.org/analysis/.

Cha, Victor D. *Alignment Despite Antagonism: The United States-Korea-Japan Triangle.* Stanford, CA: Stanford University Press, 1999.

——. "Powerplay: Origins of the U.S. Alliance System in Asia." *International Organization* 34, no. 3 (2009–2010): 158–96.

Chan, Steve. "Challenging the Liberal Order: The U.S. Hegemon as a Revisionist Power." *International Affairs* 97, no. 5 (2021): 1335–52.

——. "China and Thucydides's Trap." In *China's Challenges and International Order Transition: Beyond the "Thucydides Trap,"* ed. Kai He and Huiyun Feng, 52–71. Ann Arbor: University of Michigan Press, 2020.

——. *China's Troubled Waters: Maritime Disputes in Theoretical Perspective.* Cambridge: Cambridge University Press, 2016.

——. *China, the U.S., and the Power-Transition Theory: A Critique.* London: Routledge, 2008.

——. "Exploring Some Puzzles in Power-Transition Theory: Some Implications for Sino-American Relations." *Security Studies* 13, no. 3 (2004): 103–41.

——. "Extended Deterrence in the Taiwan Strait: Discerning Resolve and Commitment." *American Journal of Chinese Studies* 21, no. 2 (2014): 83–93.

——. "In the Eye of the Storm: Taiwan, China, and the U.S. in Challenging Times." In *Taiwan's Political Economy,* ed. Cal M. Clark, Karl Ho, and Alex C. Tan, 61–78. New York: Nova Science Publishers, 2021.

——. *Looking for Balance: China, the United States, and Power Balancing in East Asia.* Stanford, CA: Stanford University Press, 2012.

——. "More Than One Trap: Problematic Interpretations and Overlooked Lessons from Thucydides." *Journal of Chinese Political Science* 24, no. 1 (2019): 11–24.

——. "Power Shift, Problem Shift, and Policy Shift: Americans' Reactions to Global China's Rise." Unpublished manuscript.

——. "Prognosticating about Extended Deterrence in the Taiwan Strait: Implications from Strategic Selection." *World Affairs* 168, no. 1 (2005): 13–25.

——. "Thucydides's Trap?" H-Diplo/ISSF Roundtable Discussion 12-2. November 9, 2020. https://networks.h-net.org/node/28443/discussions/6721850/h-diploissf-roundtable-12-2 -thucydides%E2%80%99s-trap-historical.

——. *Thucydides's Trap? Historical Interpretation, Logic of Inquiry, and the Future of Sino-American Relations.* Ann Arbor: University of Michigan Press, 2020.

——. *Trust and Distrust in Sino-American Relations: Challenge and Opportunity.* Amherst, NY: Cambria Press, 2017.

——. "Why Thucydides' Trap Misinforms Sino-American Relations." *Vestnik RUDN, International Relations* 21, no. 2 (2021): 234–42.

Chan, Steve, Huiyun Feng, Kai He, and Weixing Hu. *Contesting Revisionism: China, the United States, and the Transformation of International Order.* Oxford: Oxford University Press, 2021.

Chan, Steve, Weixing Hu, and Kai He. "Discerning States' Revisionist and Status-Quo Orientations: Comparing China and the U.S." *European Journal of International Relations* 27, no. 2 (2019): 613–40.

Chernova, Anna, Zahra Ullah, and Rob Picheta. "Russia Reacts Angrily after Biden Calls Putin a 'Killer.'" CNN, March 18, 2021. https://www.cnn.com/2021/03/18/europe/biden-putin -killer-comment-russia-reaction-intl/index.html.

Chiang, Yi-ching, and Stacy Hsu, "U.S. Tweet Signals Level of Engagement with Taiwan Seen under Trump." Central News Agency, February 11, 2021. https://www.globalsecurity.org /wmd/library/news/taiwan/2021/taiwan-210211-cna02.htm.

China Global Television Network. "Full Text of Xi Jinping Keynote at the World Economic Forum." January 17, 2017. https://america.cgtn.com/2017/01/17/full-text-of-xi-jinping-keynote -at-the-world-economic-forum.

Chong, Ja Ian. "Popular Narratives versus Chinese History: Implications for Understanding an Emergent China." *European Journal of International Relations* 20, no. 4 (2014): 939–64.

Chong, Ja Ian, and Todd H. Hall. "The Lessons of 1914 for East Asia Today: Missing the Trees for the Forest." *International Security* 39, no. 1 (2014): 7–43.

Christensen, Thomas J. "Fostering Stability or Creating a Monster? China's Rise and U.S. Policy toward East Asia." *International Security* 31, no. 1 (2006): 81–126.

——. "Posing Problems without Catching Up: China's Rise and Challenges for U.S. Security Policy." *International Security* 25, no. 4 (2001): 5–40.

Christensen, Thomas J., and Jack Snyder. "Chain Gangs and Passed Bucks: Predicting Alliance Patterns in Multipolarity." *International Organization* 44, no. 2 (1992): 137–68.

Chubb, Andrew. "PRC Assertiveness in the South China Sea: Measuring Continuity and Change, 1970–2015." *International Security* 45 no. 3 (2020–2021): 79–121.

Chung, Ha-Joon. *Kicking Away the Ladder: Development Strategy in Historical Perspective.* London: Anthem Press, 2002.

Cioffi-Revilla, Claudio. "The Political Uncertainty of Interstate Rivalries: A Punctuated Equilibrium Model." In *The Dynamics of Enduring Rivalries*, ed. Paul Diehl, 64–97. Chicago: University of Chicago Press, 1998.

Cline, Ray S. *The Power of Nations in the 1990s: A Strategic Assessment.* Lanham, MD: University Press of America, 2002.

Colaresi, Michael. *Scare Politics: The Politics of International Rivalry.* Syracuse, NY: Syracuse University Press, 2005.

Coleman, James C. *The Mathematics of Collective Action.* Chicago: Aldine, 1973.

Colgan, Jeff D. "American Perspectives and Blind Spots on World Politics." *Journal of Global Security Studies* 4, no. 3 (2019): 300–309.

Connelly, Eileen A. J. "Blinken Dodges Question on Punishing China for Covid-19 Pandemic." *New York Post,* March 28, 2021. https://nypost.com/2021/03/28/blinken-dodges-on-punishing-china-for-covid-19-pandemic/.

Consumer News and Business Channel. "Trump: NAFTA Worst Trade Deal in History." June 28, 2016. https://www.cnbc.com/video/2016/06/28/trump-nafta-worst-trade-deal-in-history.html.

Copeland, Dale C. *The Origins of Major War.* Ithaca, NY: Cornell University Press, 2000.

Crawford, Timothy W. *Pivotal Deterrence: Third-Party Statecraft and the Pursuit of Peace.* Ithaca, NY: Cornell University Press, 2003.

Crist, Carolyn. "Investigation into Coronavirus Origins." WebMD, May 28, 2021. https://www.webmd.com/lung/news/20210527/biden-orders-investigation-into-coronavirus-origins.

Cunningham, Fiona S. "The Maritime Rung on the Escalation Ladder: Naval Blockade in a US-China Conflict." *Security Studies* 29, no. 4 (2020): 730–68.

Daalder, Ivo H., and James M. Lindsay. *America Unbound: The Bush Revolution in Foreign Policy.* New York: Wiley, 2005.

Dahl, Robert. "The Concept of Power." *Behavioral Science* 2, no. 3 (1957): 201–15.

Danilovic, Vesna. "Conceptual and Selection Bias Issues in Deterrence." *Journal of Conflict Resolution* 45, no. 1 (2001): 97–125.

Danzman, Sarah B., Thomas Oatley, and William K. Winecoff. "All Crises Are Global: Capital Cycles in an Imbalanced International Political Economy." *International Studies Quarterly* 6, no. 1 (2017): 907–23.

Davidson, Jason W. *The Origins of Revisionist and Status-Quo States.* London: Palgrave Macmillan, 2006.

De Soysa, Indra, and Paul Midford. "Enter the Dragon! An Empirical Analysis of Chinese versus US Arms Transfers to Autocrats and Violators of Human Rights." *International Studies Quarterly* 56, no. 4 (2012): 843–56.

Desch, Michael C. "America's Liberal Illiberalism: The Ideological Origins of Overreaction in U.S. Foreign Policy." *International Security* 32, no. 3 (2007–2008): 7–43.

Deutsche Welle. "US Lifts Trump Sanctions on International Criminal Court Officials." April 3, 2021. https://www.dw.com/en/us-lifts-trump-sanctions-on-international-criminal-court-officials/a-57089520.

Diehl, Paul F., ed. *The Dynamics of Enduring Rivalries.* Urbana: University of Illinois Press, 1998.

Diehl, Paul F., and Gary Goertz. *War and Peace in International Rivalry.* Ann Arbor: University of Michigan Press, 2000.

Doran, Charles, F. *Systems in Crisis: New Imperatives of High Politics at Century's End*. Cambridge: Cambridge University Press, 1991.

Doran, Charles F., and Wes Parsons. "War and the Cycle of Relative Power." *American Political Science Review* 74, no. 4 (1980): 947–65.

Drezner, Daniel W. "Perception, Misperception, and Sensitivity: Chinese Economic Power and Preferences after the 2008 Financial Crisis." In *Strategic Adjustment and the Rise of China*, ed. Robert S. Ross and Oystein Tunsjo, 69–99. Ithaca, NY: Cornell University Press, 2017.

——. *The Sanctions Paradox: Economic Statecraft and International Relations*. Cambridge: Cambridge University Press, 1999.

East, Maurice A. "Status Discrepancy and Violence in the International System." In *The Analysis of International Politics*, ed. James N. Rosenau, Vincent Davis, and Maurice A. East, 299–319. New York: Free Press, 1972.

The Economic Times. "China Slams US for Delisting Xinjiang's East Turkestan Islamic Movement as Terrorist Outfit." November 6, 2020. https://economictimes.indiatimes.com/news /defence/china-slams-us-for-delisting-xinjiangs-east-turkestan-islamic-movement-as -terrorist-outfit/articleshow/79083396.cms.

The Economist. "'Genocide' Is the Wrong Word for the Horrors of Xinjiang: To Confront Evil, the First Step Is to Describe It Accurately." February 13, 2021. https://www.economist.com /leaders/2021/02/13/genocide-is-the-wrong-word-for-the-horrors-of-xinjiang.

Edwards-Levy, Ariel. "Polls Find Most Republicans Say 2020 Election Was Stolen and Roughly One-Quarter Embrace QAnon Conspiracies." CNN, May 28, 2021. https://www.cnn.com /2021/05/28/politics/poll-qanon-election-conspiracies/index.html.

Elman, Colin. "Extending Offensive Realism: The Louisiana Purchase and America's Rise to Regional Hegemony." *American Political Science Review* 98, no. 4 (2004): 563–76.

Erickson, Andrew S., Evan B. Montgomery, Craig Neuman, Stephen Biddle, and Ivan Oelrich. "Correspondence: How Good Are China's Antiaccess/Area-Denial Capabilities?" *International Security* 41, no. 4 (2017): 202–13.

Etzioni, Amitai. "Capitalism Needs to be Re-encapsulated." *Society* 58, no. 1 (2021): 1–15.

——. "The Challenging Results of China's New Anti-Poverty Campaign: It's Not as Simple as Critics Might Have You Believe." *The Diplomat*, March 11, 2021. https://thediplomat.com /2021/03/the-challenging-results-of-chinas-new-anti-poverty-campaign/.

——. "Is America Becoming a Chauvinistic Nation?" *National Interest*, March 20, 2021. https://nationalinterest.org/feature/america-becoming-chauvinistic-nation-180660.

——. "Will the Biden Administration Embrace Trump's Extreme Anti-China Rhetoric? The New Administration Will Have to Sidestep yet Another Trump Landmine." *The Diplomat*, February 1, 2021. https://thediplomat.com/2021/02/will-the-biden-administration-embrace -trumps-extreme-anti-china-rhetoric/.

Evans, Gareth. "What Asia Wants from the Biden Administration." GlobalAsia, March 2021. https://globalasia.org/v16no1/cover/what-asia-wants-from-the-biden-administration _gareth-evans.

Evans, Peter B. *Embedded Autonomy: States and Industrial Transformation*. Princeton, NJ: Princeton University Press, 1995.

Evans, Peter B., Harold K. Jacobson, and Robert D. Putnam, eds. *Double-Edged Diplomacy: International Bargaining and Domestic Politics.* Berkeley: University of California Press, 1993.

Evans, Peter B., Dietrich Rueschemeyer, and Theda Skocpol, eds. *Bringing the State Back In.* Cambridge: Cambridge University Press, 1985.

Ewalt, David M. "The World's Most Innovative Research Institutions 2019." Reuters, September 18, 2019. https://www.reuters.com/innovation/most-innovative-institutions-2019.

Farrell, Henry, and Abraham L. Newman. "Weaponized Interdependence: How Global Economic Networks Shape State Coercion." *International Security* 44, no, 1 (2019): 42–79.

Fearon, James D. "Rationalist Explanations for War." *International Organization* 49, no. 3 (1995): 379–414.

——. "Signaling Foreign Policy Interests: Tying Hands versus Sinking Costs." *Journal of Conflict Resolution* 41, no. 1 (1997): 68–90.

——. "Signaling versus the Balance of Power and Interests: An Empirical Test of a Crisis Bargaining Model." *Journal of Conflict Resolution* 38, no. 2 (1994): 236–69.

Feaver, Peter D., Hal Brands, Rebecca F. Lissner, and Patrick Porter. "Correspondence: The Establishment and U.S. Grand Strategy." *International Security* 42, no. 2 (2019): 197–204.

Feng, Yongping. "The Peaceful Transition of Power from the UK to the US." *Chinese Journal of International Politics* 1, no. 1 (2006): 83–108.

Ferguson, Jane. "As Peace Talks with the Taliban Stall, Deadline to Withdraw U.S. Troops from Afghanistan Looms." PBS, February 20, 2021. https://www.pbs.org/newshour/show/as -peace-talks-with-the-taliban-stall-deadline-to-withdraw-u-s-troops-from-afghanistan -looms.

Fischer, Fritz. *The War of Illusions.* New York: Norton, 1975.

Fisher, Richard D., Jr. "'One China' and the Military Balance on the Taiwan Strait." In *The "One China" Dilemma,* ed. Peter C. Y. Chow, 217–56. New York: Palgrave Macmillan, 2008.

Fravel, M. Taylor. "Power Shifts and Escalation: Explaining China's Use of Force in Territorial Disputes." *International Security* 32, no. 3 (2007–2008): 44–83.

——. "Regime Insecurity and International Cooperation: Explaining China's Compromises in Territorial Disputes." *International Security* 30, no. 2 (2005): 46–83.

——. *Strong Border, Secure Nation: Cooperation and Order in China's Territorial Disputes.* Princeton, NJ: Princeton University Press, 2008.

Freedom House. "Countries and Territories." 2021. https://freedomhouse.org/countries /freedom-world/scores.

Friedberg, Aaron L. *A Contest for Supremacy: China, America, and the Struggle for Mastery in Asia.* New York: Norton, 2011.

——. "The Future of U.S.-China Relations: Is Conflict Inevitable?" *International Security* 30, no. 2 (2005): 7–45.

——. *The Weary Titan: The Experience of Relative Decline, 1895–1905.* Princeton, NJ: Princeton University Press, 1988.

Friedman, George, and Meredith LeBard. *The Coming War with Japan.* New York: St. Martin's, 1991.

Fu, Ronan Tse-min, David J. Gill, Eric Hundman, Adam P. Liff, and G. John Ikenberry. "Correspondence: Looking for Asia's Security Dilemma." *International Security* 40, no. 2 (2015): 181–204.

Fukuyama, Francis. "The Pandemic and the Political Order: It Takes a State." *Foreign Affairs,* July/August 2020. https://www.foreignaffairs.com/articles/world/2020-06-09/pandemic -and-political-order.

Galtung, Johan. "On the Effects of International Sanctions: With Examples from the Case of Rhodesia." *World Politics* 19, no. 3 (1967): 378–416.

——. "A Structural Theory of Imperialism." *Journal of Peace Research* 3 (1971): 81–117.

——. "Violence, Peace, and Peace Research." *Journal of Peace Research* 6, no. 3 (1969): 167–91.

Gamba, Virginia. *The Falklands/Malvinas War: A Model for North-South Crisis Prevention.* London: Allen & Unwin, 1987.

Gan, Nectar. "China Pushes Back on U.S. Claims that Coronavirus Originated from Wuhan Lab." CNN, May 4, 2020. https://www.cnn.com/2020/05/04/asia/china-us-coronavirus-spat -intl-hnk/index.html.

Gartner, Scott S., and Randolph M. Siverson. "War Expansion and War Outcome." *Journal of Conflict Resolution* 40, no. 1 (1996): 4–15.

Gastil, Raymond D. *Freedom in the World: Political Rights and Civil Liberties, 1978.* New York: Freedom House, 1978. https://freedomhouse.org/sites/default/files/2020–02/Freedom_in _the_World_1978_complete_book.pdf.

Gelfand, Michele, Joshua C. Jackson, Xinyue Pan, Dana Nau, Dylan Pieper, Emmy Denison, Munqith Dagher, Paul A. M. Van Lange, Chi-Yue Chiu, and Mo Wang. "The Relationship between Cultural Tightness-Looseness and COVID-19 Cases and Deaths: A Global Analysis." *Lancet Planetary Health* 5, no. 3 (2021): E135–44. https://www.thelancet.com/journals /lanplh/article/PIIS2542-5196(20)30301-6/fulltext.

Georgetown University Initiative for U.S.-China Dialogue on Global Issues. "America's Taiwan Policy: Debating Strategic Ambiguity and the Future of Asian Security." October 2, 2020. https://uschinadialogue.georgetown.edu/events/america-s-taiwan-policy-debating -strategic-ambiguity-and-the-future-of-asian-security.

Gilley, Bruce. "Not So Dire Straits: How the Finlandization of Taiwan Benefits U.S. Security." *Foreign Affairs* 89, no. 1 (2010): 44–56, 58–60.

Gilli, Andrea, and Mauro Gilli. "Why China Has Not Caught Up Yet: Military-Technological Superiority and the Limits of Imitation, Reverse Engineering, and Cyber Espionage." *International Security* 43, no. 3 (2019): 141–89.

Gilpin, Robert. *War and Change in World Politics.* Cambridge: Cambridge University Press, 1981.

Glaser, Bonnie S., Michael J. Mazarr, Michael J. Glennon, Richard Haas, and David Sacks. "Dire Straits: Should American Support for Taiwan Be Ambiguous?" *Foreign Affairs,* September 24, 2020. https://www.foreignaffairs.com/articles/united-states/2020-09-24/dire -straits.

Glaser, Charles L. "A Flawed Framework: Why the Liberal International Concept Is Misguided." *International Security* 43, no. 4 (2019): 51–87.

——. "A U.S.-China Grand Bargain: The Hard Choice between Military Competition and Accommodation." *International Security* 39, no. 4 (2015): 49–90.

GlobalSecurity.org. "Taiwan Strait: 21 July 1995 to 23 March 1996." No date. https://www.globalsecurity.org/military/ops/taiwan_strait.htm.

Glosny, Michael A. "Strangulation from the Sea? A PRC Submarine Blockade of Taiwan." *International Security* 28, no. 4 (2004): 125–60.

Gochman, Charles S. "Status, Capabilities, and Major Power Conflict." In *The Correlates of War II: Testing Some Realpolitik Models*, ed. J. David Singer, 83–123. New York: Free Press, 1980.

Goertz, Gary, and Paul F. Diehl. "Enduring Rivalries: Theoretical Constructs and Empirical Patterns." *International Studies Quarterly* 37, no. 2 (1993): 147–71.

Goh, Evelyn. "Contesting Hegemonic Order: China in East Asia." *Security Studies* 28, no. 3 (2019): 614–44.

——. "Great Powers and Hierarchical Order in Southeast Asia: Analyzing Regional Security Strategy." *International Security* 32, no. 3 (2007–2008): 113–57.

——. *The Struggle for Order: Hegemony, Hierarchy, and Transition in the Cold-War East Asia.* Oxford: Oxford University Press, 2013.

Goldstein, Avery. *Rising to the Challenge: China's Grand Strategy and International Security.* Stanford, CA: Stanford University Press, 2005.

Goldstein, Lyle, and William Murray. "Undersea Dragons: China's Maturing Submarine Force." *International Security* 28, no. 4 (2004): 161–96.

Gordon, Philip H. *Losing the Long Game: The False Promise of Regime Change in the Middle East.* New York: St. Martin's, 2020.

Gramsci, Antonio. *Selections from the Prison Notebooks of Antonio Gramsci.* New York: International Publishers, 1971.

Gries, Peter H. *China's New Nationalism: Pride, Politics, and Diplomacy.* Berkeley: University of California Press, 2012.

Gries, Peter H., and Yiming Jing. "Are the U.S. and China Fated to Fight? How Narratives of 'Power Transition' Shape Great Power War or Peace." *Cambridge Review of International Affairs* 32, no. 4 (2019): 456–82.

Gries, Peter H., and Tao Wang. "Taiwan's Perilous Futures: Chinese Nationalism, the 2020 Presidential Elections, and U.S.-China Tensions Spell Trouble for Cross-Strait Relations." *World Affairs* 183, no. 1 (2020): 40–61.

Griffiths, James. "These Uighurs Were Locked up by the US in Guantanamo. Now They're Being Used as an Excuse for China's Crackdown in Xinjiang." CNN, May 15, 2021. https://www.cnn.com/2021/05/15/china/china-xinjiang-guantanamo-uyghurs-intl-hnk/index.html.

Grigoryan, Arman. "Selective Wilsonianism: Material Interests and the West's Support for Democracy." *International Security* 44, no. 4 (2020): 158–200.

Grossman, Derek, Sheryn Lee, Benjamin Scherer, and Scott L. Kastner. "Correspondence: Stability or Volatility across the Taiwan Strait?" *International Security* 41, no. 2 (2016): 192–197.

The Guardian. "NATO Bombed Chinese Deliberately." October 17, 1999. https://www.theguardian.com/world/1999/oct/17/balkans.

——. "Truth behind America's Raid on Belgrade." November 28, 1999. https://www
.theguardian.com/theobserver/1999/nov/28/focus.news1.

——. "US Intelligence Couldn't Resolve Debate over Covid Origins—Official Report."
August 27, 2021. https://www.theguardian.com/us-news/2021/aug/27/coronavirus-origin
-us-intelligence.

Gurr, Ted R. *Why Men Rebel?* Princeton, NJ: Princeton University Press, 1970.

Haass, Richard, and David Sacks. "American Support for Taiwan Must be Unambiguous." *Foreign Affairs*, September 20, 2020. https://www.foreignaffairs.com/articles/united-states
/american-support-taiwan-must-be-unambiguous.

Hagstrom, Linus. "'Power Shift' in East Asia? A Critical Reappraisal of Narratives on the
Diaoyu/Senkaku Islands Incident in 2010." *Chinese Journal of International Politics* 5, no. 3
(2012): 267–97.

Hagstrom, Linus, and Bjorn Jerden. "East Asia's Power Shift: The Flaws and Hazards of the
Debate and How to Avoid Them." *Asian Perspective* 38, no. 3 (2014): 337–62.

Hanson, Victor D. "Lord Ismay, What Has Happened to the Prescient Post-WWII Dictum
'Russians Out, Americans In, Germans Down'?" *National Review*, July 5, 2017. https://
www.nationalreview.com/2017/07/nato-russians-out-americans-germans-down-updated
-reversed/.

Harris, Peter, and Peter L. Trubowitz. "The Politics of Power Projection: The Pivot to Asia, Its
Failure, and the Future of American Primacy." *Chinese Journal of International Politics* 14,
no. 2 (2021): 187–217.

Hart, Jeffrey. "Three Approaches to the Measurement of Power in International Relations."
International Organization 30, no. 2 (1976): 289–305.

Hauser, Jennifer, and Ivana Kottasova. "Australia Had 'Deep and Grave' Concerns about French
Submarines' Capabilities, PM Says." CNN, September 19, 2021. https://www.cnn.com/2021
/09/19/australia/aukus-australia-submarine-deal-concerns-intl/index.html.

He, Kai, and Huiyun Feng. *Prospect Theory and Foreign Policy Analysis in the Asia Pacific:
Rational Leaders and Risky Behavior*. New York: Routledge, 2012.

He, Kai, Huiyung Feng, Steve Chan, and Weixing Hu. "Rethinking Revisionism in World Politics." *Chinese Journal of International Politics* 14, no. 2 (2021): 159–86.

Hemmer, Christopher, and Peter J. Katzenstein. "Why Is There No NATO in Asia? Collective
Identity, Regionalism, and the Origins of Multilateralism." *International Organization* 56,
no. 3 (2002): 575–607.

Higgins, Trumbull. *Hitler and Russia: The Third Reich in a Two-Front War, 1937–1943*. New
York: Macmillan, 1966.

Hoffmann, Stanley. "An American Social Science." *Daedalus* 106, no. 3 (1977): 41–60.

Holsti, Ole R. "The Belief System and National Images: A Case Study." *Journal of Conflict Resolution* 6, no. 3 (1962): 244–52.

Hopewell, Kristen. "Strategic Narratives in Global Trade Politics: American Hegemony, Free
Trade, and the Hidden Hand of the State." *Chinese Journal of International Politics* 14, no. 1
(2021): 51–86.

Hornberger, Jacob G. "America: The Dictatress of the World." Mises Wire, October 9, 2017.
https://mises.org/wire/america-dictatress-world.

Horowitz, Michael C., Shahryar Pasandideh, Andrea Gilli, and Mauro Gilli. "Correspondence: Military-Technological Imitation and Rising Powers." *International Security* 44, no. 2 (2019): 185–92.

Howard, Jacqueline. "Coronavirus Likely Spread to People from an Animal—But Needs More Study, New WHO Report Says." CNN, March 30, 2021. https://www.cnn.com/2021/03/30/health/who-coronavirus-origin-report/index.html.

Hsieh, John F. S., and Emerson M. S. Niou. "Measuring Taiwan Public Opinion on Taiwanese Independence." *China Quarterly* 181, no. 1 (2005): 158–68.

Hulme, Patrick. "Taiwan, 'Strategic Clarity' and the War Powers: A U.S. Commitment to Taiwan Requires Congressional Buy-In." *Lawfare*, December 4, 2020. https://www.lawfareblog.com/taiwan-strategic-clarity-and-war-powers-us-commitment-taiwan-requires-congressional-buy.

Human Rights Watch. "US Sanctions International Criminal Court Prosecutor: Trump Administration's Action Tries to Block World's Worst Crimes." September 2, 2020. https://www.hrw.org/news/2020/09/02/us-sanctions-international-criminal-court-prosecutor.

——. "US Sanctions on the International Criminal Court: Questions and Answers." December 14, 2020. https://www.hrw.org/news/2020/12/14/us-sanctions-international-criminal-court.

Huntington, Samuel P. *The Clash of Civilizations and the Remaking of the World Order.* New York: Simon & Schuster, 1996.

Huth, Paul K., and Bruce M. Russett. "General Deterrence between Enduring Rivals: Testing Three Competing Models." *American Political Science Review* 87, no. 1 (1993): 61–73.

Ikenberry, G. John. *After Victory: Institutions, Strategic Restraint, and the Rebuilding of Order after Major Wars.* Princeton, NJ: Princeton University Press, 2001.

——. "The End of Liberal International Order?" *International Affairs* 94, no. 1 (2018): 7–23.

——. "The Future of the Liberal World Order: Internationalism after America." *Foreign Affairs* 90, no. 3 (2011): 56–68.

——. *Liberal Leviathan: The Origins, Crisis, and Transformation of the American World Order.* Princeton, NJ: Princeton University Press, 2012.

——. "The Plot against American Foreign Policy: Can the Liberal Order Survive?" *Foreign Affairs* 96, no. 3 (2017): 2–9.

——. "The Rise, Character, and Evolution of International Order." In *International Politics and Institutions in Time*, ed. Orfeo Fioretos, 59–75. Oxford: Oxford University Press, 2017.

——. "The Rise of China and the Future of the West: Can the Liberal System Survive?" *Foreign Affairs* 87, no. 1 (2008): 23–37.

Ikenberry, G. John, Michael Mastanduno, and William C. Wohlforth. "Introduction: Unipolarity, State Behavior, and Systemic Consequences." *World Politics* 61, no. 1 (2009): 1–27.

International Strategic Analysis. "The 2021 ISA Country Power Rankings." 2021. https://www.isa-world.com/news/?tx_ttnews%5BbackPid%5D=1&tx_ttnews%5Btt_news%5D=595&cHash=d37d2e848d6b79811749a619c74abebc.

Izumikawa, Yasuhiro. "Network Connections and the Emergence of the Hub-and-Spokes Alliance System in East Asia." *International Security* 45, no. 2 (2020): 7–50.

Janis, Irving L. *Groupthink: Psychological Studies of Policy Decisions and Fiascoes*. Boston: Houghton Mifflin, 1982.

Jerden, Bjorn. "The Assertive China Narrative: Why It Is Wrong and How So Many Still Bought into It." *Chinese Journal of International Politics* 7, no. 1 (2014): 47–88.

Jervis, Robert. *Perception and Misperception in International Politics*. Princeton, NJ: Princeton University Press, 1976.

——. "Thinking Systematically about China." *International Security* 31, no. 2 (2006): 206–208.

——. "Unipolarity: A Structural Perspective." *World Politics* 61, no. 1 (2009): 188–213.

Johnston, Alastair I. "China in a World of Orders." *International Security* 44, no. 2 (2019): 9–60.

——. "How New and Assertive Is China's New Assertiveness?" *International Security* 37, no. 4 (2013): 7–48.

——. "Is Chinese Nationalism Rising? Evidence from Beijing." *International Security* 41, no. 3 (2016–2017): 7–43.

——. *Social States: China in International Institutions, 1980–2000*. Princeton, NJ: Princeton University Press, 2008.

——. "Stability and Instability in Sino-US Relations: A Response to Yan Xuetong's Superficial Friendship Theory." *Chinese Journal of International Politics* 4, no. 1 (2011): 5–29.

Johnston, Alastair I., and Robert S. Ross. Conclusion to *Engaging China: The Management of an Emergent Power*, ed. Alastair I. Johnston and Robert S. Ross, 271–95. London: Routledge, 1999.

Kagan, Donald. *The Outbreak of the Peloponnesian War*. Ithaca, NY: Cornell University Press, 1969.

Kagan, Robert. "The Illusion of 'Managing' China." *Washington Post*, May 15, 2005. https://www.washingtonpost.com/wpdyn/content/article/2005/05/13/AR2005051301405.html.

Kahneman, Daniel, and Amos Tversky. "Prospect Theory: An Analysis of Decision under Risk." *Econometrica* 47, no. 2 (1979): 263–92.

Kang, David C. *China Rising: Peace, Power, and Order in East Asia*. New York: Columbia University Press, 2007.

——. *East Asia before the West: Five Centuries of Trade and Tribute*. New York: Columbia University Press, 2012.

——. "Hierarchy and Legitimacy in International Systems: The Tribute System in Early Modern East Asia." *Security Studies* 19, no. 4 (2010): 591–622.

——. "International Order in Historical East Asia: Tribute and Hierarchy beyond Sinocentrism and Eurocentrism." *International Organization* 74, no. 1 (2020): 65–93.

——. "Thought Games about China." *Journal of East Asian Studies* 20, no. 2 (2020): 135–50.

Kang, David C., and Alex Yu Ting Lin. "US Bias in the Study of Asian Security: Using Europe to Study Asia." *Journal of Global Security Studies* 4, no. 3 (2019): 393–401.

Kant, Immanuel. *Perpetual Peace: A Philosophical Note*. Translated by M. Campbell Smith. London: George Allen & Unwin, 1917. First published 1795 by Friedrich Nicolovius (Königsberg). https://www.gutenberg.org/ebooks/50922.

Kastner, Scott L. "Is the Taiwan Strait Still a Flash Point? Rethinking the Prospects for Armed Conflict between China and Taiwan." *International Security* 40, no. 3 (2015–2016): 54–92.

——. *Political Conflict and Economic Interdependence across the Taiwan Strait and Beyond.* Stanford, CA: Stanford University Press, 2009.

Kastner, Scott L., Margaret M. Pearson, and Chard Rector. *China's Strategic Multilateralism: Investing in Global Governance.* Cambridge: Cambridge University Press, 2018.

Kastner, Scott L., and Chard Rector. "National Unification and Mistrust: Bargaining Power and the Prospects for a PRC/Taiwan Agreement." *Security Studies* 17, no. 1 (2008): 39–71.

Kennedy, Paul. *The Rise and Fall of Great Powers.* New York: Vintage Books, 1987.

Keohane, Robert O., and Joseph S. Nye Jr. *Power and Interdependence.* Boston: Little, Brown, 1977.

Khong, Yuen Foong. "The American Tributary System." *Chinese Journal of International Politics* 6, no. 1 (2013): 1–47.

——. *Analogies at War: Korea, Munich, Dien Bien Phu, and the Vietnam Decisions of 1965.* Princeton, NJ: Princeton University Press, 1992.

——. "Primacy or World Order? The United States and China's Rise—A Review Essay." *International Security* 38, no. 3 (2013–2014): 153–75.

Kim, Sung Eun, and Yotam Margalit. "The Tariffs as Electoral Weapons: The Political Geography of US-China Trade War." *International Organization* 75, no. 1 (2021): 1–38.

Kim, Tongfi, Andrew Taffer, and Ketian Zhang. "Is China a Cautious Bully?" *International Security* 45, no. 2 (2020): 187–93.

Kirshner, Jonathan. "Handle Him with Care: The Importance of Getting Thucydides Right." *Security Studies* 28, no. 1 (2019): 1–24.

——. "Offensive Realism, Thucydides Trap, and the Tragedy of Unforced Errors: Classical Realism and US-China Relations." *China International Strategy Review* 1 (2019): 51–63.

——. "The Tragedy of Offensive Realism: Classical Realism and the Rise of China." *European Journal of International Relations* 18, no. 1 (2012): 53–75.

Krickovic, Andrej. "The Symbiotic China-Russia Partnership: Cautious Riser and Desperate Challenger." *Chinese Journal of International Politics* 10, no. 3 (2017): 299–329.

Krickovic, Andrej, and Chang Zhang. "Fears of Falling Short versus Anxieties of Decline: Explaining Russia and China's Approach to Status-Seeking." *Chinese Journal of International Politics* 13, no. 2 (2020): 219–51.

Kugler, Jacek, and Marina Arbetman. "Choosing Among Measures of Power: A Review of the Empirical Record." In *Power in World Politics*, ed. Richard J. Stoll and Michael D. Ward, 49–78. Boulder, CO: Lynne Rienner, 1989.

——. "Relative Policy Capacity: Political Extraction and Political Reach." In *Political Capacity and Economic Behavior*, ed. Marina Arbetman and Jacek Kugler, 11–45. Boulder, CO: Westview, 1997.

Kugler, Jacek, and William Domke. "Comparing the Strengths of Nations." *Comparative Political Studies* 19, no. 1 (1986): 39–69.

Kugler, Jacek, and Ronald L. Tammen, eds. *The Performance of Nations.* Lanham, MD: Rowman & Littlefield, 2012.

Kugler, Jacek, Ronald L. Tammen, and John Thomas. "How Political Performance Impacts Conflict and Growth." In *The Performance of Nations*, ed. Jacek Kugler and Ronald L. Tammen, 79–96. Lanham, MD: Rowman & Littlefield, 2012.

Kupchan, Charles A. *How Enemies Become Friends: The Sources of Stable Peace.* Princeton, NJ: Princeton University Press, 2010.

——. *Isolationism: A History of America's Efforts to Shield Itself from the World.* Oxford: Oxford University Press, 2020.

Kupchan, Charles A., and Peter L. Trubowitz. "A China Strategy to Reunite America's Allies." *Project Syndicate*, January 4, 2021. https://www.project-syndicate.org/commentary/biden -china-strategy-to-reunite-us-allies-by-charles-a-kupchan-and-peter-trubowitz-1-2021 -01.

——. "Dead Center: The Demise of Liberal Internationalism in the United States." *International Security* 32, no. 2 (2007): 7–44.

——. "The Home Front: Why an Internationalist Foreign Policy Needs a Stronger Domestic Foundation." *Foreign Affairs*, May-June 2021. https://www.foreignaffairs.com/articles /united-states/2021-04-20/foreign-policy-home-front.

——. "The Illusion of Liberal Internationalism's Revival." *International Security* 35, no. 1 (2010): 95–109.

Lake, David A. "Economic Openness and Great Power Competition: Lessons for China and the United States." *Chinese Journal of International Politics* 11, no. 3 (2018): 237–70.

Lake, David A., Lisa L. Martin, and Thomas Risse. "Challenges to Liberal Order: Reflections on *International Organization.*" *International Organization* 75, no. 2 (2021): 225–57.

Lampton, David M. "Reconsidering U.S.-China Relations: From Improbable Normalization to Precipitous Deterioration." *Asia Policy* 14, no. 2 (2019): 43–60.

Larson, Deborah W., and Alexei Shevchenko. *Quest for Status: Chinese and Russian Foreign Policy.* New Haven, CT: Yale University Press, 2019.

——. "Status Seekers: Chinese and Russian Responses to U.S. Primacy." *International Security* 34, no. 4 (2010): 63–95.

Lau, Stuart. "German Minister and US Envoy Clash over Huawei's Possible Participation in Germany's 5G Network." *South China Morning Post*, November 26, 2019. https://www.scmp .com/news/world/europe/article/3039320/german-minister-and-us-envoy-clash-over -huaweis-possible.

Layne, Christopher. "Kant or Cant: The Myth of the Democratic Peace." *International Security* 19, no. 2 (1994): 5–49.

——. *The Peace of Illusions: American Grand Strategy from 1940 to the Present.* Ithaca, NY: Cornell University Press, 2006.

——. "Preventing the China-U.S. Cold War from Turning Hot." *Chinese Journal of International Politics* 13, no. 3 (2020): 343–85.

——. "The Waning of U.S. Hegemony—Myth or Reality? A Review Essay." *International Security* 34, no. 1 (2009): 147–72.

Lebow, R. Ned. *Between Peace and War: The Nature of International Crisis.* Baltimore: Johns Hopkins University Press, 1981.

——. "Miscalculation in the South Atlantic: The Origins of the Falklands War." In *Psychology and Deterrence*, ed. Robert Jervis, R. Ned Lebow, and Janice G. Stein, 85–124. Baltimore: Johns Hopkins University Press, 1985.

——. *The Rise and Fall of Political Orders.* Cambridge: Cambridge University Press, 2018.

——. "Thucydides and Deterrence." *Security Studies* 16, no. 2 (2007): 163–88.

——. *Why Nations Fight: Past and Future Motivations for War*. Cambridge: Cambridge University Press, 2010.

Lebow, R. Ned, and Daniel P. Tompkins. "The Thucydides Claptrap." *Washington Monthly*, June 28, 2016. https://washingtonmonthly.com/2016/6/28/thucydides-claptrap.

Lebow, R. Ned, and Benjamin Valentino. "Lost in Transition: A Critical Analysis of Power Transition Theory." *International Relations* 23, no. 3 (2009): 389–410.

Lee, James. "Did Thucydides Believe in Thucydides' Trap? The History of the Peloponnesian War and Its Relevance to US-China Relations." *Journal of Chinese Political Science* 24, no. 1 (2019): 67–86.

Lemke, Douglas. *Regions of War and Peace*. Cambridge: Cambridge University Press, 2002.

Levin, Dov H. *Meddling in the Ballot Box: The Causes and Effects of Partisan Electoral Interventions*. Oxford: Oxford University Press, 2020.

Levy, Jack S. "Declining Power and the Preventive Motivation for War." *World Politics* 60, no. 1 (1987): 82–107.

——. "Loss Aversion, Framing and Bargaining: The Implications of Prospect Theory for International Conflict." *International Political Science Review* 17, no. 2 (1996): 177–93.

——. "Preventive War and Democratic Politics." *International Studies Quarterly* 52, no. 1 (2008): 1–24.

Levy, Jack S., and William Mulligan. "Shifting Power, Preventive Logic, and the Response of the Target: Germany, Russia, and the First World War." *Journal of Strategic Studies* 40, no. 5 (2017): 731–69.

Li, Mingjiang. "China's Non-Confrontational Assertiveness in the South China Sea." East Asia Forum, June 14, 2012. www.eastasiaforum.org/2012/06/14/china-s-non-confrontational-assertiveness-in-the-south-china-sea.

Li, Xiaojun, and Dingding Chen. "Public Opinion, International Reputation, and Audience Costs in an Authoritarian Regime." *Conflict Management and Peace Science* 38, no. 5 (2020): 543–60. https://journals-sagepub-com.colorado.idm.oclc.org/doi/pdf/10.1177/073889 4220906374.

Liao, George. "Military Balance across Taiwan Strait Slipping toward China: Development of Chinese Landing Ships Significantly Enhancing Invasion Capability." *Taiwan News*, July 14, 2020. https://www.taiwannews.com.tw/en/news/3966391.

Lieber, Keir A. "The New History of World War I and What It Means for International Relations Theory." *International Security* 32, no. 2 (2007): 155–91.

Lieber, Keir A., and Daryl G. Press. "The End of MAD: The Nuclear Dimension of U.S. Primacy." *International Security* 30, no. 4 (2006): 7–44.

Liff, Adam P., and G. John Ikenberry. "Racing Toward Tragedy? China's Rise, Military Competition in the Asia Pacific, and the Security Dilemma." *International Security* 39, no. 2 (2014): 52–91.

Lim, Ives-Heng. "The Future Instability of Cross-Strait Relations: Prospect Theory and Ma Ying-Jeou's Paradoxical Legacy." *Asian Security* 14, no. 3 (2017): 318–33.

Lin, Syaru S. *Taiwan's China Dilemma: Contested Identities and Multiple Interests in Taiwan's Cross-Strait Economic Policy*. Stanford, CA: Stanford University Press, 2016.

Lind, Jennifer. "Asia's Other Revisionist Power: Why U.S. Grand Strategy Unnerves China." *Foreign Affairs* 96, no. 2 (2017): 74–82.

Lind, Jennifer, and Daryl G. Press. "Markets and Mercantilism? How China Secures Its Energy Supplies." *International Organization* 42, no. 4 (2018): 170–204.

Lindsay, Jon R. "The Impact of China on Cybersecurity: Fiction and Friction." *International Security* 39, no. 3 (2014–2015): 7–47.

Liu, Feng. "China's Security Strategy Toward East Asia." *Chinese Journal of International Politics* 9, no. 2 (2016): 151–79.

Liu, Frank C. S. "Taiwanese Voters' Political Identification Profile, 2013–2014: Becoming One China or Creating a New Country?" *Asian Survey* 56, no. 5 (2016): 931–57.

Lopes da Silva, Diego, Nan Tian, and Alexandra Marksteiner. "Trends in World Military Expenditure, 2020." SIPRI Fact Sheet. Solna: Stockholm International Peace Research Institute, 2021.

Lukes, Steven. *Power: A Radical View.* Houndmills, UK: MacMillan, 1975.

MacDonald, Paul K., and Joseph M. Parent. "Graceful Decline? The Surprising Success of Great Power Retrenchment." *International Security* 35, no. 4 (2011): 7–44.

——. "The Road to Recovery: How Once Great Powers Became Great Again." *Washington Quarterly* 41, no. 3 (2018): 21–39.

——. *Twilight of Titans: Great Power Decline and Retrenchment.* Ithaca, NY: Cornell University Press, 2018.

Mack, Andrew. "Why Big Nations Lose Small Wars: The Politics of Asymmetric Conflict." *World Politics* 27, no. 2 (1975): 175–200.

MacMillan, Margaret. *The War That Ended Peace.* New York: Random House, 2013.

Maddison, Angus. "Historical Statistics of the World Economy: 1–2006 AD." 2010. http://www.ggdc.net/maddison/Historical_Statistics/horizontal-file_02-2010.xls

Mahbubani, Kishore. *Has China Won? The Chinese Challenge to American Primacy.* New York: Hachette, 2020.

——. "Was Trump Right or Wrong on China? Biden's Answer Will Shape the Future." *GlobalAsia*, March 2021. https://globalasia.org/v16no1/cover/was-trump-right-or-wrong-on-china-bidens-answer-will-shape-the-future_kishore-mahbubani.

Mansfield, Edward D., and Jack Snyder. "Democratic Transitions, Institutional Strength, and War." *International Organization* 56, no. 2 (2002): 297–337.

——. "Democratization and the Danger of War." *International Security* 20, no. 1 (1995): 5–38.

——. *Electing to Fight: Why Emerging Democracies Go to War.* Cambridge, MA: MIT Press, 2005.

Maoz, Zeev. *Networks of Nations: The Evolution, Structure, and Impact of International Networks, 1816–2001.* Cambridge: Cambridge University Press, 2010.

Martin, Michael, and Tinbete Ermyas. "Former Pentagon Chief Esper Says Trump Asked About Shooting Protestors." NPR, May 9, 2022. https//www.npr.org/2022/05/09/1097517470/trump-esper-book-defense-secretary.

Marx, Karl. "Eighteenth of Brumaire of Louis Napoleon." New York: International Publishers, 1963. First published 1852. https://archive.org/details/eighteenthbrumai017766mbp.

Mastanduno, Michael. *Economic Containment: Cocom and the Politics of East-West Trade.* Ithaca, NY: Cornell University Press, 1992.

Masters, Jonathan. "Trump's Threat to Use the Military Against Protestors: What to Know." New York: Council on Foreign Relations, June 5, 2020. https://www.cfr.org/in-brief/trumps -threat-use-military-against-protesters-what-know.

Mastro, Oriana S. "The Taiwan Temptation: Why Beijing Might Resort to Force." *Foreign Affairs* 100, no. 4 (2021): 58–67.

McDermott, Rose. *Risk-Taking in International Relations: Prospect Theory in American Foreign Policy.* Ann Arbor: University of Michigan Press, 1998.

Mearsheimer, John L. "Bound to Fail: The Rise and Fall of the Liberal International Order." *International Security* 43, no. 4 (2019): 7–50.

——. "China's Unpeaceful Rise." *Current History* 105, no, 690 (2006): 160–62.

——. "The Gathering Storm: China's Challenge to US Power in Asia." *Chinese Journal of International Politics* 3, no. 4 (2010): 381–96.

——. "Taiwan's Dire Straits." *National Interest* 130 (March-April 2014): 29–39.

——. *The Tragedy of Great Power Politics.* New York: Norton, 2001.

——. *Why Leaders Lie: The Truth about Lying in International Politics.* Oxford: Oxford University Press, 2011.

Mearsheimer, John J., and Stephen M. Walt. "An Unnecessary War." *Foreign Policy*, 134 (January/February 2003): 50–59.

Medeiros, Evan S. *China's International Behavior: Activism, Opportunism, and Diversification.* Santa Monica, CA: RAND Corporation, 2009.

Mercer, Jonathan. *Reputation and International Politics.* Ithaca, NY: Cornell University Press, 1996.

Merritt, Richard L., and Dina A. Zinnes. "Alternative Indexes of National Power." In *Power in World Politics*, ed. Richard J. Stoll and Michael D. Ward, 11–28. Boulder, CO: Lynne Rienner, 1989.

——. "Validity of Power Indices." *International Interactions* 14, no. 2 (1988): 141–51.

Midlarsky, Manus I. *On War: International Violence in the International System.* New York: Free Press, 1975.

Ministry of Foreign Affairs, People's Republic of China. "Set Aside Dispute and Pursue Joint Development." Diplomatic History, Events and Issues, November 2000. https://www.fmprc .gov.cn/mfa_eng/ziliao_665539/3602_665543/3604_665547/200011/t20001117_697808 .html.

Modelski, George, and William R. Thompson. *Leading Sectors and World Powers: The Coevolution of Global Politics and Economics.* Columbia: University of South Carolina Press, 1996.

Monmouth University Polling Institute. "Doubt in American System Increases." West Long Branch, NJ: Monmouth University, November 12, 2021. https://www.monmouth.edu /polling-institute/reports/monmouthpoll_us_111521/.

Montgomery, Evan B. "Contested Primacy in the Western Pacific: China's Rise and the Future of U.S. Power Projection." *International Security* 38, no. 4 (2014): 115–49.

Morgenthau, Hans J. *Politics among Nations: The Struggle for Power and Peace.* New York: Knopf, 1960.

Morris, Kyle. "Milley Secretly Called Chinese Officials Out of Fear Trump Would 'Attack' in Final Days: Book Claims." Fox News, September 14, 2021. https://www.foxnews.com

/politics/milley-secretly-called-chinese-officials-out-of-fear-trump-would-attack-in
-final-days-book-claims.

Moyer, Jonathan D., Collin J. Meisel, Austin S. Matthews, David K. Bohl, and Mathew J. Burrows. *China-US Competition: Measuring Global Influence.* Washington, DC: Scowcroft
Center, Atlantic Council and Frederick Pardee Center for International Futures, University of Denver, 2021. https://www.atlanticcouncil.org/wp-content/uploads/2021/06/China
-US-Competition-Report-2021.pdf.

Mueller, Karl P., Jason J. Castillo, Forrest E. Morgan, Negeen Pegahi, and Brian Rosen. *Striking First: Preemptive and Preventive Attack in U.S. National Security Policy.* Santa Monica,
CA: RAND, 2006.

Murray, Michelle. "Identity, Insecurity, and Great Power Politics: The Tragedy of German
Naval Ambition before the First World War." *Security Studies* 19, no. 4 (2010): 656–88.

——. *The Struggle for Recognition in International Relations: Status, Revisionism, and Rising
Powers.* New York: Oxford University Press, 2019.

National Public Radio (NPR). "Trump Calls Governors Weak, Urging Them to 'Dominate' to
Quell Violence." June 1, 2020. https://www.npr.org/2020/06/01/867063007/trump-calls
-governors-weak-and-urges-them-to-dominate-violent-protesters.

Nature Index. "The Top 10 Research Institutions for 2018." June 20, 2019. https://www
.natureindex.com/news-blog/ten-global-institutions-universities-twenty-nineteen
-annual-tables.

News18. "'Unacceptable Behaviour among Allies': Snubbed over Submarines Deal, France
Recalls Envoys from Oz, US." September 19, 2021. https://www.news18.com/news/world
/france-recalls-ambassadors-to-australia-us-in-escalating-row-4216139.html.

Nincic, Miroslav. *The Logic of Positive Engagement.* Ithaca, NY: Cornell University Press, 2011.

Norrlof, Carla, and William C. Wohlforth. "*Raison de l'Hégémonie* (The Hegemon's Interest):
Theory of the Costs and Benefits of Hegemony." *Security Studies* 28, no. 3 (2019): 422–50.

Nye, Joseph S., Jr. *Bound to Lead: The Changing Nature of American Power.* New York: Basic
Books, 1990.

——. *The Paradox of American Power.* New York: Oxford University Press, 2002.

——. "The Rise and Fall of American Hegemony: From Wilson to Trump." *International
Affairs* 95, no. 1 (2019): 63–80.

——. *Soft Power: The Means to Success in World Politics.* New York: Public Affairs, 2004.

Oatley, Thomas, William K. Winecoff, Sarah B. Danzman, and Andrew Pennock. "The Political
Economy of Global Finance: A Network Model." *Perspectives on Politics* 11, no. 1 (2013): 133–53.

Office of the Secretary of Defense. *Military and Security Developments Involving the People's
Republic of China 2020: Annual Report to Congress.* Washington: U.S. Department of
Defense, 2020. https://media.defense.gov/2020/Sep/01/2002488689/-1/-1/1/2020-DOD-CHI
NA-MILITARY-POWER-REPORT-FINAL.PDF.

O'Hanlon, Michael E. "Why China Cannot Conquer Taiwan." *International Security* 25, no. 2
(2000): 51–86.

O'Hanlon, Michael E., Lyle Goldstein, and William Murray. "Correspondence: Damn the Torpedoes: Debating Possible U.S. Navy Losses in a Taiwan Scenario." *International Security*
29, no. 2 (2004): 202–206.

Olson, Mancur, Jr. *The Logic of Collective Action*. Cambridge, MA: Harvard University Press, 1965.

——. *The Rise and Decline of Nations: Economic Growth, Stagflation, and Social Rigidities*. New Haven, CT: Yale University Press, 1982.

Oren, Ido. *Our Enemies and US: America's Rivalries and the Making of Political Science*. Ithaca, NY: Cornell University Press, 2003.

Organski, A. F. K. *World Politics*. New York: Knopf, 1958.

Organski, A. F. K., and Jacek Kugler. "The Costs of Major Wars: The Phoenix Factor." *American Political Science Review* 71, no. 4 (1977): 1347–66.

——. *The War Ledger*. Chicago: University of Chicago Press, 1980.

Pan, Chengxin. *Knowledge, Desire and Power in Global Politics: Western Representations of China's Rise*. Cheltenham, UK: Edward Elgar, 2012.

Pan, Hsin-Hsin, Wen-Chin Wu, and Yu-Tzung Chang. "How Chinese Citizens Perceive Cross-Strait Relations: Survey Results from Ten Major Cities in China." *Journal of Contemporary China* 26, no. 106 (2017): 616–31.

Pang, Xun, Linda Liu, and Stephanie Ma. "China's Network Strategy for Seeking Great Power Status." *Chinese Journal of International Politics* 10, no. 1 (2017): 1–29.

Paul, T. V., ed. *Accommodating Rising Powers: Past, Present, and Future*. Cambridge: Cambridge University Press, 2016.

——. "The Accommodation of Rising Powers in World Politics." In *Accommodating Rising Powers: Past, Present, and Future*, ed. T. V. Paul, 3–32. Cambridge: Cambridge University Press, 2016.

——. *Restraining Great Powers: Soft Balancing from Empires to the Global Era*. New Haven, CT: Yale University Press, 2018.

Paul, T. V., and Markus Kornprobst, eds. "Deglobalization and the International Order." Special issue, *International Affairs* 97, no. 5 (September 2021).

Pepinsky, Thomas, and Jessica C. Weiss. "The Clash of Systems? Washington Should Avoid Ideological Competition with Beijing." *Foreign Affairs*, June 11, 2021. https://www.foreignaffairs.com/articles/united-states/2021-06-11/clash-systems.

Perlroth, Nicole. *This Is How They Tell Me the World Ends: The Cyber-Weapons Arms Race*. New York: Bloomsbury, 2020.

Platias, Athanassios, and Vasilis Trigkas. "Unravelling the Thucydides' Trap: Inadvertent or War of Choice?" *Chinese Journal of International Politics* 14, no. 2 (2021): 187–217.

Pomeroy, Caleb, and Michael Beckley. "Correspondence: Measuring Power in International Relations." *International Security* 44, no. 1 (2019): 197–200.

Pomfret, John. "China Finds Bugs on Jet Equipped in U.S." *Washington Post*, January 19, 2002. https://www.washingtonpost.com/archive/politics/2002/01/19/china-finds-bugs-on-jet-equipped-in-us/65089140-2afe-42e0-a377-ec8d4e5034ef/.

Ponciano, Jonathan. "The Largest Technology Companies in 2019: Apple Reigns as Smartphones Slip and Cloud Services Thrive." *Forbes*, May 15, 2019. https://www.forbes.com/sites/jonathanponciano/2019/05/15/worlds-largest-tech-companies-2019/.

Porch, Douglas. "The Taiwan Strait Crisis of 1996." *Naval War College Review* 52, no. 3 (1999): 1–34.

Porter, Patrick. "Why America's Grand Strategy Has Not Changed: Power, Habit, and U.S. Foreign Policy Establishment." *International Security* 42, no. 4 (2018): 9–46.

Posen, Barry R. "Command of the Commons: The Military Foundation of U.S. Hegemony." *International Security* 28, no. 1 (2003): 5–46.

Powell, Robert. *In the Shadow of Power: States and Strategies in International Politics*. Princeton, NJ: Princeton University Press, 1999.

——. "War as a Commitment Problem." *International Organization* 60 no. 1 (2006): 169–203.

Power, Samantha. "Bystander to Genocide." *The Atlantic*, September 2001. https://www.theatlantic.com/magazine/archive/2001/09/bystanders-to-genocide/304571/.

Prestowitz, Clyde V., Jr. *Trading Places: How We Are Giving Our Future to Japan and How to Reclaim It*. New York: Basic Books, 1990.

Pu, Xiaoyu. *Rebranding China: Contested Status Signaling in the Changing Global Order*. Stanford, CA: Stanford University Press, 2019.

Purdie, Edie. "Tracking GDP in PPP Terms Shows Rapid Rise of China and India." *Data Blog* (World Bank blog), October 19, 2019. https://blogs.worldbank.org/opendata/tracking-gdp-ppp-terms-shows-rapid-rise-china-and-india.

Putnam, Robert D. *Bowling Alone: The Collapse and Revival of American Society*. New York: Simon & Schuster, 2000.

——. "Diplomacy and Domestic Politics: The Logic of Two-Level Games." *International Organization* 42, no. 3 (1988): 427–60.

Qi, Haixia. "Disputing Chinese Views on Power." *Chinese Journal of International Politics* 10, no. 2 (2017): 211–39.

Quek, Kai, and Alastair I. Johnston. "Can China Back Down? Crisis De-escalation in the Shadow of Popular Opposition." *International Security* 42, no. 3 (2017–2018): 7–36.

Rahe, Paul A. "Sparta Ascendant, Athens Rising: Alliance, Ambivalence, Rivalry, and War in a Tripolar World." In *Disruptive Strategies: The Military Campaigns of Ascendant Powers and Their Rivals*, ed. David Beekwy, 13–42. Stanford, CA: Hoover Institution Press, 2021.

Raiffa, Howard. *The Art and Science of Negotiation*. Cambridge, MA: Harvard University Press, 1982.

Rauch, Carsten. "Challenging the Power Consensus: GDP, CINC, and Power Transition." *Security Studies* 26, no. 4 (2017): 642–64.

Ray, James L. "Status Inconsistency and War Involvement Among European States, 1816–1970." *Peace Science Society Papers* 23 (1974): 69–80.

Reiff, Nathan. "10 Biggest Telecommunications Companies." Investopedia, January 13, 2021. https://www.investopedia.com/articles/markets/030216/worlds-top-10-telecommunications-companies.asp.

Reiter, Dan. "Exploding the Powder Keg Myth: Preemptive Wars Almost Never Happen." *International Security* 20, no. 2 (1995): 5–34.

Renshon, Jonathan. *Fighting for Status: Hierarchy and Conflict in World Politics*. Princeton, NJ: Princeton University Press, 2017.

——. "Status Deficits and War." *International Organization* 70, no. 3 (2016): 513–50.

Resnick, Brian. "Please, Trump: Keep Telling Your Supporters the Covid-19 Vaccines Work." *Vox*, March 18, 2021. http://maristpoll.marist.edu/wp-content/uploads/2021/03/NPR_PBS -NewsHour_Marist-Poll_USA-NOS-and-Tables_202103091124.pdf#page=3.

Reuters. "Timeline: U.S. Arms Sales to Taiwan in 2020 Total $5 billion amid China Tensions." December 7, 2020. https://www.reuters.com/article/us-taiwan-security-usa-timeline/ti meline-u-s-arms-sales-to-taiwan-in-2020-total-5-billion-amid-china-tensions-idUSKB N28IoBF.

Reuveny, Rafael, and William R. Thompson. *Growth, Trade, and Systemic Leadership*. Ann Arbor: University of Michigan Press, 2004.

Richardson, Lewis F. *Arms and Insecurity*. Pittsburgh, PA: Boxwood Press, 1960.

Richelson, Jeffrey T., ed. "The Snowden Affair: Web Resources the Latest Firestorm Over the National Security Agency." Washington, DC: National Security Archive, George Washington University, September 4, 2013. https://nsarchive2.gwu.edu/NSAEBB/NSAEBB436/.

Rigger, Shelley. *Why Taiwan Matters: Small Island, Global Powerhouse*. Lanham, MD: Rowman & Littlefield, 2011.

Rising Power Initiative. "RPI Policy Alert: Rising Powers React to Contentious U.S.-China Relations: A Roundup." Washington, DC: George Washington University, March 2021. https://www.risingpowersinitiative.org/publication/rising-powers-react-to-contentious -u-s-china-relations-a-roundup/.

——. "RPI Policy Alert: Rising Powers React to Biden-Suga Summit." Washington, DC: George Washington University, April 2021. https://www.risingpowersinitiative.org/publication /rising-powers-react-to-biden-suga-summit/.

Romberg, Alan D. *Rein in at the Brink of the Precipice: American Policy Toward Taiwan and U.S.-PRC Relations*. Washington, DC: Stimson Center, 2003.

Rosato, Sebastian. "The Inscrutable Intentions of Great Powers." *International Security* 39, no. 3 (2015): 48–88.

——. "Why the United States and China Are on a Collision Course." Cambridge, MA: Belfour Center for Science and International Affairs, Harvard Kennedy School, 2015. https://www .belfercenter.org/publication/why-united-states-and-china-are-collision-course.

Ross, Robert S. "The 1995–96 Taiwan Strait Confrontation: Coercion, Credibility, and the Use of Force." *International Security* 25, no. 2 (2000): 87–123.

——. "Navigating the Taiwan Strait: Deterrence, Escalation Dominance, and US-China Relations." *International Security* 27, no. 2 (2002): 48–85.

Rousseau, David. *Identifying Threats and Threatening Identities: The Social Construction of Realism and Liberalism*. Stanford, CA: Stanford University Press, 2006.

Russett, Bruce M. "The Mysterious Case of Vanishing Hegemony: Or, Is Mark Twain Really Dead?" *International Organization* 39, no. 2 (1985): 207–31.

Russett, Bruce M., and John R. Oneal. *Triangulating Peace: Democracy, Interdependence and International Organizations*. New York: Norton, 2001.

Sanders, Phillip C., and Scott L. Kastner. "Bridge over Troubled Water? Envisioning a China-Taiwan Peace Agreement." *International Security* 33, no. 4 (2009): 87–114.

Sands, Geneva, Kylie Atwood, Stephen Collinson, and Kevin Bohn. "US Government Report Assesses China Intentionally Concealed Severity of Coronavirus." CNN, May 4, 2020.

https://www.cnn.com/2020/05/03/politics/mike-pompeo-china-coronavirus-supplies
/index.html.

Sarotte, M. E. "China's Fear of Contagion: Tiananmen Square and the Power of European Example." *International Security* 37, no. 2 (2012): 156–82.

Sartori, Anne E. *Deterrence by Diplomacy.* Princeton, NJ: Princeton University Press, 2005.

——. "The Might of the Pen: A Reputation Theory of Communication in International Disputes." *International Organization* 56, no. 1 (2002): 121–49.

Saull, Richard. "Rethinking Hegemony: Uneven Development, Historic Blocs, and the World Economic Crisis." *International Studies Quarterly* 56, no. 2 (2012): 323–38.

Schake, Kori. *Safe Passage: The Transition from British to American Hegemony.* Cambridge, MA: Harvard University Press, 2017.

Schelling, Thomas. *Arms and Influence.* New Haven, CT: Yale University Press, 1966.

Schuster, John M. "The Deception Dividend: FDR's Undeclared War." *International Security* 34, no. 3 (2010): 133–65.

Schweller, Randall L. "Democratic Structure and Preventive War: Are Democracies More Pacific?" *World Politics* 44, no. 2 (1992): 235–69.

——. "Opposite but Compatible Nationalisms: A Neoclassical Realist Approach to the Future of US-China Relations." *Chinese Journal of International Politics* 11, no. 1 (2018): 23–48.

——. "The Problem of International Order Revisited: A Review Essay." *International Security* 26, no. 1 (2001): 161–86.

——. "Rising Powers and Revisionism in Emerging World Orders." *Russia in Global Affairs,* 2015. http://eng.globalaffairs.ru/valday/Rising-Powers-and-Revisionism-in-Emerging
-International-Orders-17730.

——. *Unanswered Threats: Political Constraints on the Balance of Power.* Princeton, NJ: Princeton University Press, 2006.

Senese, Paul D., and John A. Vasquez. *The Steps to War: An Empirical Study.* Princeton, NJ: Princeton University Press, 2008.

Shambaugh, David. "A Matter of Time: Taiwan's Eroding Military Advantage." *Washington Quarterly* 23, no. 2 (2000): 119–33.

Sharp, Travis, John S. Meyers, and Michael Beckley. "Correspondence: Will East Asia Balance against Beijing?" *International Security* 43, no. 3 (2018–2019): 194–97.

Shea, Patrick E. "Financing Victory: Sovereign Credit, Democracy, and War." *Journal of Conflict Resolution* 58, no. 5 (2014): 771–85.

Shi, Jiangtao. "Inevitable War? China, America, and Their Next Battlegrounds." Inkstonenews, May 21, 2020. https://www.inkstonenews.com/politics/inevitable-war-china-america-and
-their-next-battlegrounds/article/3085414.

Shifrinson, Joshua I. R., and Michael Beckley. "Correspondence: Debating China's Rise and U.S. Decline." *International Security* 37, no. 3 (2012–2013): 172–81.

Shirk, Susan L. *China, Fragile Superpower: How China's Internal Politics Could Derail Its Peaceful Rise.* Oxford: Oxford University Press, 2007.

Silove, Nina. "The Pivot before the Pivot: U.S. Strategy to Preserve the Power Balance in Asia." *International Security* 40, no. 4 (2016): 45–88.

Silver, Laura, Kat Devlin, and Christine Huang. "Most Americans Support Tough Stance toward China on Human Rights, Economic Issues." Washington, DC: Pew Research Center, March 4, 2021. https://www.pewresearch.org/global/2021/03/04/most-americans-support-tough-stance-toward-china-on-human-rights-economic-issues/.

Silverstone, Scott A. *Preventive War and American Democracy.* London: Routledge, 2007.

Singer, J. David, Stuart Bremer, and John Stuckey. "Capability Distribution, Uncertainty, and Major Power War, 1820–1965." In *Peace, War, and Numbers,* ed. Bruce M. Russett, 19–48. Beverly Hills, CA: SAGE, 1968.

Sinkkonen, Elina. "Nationalism, Patriotism, and Foreign Policy Attitudes among Chinese University Students." *China Quarterly* 216 (2013): 1045–63.

Slotkin, Jason. "Report on Khashoggi Killing Prompts Calls for Penalties Against Crown Prince." National Public Radio, February 27, 2021. https://www.npr.org/2021/02/27/972141908/report-on-khashoggi-killing-prompts-calls-for-penalties-against-crown-prince.

Smeltz, Dina, Ivo Daalder, Karl Friedhoff, Craig Kafura, and Brandon Helm. *Rejecting Retreat: Americans Support US Engagement in Global Affairs.* Chicago: Chicago Council on Global Affairs, 2019. https://www.thechicagocouncil.org/sites/default/files/2020-11/report_ccs19_rejecting-retreat_20190909.pdf.

Snider, Lewis W. "Identifying the Elements of State Power: Where Do We Begin?" *Comparative Political Studies* 20, no. 3 (1987): 314–56.

Snyder, Jack. *Myths of Empire: Domestic Politics and International Ambition.* Ithaca, NY: Cornell University Press, 1993.

Snyder, Jack, and Erica D. Borghard. "The Cost of Empty Threats: A Penny, Not a Pound." *American Political Science Review* 105, no. 3 (2011): 437–56.

Solingen, Etel. "Domestic Coalitions, Internationalization, and War: Then and Now." *International Security* 39, no. 1 (2014): 44–70.

——. "Pax Asiatica versus Bella Levantina: The Foundations of War and Peace in East Asia and the Middle East." *American Political Science Review* 101, no. 4 (2007): 757–80.

——. *Regional Orders at Century's Dawn: Global and Domestic Influences on Grand Strategy.* Princeton, NJ: Princeton University Press, 1998.

Stankiewicz, Kevin. " 'They Owe Trillions'—Steve Bannon Says China Must Be Held Accountable for Coronavirus Spread." CNBC, April 30, 2020. https://www.cnbc.com/2020/04/30/steve-bannon-china-must-be-held-accountable-for-coronavirus-spread.html.

Starrs, Sean. "American Economic Power Hasn't Declined—It Globalized! Summoning the Data and Taking Globalization Seriously." *International Studies Quarterly* 57, no. 4 (2013): 817–30.

Statistics Times. "Comparing United States and China by Economy." May 15, 2021. http://statisticstimes.com/economy/united-states-vs-china-economy.php.

Stein, Arthur A., and Richard Rosecrance, eds. *The Domestic Bases of Grand Strategy.* Ithaca, NY: Cornell University Press, 1993.

Strange, Susan. "The Persistent Myth of Lost Hegemony." *International Organization* 41, no. 4 (1987): 551–74.

Struver, Georg. "China's Partnership Diplomacy: International Alignment Based on Interest or Ideology." *Chinese Journal of International Politics* 10, no. 1 (2017): 31–65.

Swaine, Michael D., and Ashley L. Tellis. *Interpreting China's Grand Strategy: Past, Present, and Future*. Santa Monica, CA: RAND, 2000.

Taber, Charles S. "Power Capability Indexes in the Third World." In *Power in World Politics*, ed. Richard J. Stoll and Michael D. Ward, 29–48. Boulder, CO: Lynne Rienner, 1989.

Taiwan Documents Project. "Shanghai Communiqué: Joint Communique of the United States of America and the People's Republic of China." February 28, 1972. http://www.taiwandocuments.org/communique01.htm.

Tammen, Ronald L., Jacek Kugler, and Douglas Lemke. "Foundations of Power Transition Theory." In *Oxford Encyclopedia of Empirical International Relations*, ed. William R. Thompson. Oxford: Oxford University Press, 2017. https://oxfordre.com/politics/view/10.1093/acrefore/9780190228637.001.0001/acrefore-9780190228637-e-296.

Tammen, Ronald L., Jacek Kugler, Douglas Lemke, Allan Stam III, Mark Abdollahian, Carole Alsharabati, Brian Efird, and A. F. K. Organski. *Power Transitions: Strategies for the 21st Century*. New York: Chatham House, 2000.

Tellis, Ashley J. "Overview: Assessing National Power." In *Foundations of National Power in the Asia-Pacific*, ed. Ashley J. Tellis, Alison Szalwinski, and Michael Willis, 2–21. Seattle: National Bureau of Asian Research, 2015. https://www.nbr.org/wp-content/uploads/pdfs/publications/sa15_overview_telllis.pdf.

Tellis, Ashley J., Janice Bially, Christopher Layne, and Melissa McPherson, *Measuring National Power in the Postindustrial Age*. Santa Monica, CA: RAND, 2000.

Thompson, William R. "A Streetcar Named Sarajevo: Catalysts, Multiple Causation Chains, and Rivalry Structures." *International Studies Quarterly* 47, no. 3 (2003): 453–74.

Thurston, Anne F. *Engaging China: Fifty Years of Sino-American Relations*. New York: Columbia University Press, 2021.

Tierney, Dominic. "Does Chain-Ganging Cause the Outbreak of War?" *International Studies Quarterly* 55, no. 2 (2011): 285–304.

Timsit, Annabelle. "Xi Jinping Sends Warning to the US at Davos." World Economic Forum. January 25, 2021. https://qz.com/1962084/read-xi-jinpings-speech-at-the-2021-davos-forum/.

Tingley, Dustin. "Rising Power on the Mind." *International Organization* 71, no. S1 (2017): S165–88.

Toft, Monica D. "Why Is America Addicted to Foreign Interventions?" *National Interest*, December 10, 2017. https://nationalinterest.org/feature/why-america-addicted-foreign-interventions-23582.

Tomz, Michael. "Domestic Audience Costs in International Relations: An Experimental Approach." *International Organization* 61, no. 4 (2007): 821–40.

——. *Reputation and International Cooperation: Sovereign Debt across Three Centuries*. Princeton, NJ: Princeton University Press, 2007.

Trachtenberg, Marc. "Audience Costs: An Historical Analysis." *Security Studies* 21, no. 1 (2012): 3–42.

——. "Preventive War and U.S. Foreign Policy." *Security Studies* 16, no. 1 (2007): 1–31.

Treisman, David. "Rational Appeasement." *International Organization* 58, no. 2 (2004): 344–73.

Trigkas, Vasilis. "Aircraft Carriers in the Taiwan Strait." *The Diplomat*, 2014. https://the diplomat.com/2014/12/aircraft-carriers-in-the-taiwan-strait/.

Tyler, Patrick. *A Great Wall, Six Presidents and China: An Investigative History*. New York: Perseus, 1999.

U.S. News and World Report. "2021 Best Global Universities Rankings." 2021. https://www .usnews.com/education/best-global-universities/rankings.

Van Evera, Stephen. *Causes of War: Power and the Roots of Conflict*. Ithaca, NY: Cornell University Press, 1999.

——. "The Cult of Offensive and the Origins of the First World War." *International Security* 9, no. 1 (1984): 58–107.

Vasquez, John A. "The Realist Paradigm and Degenerative versus Progressive Research Programs: An Appraisal of Neotraditional Research on Waltz's Balancing Proposition." *American Political Science Review* 91, no. 4 (1997): 899–912.

——. *The War Puzzle*. New York: Cambridge University Press, 1993.

——. *The War Puzzle Revisited*. Cambridge: Cambridge University Press, 2009.

——. "When Are Power Transitions Dangerous? An Appraisal and Reformulation of Power Transition Theory." In *Parity and War: Evaluations and Extensions of the War Ledger*, ed. Jacek Kugler and Douglas Lemke, 35–56. Ann Arbor: University of Michigan Press, 1996.

——. "Whether and How Global Leadership Transitions Will Result in War: Some Long-Term Predictions from Steps-to-War Explanation." In *Systemic Transitions: Past, Present, and Future*, ed. William R. Thompson, 131–60. New York: Palgrave Macmillan, 2009.

Vasquez, John A., and Marie T. Henehan. *Territory, War, and Peace*. New York: Routledge, 2011.

Voeten, Erik. "Resisting the Lonely Superpower: Responses of States in the United Nations to U.S. Dominance." *Journal of Politics* 66, no. 3 (2004): 729–54.

Vogel, Ezra F. *Japan as Number One: Lessons for America*. Cambridge, MA: Harvard University Press, 1979.

Voice of America News. "Obama: US, Not China, Should Set Pacific Trade Rules." May 3, 2016. https://www.voanews.com/a/obama-united-states-pacific-trade-rules/3313875.html.

Volgy, Thomas J., and Stacey Mayhall. "Status Inconsistency and International War: Exploring the Effects of Systemic Change." *International Studies Quarterly* 39, no. 1 (1995): 67–84.

Wachman, Alan. *Why Taiwan? Geostrategic Rationales for China's Territorial Integrity*. Stanford, CA: Stanford University Press, 2007.

Walker, Robert B. J. *Inside/Outside: International Relations as Political Theory*. Cambridge: Cambridge University Press, 1995.

Wallace, Michael D. *War and Rank among States*. Lexington, KY: Heath, 1973.

Waltz, Kenneth N. *Theory of International Politics*. Reading, MA: Addison-Wesley, 1979.

Wang, Jisi. "The Plot Against China? How Beijing Sees the New Washington Consensus." *Foreign Affairs* 100, no. 4 (2021): 48–57.

Wang, T. Y. "Changing Boundaries: The Development of the Taiwan Voters' Identity." In *The Taiwan Voter*, ed. Christopher H. Achen and T. Y. Wang, 45–70. Ann Arbor: University of Michigan Press, 2017.

——. "Strategic Ambiguity or Strategic Clarity? US Policy Toward the Taiwan Issue." *Taiwan Insight*, June 7, 2021. https://taiwaninsight.org/2021/06/07/strategic-ambiguity-or-strategic-clarity-us-policy-towards-the-taiwan-issue/.

Wang, T. Y., and I-Chou Liu. "Contending Identities in Taiwan: Implications for Cross-Strait Relations." *Asian Survey* 44, no. 4 (2004): 568–90.

Wang, Yong. "If Biden Gets China Right: A World of Opportunities Awaits." *GlobalAsia*, March 2021. https://globalasia.org/v16no1/cover/if-biden-can-get-china-right-a-world-of-opportunities-awaits_wang-yong.

Wang, Yuan-kang. *Harmony and War: Confucian Culture and Chinese Power Politics*. New York: Columbia University Press, 2010.

——. "The Durability of a Unipolar System: Lessons from East Asian History." *Security Studies* 29, no. 5 (2020): 832–63.

——. "Taiwan Public Opinion on Cross-Strait Security Issues: Implications for U.S. Foreign Policy." *Strategic Studies Quarterly* 7, no. 2 (2013): 93–113.

Wang, Zheng. *Never Forget National Humiliation: Historical Memory in Chinese Politics and Foreign Relations*. New York: Columbia University Press, 2012.

Ward, Steven. *Status and the Challenge of Rising Powers*. Cambridge: Cambridge University Press, 2017.

Wayman, Frank, J. David Singer, and Gary Goertz. "Capabilities, Allocations, and Success in Militarized Disputes and Wars, 1816–1976." *International Studies Quarterly* 27, no. 4 (1983): 497–515.

Weibel, Erik. "Dependency Revisited: International Markets, Business Cycles, and Social Spending in the Developing World." *International Organization* 60, no. 2 (2006): 433–69.

Weisman, Jonathan, and Reid J. Epstein. "G.O.P. Declares Jan. 6 Attack 'Legitimate Political Discourse.'" *New York Times*, February 4, 2022. https://www.nytimes.com/2022/02/04/us/politics/republicans-jan-6-cheney-censure.html

Weiss, Jessica C. "Can the U.S. Sue China for Covid-19 Damages? Not Really. Here's How This Could Quickly Backfire." *Washington Post*, April 29, 2020. https://www.washingtonpost.com/politics/2020/04/29/can-us-sue-china-covid-19-damages-not-really-this-could-quickly-backfire/.

——. "How Hawkish Is the Chinese Public? Another Look at 'Rising Nationalism' and Chinese Foreign Policy." *Journal of Contemporary China* 28, no. 119 (2019): 679–95.

——. *Powerful Patriots: Nationalist Protest in China's Foreign Relations*. Oxford: Oxford University Press, 2014.

Weiss, Jessica C., and Alan Dafoe. "Authoritarian Audiences, Rhetoric, and Propaganda in International Crises: Evidence from China." *International Studies Quarterly* 63, no. 4 (2019): 963–73.

Welch, David. "Can the United States and China Avoid a Thucydides Trap?" E-International Relations, 2015. https://www.e-ir.info/2015/04/06/can-the-united-states-and-china-avoid-a-thucydides-trap/.

Wendt, Alexander. "Anarchy Is What States Make of It: The Social Construction of Power Politics." *International Organization* 46, no. 2 (1992): 391–425.

Westcott, Ben. "US Military Considered Using Nuclear Weapons against China in 1958 Taiwan Strait Crisis, Leaked Documents Show." CNN, May 24, 2021. https://www.cnn.com /2021/05/24/china/us-china-taiwan-1958-nuclear-intl-hnk/index.html.

The White House. "The National Security Strategy of the United States of America: September 2002." Washington: U.S. State Department, 2002. https://2009-2017.state.gov/docu ments/organization/63562.pdf.

Winecoff, William K. "Structural Power and the Global Financial Crisis: A Network Analytical Approach." *Business and Politics* 17 (2015): 495–525.

Wohlforth, William C. "The Perception of Power: Russia in the Pre-1914 Balance." *World Politics* 39, no. 3 (1987): 353–81.

Wolf, Albert B., and M. Taylor Fravel. "Correspondence: Structural Sources of China's Territorial Compromises." *International Security* 31, no. 2 (2006): 206–208.

Wolf, Reinhard. "Rising Powers, Status Ambitions, and the Need to Reassure: What China Could Learn from Imperial Germany's Failures." *Chinese Journal of International Politics* 7, no. 2 (2014): 185–219.

Wolfowitz, Paul. "Bridging Centuries–Fin de Siècle All over Again." *Wall Street Journal*, June 10, 1997. https://www.wsj.com/articles/SB865919411252495500.

Woodward, Bob, and Robert Costa. *Peril*. New York: Simon & Schuster, 2021.

Wright, Jasmine. "Biden Commits to 'Free, Open, Secure' Indo-Pacific in Rare Op-ed with 'Quad' Members." CNN, March 14, 2021. https://www.cnn.com/2021/03/14/politics/biden -modi-morrison-suga-quad-op-ed/index.html.

Wrong, Dennis H. *Power: Its Forms, Bases, and Uses*. New Brunswick, NJ: Transaction, 1995.

Wu, Yu-Shan. "Heading Towards Troubled Waters? The Impact of Taiwan's 2016 Elections on Cross-Strait Relations." *American Journal of Chinese Studies* 23, no. 1 (2016): 59–75.

Xin, Qiang. "Having Much in Common? Changes and Continuity in Beijing's Taiwan Policy." *Pacific Review* 33, no. 6 (2021): 926–45.

——. "Selective Engagement: Mainland China's Dual Track Taiwan Policy." *Journal of Contemporary China* 29, no. 124 (2020): 535–52.

Xinhuanet. "China Welcomes Helpful Suggestions, but Won't Accept Sanctimonious Preaching: Xi." July 1, 2021. http://www.xinhuanet.com/english/special/2021–07/01/c_1310037332 .htm.

Yan, Xuetong. "The Instability of China-US Relations." *Chinese Journal of International Politics* 3, no. 3 (2010): 263–92.

Yang, Yuan. "Escape from both the 'Thucydides Trap' and the 'Churchill Trap': Finding a Third Type of Great Power Relations under the Bipolar System." *Chinese Journal of International Politics* 11, no. 2 (2018): 193–235.

Yang, Zhong. "Explaining National Identity Shift in Taiwan." *Journal of Contemporary China* 25, no. 99 (2016): 336–52.

Yicai Global. "China 'Lacks the Gene' to Fall into Thucydides Trap, Says Xi Jinping." September 20, 2017. https://yicaichina.medium.com/china-lacks-the-gene-to-fall-into-the-thu cydides-trap-says-xi-jinping-ccade48ac392.

Yoder, Brandon K. "Hedging for Better Bets: Power Shifts, Credible Signals, and Preventive Conflict." *Journal of Conflict Resolution* 63, no. 4 (2019): 923–49.

YouTube. "It Is Not Up to the U.S. Alone to Evaluate its Democracy: Yang Jiechi." May 19, 2021. https://www.youtube.com/watch?v=ETOfymWVShM.

Yu, Matt, and Hsiu-chuan Shih. "Public Less Confident U.S. Coming to Taiwan's Defense: Survey." Central News Agency, March 30, 2022. https//focustaiwan.tw/politics/202204300009.

Zakaria, Fareed. "The Divided States of America." YouTube, February 10, 2021. https://www.youtube.com/watch?v=7szHDdPdEfs.

——. "On Domestic Front, Biden Is All Ambition. Why Not Foreign Policy?" *Washington Post*, February 11, 2021. https://fareedzakaria.com/columns/2021/2/11/on-the-domestic-front-biden-is-all-ambition-why-not-on-foreign-policy.

——. "The New China Scare: Why America Shouldn't Panic about Its Latest Challenger." *Foreign Affairs* 99, no. 1 (2020): 52–69.

——. "Opinion: Is Biden Normalizing Trump's Foreign Policy?" *Washington Post*, September 16, 2021, https://www.washingtonpost.com/opinions/2021/09/16/is-biden-normalizing-trumps-foreign-policy/.

Zarakol, Ayse. "Use of Historical Analogies in IR Theory." H-Diplo/ISSF Roundtable Discussion 12–2. November 9, 2020. https://networks.h-net.org/node/28443/discussions/6721850/h-diploissf-roundtable-12-2-thucydides%E2%80%99s-trap-historical.

Zelleke, Andy. " 'Strategic Clarity' Won't Solve the United States' Taiwan Dilemma: An Open Commitment to Defend Taiwan Won't Mean Much Unless the U.S. Has the Certain Capacity to Do So." *The Diplomat*, October 2, 2020. https://thediplomat.com/2020/10/strategic-clarity-wont-solve-the-united-states-taiwan-dilemma/.

Zhang, Ketian. "Cautious Bully: Reputation, Resolve, and Beijing's Use of Coercion in the South China Sea." *International Security* 44, no. 1 (2019): 117–59.

Zhu, Tian. *Catching Up to America: Culture, Institutions, and the Rise of China.* Cambridge: Cambridge University Press, 2021.

INDEX